The Battle Cry
of Freedom

The Battle Cry of Freedom

*The New England Emigrant Aid Company
in the Kansas Crusade*

by

Samuel A. Johnson

GREENWOOD PRESS, PUBLISHERS
WESTPORT, CONNECTICUT

Library of Congress Cataloging in Publication Data

Johnson, Samuel A
  The battle cry of freedom.

  Reprint of the ed. published by the University of
Kansas Press, Lawrence.
  Bibliography: p.
  Includes index.
  1. New England Emigrant Aid Company, Boston.
2. Kansas--History--1854-1861. 3. Slavery in the
United States--Anti-slavery movements. I. Title.
[F685.J75 1977]   978.1'02   77-11619
ISBN 0-8371-9813-5

Originally published in 1954 by University of Kansas Press,
Lawrence

Reprinted with the permission of The Regents Press of Kansas

Reprinted in 1977 by Greenwood Press, Inc.

Library of Congress catalog card number   77-11619

ISBN 0-8371-9813-5

Printed in the United States of America

TO

FREDDIE

Preface

This is the story of the New England Emigrant Aid Company in the Kansas Crusade. It may be straining a point to call the role of this organization a crusade, but crusade it certainly was to the men who were engaged in it. The story is worth telling, first of all, because it is interesting. Even the reader who has no particular interest in this bit of history will find in the struggles of the leaders of the Emigrant Aid Company to carry on the battle against slavery, in the face of obstacles and discouragements that would have driven most people to give up in despair, a real human interest story.

This story is also worth telling, though, because it fills a gap in American history. In the early days of the Company there was much confusion, and there has been much disagreement among historical writers since that period, as to what influence, if any, it exercised in the chain reaction of events that led up to the Civil War. This study tries to clear up some of the confusion and to point out the relationship of the Company and its leaders to the Kansas Conflict, to the Benton fight in Missouri, and to national politics, including the launching of the Republican party.

It is particularly fitting to tell the story at this time. It was just a hundred years ago, as this book goes to press, that Kansas Territory was opened to settlement and parties of Emigrant Aid Company settlers made their way to Kansas to launch the towns of Lawrence, Topeka, and Manhattan. This book is published during the centennial of both Kansas and the Emigrant Aid Company.

In order to place the role of the Company in perspective, I have recounted the main happenings in the Kansas struggle down to the autumn of 1856, when Governor Geary brought relative peace to Kansas. For the sake of completeness, and for sheer human interest, the story of the Company itself is carried through to the end. However, since the Company ceased to be a major factor in Kansas political events after Geary's time, the later events of Kansas territorial history—such as the taking over of the territorial government by the Free State party, the Lecompton Constitution episode, the violence of 1858 and 1859, and the schism in the Free State party of which the Lane-Robinson feud was a part—are not covered except for incidental mention.

The research for the writing of this book extended over many years, being carried on both in university seminars and independently. The subject was suggested to me originally by Professor Arthur Meier Schlesinger, Sr., now of Harvard University. Portions of the study were supervised by the late Professor Frank H. Hodder and Professor James C. Malin of the University of Kansas, and the late Professors Frederick L. Paxson and Carl Russell Fish, then of the University of Wisconsin. Professor Robert F. Moody of Boston University graciously lent me extensive notes he had taken on the Amos A. Lawrence papers in Boston. The original manuscript was read and criticized by Professor Curtis P. Nettels, now of Cornell University.

I am deeply indebted to Nyle H. Miller, now Secretary of the Kansas State Historical Society, and to past and present members of the staff of that organization for their help in making available material in the Library and Archives of the Society. The illustration on the jacket, showing the Free State Hotel in Lawrence after the sack of May 21, 1856, and all but one of the illustrations in the text were supplied by Mr. Miller and the Kansas State Historical Society. For the other illustration, the portrait of Edward Everett Hale, I am indebted to the Boston Athenaeum and its Director, Mr. Walter Muir Whitehill. I also wish to express my sincere appreciation of the splendid co-operation of the University of Kansas Press in preparing the book for publication.

Most of all, however, I am indebted to my wife, Winifred Feder Johnson (the "Freddie" of the dedication), without whose inspiration this book would never have been written. Besides giving all possible help and encouragement at every stage of the study, she has rendered indispensable assistance in the preparation of the manuscript. Needless to say, any faults in composition and any errors of fact or of judgment in the book are my own.

—S.A.J.

St. Louis, Missouri
July 15, 1954

Contents

                                                                    PAGE
PREFACE vii

CHAPTER

   I. THE CHALLENGE   3
  II. THE CRUSADERS   16
 III. THE WEAPONS OF OUR WARFARE   33
  IV. LAUNCHING THE KANSAS CRUSADE   51
   V. DRIVING DOWN THE STAKES   72
  VI. DRAWING THE BATTLE LINES   92
 VII. THE SINEWS OF WAR 111
VIII. WAR TO THE KNIFE 134
  IX. BEHIND THE LINES 161
   X. KNIFE TO THE HILT 181
  XI. "BLEEDING KANSAS" 208
 XII. THE END OF THE CRUSADE 231
XIII. THE LOAVES AND FISHES 254
 XIV. DOTAGE 272
  XV. DIVIDENDS 287

NOTES 304
BIBLIOGRAPHY 332
INDEX 342

ILLUSTRATIONS

                                                            FACING PAGE
ELI THAYER 20
AMOS A. LAWRENCE 20
THOMAS H. WEBB 20
EDWARD EVERETT HALE 20
CHARLES ROBINSON 21
SAMUEL C. POMEROY 21
JAMES H. LANE 21
DAVID R. ATCHISON 21
TERRITORIAL CAPITOL AT PAWNEE 36
SHAWNEE MISSION 36
LAWRENCE ABOUT 1857 37
THE ABBOTT HOWITZER 37

MAPS

SETTLED AREA OF KANSAS TERRITORY   2
SCENE OF THE KANSAS CONFLICT 184

The Battle Cry
of Freedom

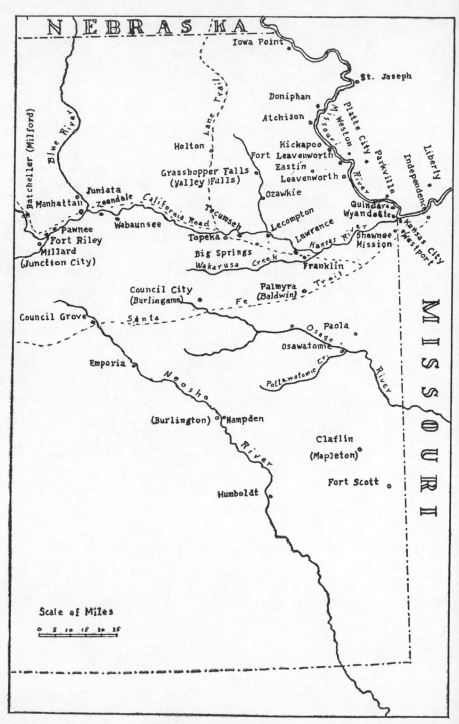

Settled Area of Kansas Territory

CHAPTER I

The Challenge

BACK IN 1820, Thomas Jefferson is reputed to have said that the popular excitement created by the debates over the bill to admit Missouri startled him like a fire bell in the night. Had Jefferson been alive in 1854, his fire bell of 1820 would have seemed but a feeble tinkle compared with the excitement aroused by the Kansas-Nebraska bill. As the bill worked its laborious way through Congress, feeling throughout the Union was intense. The North generally, and particularly those elements which had become tinged with free-soilism, saw in the repeal of the Missouri Compromise the breach of a solemn compact: a fiendish conspiracy to foist the hated institution of slavery upon a region which, in their minds, God and man had dedicated to freedom. On January 24, 1854, while the measure was still being debated in the Senate, a number of Democratic senators and representatives of free-soil leanings published "An Appeal of the Independent Democrats in Congress to the People of the United States," in which the bill was denounced as "a gross violation of a sacred pledge" and as being a part of a plot to exclude free laborers and Old World immigrants from the unoccupied area and to "convert it into a dreary region of despotism inhabited by masters and slaves." In all parts of the North party lines were shattered. Newspapers of nearly every shade of political opinion took up the cry of the "Independent Democrats in Congress." During May and June, protest meetings, similar to the famous one at Ripon, Wisconsin, were held in almost every community in the free states to denounce this new atrocity of the "slave power" and to choose delegates to state conventions which, in turn, were to plan political action to check the further extension of slavery into the territories. The flames of discontent were fanned by indignation over the numerous fugitive slave cases

[3]

which vied with the Kansas-Nebraska bill for front-page space in the newspapers of the day.

This excitability of the North on the question of the extension of slavery may be attributed in some measure to the abolitionist propaganda which had been making headway for two decades and was being reinforced at the moment by the unpopularity of the Fugitive Slave Law. It was nursed and encouraged, of course, by ambitious politicians who hoped to capitalize on it for their own advancement. Nevertheless, its roots struck deep into the social and economic life of the section. In the Northeast, where industry was developing rapidly, the businessmen opposed the formation of more slave states partly because they found free states better customers, but chiefly because they had become convinced that the continued control of the federal government by the slave capitalism of the South was inimical to their interests. Not only was the "slave power" jealous of Northern economic progress and seeking to turn every possible advantage to the South, but, most important of all, it denied them their much-desired tariff protection. The farmers of the Ohio valley disliked Southern political control because it refused them a homestead law which would give them or their sons free farms, and they felt that the development of slave-holding communities north of 36° 30′ would shut them out of a part of the public domain which they had long regarded as a sort of promised land.

Though the South was less excited than the North, Southerners generally were in a fighting mood. Most of their editors and politicians were telling them that the South had been decidedly worsted in the Compromise of 1850, and they were anxious to regain the lost ground. The slave-holding small farmers of western Missouri, like their antislavery brethren of the Old Northwest, coveted the near-by land, so long closed to them by the Indian frontier, but elsewhere in the slave states people showed but little inclination actually to occupy Kansas Territory.[1] For political reasons the Southern planter desired that Kansas be a slave state. He saw in the rising industrial capitalism of the North a civilization wholly at variance with his own semifeudal culture. Although he envied this new order, he also feared it, for it threatened to strangle him with a protective tariff, and ultimately to destroy the "peculiar institution" upon which not only his prosperity but his whole social system rested. The exasperating violations of the Fugitive Slave Law in the North he considered indicative of what he might expect if Northern influences ever should become dominant at Washington. In the face of the growing wealth and population north of the Ohio River, the Southern planter felt that the only protection that existed for his institutions and his property was the traditional balance in the Senate between the free and slave states. But the loss of California had upset this balance, and under the "squatter sovereignty" provisions of the Compromise of 1850, there seemed every prospect that New Mexico and Utah would enter the Union as free states. The only possibility of restoring the balance appeared to be to break down the Missouri Compromise and to secure a slave state north of 36° 30′. Hence the ardor with which the Southern congressmen supported the Kansas-Nebraska bill, and hence the determination to have Kansas a slave state.[2] With Kansas, extending to the crest of the Rockies, safely in Southern hands, the "abolitionist"* migration to the Southwest would be blocked, and the South, with the Senate balance restored, could forever prevent the admission of another free state without a slave state to balance it. On the other hand, there was a widespread feeling in the South that if Kansas should be lost, Missouri might be "abolitionized" by the influx of free-soil settlers and the ease with which slaves could escape; with Missouri lost, the worst was to be expected.[3] Said an anonymous writer in *De Bow's Review,* "If Kansas is not secured, there will never be another slave state, and

---

*To Southern people of the 1850's anyone opposed to the extension of slavery was an abolitionist. In the North, on the other hand, the term was applied only to radicals of the stripe of William Lloyd Garrison, who demanded the immediate and unconditional abolition of slavery as a moral principle, even if a consequence should be the destruction of the Union.

the abolitionists will rule the nation; the Union will then become a curse rather than a blessing."[4]

Thus Kansas was indeed a prize worth fighting for. If the South was less excited in the early summer of 1854, it was because it seemed inevitable to the people of both sections that the prize should go to the South. Southerners depended upon the proximity of Missouri to win the battle before the North could get ready to strike. There was much talk, both North and South, of a "law of parallels," according to which population moved westward along parallels of latitude carrying its institutions with it,—and Kansas lay directly west of Missouri, with no natural barrier between. With no railroads across Iowa or Missouri, the Northern settler must make a long expensive journey overland or by steamboat to reach Kansas, while the Missourian needed only to ferry the Missouri River, or, south of the mouth of the Kansas, to step across an imaginary line. Thus it was everywhere taken for granted, in the South with joy and in the North with consternation, that the people of Missouri would cross the border and possess the land before Northern settlers could arrive. Then, too, it was widely assumed in the South, and particularly along the Missouri frontier, that the purpose of dividing the newly organized area into two territories, Kansas and Nebraska, was to give the former to the North and the latter to the South. From this it was assumed that the Northern migration should be content to go to Nebraska, leaving Kansas to the friends of slavery.*

The tone of the Northern press was gloomy. Most of the papers published correspondence or editorials asserting that Kansas must become a slave state. Everyone was demanding that something be done, but no one seemed to know quite what to do. In general, the proposals were for political action: the formation of a new political party, the re-enactment of the Missouri

---

*So testified nearly every pro-slavery witness before the Howard Congressional Committee in 1856. The late Professor F. H. Hodder of the University of Kansas has shown that the real purpose of the division of the territory was to provide alternate routes for the proposed Pacific Railway (F. H. Hodder, "The Railroad Background of the Kansas-Nebraska Act," *Mississippi Valley Historical Review* XII, June, 1925, 3-22).

Compromise, the repeal of the Fugitive Slave Law. The whole idea of squatter sovereignty was denounced as tricky and a fraud. To be sure, William H. Seward had declared in the Senate on May 25, 1854, at the time of the final passage of the Kansas-Nebraska Act: "Come on then, Gentlemen of the Slave States; since there is no escaping your challenge, I accept it in behalf of the cause of freedom. We will engage in competition for the virgin soil of Kansas, and God give the victory to the side which is stronger in numbers as it is in the right."[5] But only here and there was an editorial voice raised to echo this sentiment.

But there was at least one man who was willing to accept the challenge; indeed, these words of Seward's might well have been his. That man was Eli Thayer, a Yankee schoolmaster of Worcester, Massachusetts. Stephen A. Douglas had said in the course of the debate on the Nebraska bill that its effect would be to transfer the slavery question from the halls of Congress to the prairies of Kansas and Nebraska. Thayer appeared to take him at his word. To Eli Thayer, squatter sovereignty was a challenge and an opportunity. Instead of weeping over the Missouri Compromise and seeking vainly for its restoration, he would organize emigration, fill Kansas Territory with a free-labor population, and beat the South at its own game. As early as February, 1854, while the Congressional debate on the Kansas-Nebraska bill was at its height, he conceived the idea of forming a corporation to organize and facilitate emigration from New England to Kansas, and by making investments in the territory in the form of mills, hotels and other enterprises for the accommodation of settlers, to attract migration from all parts of the North.

Before the national House of Representatives had even begun its debates on the Kansas-Nebraska bill, Thayer had launched his project for an Emigrant Aid Company in the legislature of Massachusetts. A full month before the enactment of that measure he had secured his first charter. By the end of July, in the face of all but overpowering obstacles, the Emigrant Aid Company had become a going concern and had sent its first colony to Kansas. By autumn similar organizations, formed in imitation of Thayer's company, had sprung up in various parts of the North, and the politicians in western Missouri were denouncing the whole group of them under the all-embracing name of "The Emigrant Aid Society" for shipping "armies of hirelings" to Kansas. And before the Kansas struggle ended, even the President of the United States was placing the blame for all the trouble on these societies.

That Thayer and his company made an impression is obvious. One cannot read even the most cursory account of the Kansas conflict without being confronted at every turn with claims for and charges against the New England Emigrant Aid Company. According to the pro-slavery leaders, it was the cause of all the trouble. According to its friends, it saved Kansas to freedom and produced that wave of antislavery sentiment which launched the Republican party and forced the issue into civil war. "No man," says Thayer, "unless he be ignorant of the facts in the Kansas struggle, or completely blinded by malice or envy, will ever attempt to defraud the Emigrant Aid Company of the glory of having saved Kansas by defeating the slave power in a great and decisive contest."[6]

What manner of man was this Eli Thayer, and what sort of men were associated with him in his enterprise? Although he claimed direct descent from John Alden and Priscilla, Eli Thayer was born poor. He worked his way through Worcester County Manual Labor High School (later Worcester Academy) and Brown University. Beginning his active career in 1845 as a teacher in Worcester Academy, he soon became its principal. In 1849 he opened a school of his own, Oread Collegiate Institute in Worcester, one of the first of the country's schools for the higher education of women. He served his home town of Worcester as schoolboard member and alderman, and in 1854, at the age of thirty-five, he was a member of the lower house of the state legislature of Massachusetts for the Worcester district.[7] He had made his way entirely by his own efforts, and at the time he projected his Kansas venture he was reputed to have amassed moderate wealth.[8]

The late William E. Connelley* characterized Thayer as "a visionary, given to fantastic money-making schemes,"[9] and one of the men most closely associated with him in one phase of the Emigrant Aid enterprise declared, "He loved notoriety and noise, and was a born speculator."[10] It is difficult to read Thayer's own writings or an account of his life without agreeing with both of these characterizations. At various times he projected a number of schemes based on his idea of organized emigration; he actually launched such a project for colonization in western Virginia, founded the town of Ceredo, and later claimed the credit for saving West Virginia to the Union.[11] He always claimed all the credit for everything. Amos A. Lawrence was constantly criticizing him for talking too much, proclaiming grandiose plans which could not be carried out, and making extravagant promises which could not be fulfilled. With all his talk about millions, he rarely advanced any money of his own; in the entire career of the Emigrant Aid Company, he paid in only four hundred dollars for stock, while he drew over five thousand dollars from the Company treasury in Commissions.[12]

There has been some speculation as to where Thayer got his idea of promoted emigration. It has been hinted in some quarters that he was inspired by Seward's famous Senate speech of May 25, 1854, already mentioned, but inasmuch as the first charter for an emigrant aid company was issued more than a month before Seward's pronouncement, this explanation is out of the question. There was nothing particularly new in the general idea of promoted emigration and corporate colonization; both of these

---

*W. E. Connelley, for many years secretary of the Kansas State Historical Society and a prolific writer on early Kansas history, was one of the most severe critics of Thayer, Robinson, and all others connected with the New England Emigrant Aid Company. In all his writings on the Kansas struggle, Connelley showed a strong partisanship for James H. Lane.

[9]

devices had been employed in the settlement of North America by the English. Yet nothing indicated that Thayer was consciously imitating this early history. In 1845 Edward Everett Hale had prepared a pamphlet entitled *How to Conquer Texas before Texas Conquers Us,* in which he had advocated organized emigration to Texas and investments there as a means of checking the advance of slavery.[13] His plan differed from Thayer's mainly in that it did not contemplate the formation of a corporation to accomplish the object. One might suppose that Thayer, who was Hale's close neighbor in Worcester, was familiar with this pamphlet and borrowed from it, but Hale, in his later writings, specifically states the contrary.[14] Thayer's own explanation of the inception of the idea was that "suddenly it came upon me like a revelation."[15] No doubt this was oversimplifying the matter, but the evidence is conclusive that the definite plan for an emigrant aid company to stimulate the settlement of Kansas by advocates of a free state was Thayer's own.

His motives in launching the project were probably mixed. At the time he was usually branded by all who opposed his plans as an abolitionist fanatic, but his bitterness toward the professed abolitionists, both then and later in life, makes it clear that he did not regard himself as one of them. His later critics have usually asserted that the whole enterprise was only a speculative money-making scheme. That he hoped to make money out of it, he was always free to admit. He so stated in his first prospectus of the Company.[16] He so testified before the Howard Congressional Committee in 1856.[17] And writing thirty years after the Kansas conflict he declared, ". . . the enterprise was intended to be a money-making affair as well as a philanthropic undertaking . . . . In all my emigration schemes I expected to make the results return a profitable dividend in cash."[18] Another motive which in all probability influenced him, one of which he himself says nothing and of which his critics say little, was the hope of profiting politically. That he had political ambitions is obvious from his entire career. In 1856 he was elected to Congress, largely on the strength of his Emigrant Aid Company activities, and from that moment forth, although he did not sever his official connections with the organization, he lost interest in it and had very little to do with its later activities. But along with these motives, Thayer always asserted most emphatically, and his friends have always asserted for him, that he had a deep and genuine desire to check the expansion of slavery. If he was not sincere in this desire, he at least was able to convince others of his sincerity, and to enlist in his project many men who were prompted by no other motive.

Those to whom Thayer first appealed and whom he induced to join him in his first petition for a charter were, for the most part, aspiring politicians who presumably were animated by a political motive. The one notable exception, the only one of the first petitioners other than Thayer who sustained an active interest in the enterprise and served on its Board of Directors throughout the period of the Kansas crusade, was Dr. Samuel G. Howe, widely known reformer and philanthropist, and husband of the equally well-known Julia Ward Howe. Howe, a graduate of Brown University and Harvard Medical School, had served through the Greek war for independence as a surgeon, had founded the Boston Institution for the Blind, and had contributed much in time and money toward prison reform and the education of defectives. He founded and edited the *Boston Commonwealth,* an antislavery (but not Garrisonian abolitionist) newspaper. Howe was typical of the men who ultimately took hold of the Emigrant Aid Company and carried on its work through the critical years.[19]

One of the first men to "enlist for war" under Thayer's banner was the Reverend Edward Everett Hale, then a young Unitarian minister of Worcester. As he said in his own autobiography, the instant he heard of Thayer's plan, he called upon him and offered to "take hold anywhere."[20] He called himself Thayer's "man Friday." A zealot in the antislavery cause, Hale became the chief propagandist and historian of the Emigrant Aid Company. He had but little money to offer, but no man contributed more liberally of his time and energy. By August of 1854, he had ready for the press a book, *Kanzas and Nebraska,* written to promote the interests of the Emigrant Aid Company. He made dozens of speeches and wrote numerous articles for newspapers and magazines on behalf of the Company. It was he who devised and carried through the plan to enlist the clergy of New England in the enterprise. Hale was the only man who sustained his interest in the Company to the very end. More than anyone else he assumed the responsibility of keeping up a shadow of organization during the Civil War years, and he had a prominent part in the effort to revive the Company after the war. Finally, he preserved the papers and effects of the Company for posterity. It was his proud boast in his old age that the Emigrant Aid Company still existed and that he was its president.[21]

Thayer and Hale might furnish the inspiration for the movement, but if any success were to be attained something more substantial than inspiration was needed. This "material aid," as Lawrence called it, could come only from the merchants of Boston and its vicinity. The man to whom Thayer gives all the credit for getting him a hearing with the businessmen was John M. S. Williams, a Virginian by birth, of the mercantile firm of Glidden and Williams. Thayer tells how, when he had labored long and seemingly in vain to interest the people of Boston in his enterprise, Williams came forward with an offer of a ten thousand dollar subscription, and then used his influence with the businessmen to bring others in.[22] Williams became one of the trustees under the temporary organization, and was a vice president during the whole active period of the corporation. Only Lawrence gave more liberally of his means, and Williams gave much more willingly. Again and again he paid privately for things for which the Company got credit and he never refused a demand for money. On numerous occasions Lawrence chided him for overliberality, at one time sending back a check for three hundred dollars with the remark that it was both poor policy and cruelty to ride a free horse to death.[23] So far as the records show, Williams never objected to the Company's investing its money with a view to at least returning the investment, but it is clear that his primary interest was in making Kansas free. Yet he was the most pessimistic of the crusaders. In October, 1854, he sent in a check for one hundred dollars as his "farewell offering to liberty,"[24] and at the end of 1856 Dr. Webb wrote, "I find but one despondent man among us; that is our friend J. M. S. Williams."[25]

The man who bore the greatest burden of the Aid Company, other than financial, was Thomas H. Webb, M.D., secretary of the Company from its inception to his death in 1866. A native of Providence, he was a classmate of Dr. S. G. Howe at Brown University, and later went through Harvard Medical School. His interest, however, was in science and history rather than in medicine, and he failed financially as a physician. He was active in several scientific and historical societies and contributed to Rofn's *Antiquitates Americanae.* He was one of the founders of the Providence Athenaeum and was its first librarian. For a time he edited the *Providence Journal.* Later he was connected with Horace Mann's *Common School Journal.* In 1850 he was secretary of the commission to survey the Mexican boundary. After the secretaryship of the Emigrant Aid Company had ceased to be a full-time job he became secretary of the Massachusetts Institute of Technology, a position which he held until his death.[26] As secretary of the Aid Company he literally broke his health with hard work.[27] In addition to his office work and correspondence, he prepared a pamphlet, *Information for Kansas Emigrants,* which he revised through twenty editions; it was universally regarded at the time as the most thorough and reliable of the numerous settlers' handbooks. Although he received a small salary, no one ever doubted the altruism of his motives. Lawrence characterized him as "the truest man of all."[28]

Each of these men carried his full share of the load, but the one who contests with Thayer the distinction of being what James Ford Rhodes called the "soul of the enterprise," was Amos A. Lawrence. Lawrence was the opposite of Thayer in almost every particular. At the time of his association with the Emigrant Aid Company he was looked upon as one of Boston's leading men of affairs, heading the commercial house founded by his father which had established the industrial towns of Lawrence and Lowell, Massachusetts. Considered wealthy, he was a philanthropist on principle, contributing to everyone who appealed to him in a worthy cause; indeed, one biographer declares that he gave away four times the fortune his father left him.[29] He was conservative in temperament and affiliations: an Episcopalian in religion, and a "Hunker Whig" in politics. He rejected all forms of radicalism, including Garrisonian abolitionism, though he was a stout opponent of the extension of slavery. He opposed the formation of the Republican party because it was sectional, voting for Fillmore in 1856 (despite his abhorrence of the narrower aspects of "Know-Nothingism") and for Bell and Everett in 1860. That he was utterly devoid of political ambitions is indicated by the fact that he declined the Know-Nothing nomination for governor of Massachusetts on two occasions when the party had a chance of success, and finally accepted the nomination when he knew that success was impossible, in the hope of rallying conservative sentiment against sectional parties. Lawrence may have been somewhat inconsistent in his views, but he always stood staunchly for what he regarded as sound principles.

However much one may be led to question Thayer's sincerity of purpose, there can be no doubt of Lawrence's. He was anxious to prevent the extension of slavery into Kansas, and he looked upon the Emigrant Aid Company as only one of several means to that end. He made many contributions apart from those to the Company. Exact in his own business affairs, he disliked

Thayer's whole plan of a commercial enterprise and consented to it with reluctance. He much preferred to carry on the whole venture as a co-operative society with no investment features whatever. He never expected the Company stock to pay; he regarded his own subscriptions to the stock as contributions to the cause, and he advised others not to invest more than they could afford to lose.

Lawrence was one of the trustees under the temporary association and was treasurer of the Company until the spring of 1857. He advanced out of his own pocket all the money that passed through the Company treasury during the first three months of its activity. During his entire treasurership he was frequently called upon to meet drafts for which there were no funds; he usually grumbled, but he always paid. On several occasions the Company was in debt to him for overdrafts as much as six thousand dollars. Besides making numerous outright donations to the Company and to various other phases of the Kansas work (including one gift of ten thousand dollars to found the college that finally became the University of Kansas), Lawrence paid for more than four hundred shares of Emigrant Aid Company stock (at a cost of eight thousand dollars), but he gave away all but a hundred and twenty-five shares. In a word, during the critical years of the Kansas conflict, it was Amos A. Lawrence who was the chief pecuniary support and conservative balance wheel of the New England Emigrant Aid Company.[30]

It was these men, and others like them who will be introduced as the account proceeds, that, raising the battle cry of freedom, accepted the challenge flung out by the passage of the Kansas-Nebraska Act. Believing that they could turn the enemy's weapon of squatter sovereignty against his own ramparts, they launched what was to them a holy war, a crusade against what they all felt to be an iniquitous institution. Their goal was not merely to save Kansas to freedom, but to block forever the further expansion of slavery and, as Lincoln was to phrase it so aptly a few years later, to "put it in the way of ultimate extinction."

CHAPTER II

The Crusaders

A S ALREADY INDICATED, Thayer began to lay his plans and to marshal his crusaders as soon as it became apparent that the bars of the Missouri Compromise were to be let down. He hoped to have his organization completed and be ready to begin operations the instant Kansas Territory should be opened to settlement. But he soon discovered that the problem was far less simple than he had supposed. Those who joined him in the first outburst of enthusiasm recoiled when cash was called for. Men of means who became interested in his project were cautious and had ideas of their own. Weeks dragged by while businessmen, who were willing to throw their weight into the balance against the extension of slavery, but who objected to being made a cat's-paw of politics, wrangled with politicians who were attracted to the venture by its vote-catching possibilities. For a time it seemed that the Emigrant Aid Company was to die in its swaddling clothes. Three months elasped before even a temporary organization could be effected, and it was a full year after Thayer's first application for a charter before the New England Emigrant Aid Company took final form.

Early in March, 1854, after the Kansas-Nebraska bill had passed the Senate, but before it was considered in the House of Representatives, Thayer made his first definite move by circulating a petition for a charter. His original petition contained sixty-two signatures, twenty-six being those of members of the legislature of Massachusetts. The petition proposed a capitalization of $10,000,000 and stated the purpose of the projected corporation to be "to aid and protect emigrants from New England or from the Old World in settling in the West, and to secure to them in their new homes the advantages of education and the rights and privileges of free labor."[1] The aim most talked of in the early discussion was the protection of the emigrant against tricksters. A bill for the incorporation of The Massachusetts Emigrant Aid Company, introduced by Thayer and sponsored by others of the petitioners who were members of the legislature, received the governor's signature April 26, 1854.[2] Only twenty of the petitioners were named as incorporators. Most of them were local politicians or merchants. Two, Charles Allen and Stephen C. Phillips, were members of Congress. One, S. G. Howe, was already nationally prominent, and three others, Anson Burlingame, Henry Wilson, and Alexander H. Bullock, were destined soon to become so. Only Thayer and Howe took any further part in the organization of the Emigrant Aid Company.[3]

This act of incorporation, or charter, as it was commonly called, created a corporation "for the purpose of assisting emigrants to settle in the West." The company was authorized to issue capital stock to an amount not exceeding $5,000,000, divided into hundred-dollar shares, assessable at four dollars a share the first year and ten dollars each year thereafter. No stockholder could cast votes for more than fifty shares of his own and fifty voted by proxy.[4]

The incorporators met May 3, 1854, at the State House in Boston, accepted the charter, and appointed a committee to draw up a plan of operations. On or about May 18 another meeting was held, to hear the report of this committee and to launch a campaign for funds. At this meeting, Dr. Thomas H. Webb, soon to become secretary of the organization, was employed to solicit stock subscriptions. But almost at once difficulties began to develop. While the incorporators were willing enough to lend the prestige of their names, they were not in a hurry to obligate themselves financially. A week after this meeting Webb complained in a letter to Thayer that not one of the incorporators had subscribed for a single share of stock, and that he could not get them to co-operate in his efforts even to the extent of introducing him to men of means.[5]

[17]

During the early part of June several meetings of the incorporators and their "associates" were held. By-laws were adopted, Dr. Webb was chosen secretary, and committees were appointed to solicit stock subscriptions outside Boston. But at each successive meeting it became more apparent that the incorporators were unwilling to assume the financial obligations which would be necessary to complete an organization. Finally, at a meeting on June 12, the nominating committee reported that it was unable to select a board of directors, and recommended that the charter be laid aside until it could be amended. A series of articles were adopted organizing an emigrant aid company as a private association under trustees. Eli Thayer and Amos A. Lawrence were designated as trustees from Boston to serve with a third, to be selected from New York. [6]

In explaining the impasse of June 12, Thayer declared, in his later account of the enterprise, that "some of the corporators feared that they might become personally responsible and had withdrawn."[7] The difficulty seems to have been that under the then existing corporation laws of Massachusetts (as under the laws of practically all states today), subscribers to the stock of a corporation, while not liable beyond the amount of their subscription, *were* liable for any unpaid balance on their stock. Since the enormous capitalization was intended, as Hale said, only to "strike terror into the enemy," with only 4 per cent assessed the first year, the liability of each subscriber would have been many times the amount of his actual investment. Then, too, besides the general unwillingness to assume such liability, there must have been a feeling, as Thayer pointed out in his testimony before the Howard Committee, that the obligation to continue payments over a ten-year period was an unwise and unnecessary burden.[8]

One of the "associates" who had joined the incorporators in the preliminary efforts to organize under the charter was Patrick T. Jackson, a merchant of Boston. He it was who enlisted Amos A. Lawrence in the enterprise. During the week when the incorporators were haggling over liability, Jackson persuaded Lawrence in private conversations that the project "was just about dying for want of concerted action and for want of business knowledge on the part of those who had started it."[9] On June 10 he wrote Lawrence a long letter explaining that in view of the difficulties it had been decided to abandon the charter until the next session of the legislature could amend it, and in the meantime to organize a private company under three trustees. He urged Lawrence to serve as one of the trustees, saying, "You can do us more good than anyone else."[10] Lawrence replied the same day, agreeing to serve.[11] This acceptance was reported at the meeting of June 12 and a tentative organization was formed under Articles of Association.

These articles provided for a private company with a capital stock of $200,000 in fully paid twenty-dollar shares. Management of the company and custody of the funds were vested in a board of three trustees, who were forbidden to incur debts beyond the amount of paid-in capital. Each trustee was to be liable only for his own official acts. A consulting board or council of fifteen was chosen to assist and advise the trustees.[12] Thus it was hoped to avoid the objections raised to the charter and to save the enterprise from utter collapse.

About the middle of May, while things still appeared to be going well in Boston, Thayer went to New York to launch the movement there. He evidently had considerable success in making converts. On May 29 Horace Greeley began a series of editorials in the *Tribune* under the caption "A Plan of Freedom," endorsing the scheme. A delegation from New York was present at the meeting of June 7, at which a committee was appointed to organize New York City. During the next few days the names of three prominent New York businessmen, Peter Cooper, George Niebold, and Moses H. Grinnell, were sent to Boston with a statement that these men were ready to serve as directors.[13] According to Thayer's own account, written more than thirty years later, he was still in New York and had obtained $200,000 of stock subscriptions when he received word of the decision in Boston to abandon the charter. The news, he said, struck him "like a thunderbolt," for it would mean the loss of these New York subscriptions. He hastened back to Boston to try to save the charter.[14] When he arrived on the scene of action, he must have realized at once the hopelessness of the situation, for P. T. Jackson, in his letter to Lawrence on June 10, stated that Thayer had agreed to serve as a trustee under the new plan, or, if it should seem best, to step aside in favor of another.

It was the hope and expectation of all the Massachusetts promoters that the New York men would fall in with the new scheme. Grinnell was selected as the New York trustee, and at a meeting in Boston on June 19, this selection was announced and an organization completed. But Grinnell refused to serve, and a long letter from Lawrence pleading with him to reconsider failed to persuade him.[15]

Not only Grinnell, but the entire New York group, objected to the plan of operating without a charter. A letter from Thayer to Lawrence, dated June 22, indicated that Thayer had discussed the matter at length with members of the New York committee and that, despite all the safeguards inserted in the Articles of Association, they were fearful of personal liability in an unincorporated company.* Thayer concluded this portion of his letter with the observation, "I begin to despair of doing anything beyond our own State except under a charter."[16] He was convinced that the New York people could not be held in line without a charter, while the Massachusetts men would not object to a charter that would obviate the deficiencies of the old one. Accordingly, he set to work to obtain a new one with as little delay as possible. The Massachusetts legislature had adjourned and would not meet again until the following winter. The next logical place to

---

* As well they might be, since an unincorporated joint stock company is legally a partnership in which each member is liable for all debts of the association.

Charles Robinson

Samuel C. Pomeroy

James H. Lane

David R. Atchison

Eli Thayer

Amos A. Lawrence

Thomas H. Webb

Edward Everett Hale

seek a charter would be New York, but the New York legislature was not in session. Since the only legislature near at hand that was then meeting was that of Connecticut, Thayer determined, in consultation with some of the New York committee, to apply for a charter in that state. In the letter to Lawrence just referred to, he said that he had sent a lawyer to Connecticut to procure a charter, and that if successful in obtaining it, they might use it or not as seemed best.

The act of incorporation must have been rushed through the Connecticut legislature with rare dispatch, for on June 29, exactly a week after his letter announcing that he had sent a lawyer to apply for it, Thayer sent Lawrence a copy of the charter.[17] The new charter retained the $5,000,000 authorized capitalization, but omitted the earlier provisions for division into shares and for annual assessments.[18] By issuing the stock in small amounts to be paid in full at once, the objections raised in regard to the first charter would be avoided. Thayer stated his own preference for ten-dollar shares, although the secretary of the New York committee favored five-dollar units, saying he could get the whole capital taken in such shares by farmers and mechanics.[19]

At first Lawrence and Jackson, who had become, along with Thayer, the prime movers in Boston, did not object to going ahead with the Connecticut charter. Indeed, it appears that at this juncture it was agreed to abandon the tentative organization effected June 12 under the Articles of Association, and to organize under the charter.[20] All efforts to fill Grinnell's place on the board of trustees were dropped. Stock-subscription blanks were printed and arrangements were made for a meeting to be held in New Haven to accept the charter and form a new organization. Both Lawrence and Jackson participated in these preparations. In fact, Jackson assumed the principal responsibility, going so far as to submit to Lawrence for his approval a list of five Boston directors (including the names of Lawrence and Thayer) to serve in the new company.[21]

[21]

However, the hope of organizing Boston under this charter proved illusory. On July 5 Lawrence wrote to Thayer that he had that day "seen or heard from nearly all the gentlemen interested in the organization of an emigrant aid society" and that subscriptions could not be had under it. "Finally," he added, "Mr. Jackson came in with the same report. He is very much discouraged."[22] Jackson must have been very much discouraged indeed, for from this point he refused to have anything further to do with the movement. It was nearly two years before his name again appeared in the records of the Emigrant Aid Company.

Here, truly, was an impasse. The New York men would not go on without a charter; the Boston men would not go on with one. Lawrence, at least, was persuaded that the two groups must part company and each go its own way. In his letter of July 5 to Thayer he continued, "The New York people must take that [the Connecticut charter] and we must begin anew as a charitable society with a Massachusetts organization." During the next twenty-four hours Thayer must have replied, orally or in a letter that is not preserved, that he was unwilling to give up the effort to include the Boston group in the new organization and that he considered the Articles of Association to have been already abandoned. At any rate, Lawrence wrote to him again the next day, "I hope you will be able to go on with the Connecticut charter, but I think you can not do much in Boston. People here are willing to pay down money, but will not subscribe for stock. The old articles having been given up, please to consider me out of office and not a candidate under the organization as a stock company."[23] Nevertheless Lawrence did not entirely eliminate himself as Jackson had done, for a week later Thayer wrote to him in regard to the New Haven meeting, asking him to select the names of persons for Massachusetts directors.[24]

The new Haven meeting was duly held July 18 or 19.[25] Neither Lawrence nor Thayer was present. Thayer desired to attend, but, after much urging from Lawrence, he had gone to

Buffalo with the "Pioneer Party" of Kansas settlers.* The meeting was under the management, for the most part, of the New York promoters, particularly R. N. Havens, although some prominent leaders of New Haven, such as Timothy Dwight, took an active part. Benjamin F. Butler presided. The Connecticut charter was accepted, by-laws were adopted, and officers were elected. Eli Thayer was chosen president; R. N. Havens of New York and William H. Russell of New Haven, vice presidents; A. A. Lawrence, treasurer; and Thomas H. Webb, secretary. It was voted to maintain offices in New York, Boston and New Haven. Obviously it was the intention to merge the nebulous organization already functioning after a fashion in Boston into the new company. But, as will be noted presently, Thayer had already yielded to Lawrence on the question of separate organization for Massachusetts, and Lawrence had made up his mind to have nothing to do with the New York and Connecticut company. As soon as he was notified officially of his selection as treasurer of the company, he wrote to Havens (the active head) declining to serve, giving as his excuse that his duties as treasurer of the Boston association would require all the time he could give to the work.²⁶ This completed the divorcement of the Boston and New York companies, although for several months Thayer continued his active connection with both.

Something of the later career of the New York company will be discussed in another chapter, but one other aspect of the Connecticut charter deserves brief mention at this point. The error has crept into some later writings, including Channing's *History of the United States*,²⁷ that the permanent charter of the New England Emigrant Aid Company was issued by Connecticut. The only possible sources of this error are the fact of the existence of a Connecticut charter, and rather hazy references to all the charters in some of the early accounts. That the New England

*Discussed on page 52.

Emigrant Aid Company was chartered by Masschusetts is as certain as that the Company ever existed.

In the opinion of Professor Robert F. Moody, "Thayer evidently did not take seriously" Lawrence's resignation of July 6.[28] Whether this was the situation or whether the two reached some sort of understanding, there is no way of knowing. During the next week, on July 8 and 11, Lawrence wrote Thayer two letters relative to the "Pioneer Party," scheduled to start on the seventeenth; in neither of these did he say any more about resigning. At all events, on July 15, for no reason that is apparent in the extant correspondence, Lawrence wrote to Thayer definitely resigning.[29] As Professor Moody sees it, this was a bit of strategy on Lawrence's part to get Thayer to accede to his views, and it "evidently convinced Thayer that, in order to have Lawrence's support, the Massachusetts group must be separately organized."[30] That Thayer, having lost the support of Jackson, would be anxious to retain at almost any cost the active co-operation of a man of Amos A. Lawrence's wealth and prestige is self-evident. Accordingly Thayer wrote Lawrence July 17 from Worcester, on the eve of his departure for Buffalo and the very day before the scheduled meeting at New Haven, that he had become convinced from expressions of opinion by Boston and Roxbury men that it was desirable to go on under the Articles of Association and fill the vacancy on the board of trustees occasioned by Grinnell's refusal to serve. He was willing to leave the selection of the new trustee to Lawrence, although he suggested Mr. Jackson, and even offered to vacate his own place and so make room for another, if Lawrence should think best: "The truth is," he continued, "the private company is still in existence in the estimation of the citizens and they subscribe for stock under that belief; at least some of them do."[31] Lawrence replied under the same date: "I can not answer about the organization. We are very peculiar here [Boston] in business transactions and very exact. Therefore

[24]

I am inclined to think we must go on by ourselves if at all. What is wanted now is cash."[32]

Sometime between the date of these letters and July 24, Lawrence, presumably acting on a suggestion in Thayer's letter that he might be able to "start something better," drew up a constitution for an "Emigrant Aid Society" and an "Indenture" to be signed by its trustees.[33] As already suggested in the introductory chapter, Lawrence was opposed to the whole idea of a commercial company, preferring that the emigrant aid enterprise operate as a philanthropic society with an open membership, which should depend on donations for its revenue. He believed, as he had previously written Thayer, that Boston businessmen, preferring like himself not to mix their philanthropy with business, would "pay down money, but [would] not subscribe for stock." This drafted constitution and indenture embodied his ideas. There was to be no capital stock, and anyone could become a member of the projected society by signing the constitution and paying dues.

A meeting of all interested persons was held in Boston on July 24 after Thayer's return from Buffalo. Lawrence's constitution with its plan for an open society was rejected.* The old Articles of Association of June 12, revised under the title Articles of Agreement and Association, were adopted as the basis of organization. These provided for an unincorporated joint-stock company under the name *The Emigrant Aid Company* with a capitalization of $200,000, divided into twenty-dollar shares. All subscriptions were conditioned upon 2,500 shares being subscribed by September 10, 1854, after which time shares were assessable up to their full value. The Council of Fifteen was eliminated and entire direction was vested in a board of three trustees, named

---

*On the back of the orginal draft, which Professor Moody found among the Lawrence papers, there is endorsed in Lawrence's handwriting, "Form of a constitution of an Emigrant Aid Society. July, 1854. The persons interested thought a stock company would be preferable." In a later incomplete draft of a letter to J. M. S. Williams, Lawrence wrote, "I prepared another plan and went to the next meeting with it. That was not accepted" (Moody notes).

in the articles, to serve until removed by a two-thirds majority of the stockholders. Amos A. Lawrence, J. M. S. Williams, and Eli Thayer were named as trustees for life.³⁴ If Jackson was ever approached on the subject of serving as a trustee he evidently declined. Immediately after this general session the trustees met to complete their organization. Dr. Webb was chosen secretary of the Company and of the trustees at a salary of $1,000 a year. Lawrence was formally elected treasurer. Provision was made for weekly meetings of the trustees.³⁵

This was the organization under which the Company functioned during the remainder of 1854 and until March 5, 1855, when it gave way to a corporate organization under a second Massachusetts charter. At the seventh weekly meeting of the trustees, September 16, it was voted, on motion of Thayer, that the words "of Massachusetts" be added to the name, making it read "The Emigrant Aid Company of Massachusetts." At the same time it was voted to request the company operating in New York City under the Connecticut charter similarly to designate itself.³⁶ Shortly after this the New York company assumed the name The Emigrant Aid Company of New York and Connecticut.

When the Massachusetts legislature met in January, 1855, the trustees petitioned for a new charter. A question has been raised in some quarters as to the motive of this action.* It seems fairly clear that, while it had been the intention from the very beginning of the "Voluntary Association" to apply for another Massachusetts charter at the first opportunity, the real purpose was to free the subscribers from the liability which the law imposes on every stockholder of an unincorporated joint-stock company

---

* Professor Moody ventures the opinion that the trustees sought a new charter to escape the personal liability which each had assumed the previous September for $10,000 worth of stock, underwritten, as will be explained more fully in a later chapter, to make possible an assessment on the subscriptions. No assessment could be levied, according to the Articles of Agreement and Association, unless $50,000 should be subscribed by September 1, 1854. Since only $20,000 had been subscribed by that date, the trustees made up the $30,000 deficiency by each subscribing for $10,000.

(which is legally a partnership) for all debts of the association.*

"An Act to Incorporate the New England Emigrant Aid Company" became a law February 21, 1855. Naming only the three trustees and Dr. Webb with their "associates, successors and assigns" as incorporators, a corporation was created "for the purpose of directing emigration Westward, and aiding in providing accommodations for the emigrants after arriving at their places of destination, and for other purposes." Capitalization was limited to $1,000,000, and real estate holdings in Massachusetts to $20,000. As in the Connecticut charter, the old provisions for division of capital into shares and for the basis of stock assessments were omitted.[37] In fact, the close resemblance of this charter to the one granted by Connecticut suggests that the real objection of the Boston men to acting under the Connecticut corporation may have been less a matter of concern as to the suitability of the charter than a disinclination to join with certain of the New York promoters. A clipping from the New York correspondence of the *Boston Post* under the date line of October 18, 1854, in which the New York promoters are characterized as "obscure politicians seeking a new ground for self-advancement,"[38] strengthens this suspicion.

The trustees at once (February 24) called a meeting for March 5, 1855, to accept the charter and to form an organization under it.[39] Even before this formal action, the trustees had set out to construct a slate of officers and directors for the new corporation. As early as February 20 Lawrence had written to J. M. S. Williams suggesting the names of George Upton and John Lowell as Boston directors and saying that he was writing to neighboring

---

* A circular letter to the stockholders advising them of the action (copy in Collected Pamphlets) states that the trustees had petitioned for a charter "in accordance with the wishes of the stockholders to avoid the personal liability to which they are now subjected." A circular addressed to the New England clergymen a few months later (copy among Aid Company Papers) states that, under the Charter, "no stockholder is liable in any event for anything beyond his first investment." A clause had been inserted in the Articles of Agreement and Association that a stockholder should not be liable beyond the amount of his subscription, but that such a reservation was void as to outsiders at common law must have been known to businessmen of the standing of Lawrence and Williams.

towns for the names of the best men there.[40] On February 28 he wrote to George Upton urging him to accept the presidency of the new company.[41] On March 2 he again wrote to Williams, this time suggesting William B. Spooner, John Lowell, and Dr. Samuel Cabot as Boston directors. Stating that Upton would not serve, he proposed John Carter Brown of Providence for president. "The president," he declared, "should be a conservative man, an old Hunker [Whig] if possible. Neither Thayer nor yourself is 'old fogy' enough for the place."[42] Thus it is clear that the personnel of the new corporation was hand-picked by the old trustees and that the selections were made with a view to creating a favorable impression. The large Board of Directors (the by-laws specified not less than twenty-five) was intended for show, with a small group of what Lawrence called "working directors" (finally designated "executive committee") actually to manage affairs. These dummy directors were to be men of prominence in the various localities in which the Company was seeking stock subscriptions, and their names were to be used to lend prestige and the appearance of stability to the organization. In several instances men who were not even stockholders were carried as directors for several years. Above all, the president, a mere figurehead whose chief function was to lend the prestige of his name, must be distinguished for his wealth and influence, and must be free from the slightest taint of political radicalism. Lawrence, at least, did not intend that the officers of this company should ever be ridiculed as "obscure politicians seeking a new ground for self-advancement."

John Carter Brown, slated for the presidency, was a wealthy merchant of the firm of Brown and Ives of Providence, Rhode Island. He was the son of Nicholas Brown, one of the founders of the firm, whose gifts to Rhode Island College had led to the changing of the name of that institution to Brown University. John Carter Brown was also a benefactor of the University, and his memory is preserved on the campus by the John Carter Brown

Library, provided for in his son's will. His hobby was the collection of rare books. Like Lawrence, Brown was interested in the Emigrant Aid Company only as a weapon with which to combat the extension of slavery. One of the heaviest stockholders, he regarded his subscriptions as contributions to a cause, never expecting or apparently desiring that the stock should ever yield him a pecuniary return. He remained president of the Emigrant Aid Company as long as it was interested in Kansas. While his position was larely nominal, he always took an active interest in the affairs of the Company, usually attended directors' meetings, and was always ready to advance money or give time and effort to the work.[43]

The meeting for organization was held on Monday, March 5, 1855, at the Company's new office at No. 3 Winter Street, Boston. After formal acceptance of the charter by the four incorporators, these proceeded to elect twenty-five "associates." Whether the list, presented by Thayer, was composed of persons present or of those whom it was designed to make directors is not clear, since there would be much overlapping. At any rate, the names were identical with those placed on the original roster of directors, with the addition of John Carter Brown, George B. Upton, Samuel B. Tobey, and Calvin E. Stowe (husband of Harriet Beecher Stowe, and prominent in his own right as a clergyman). It may be assumed that Upton, Tobey, and Stowe refused to serve as directors. Upton and Tobey were added to the list a year later and served throughout the remaining active life of the Company. Stowe, who held twenty shares of stock, continued to attend stockholders' meetings and to take an active interest in Company matters, but was never made a director, probably because he declined to serve.

Having thus enlarged the personnel of the Company, the meeting proceeded to organize by the adoption of by-laws and the election of officers. The code of by-laws, presented by Amos A. Lawrence, provided for the usual officers (two vice presidents) and a board of at least twenty-five directors, three of whom were to be the president and two vice presidents *ex officio*. The secretary, in addition to the usual duties of the office, was to have charge of arranging for the transportation of settlers (a function that Dr. Webb was already performing under the trustees). The treasurer was forbidden to incur any debt or to make any payment without the money in hand; this provision, never observed, was intended to stop the advances of cash which Lawrence had been making under the trusteeship. The capital stock was to be divided into twenty-dollar shares, with provision for the issuance of certificates and the transfer of shares. It was provided that there should be an annual meeting of stockholders on the Tuesday before the last Wednesday in May, with special meetings to be called by the secretary on the request of one-fourth of the directors. One-sixth of all paid-in stock should constitute a quorum. There was to be a meeting of the directors at least once each quarter, with five constituting a quorum. The directors were authorized to appoint "such committees of their number as may be requisite," and this was construed to permit the appointment of an executive committee which should perform all the usual functions of a board of directors.[44]

The following officers were elected: John Carter Brown of Providence, president; Eli Thayer of Worcester and J. M. S. Williams of Cambridge, vice presidents; Amos A. Lawrence, treasurer; and Thomas H. Webb, secretary. In addition to the three senior officers, who were directors *ex officio*, twenty-one directors were named in accordance with a prearranged slate.* It was voted that all stockholders of the Emigrant Aid Company of Massachu-

---

*The directors were: William B. Spooner, Samuel Cabot, Jr., and John Lowell, all of Boston; William J. Rotch, New Bedford; J. P. Williston, Northampton; William Dudley Pickman, Salem; Richard P. Waters, Beverly; R. A. Chapman, Springfield; John Nessmith, Lowell; Alvah Crocker, Fitchburg (who declined to serve); Moses Davenport, Newburyport; Charles H. Bigelow, Lawrence; Dr. Nathan Durfee, Fall River; William Willis, Portland, Maine; Franklin Muzzy, Bangor, Maine; John D. Lang, Vasselboro, Maine; E. P. Walton, Montpelier, Vermont; Joseph Gilmore, Concord; Ichabod Goodwin, Portsmouth, New Hampshire; Thomas H. Edwards, Keene, New Hampshire; Albert Day, Hartford, Connecticut.

setts be admitted as stockholders of the New England Emigrant Aid Company by exchanging their stock share for share. Lawrence then presented a report of the treasury under the old organization, and the meeting adjourned.[45] A bare quorum of the newly elected directors met immediately and named an executive committee composed of J. M. S. Williams, Eli Thayer, Dr. Samuel Cabot, and R. P. Waters.[46]

Since the by-laws called for twenty-five directors, there was one vacancy, and the refusal of one of those elected to serve created a second vacancy. Accordingly an adjourned meeting of the stockholders on June 1, 1855, added the names of Le Baron Russell, and Charles J. Higginson, both of Boston, to the list of directors,[47] and at a directors' meeting on June 9, both of these were added to the executive committee.[48]

Thus, through many tribulations and in the face of crushing discouragements, there was organized what might be called the general staff of the Kansas crusade. The movement was rescued from becoming the plaything of petty politics and so probably saved from the oblivion that was soon to overtake the New York and Connecticut Company. In the struggle to perfect a workable organization, control of the enterprise passed from schemers like Thayer and zealots like Hale to stable men of affairs who, while no less sincere in their loyalty to the cause, could be depended on to conduct the crusade calmly and on a high moral plane. The original directors, all hand-picked by Lawrence, all measured up in varying degrees to the standard he had set for the president: they were prominent, well-to-do, and free from any taint of radicalism. Abolitionists were shunned as though they had been lepers. The Boston directors, on whose shoulders fell the real burden of management, were all leading citizens of their day. Lowell and Cabot belonged to the old aristocracy referred to in the familiar jest about Boston, "where the Lowells speak only to Cabots, and the Cabots speak only to God." Russell and Higginson also were members of "first families." Both Cabot and Russell

[31]

were among Boston's foremost physicians. Lowell was a practicing lawyer, and later became a United States district judge. William B. Spooner, who was added to the executive committee in the spring of 1856, was a merchant and philanthropist. In his will, he left a sum of money to the University of Kansas which was used, in part, to build Spooner Library, now the University Museum of Fine Arts. Waters, the only member of the executive committee other than Thayer who did not live in Boston, was a merchant of Salem. Perhaps it is straining a point to call such men crusaders, but they were engaged in conducting a movement which certainly partook of the character of a crusade and which was to leave a lasting imprint on the history of their country.

CHAPTER III

The Weapons of Our Warfare

F OR THE WEAPONS of our warfare are not carnal," Saint Paul proclaimed to the Corinthians, "but are mighty through God to the pulling down of strongholds." It is not recorded that any of the leaders of the Emigrant Aid Company ever thought of this text in connection with their plans, but something like this must have been in the minds of Thayer and his associates when they were mapping their campaign. True enough, before the Kansas crusade should end, these knights of freedom were to be toying with no less carnal weapons than Sharps rifles, but in their original program there was no place for the shedding of blood. Their soldiers were to be peaceful settlers; their bullets, ballots; their fortresses, hotels, schools, and churches; and their heavy artillery, sawmills. Of course, like the mail-clad knights who had sought to reclaim the Holy Land from the Saracen, they were not averse to profiting from their conquest, but their battle cry was FREEDOM.

The plan on which they proposed to operate may be briefly summarized: first, to promote migration from the Northeast by supplying information, by securing for the emigrant reduced rates of transportation, and by organizing the prospective settlers into conducted parties for travel; second, to attract settlers into Kansas from all parts of the North by establishing in that territory mills, hotels, schools, churches, and other enterprises which would mitigate the hardships of pioneering; third, to seek to realize from these properties and from the sale of town lots which might be donated to the Company by parties of settlers, a return to the stockholders on the money invested. This plan appeared perfectly feasible on its face. In a period when thousands of persons were migrating westward every year, it seemed certain that a responsible organization which should advertise Kan-

[33]

sas, assist migration thither, and pour into the territory the bait of a large capital investment would be able to fill Kansas with enough settlers to outvote the pro-slavery squatters from Missouri and the South. And this very ingathering of population must inevitably increase the value of the Company's property holdings in the territory. Of course no one foresaw the financial difficulties that were to hamper the Company's operations, the outbreak of violence in Kansas that was to drag it into the swirl of national politics, or the economic depression that was to wipe out the value of its holdings. In the summer of 1854 all was rosy. The problem of organization appeared to have been solved, and the success of the enterprise seemed assured.

The first task that the Company set for itself was that of aiding and directing migration to Kansas. At first, at least, the aim was not so much to persuade people to migrate as to persuade those who might be migrating of their own accord to settle in Kansas. Thayer, in his various writings, always spoke of "directing" migration. Edward Everett Hale, in his *Kanzas and Nebraska,* published in August, 1854, declared the purpose of the Company to be "to secure for Kansas a fair proportion of the western emigration."[1] It was an early intention, never entirely given up, to divert some portion of the German and Irish immigration to Kansas. Contemporary newspaper accounts of the Emigrant Aid Company always referred to such an aim. Writing to his father, May 11, 1854, Hale said, "You know how it [the emigrant aid project] has interested me as a means of helping these German and Irish people westward without suffering."[2] Another objective stressed in the early petitions for charters and frequently mentioned in the early correspondence was the protection of emigrants to the West against frauds commonly practiced on them. In an official draft of instructions prepared by Lawrence on behalf of the trustees in August, 1854, Dr. Robinson, as agent of the Company, is directed to try to secure the co-operation of railway companies to stop frauds practiced on emigrants "by 'runners' and others who receive pay for making sale of tickets, or who sell fraudulent tickets."[3]

The first thing the Company set about to do in aid of emigration was to secure reduced rates of transportation. The Boston office undertook to obtain special railway rates as far west as St. Louis. The negotiations with the steamboat owners for river passage from St. Louis to Kansas City were left to a forwarding agent in St. Louis. There are preserved a large number of letters from both Dr. Webb and Lawrence to railway executives seeking reduced fares. These appear to have been a relatively easy matter to arrange the first year; after that the railway companies began to enter into agreements among themselves not to make reductions, and it became necessary for Webb to resort to all sorts of stratagems. Until the summer of 1856 the Aid Company was usually able to offer a rate of twenty-five dollars to St. Louis— about ten dollars lower than the regular fare. Steamboat rates to Kansas City varied from ten to twelve dollars, depending on the season and the condition of the river. Anson J. Stone, the assistant treasurer, testified before the Howard Committee in June, 1856, that the transportation companies made the same reduction to the Emigrant Aid Company that they made to "all other companies, picnic parties, conventions, etc."[4] Lawrence testified at the same time that the reductions averaged about 15 per cent for the entire trip.[5] The usual procedure was for Dr. Webb to purchase the tickets in wholesale lots, ordinarily twenty at a time, from the Boston passenger agents of the railways, with the privilege of returning any that might not be used. He then offered them for sale in the Emigrant Aid Company office, or sent them out to branch Kansas leagues for sale. At times he procured tickets for privately organized parties in various parts of New England. During 1856 he worked in close co-operation with William Barnes, secretary of the New York State Kansas Committee, each securing tickets for the other. These tickets were always sold to the emigrant at cost. The money received for their sale was

[35]

handled entirely by Dr. Webb, and did not pass through the Company treasury. Contrary to the impression created by most writings on the subject of the Emigrant Aid Company, this sale of tickets did not cease with the difficulties of 1856, but continued through 1859.[6] Hale retails the yarn, for whatever it may be worth, that two of the pro-slavery governors of Kansas, Walker and Stanton, made the trip out on Emigrant Aid Company tickets.[7]

Of course no project to stimulate or direct migration could overlook the possibilities of information service and propaganda. From the time of the earliest tentative organization, Dr. Webb maintained an office in Boston, located temporarily in the rooms of the Massachusetts Historical Society, as an information bureau. Early in August, 1854, a propaganda document, *Organization, Objects and Plan of Operations of the Emigrant Aid Company,* was printed in pamphlet form, with description of Kansas Territory by Charles Robinson, and distributed to prospective emigrants.[8] It was revised and reissued from time to time until March of 1855, when it was replaced by Dr. Webb's *Information for Kansas Emigrants.* Hale's *Kanzas and Nebraska,* issued in August, 1854, as propaganda for the Emigrant Aid Company, has already been mentioned. Thayer, Hale, and others made speaking tours to different parts of New England. In their speeches they mingled with their plea for funds to "save Kansas" glowing descriptions of Kansas as a place for settlement. The answer to the question, frequently raised, whether or not the Aid Company engaged in recruiting, depends upon what one means by that term. The Company certainly engaged in extensive propaganda to advertise Kansas and promote migration, but its officers always denied there was any personal solicitation. In describing the Company's information service before the Howard Committee, Anson J. Stone declared that this activity was limited to answering questions and supplying pamphlets. "We never urge them to go," he said.[9]

[36]

Territorial Capitol at Pawnee

Shawnee Mission

Lawrence about 1857

The Abbott Howitzer

Whenever a sufficient number of emigrants were ready, Dr. Webb organized them into a party and placed a conductor in charge to make all necessary arrangements along the route. Much was said in all of the Company's advertising and propaganda about the advantages of traveling in conducted parties, and many of the emigrants testified before the Howard Committee that the arrangement had been of great benefit to them. Parties varied in size from a dozen or so to over a hundred. After the work got well under way, Dr. Webb designated Tuesday as "party day" and endeavored to have a group ready to start on that day each week. The conductors, to whom the transportation companies always gave passes, were at first officers or regular agents of the Company. Later it was the usual practice to place a dependable member of the party in charge. After the first year, Kansas settlers who had returned East on private business frequently sought this means of returning to Kansas without cost to themselves, or perhaps one might better say of earning their passage to Kansas. When a party arrived in Kansas City it was met by an agent of the Company who looked after the baggage, arranged for temporary accommodations, supplied information about available lands, and recommended a place of settlement.[10]

In the days of the Kansas conflict, one of the questions most frequently discussed on the border was that of the relation to the Company of the settler who migrated under Emigrant Aid Company auspices. More testimony was offered to the Howard Committee on this point than on any other matter touching Aid Company activities. Enemies of the Company were constantly circulating stories that it was shipping paupers to Kansas, sending armies of hirelings, paying people to migrate, and even sending New Englanders only to vote and return. On the other hand, discontented individuals who had migrated in Aid Company parties often complained that they had been misled by false promises, overcharged, neglected, or otherwise badly dealt with. These charges and complaints will be later examined in detail. For the present it must suffice to indicate the general policy of the Company in dealing with its emigrants.

Edward Everett Hale, writing nearly half a century after the Kansas conflict, stated bluntly, "We never gave a penny to a settler unless he was engaged to do work for us."[11] It certainly was never a part of the Company's policy to render pecuniary aid of any sort to prospective settlers. In the Company letter books there are letterpress copies of literally dozens of letters written by Dr. Webb to prospective emigrants in response to inquiries, in each of which he states that the Company offers no financial assistance to those who go in its parties. Numerous letters in the Company's files making inquiry about monetary aid are endorsed in Dr. Webb's handwriting, "Answered by sending pamphlet." And the "pamphlet" stated specifically, "The Company . . . has not paid, neither does it intend to pay, in whole or in part, the expenses of transporting individuals to, or of supporting them after their arrival in the Territory."[12] Every officer of the Company who testified before the Howard Committee said the same thing,[13] and every settler whose testimony is recorded, and who made it clear that he was a bona fide Aid Company emigrant, declared that the only help he received was a reduction in fare and the convenience of traveling in a conducted party. There were, indeed, some settlers who testified that they had received financial assistance from "the Emigrant Aid Society," but this may be explained by the facts that on the frontier all emigrant-aid organizations were confused under this general title and that some such organizations are known to have paid the expenses of emigrants.

A few instances have come to light, less than a dozen in all, of the advancement of funds to individuals by the Company or its officers. Some of these undoubtedly were advances on wages. On several occasions the Company sent out trained technicians to set up its mills, and it would not be surprising if these men should insist that the Company advance money for their expenses to

Kansas. One contract has been found in which Williams, on behalf of the Company, advanced fifty dollars to two brothers who agreed to work it out on one of the Company's mills.[14] In other cases the correspondence shows that the Company was merely acting as forwarding agent for private donors who sent money to the Boston office with a request that it be sent on to individuals or used to aid certain persons in "fitting out" parties. On one or two occasions the Company as such appears to have made personal loans to individuals,* but these were exceptional cases.

There were some settlers, too, who said that they had been required to pledge their votes to the free-state cause before the "Emigrant Aid Society" would assist them. But here again the explanation lies in the indiscriminate application of the term "Emigrant Aid Society" to all organizations functioning in the colonization of Kansas. Some such organizations undoubtedly did require such a pledge, but there is abundant evidence that the New England Emigrant Aid Company never exacted any promise of any sort from its colonists, and that it extended its facilities to all who applied, with no questions asked as to their political opinions or their intentions for the future.† Although the Company made no secret of its hope and expectation that those who went to Kansas under its auspices would remain as permanent settlers, these were never bound by a written or oral agreement.[15] Neither did the Company presume to dictate to its colonists where they should settle in Kansas, though it did offer them the services and advice of its agents. As Lawrence told the Howard Committee, all connection between the emigrant and the Company ceased upon arrival of the settler in the territory.[16] It seems scarcely necessary to add that the New England Emigrant Aid Company did not, as did certain other

---

*E.g., a loan of $100 to Jerome B. Taft, who on sundry occasions acted as agent for the Company in local matters in Kansas (Aid Company Records, Book I, 41).

†The same kinds of evidence might be marshalled on this point as were cited in relation to pecuniary aid: Webb's letters, testimony before the Howard Committee, and public declarations, as in Webb's *Information*, 5th and later editions, 7-8.

associations, require persons who migrated under its auspices to become stockholders of the Company. In fact, Dr. Webb's pamphlet advised the prospective emigrant against putting money into stock unless he had abundant means, because he would probably need all his available cash after he reached Kansas.[17]

A number who went to Kansas as members of Company parties complained that they had been defrauded or misled by false promises. That misunderstanding should arise was probably inevitable; in many instances evidence is at hand to show exactly how the difficulties arose. A part of the trouble came from the fact that the Boston office never knew exactly what was going on in Kansas. In part, too, the fault lay with the emigrants themselves; many a New Englander who had never been west of the Hudson conjured up for himself visions of Kansas as an earthly paradise, only to be violently disillusioned by actual frontier conditions. But the principal bit of fire behind all the smoke was the tendency of certain spokesmen of the Company, Thayer and Hale especially, to talk far too glibly of the wonderful things the organization planned to do. Lawrence frequently chided them for making promises that could not be fulfilled. For example, he wrote to Hale February 25, 1855: "You have a way of doing things in Worcester which is certainly different from ours here [Boston]; and which, to say the least, we do not like as well as our own . . . I will . . . not more than allude to the representations which have been made as to the facilities which the Emigrant Aid Society will afford to settlers on the road, and after reaching the Territory, and which will prove wholly delusive, and must react upon all connected with it to our confusion and dismay . . . . Notices have been spread through the papers that parties will be sent twice a week, commencing March 6th, that the fare will be only $25 (it will be $25 to St. Louis and probably $40 to any settlement in Kansas, at least for the first parties), all of which is untrue and impossible, and creates confusion and distrust."[18] Nevertheless, it was always the clear policy of the Company as such to warn emigrants of the hardships they must face and to promise nothing beyond cheap fares, conducted parties, and the advice of agents on the ground. Dr. Webb took advantage of every opportunity, in his pamphlet and in answering letters of inquiry, to dissuade persons from going to Kansas without some reserve of cash, and to make clear that the Company could not promise employment to anyone.[19]

This is not the proper point at which to discuss in detail the investments of the Emigrant Aid Company in Kansas, but it is within the scope of the present chapter to note the general policies of the Company in this regard. A little folder, issued apparently in 1855 to stimulate stock subscriptions, sets forth the avowed objects of the Company. After mentioning the services to emigrants already described, it adds: "To secure for their accommodation, by purchase or otherwise, advantageous locations for landing places and for outfitting purposes; to erect hotels for the convenience of settlers and travelers; to erect, or aid individuals in erecting and conducting saw mills, grist mills, machine shops and similar establishments essential in new settlements, and to aid in the erection of school houses and churches."[20] During the first two years of its activity, the period of the Kansas conflict, the Company concentrated its investments in hotels and mills. It bought a hotel in Kansas City and built one in Lawrence. It purchased and sent to Kansas machinery for several sawmills and at least three grist mills, together with steam engines for their operation. Additional mill machinery, such as lath machines and shingle machines, was sent out from time to time. Except its hotel, temporary shacks for the accommodation of settlers, a frame office building in Lawrence and shelters for its mills, the Company constructed no buildings prior to 1857. Its agents gave what help and encouragement they could in the organization of churches and the establishment of schools, but before 1857 no cash was expended for these purposes. On numerous occasions the Emigrant Aid Company was called to aid in local development projects in

Kansas, such as bridges, hotels, boat lines, stagecoach lines, and colleges. Sometimes the Company was asked to take stock in these ventures, sometimes to make loans, and occasionally to finance them outright. Certainly there was nothing about such assistance that would have been out of keeping with the fundamental policies of the Company, since these enterprises would have served to attract and hold settlers and, for that reason, to enhance the value of the Company's property. As will appear later, the Company did, beginning in 1857, assist some such local projects, but during the first two years of its operation its funds were never adequate for its own development plans, so that it had no means available with which to aid these local activities.[21]

The Company has often been accused of speculating in land, and even of existing primarily for that purpose.[22] Beginning in 1857 it did make some speculative purchases, but during the first two years there is no record of the expenditure of even a dollar for real estate, except the Kansas City hotel. Nevertheless the Company acquired a number of town lots in its settlements by gift of the town associations formed by its settlers. Commonly, when such a town association was formed, certain lots or town shares would be assigned to the Emigrant Aid Company on condition that it locate a mill or make some other improvement in the settlement. These town associations, said Thayer, "would have given similar advantages to any person or company of men who would have made improvements."[23] This was a common usage in frontier communities, and some of these same towns made comparable grants to other organizations or individuals in return for promises to establish industries.

Of course the acquisition of town lots in this manner with a view to ultimate financial gain was speculation of a sort. The fact would seem to be that, while most of the leaders of the emigrant aid project did not consider land speculation to be one of the Company's major purposes, land deals were not inconsistent with the aim of making the whole venture pay a return to the stockholders. Thayer was always anxious for the Company to purchase any land that promised a profit, and even Lawrence raised no serious objection to the idea if the money should be available and the transaction could be handled in a manner that would neither hamper the regular work of the Company nor discredit it with the public. Until the question of slavery in Kansas was settled, he objected to officers and directors of the Company engaging in private land speculations in the territory and refrained from doing so himself (although he had extensive holdings in Wisconsin and other western regions); but in the fall of 1856, when the free-state cause appeared secure, he withdrew his objections and even himself took a flyer in a venture, the Kansas Land Trust, which involved several of the Aid Company directors.

At the very beginning of the Company's operations, in August, 1854, Robinson (one of the Kansas agents) had an opportunity to buy for the Company a promising tract in Kansas City. At first Lawrence wrote him to secure an option, but a week later he advised Robinson that for lack of funds the purchase could not be made.[24] On August 26 he presented a lengthy memorandum on the matter to the trustees. In this he protested against the purchase because the money was not in sight and because he felt that "the company's interest in land should be small" and in scattered tracts which might be sold to the emigrants "at prime cost" to stimulate activity and help pay for the agencies. But he objected further, "Because this purchase of land and building is for the purpose of speculating, to make a profit; and is not necessary to accomplish the object for which the society was formed. It is using the good name of the company to create a rise in value in the neighborhood of our purchases; and if the trustees themselves should be considerable holders of stock they would be liable to the imputation of using the credit of the company for their own interests. If successful, we should injure the reputation which we ought to obtain of being disinterested laborers in a

[43]

good cause; if unsuccessful, we should be blamed by the other stockholders, who will consider themselves deceived by our representations."[25]

This apparently was an honest and accurate statement of Lawrence's views at the moment, but that his principles on this subject were more elastic than on most other matters is suggested by another incident that occurred the following spring. In April, 1855, at a time when the Company faced a dire financial stringency, the Kansas agents proposed the purchase of a large parcel of Kansas half-breed Indian lands. In response to the proposal Lawrence wrote to Pomeroy: "Do not fear to buy the Kaw lands freely for the company. The company needs something to make money with . . . . I will pay an overdraft on that."[26] Only the refusal of the Indian agent to ratify prevented the completion of the deal. The piling up of overdrafts on the Company treasury, which he was called upon to pay, must have been making a dent in Lawrence's scruples. At all events the fact that the Emigrant Aid Company spent no money on land ventures during the two critical years was less a matter of conscience than of lack of cash. Still the very fact that its limited funds were not diverted from other purposes to this use is a good indication that land speculation was, at most, only incidental to its wider program. This agrees essentially with the oft-repeated statement of various spokesmen of the Company that "it had not been organized for the purposes of a land company."[27]

To avoid confusion, something should be said about the Kansas Land Trust, which one writer calls the "land investing affiliate" of the Emigrant Aid Company.[28] Near the end of September or early in October, 1856, after Geary had quieted the turmoil in Kansas, a co-operative association was formed under this title to make speculative investments in Kansas land. Twenty-six persons or firms, all but one of them from New England or New York City, subscribed $22,000 in hundred-dollar shares. The list of subscribers contained the names of two directors of the Emigrant Aid Company, W. D. Pickman and J. P. Williston, and of the firm of Glidden and Williams, of which J. M. S. Williams was a member. Lawrence was not listed as a subscriber, but he was probably financially interested in some way. Management of the trust was vested in three trustees, Amos A. Lawrence, B. B. Storer, and W. D. Pickman. Shortly after he resigned his Aid Company agency, Charles Robinson was appointed Kansas agent of the Trust at a salary of $1,000 a year, with expense allowance and commissions. In September, 1857, the subscribers were repaid one-half of their investment, but whether this money had not been used or had been invested, this dividend representing the proceeds of sales, is not clear. About the same time a deal was arranged to sell out the holdings of the Trust in Kansas to Robinson for $15,000 on three $5,000 notes; but shortly after this the nationwide depression hit Kansas, so that Robinson was unable to sell the land and meet his notes.[29] The present study has not revealed the final outcome of the venture.

Despite the overlapping of personnel, it is hardly accurate to refer to the Land Trust as the Aid Company's "land investing affiliate." The Company, as such, had no interest in it. Only four persons prominently connected with the Company had anything to do with it, though some of the other members may have held small blocks of stock in the Aid Company. None of the executive committee of the Company were members of the Trust, and the two directors who were attended directors' meetings only irregularly. There is no evidence of co-operation between the organizations or of the use by either of the agencies of facilities of the other, Robinson having severed his connection with the Aid Company before he entered the service of the Land Trust. It is possible, of course, that a more exhaustive study of the Kansas Land Trust might reveal a closer connection, but, on the basis of information at hand, it would seem that the affiliation was limited to an overlapping of personnel.

For half a century there has raged among historians, amateur and professional, a controversy as to whether the Emigrant Aid Company was a philanthropic undertaking or a money-making scheme. As should be clear from what has already been said, at least in some measure it was both. Spokesmen for the Company in their later writings, although they mentioned the money-making aspect of the enterprise, usually stressed the philanthropic side. Thayer lamented that his associates had rejected his speculative plans because they feared "that people might say that we were influenced by pecuniary considerations in our patriotic work for Kansas . . . . So we went on the charity plan, and were never one half so efficient as we would have been by the other method."[30] Robinson declared, "As people would no longer take stock in the Aid Company as a business venture, the churches and people subscribed from considerations of patriotism and philanthropy."[31]

The late W. E. Connelley sounded the keynote for the antagonists of the Company when he asserted: "It was organized for speculative purposes. Making Kansas a free state was incidental in its design, and was an issue principally to induce people to subscribe for stock and contribute money. Large dividends for the stockholders constituted the main purpose."[32] Perhaps Connelley was right so far as Thayer's original plan was concerned, but evidence of several kinds indicates that he was in error as to the dominant purpose of the Company during the period of the Kansas conflict.

The fact that the organizers preferred Thayer's stock-company plan to Lawrence's plan for an emigrant aid society might be construed as supporting the view that the profit motive was paramount. However, there are various plausible explanations of this preference that are not inconsistent with a philanthropic motive. The stock plan would be more systematic and businesslike; the managers would know more definitely upon what they might depend. The subscriber to stock was legally obliged to pay for it; the person who pledged a donation was not. Possession of stock carrying an interest in Company property would create a loyalty on the part of the stockholder that no mere contributor would be likely to feel. And then there was the problem of the property itself; in the very nature of the program, a certain amount of it must be acquired, and it would surely be more feasible to return this property to a body of stockholders, when the purpose of the enterprise was achieved, than to dispose of it otherwise. So the form of organization as a stock company, although it may indicate that the profit motive was present, does not of necessity rule out the primacy of a philanthropic aim.

On the other hand, as has been pointed out, the men who carried the heaviest burden of the actual operation of the Company during the two critical years were motivated largely, if not entirely, by an interest in the cause of free Kansas. Amos A. Lawrence and John Carter Brown, who bore the largest financial load during these years, were prompted solely by this motive, and neither desired nor expected that their stock would pay. Williams and Hale were enthusiasts in the cause; they both *hoped* that the stock would at least return the principal invested, but Williams gave too lavishly of his somewhat limited means to be accused of acting from a selfish motive, while Hale's holdings were so small that his financial stake in the Company was inconsequential. Dr. Webb, the only one of the group employed on a salary, really *expected* the stock to earn a dividend, but no one can read his hundreds of letters, written to all sorts of persons under all sorts of conditions, and retain any doubt of his sincerity in the cause of freedom. Such limited information as is available about the other active leaders indicates that the same statement is true of them: they hoped, or possibly expected, that the stock could be made to pay, but regarded this as a secondary consideration. Only Thayer among the real managers emphasized the prospect of financial gain, but his investment in the Company was so small as to suggest that he may have been prompted less by a real hope of profit than by pique that his original idea had been tampered with.

[47]

Something of the fundamental nature of the Company may be learned from the stock itself. If the enterprise really was, as Connelley and others have asserted, primarily a money-making scheme, one would expect the promoters to hold large blocks of stock. Instead, the only three active managers who held any considerable amounts of stock, Lawrence, Brown and Williams,* are known to have been actuated by a motive other than the profit motive, whereas Thayer, who talked most about money-making, although he subscribed at one time or another for some four hundred shares, actually paid for and retained only twenty.[33] Moreover the stock ledger of the Company shows that the vast majority of the stockholders held from one to five shares each. There were sixty-eight persons who held twenty-five or more shares each, but only thirty-five who had as many as fifty shares. Nine persons held 100 or more each; four, 125; and one, 150. None of these larger stockholders, however, with the exception of the three just mentioned, were among the early promoters. Considerably less than half of the 8,346 shares issued were held in lots of twenty-five or more, and less than a third in blocks of fifty or more. This wide distribution of the stock would surely suggest, though of course it does not prove, that the stock was not generally regarded as either a good investment or an attractive speculation. In all probability the person who bought one to five shares, like the people who bought the small-denomination war bonds during the two world wars, looked upon this purchase less as an investment than as a contribution to a cause, even though he may have hoped or possibly expected to receive back his principal and perhaps some additional return. Indeed Dr. Webb wrote in letter after letter, "If those who are able will give of their abundance, or rather loan by subscribing to stock, we shall be enabled to arrest the further progress of the blighting curse of slavery."[34]

Appeals for stock subscriptions were made on both bases. Al-

---

* Brown and Lawrence held 125 shares ($2,500) each, and Williams 100 shares ($2,000). Lawrence paid for 405 shares, but gave most of them away.

though Thayer, in his speeches, was given to stressing the investment feature, much to the discomfiture of Lawrence, all the extant pamphlets, all the resolutions of the executive committee,
and practically all the newspaper accounts of public meetings
agree that the plea was for aid in saving Kansas, with only incidental reference to the possibility of financial returns. The very
limited number of stock transfers shown in the stock registers
tends to disprove Connelley's charge of extensive jobbing in the
Company's stock.[35] Nearly all the transfers were made by either
Lawrence or Thayer. Those of Lawrence are known to have been
gifts, made, apparently, to stimulate interest in the Company.
There is no adequate explanation of Thayer's numerous transfers except W. H. Carruth's guess "that he subscribed on occasion
to set the ball rolling, and then persuaded others to relieve him."[36]
Without assuming that Thayer would have been above jobbing in
the Company's stock, one cannot see how he could have done so
when the Company never issued its stock at less than par, and
when no buyer could have been found for it at more than par.

One cannot, of course, determine what motive induced the
individual stockholder to subscribe or what value he placed upon
his stock. Obviously, as Hale said, "Some did and some did not
expect returns."[37] It is probably significant, however, that nearly
all the larger subcriptions were made during the summer of
1856, the "Bleeding Kansas" days, when the excitement of the
nation over the Kansas conflict had reached fever heat, and that
subscriptions stopped entirely with the restoration of quiet in
Kansas, even though the early part of 1857, before the economic
depression descended on the country, was the period when the
Company's prospects of financial success were the brightest.

There is one other bit of circumstantial evidence that may
have some bearing on the fundamental purpose of the Company.
There was never a time, from Thayer's first petition for incorporation until the final expiration of the last charter, when the official
name of the organization was not Emigrant Aid *Company*. Nev-

ertheless, it was frequently referred to, even by those most intimately connected with it, as the Emigrant Aid *Society*. In their correspondence, in their testimony before the Howard Committee, and indeed everywhere except in strictly official documents, Lawrence, Thayer, and the others used the terms interchangeably. This would suggest that even the most active managers of the Emigrant Aid Company thought of it rather as a benevolent association than as a commercial enterprise.

But without doubt the best test of the real aim of the concern is to be found in a record of its actual operations. These operations will be traced in some detail, but it may be stated here that during the first two years, although the trustees and executive committee were ever mindful of their responsibility for the stockholders' money and tried to manage affairs with a view to returning at least the original investment, they consistently placed the emphasis on the crusading aspect of the venture. In the fall of 1856, when the purpose of saving Kansas to freedom was considered to have been achieved, the emphasis was shifted. From that time on, efforts were concentrated on financial returns. It may be stated categorically, then, that the purpose of the Company was first to block the extension of slavery into Kansas, and then to earn a profit or at least save the investment.

Such was the equipment with which the Emigrant Aid Company entered upon its crusade for freedom in Kansas. Armed only with propaganda, a small capital investment, and a scheme for aiding and encouraging migration, and with FREEDOM for its battle cry, the Company set forth on its crusade to rescue Kansas from "the minions of the slave power."

CHAPTER IV

Launching the Kansas Crusade

LUCKILY THE PROMOTERS of the Company did not delay the launching of their Kansas crusade until they had overcome all the difficulties of organization or even until their plans were fully matured. Obviously the first step in the actual work of colonizing Kansas must be to spy out the land. Just as soon as a tentative organization had been formed in June, 1854, Lawrence and Thayer, without awaiting the selection of a third trustee, engaged Dr. Charles Robinson and Charles H. Branscomb to visit Kansas Territory on behalf of the embryonic Emigrant Aid Company for the purpose of making observations. Lawrence advanced the money for their expenses.

Robinson and Branscomb left Boston late in June and reached the village of Kansas (Kansas City) early in July.[1] Here they separated, Robinson continuing up the Missouri River to Fort Leavenworth and Branscomb going up the Kansas River to Fort Riley. Each was to observe the character of the country, investigate Indian land titles, and note locations suitable for settlements. While in Kansas City, probably on the return trip, Robinson discussed with several residents of the village various proposals to buy property for the Company and to establish a forwarding agency. From Gaius Jenkins, who a few months before had bought the Gillis House, the largest hotel in the settlement, he obtained an option on that property. From J. Riddlesbarger, a warehouseman, he secured an offer to act as forwarding agent for the Company.[2] Late in July both Robinson and Branscomb started back to the East. At Buffalo, New York, they met the pioneer party of settlers, conducted that far by Thayer. Branscomb returned to Kansas with the party as conductor, while Robinson and Thayer hastened on to Boston, where Robinson set about preparing a description of Kansas Territory for the Company's pamphlet.

While this spadework was being done in Kansas and on the border, preparations were under way in Boston for the sending of this first party of settlers. About the same time that Robinson and Branscomb started on their mission, Dr. Webb opened a temporary office in the rooms of the Massachusetts Historical Society, of which he was a member. Here he received all inquirers and gave out information. A few days later Thayer, in his quixotic manner, announced July 17 as the date of departure of the first party, but he failed to work out any details. Ten days before the party was to start, there were still no plans and, as usual, Lawrence had to take the matter in hand. He had already urged Thayer to go along as conductor, but to no avail. On July 8 he wrote to Thayer: "I am very much mortified that I should thoughtlessly have committed myself to a scheme which, without my personal effort, seems likely to fail. The expedition of the 17th has been proclaimed and I supposed when I became a party to it that plans were made for carrying it out; but the greatest exertion now seems to be required to prepare the details. This I am now making, and it shall go if I have to go with it myself. The train will leave at 2:15 on the 17th . . . . You must go at least as far as Buffalo. It will not answer to make plans so definitely and allow them to fail. I hope we shall be more careful hereafter."[3]

Thayer did not wish to conduct the party, because he was anxious to attend the organization meeting in New Haven on the eighteenth, but under Lawrence's urging he reluctantly consented to go as far as Buffalo. When the seventeenth arrived the party started. It is not quite clear just how many left Boston, but when the group reached Kansas it consisted of twenty-nine men. At Rochester, New York, the colony was joined by two men who were destined to loom large in the early history of Kansas, Dr. John Doy and D. R. Anthony.* At Kansas City the party was

---

*Famous in his day for his efforts in aiding runaway slaves to escape and for his spectacular rescue from the St. Joseph, Missouri, jail. See John Doy, *The Narrative of John Doy* (New York, 1860). D. R. Anthony was the brother of the noted feminist Susan B.

joined by James Blood, who had preceded them as a sort of unofficial agent of the Emigrant Aid Company. Traveling by ox
team along the south bank of the Kansas River, they reached
the present site of Lawrence about noon of August 1, 1854. The
place had been selected by Blood and Branscomb as being the
first desirable location on the Kansas River to which the Indians
had ceded their rights. The settlers camped on a hill overlooking
the site selected, naming it Mount Oread in memory of Thayer's
Oread Collegiate Institute in Worcester. Two of the men at once
became homesick and returned to the East; the others staked out
claims and began the erection of cabins.[4] The advance guard had
taken up its position and was digging in.

While the pioneer party was making its way to Kansas, a
working organization of the Company had finally been achieved
under the Articles of Agreement and Association. No sooner was
this "voluntary association" set in motion than the trustees turned
to the task of setting up machinery to carry on their colonizing
activities. The first step was the appointment of agents to repre-
sent the Company on the ground. At their second meeting, on
August 7, 1854, Robinson, who was already in the service of the
Company, was appointed a general agent for Kansas Territory
at a salary of $1,000 a year and two and one-half per cent com-
mission on all sales and receipts.[5] Robinson at the time was a
physician and newspaper man of Fitchburg, Massachusetts. He
had attended one of Thayer's early meetings and had offered his
services in Kansas. Thayer appears to have been impressed by
him at once and Lawrence, after inquiring of acquaintances in
Fitchburg, decided that Robinson would do.[6] Down to the time
when he entered the service of the Emigrant Aid Company, Robinson's career had been somewhat erratic. Leaving Amherst College in the middle of his second year, ostensibly because of bad

Anthony and an active free-state leader, who later became prominent as editor, politician,
and leading citizen of Leavenworth and whose son, D. R. Anthony, Jr., was for a number of years a Representative in Congress from the Leavenworth district.

eyes, he had studied medicine in the office of a physician. From 1843 until 1845 he practiced medicine in Belchertown, Massachusetts. In 1845 he moved to Springfield, where, a few months later, his first wife died. In the spring of 1846 he moved to Fitchburg and took up medical practice. In 1849 he went overland to California as physician to a Boston party of gold-seekers; in this he was motivated, according to his official biographer, by the hope of improving his health.[7] There, in 1850, he became the principal leader of the Sacramento squatter riot.[8] Although he was elected to the California legislature, he returned to Fitchburg in 1852, resumed his practice of medicine, and began the editing of the *Fitchburg News*. At that time he married as his second wife Sara D. T. Lawrence, a distant relative of Amos A. Lawrence. Despite the contrary statement of certain of his biographers, he does not appear to have been an outstanding success as a physician; he never joined a medical society, nor did he, in his later life in Kansas, ever resume his practice.

Robinson's character is too controversial to risk a definite estimate of it in an account in which he moves only as a secondary figure. According to his friends he was a hero and a self-sacrificing patriot; according to his enemies he was a self-seeking adventurer. Perhaps he was something of both. That he was shrewd and capable his friends and enemies agree. That he had political ambition and a penchant for money-making is obvious. That he was the moving spirit and most effective leader of the Kansas free-state movement is scarcely open to question.* That he was as sincere in his antislavery sentiments as a politician is ever likely to be may be fairly assumed. He was probably "law honest"; charges of outright dishonesty have been made repeatedly by his detractors, but they have never been adequately proved.† The

---

* Connelley and other partisans have questioned it, however, according this distinction to James H. Lane.

† In 1862, during Robinson's term as governor of Kansas, articles of impeachment were brought against him by the state House of Representatives, charging complicity in a sale of state bonds which had been made under very suspicious circumstances. Although the state treasurer and state auditor were convicted, Governor Robinson was acquitted, only

present study has revealed nothing that would convict Robinson of ever having defrauded the Emigrant Aid Company, although he did on occasion drive a sharp bargain with it, and he undoubtedly capitalized his connection with the Company to further his own fortunes, both political and financial. At any rate the principal officers of the Company maintained complete confidence in him to the end; in 1857 Lawrence wrote to a correspondent, "Governor Robinson is more reliable than any [other] man who has gone to Kansas, so far as my experience with him and others has enabled me to form an opinion."[9]

At the same meeting of the trustees at which Robinson was appointed, Lawrence was directed to draw up instructions for his trip to Kansas. These instructions were duly prepared under date of August 9, 1854. Robinson was directed: (1) to arrange with railway companies and steamboat owners for reduced fares for parties of emigrants to Kansas; (2) to try to secure the co-operation of railway companies to stop the frauds practiced on emigrants; (3) to select men or firms for forwarding agents along the way; (4) to inquire at Buffalo and elsewhere as to the cost of steam engines of various power and the cost of their transportation to Kansas; (5) to get the refusal of property necessary for the accommodation of emigrants.[10] He left Boston on August 29, 1854, as conductor of the second party of settlers, reaching the Wakarusa settlement, as the infant colony of Lawrence was then known, on September 12. From that time until the fall of 1856 he was one of the three general agents of the Emigrant Aid Company. He maintained headquarters in Lawrence. His particular charge was the location of settlements, the care of settlers, and custody of the Company's property in the territory.

At the fifth meeting of the trustees, August 26, 1854, Samuel C. Pomeroy and Charles H. Branscomb were appointed general agents of the Company. Each was to receive an annual salary

---

three senators voting for his conviction. His friends claimed that the charges were fabricated for political purposes by his rival James H. Lane (C. A. M. Ewing, "Early Kansas Impeachments," *Kansas Historical Quarterly*, August, 1932, 307-35).

of $1,000 with allowance for expenses. In addition Pomeroy was allowed a commission of 10 per cent of the net profit on all sales and collections he should make. Branscomb was allowed 2½ per cent commission on the gross amount of his sales and collections. Dr. Webb was directed to draft instructions for each of the agents along general lines laid down by the trustees.[11]

Pomeroy was a native of Southampton, Massachusetts, a member of an old New England family, and an alumnus of Amherst College. At the time he made his connection with the Emigrant Aid Company he had attained some little distinction as an antislavery politician, having had a part in the formation of the Liberty party in Masachusetts, and having served in the legislature of his state as a Free Soiler.[12] He appears to have known his way about political Washington and to have been on intimate, though not very cordial, terms with President Pierce. According to his own statement he had determined to go to Kansas on his own account when some of his friends persuaded him to associate himself with the Emigrant Aid Company. He declared that he was interested in the agricultural and commercial possibilities of the territory, in a route for the Pacific Railway and in mills and roads, but most of all in keeping slavery out.[13]

Pomeroy's character is even more of an enigma than that of Robinson. It is clear from his letters that he had an exalted opinion of himself. Rabidly antislavery in all his public utterances, he liked to flaunt his courage and his patriotism. That he possessed no excess of physical courage is suggested by the fact that on at least two occasions when he was confronted with bodily danger he surrendered to the enemy. In many ways he was undoubtedly a valuable man to the Company. He was an effective public speaker and was frequently called home from the border and sent on speaking tours through the East. His political experience and his associations in the national capital made him a useful lobbyist; at least two different times he was sent to Washington on missions that were essentially political in character. Yet, despite the fact that he was made a sort of general manager for the Company in Kansas and was given a wider discretion in the handling of Company money than any other one man, not even excluding Lawrence, he appears to have had very little financial acumen. As in the case of Robinson, although there is no tangible proof that he ever defrauded the Company, he was certainly lax in the handling of Company funds; as William Herbert Carruth expressed it, "he was reckless with drafts."[14] To say the least, he was a poor manager. His accounts were always in a chaotic condition, so that no accountant who has examined such of them as are preserved can make head or tail of them. In 1857 the suspicions of the directors were aroused by his handling of affairs in Atchison, but he was able to regain their confidence and to retain his agency until the Company closed out its Kansas holdings. In 1861 he was openly accused of graft in the handling of relief funds, but was exonerated by an investigating committee. During the next few years, while he was United States Senator from Kansas, he was involved in several political intrigues that look a bit shady, and finally in 1871 he was defeated for re-election to the Senate by what purported to be an exposé of an attempt on his part to bribe legislators. His friends always maintained that these charges were trumped up by his enemies to bring about his political undoing. Perhaps they were. It may be of some significance that Pomeroy, unlike Robinson, never established a real home in Kansas, his wife joining him there only for short periods, and that as soon as he was discredited by his failure of re-election to the Senate he left Kansas, never to return.

According to the plan laid down by the trustees in their meeting of August 26, 1854, Pomeroy was to be financial agent or Kansas treasurer of the Company, with headquarters in Kansas City. With the approval of either of the other agents, he was authorized to purchase real estate to an amount not exceeding $40,000, to buy not more than six sawmills and one grist mill, and to cause receiving houses to be erected. He was permitted

[57]

to draw on Amos A. Lawrence, treasurer of the Company, at five days' sight up to a total amount of $10,000, but his drafts were to be drawn only when authorized by telegraph, and must be signed by one other agent. He was to incur no debt on behalf of the Company except for real estate, and not in excess of the amount specified. Deeds to real estate were to be made to him and one other agent in trust for the Company. He was instructed to keep himself informed as to Indian titles to land, and to keep the trustees advised of his doings by frequent correspondence. He was further directed to have a schoolhouse built in each settlement, and to encourage the establishment of churches by all suitable means.[15] He went to Kansas with the party of settlers who left Boston August 29, 1854.

The least important and also the least satisfactory of the original general agents of the Company was Charles H. Branscomb of Holyoke, Massachusetts. He was a graduate of Dartmouth College and had studied law at Cambridge Law School.[16] At the time of his employment by the Emigrant Aid Company he was in his early thirties and had been practicing law for six years. At first he was used as liaison man between Boston and Kansas, conducting two parties in the fall of 1854. During the winter of 1854-55 he appears to have helped Dr. Webb in the office, to have made trips to interview railway passenger agents, and to have done other errands too important to be entrusted to irresponsible messengers. For a time during the summer of 1855, while Dr. Webb was in Kansas, Branscomb acted as secretary of the Company. In December of that year he was commissioned a stock-subscription agent, and for the next two months worked with Thayer soliciting in New York. Early in March of 1856 he was recalled to Boston to assist in the organizing and dispatching of emigrant parties. A little later in the month he was sent to St. Louis to make contracts with steamboat owners. In June he was sent to Kansas to take charge of Company affairs while Robinson was in prison and Pomeroy was in the East. The following October, after Robinson's resignation, Branscomb was sent back to Kansas a permanent resident agent, a position which he occupied for about a year. Late in the summer of 1857 it was discovered that Branscomb was padding his expense account, and he was asked to resign. After he had been superseded in his agency by Martin F. Conway, other irregularities came to light. He had grossly violated his instructions in the disposal of Company property; he had neglected other properties, failing to collect rents and allowing buildings and machinery to fall into disrepair; finally, he did not account for about a thousand dollars of Company money.[17] Despite all this, it seems likely that Branscomb was less dishonest than incompetent. After his dismissal from Company employment he served in the Kansas territorial legislature and later, having moved to St. Louis, in the legislature of Missouri. Ultimately he entered the diplomatic service, in which he appears to have had an honorable though not distinguished career.

Arrangements were made with warehousemen, B. Slater in St. Louis and J. Riddlesbarger in Kansas City, to act as forwarding agents of the company. Their function was merely to receive, store, and reship freight and settlers' baggage, and to act as bankers in cashing and forwarding drafts drawn on the Company by its general agents. They were allowed no discretionary power in the handling of Company business, and were paid only the usual commissions charged for such services. Temporary agents were employed from time to time, both in Kansas and in the East. Some of these will be mentioned by name as occasion arises. Generally speaking, they were of little importance.

While the entering wedge was being driven into Kansas Territory by the sending of settlers and agents, the trustees were launching a propaganda campaign and financial drive to rally Eastern opinion and money in support of their effort. Beginning early in September, 1854, and continuing through the fall and winter, Thayer spent a great deal of time lecturing in various parts of

[59]

New England. Sometimes he made a special trip out of Boston to hold a meeting; sometimes he went on tours lasting several weeks. He was usually accompanied by either Branscomb or E. B. Whitman, who was employed for several months as a stock-subscription agent. The usual plan was to make advance arrangements for a "Kansas meeting," called by a local committee and presided over by some prominent citizen of the community. The meetings were extensively advertised and, according to the newspaper accounts, were generally well attended. Thayer would address such a meeting at considerable length, telling the story of the Emigrant Aid Company and its plans, urging emigration to Kansas, and suggesting the formation of a local "Kansas League" in support of the Company. Branscomb or Whitman would then follow with a shorter talk pleading for subscriptions to the stock of the Company. After the speaking the meeting could usually be depended upon to organize itself into a Kansas League, adopt the form constitution supplied by Thayer,* and elect officers. Frequently committees were appointed to solicit subscriptions to the stock of the Emigrant Aid Company.[18]

Just how many such meetings were held or how many subsidiary leagues were formed cannot be determined. Some communities organized leagues without receiving a visit from Thayer, getting their information from the Company's pamphlet and through correspondence with Dr. Webb. About two dozen such leagues can be identified by name, but it is certain that a much greater number existed. Some of them were very active throughout the period of the Kansas conflict; others appear to have done little more than organize. Each league was pledged by its constitution to promote antislavery emigration to Kansas and "to cooperate with the Emigrant Aid Company in the colonization of Kansas with freemen."[19] Each had a "Master of Emigra-

---

* Thayer carried printed forms of a constitution for Kansas Leagues, an exact copy, with blanks left for proper names, of the constitution of the Worcester County Kansas League, which Thayer, Hale, and others had organized in the summer of 1854. Several copies are preserved among the Aid Company Papers.

tion" whose duty it was to procure tickets for prospective emigrants from the Company office in Boston. Some of these leagues contributed considerable accessions to the Company parties. Perhaps half a dozen of them organized parties of their own. One of the earliest of these was the Hampton County Colony which settled at Burlington, Kansas; probably the most notable was the "Beecher's Bible Rifle" colony which settled Wabaunsee.

The first propaganda publication of the Emigrant Aid Company was the pamphlet *Organization, Objects and Plan of Operations of the Emigrant Aid Company,* to which reference has already been made. To trace the genesis of this pamphlet it is necessary to go back to the meeting of the incorporators of the Massachusetts Emigrant Aid Company on May 4, 1854. At that meeting a committee, consisting of Eli Thayer, Alexander H. Bullock, Edward Everett Hale, Richard Hildreth, and Otis Clapp, was appointed to prepare a plan of operations for the Company. A week later a report of the committee was presented at an adjourned meeting. The "Plan" had been sketched by Thayer and put into literary form by Hale.[20] It recited the contemplated benefits to the emigrants, to the country, and to the Company, and recommended that the directors should: (1) advertise immediately for rates to transport twenty thousand emigrants to Kansas; (2) conduct a boarding house with a capacity of three hundred; (3) send to Kansas a sawmill, a grist mill and other machinery; (4) establish a weekly newspaper; and (5) when Kansas should become a free state, dispose of the Company's interests there, declare a dividend, and select a new field in which to build another free state. In this last connection, the plan suggests that the Company might continue its efforts until it had erected a cordon of free states from Kansas to the Gulf of Mexico.[21] Sometime during the summer of 1854, while the organization of the Company was still in a nebulous form, this report, along with some sketches of the Kansas region which Robinson had written five years before, was printed as a thirty-two page pamphlet under the title *Nebraska and Kansas: Report of the Committee of the Massachusetts Emigrant Aid Company, with the Act of Incorporation and Other Documents.* A second edition was printed later. At the first meeting of the trustees, July 24, the secretary was directed to prepare a new pamphlet. This new pamphlet turned out to be only a slight revision of the former one with some additions. The "Report" was abridged somewhat, Robinson's description of Kansas was rewritten in the light of his recent trip, and some further description by George S. Park of Parkville, Missouri, was added, along with notices of the Company parties and settlements. This revision was published under the title, *Organization, Objects and Plan of Operations of the Emigrant Aid Company.* It was presented at the second meeting of the trustees, August 7, 1854. It ran through at least four editions.[22] In the third edition there was added a form constitution for auxiliary Kansas Leagues. This pamphlet was distributed free at the Boston office and was sent to newspapers and the various Kansas Leagues. So great was the demand of the local leagues for copies for distribution that the trustees felt obliged to make a ruling that auxiliary societies must pay for copies ordered in quantity.[23] Dr. Webb had it translated into German for use both in Germany and in the United States.[24] In March, 1855, it was superseded by Webb's *Information for Kansas Emigrants.*

On August 21, 1854, Hale's *Kanzas and Nebraska* appeared. As has been indicated, its preparation was undertaken in the interest of the Emigrant Aid Company, and a preliminary newspaper announcement states that it was being published "under the sanction of the Emigrant Aid Society."[25] Copies were offered for sale at the Company office in Boston. The book appears to have had considerable influence in stimulating interest in the Company and in promoting migration.

The propaganda value of songs was not overlooked. In August of 1854 John Greenleaf Whittier wrote, for the benefit of the emigrant aid effort, his well-known "Song of the Kansas Emigrant," to be sung to the tune of "Auld Lang Syne." As the train bearing the second party of Aid Company emigrants pulled out of the Boston station, August 29, the members of the party sang:

"We cross the prairies as of old
The Pilgrims crossed the sea,
To make the West, as they the East,
The homestead of the free."

During the following February, Dr. Webb offered a prize of fifty dollars for the best song that should be submitted. There were eighty-eight entries. The prize was awarded to Lucy Larcom, a teacher in the Wheaton Female Seminary at Norton, Massachusetts. Her song, "Call to Kansas," was, by her own admission, inspired by Whittier's earlier composition.[26] A little folder, *Lays of the Emigrants,* containing these two songs and a few others, was printed and distributed to members of emigrant parties.[27]

All these efforts were calling for money. Printing bills and office expenses were considerable. The lecture tours involved some expenditures. Salaries were piling up at the rate of almost four hundred dollars a month. In Lawrence, Robinson was spending money to buy out a squatter on the site and to erect temporary shacks, as well as for other incidental items. At Kansas City Pomeroy had to meet freight bills, payments on the hotel, and the cost of mills. But money was slow coming in. Indeed, all the money expended by the Company up to the middle of September, 1854, was advanced by Amos A. Lawrence out of his own funds. Some subscriptions to stock had been made under the tentative organization, but during the period of uncertainty that followed no effort was made to collect them. As soon as the trusteeship was launched, however, a drive for funds was begun. One William A. White was appointed a stock-subscription collector at a commission of 1 per cent on all collections above the first

$10,000, and Williams and Webb were directed to prepare a circular.[28] Lawrence and Williams worked diligently endeavoring to secure subcriptions from Boston businessmen, while in his lectures Thayer pleaded for funds as well as for emigrants.[29]

The result of all this effort was sadly disappointing. At this early stage the talk of profits from land values seems to have retarded rather than aided the subscription drive. As early as August 15 Lawrence wrote to Robinson that the people of Boston had little confidence in landed stocks,[30] and on September 2 he wrote to Williams, "The failure of our stock subscription is not to be wondered at in this community which has suffered so severely from land companies of various kinds."[31] In the same letter he reported a "complete stoppage of stock subscriptions." Only $20,000 had been subscribed, but according to the Articles of Agreement and Association no assessment could be levied on the stock unless $50,000 should be subscribed by September 1. Accordingly, in response to a suggestion of Williams that the trustees "take hold personally and put the subscription up to $50,000," Lawrence proposed that each of the trustees underwrite or become personally responsible for $10,000. On this dubious basis the trustees declared that the required amount had been subscribed, and proceeded to assess the stock. All subscriptions of less than $200 each were called in full; $10 a share (one-half) was levied upon all subscriptions of more than $200.[32] But money came in slowly. On September 24 not enough had been received to pay a draft from Pomeroy, and again Lawrence had to advance his own funds. Lawrence was desperate, and decided to appeal to the clergy. Early in October he issued over his own signature a circular to New England clergymen urging them to get behind the movement and assist in the organization of auxiliary societies.[33] On October 30 he wrote to Professor Packard of Bowdoin College to ask whether something could be done in the colleges.[34]

Thus the financial struggle went on. On November 7 Lawrence wrote to Dr. Webb that it was absolutely necessary that

Pomeroy have more money, and that the cash receipts or even the unpaid subscriptions would scarcely meet running expenses. He expected that the trustees would have to pay the $30,000 they had guaranteed. Another assessment on the stock would yield less than the first, since they had already undertaken to collect in full the subscriptions of less than $200. He was still willing to do his share individually with the other trustees, but he felt that they had done enough in assuming responsibility for the $30,000. He feared it would be necessary to sell property in Kansas and reinvest.[35] At the end of the year Lawrence had paid overdrafts to an amount in excess of $6,000. At that time he recorded in his diary: "Kansas drafts came in; no money in the treasury and never have had, and no money of my own, so I transferred some manufacturing company's stock to be sold and pay them. If Kansas should not be a free State, I shall lay it to heart and to my pocket too."[36]

If it is true that imitation is the sincerest form of flattery, the Emigrant Aid Company of Massachusetts had ample reason to feel flattered, for within a year there were at least half a dozen organizations more or less resembling it scattered through the northeastern part of the country. Most of these were apparently inspired by reports of the Boston organization, and several sought affiliation with it. The first of these to appear was an association of antislavery congressmen, formed in Washington, D. C., on May 29, 1854. Whether it was suggested by Thayer's early efforts cannot be determined with certainty, but such a possibility is hinted by the fact that its president, John Z. Goodrich, was a representative from Massachusetts. This organization, calling itself the Union Emigration Society, was largely political in character and was of short duration. Two years later one of its directors, Daniel Mace, testifying before the Howard Committee, could remember little about it.[37] A few dollars were raised from membership dues and expended on the issue of a circular urging freesoil emigration to Kansas, and pleading with Northern people to elect antislavery congressmen.[38] Late in July of 1854 Goodrich wrote to Lawrence proposing that the two organizations merge, but the trustees of the Emigrant Aid Company wisely declined the invitation.[39]

The origin of the Emigrant Aid Company of New York and Connecticut has already been sketched. R. N. Havens, its vice-president, was the active head of the organization in New York. Moses H. Grinnell was elected treasurer after Lawrence refused to serve. During the summer and fall of 1854 an occasional puff appeared in the New York papers, but nothing of a tangible nature seems to have been accomplished. In October Dr. Webb wrote to Pomeroy that it was rumored that the New York Company was at last to begin operations,[40] but if it really did anything no report of its activities got into the newspapers. As late as the first of March, 1855, a representative of this company went to Boston with a letter of introduction from Theodore Dwight to Thayer to propose a plan of co-operation with the Boston Company, but nothing came of the proposal.[41] By the summer of 1855 the Emigrant Aid Company of New York and Connecticut had ceased to be mentioned, and Havens had to admit its failure. The fault seems to have been, as previously noted, that the direction of the enterprise fell into the hands of self-seeking politicians, so that it lost the confidence of practical men of affairs. Most of its more responsible promoters later became stockholders and some of them directors in the New England Emigrant Aid Company. But before its untimely demise it had given rise to two other organizations which were actually to function in a small way in the colonization of Kansas. The New York Kansas League grew out of the New York and Connecticut Emigrant Aid Company, and the American Settlement Company grew out of the New York Kansas League.

On August 3, 1854, after a preliminary meeting a week earlier, a meeting was held in New York City to form a Kansas League. The gathering was called to order by R. N. Havens and was addressed at length by Thayer. The constitution of the Worcester

County Kansas League was adopted entire, including the clause pledging co-operation with the Emigrant Aid Company; and a roster of officers was chosen which included Theodore Dwight as secretary and Thaddeus Hyatt as a member of the board of directors. This league is known to have sent a delegation to join the second Massachusetts Emigrant Aid Company party of settlers at Albany August 30, 1854,[42] and it may have furnished contingents to other parties. In December, 1854, the League made a definite proposal of co-operation with the Massachusetts Emigrant Aid Company, but in view of the earlier unfortunate experience in attempting to work with the New York men, the trustees declined the offer.[43] After this the League affiliated itself with the American Settlement Company and continued to function until 1856, when it merged itself into the wider emigrant aid movement of that year.[44]

The American Settlement Company was formed in September, 1854, by some of the men interested in the New York Kansas League. After some shifting about, the officers were Theodore Dwight, president; J. E. Snodgrass, vice-president; George Walter, superintendent; A. H. Jocelyn, secretary; D. C. Van Norman, treasurer. It was organized as an unincorporated joint-stock company. The shares were five dollars each and no individual could hold more than six shares. Every settler was required to be a stockholder, and each share entitled the holder to one lot in the Company's settlement in Kansas. The Settlement Company proposed to settle a county in Kansas, sending its emigrants through the facilities of the New York Kansas League.[45] The American Settlement Company founded a town, Council City (present Burlingame), and maintained an agent in Kansas until 1856.* Its superintendent, George Walter, who was also Master of Emigration of the New York Kansas League, maintained an office at 110 Broadway, New York, where he gave out information

---

* The agent was Loton Smith until 1855. After that it was J. M. Winchell. Both were members of the Board of Directors.

[67]

and sold tickets at reduced fares, much after the manner of Dr. Webb is Boston. He also issued an emigrants' handbook entitled *History of Kansas*.[46] The Settlement Company proposed to establish a mill, build a hotel, and make other improvements in Council City, but these never materialized. The vice-president, Dr. J. E. Snodgrass, went about delivering Kansas lectures throughout the middle states, much as Thayer was doing in New England. One tour took him into Pennsylvania and another into Maryland.[47]

A mass meeting in Albany, New York, on July 28, 1854, appointed a committee to draw up plans for a Kansas League. At another mass meeting, on August 30, called to welcome the second Emigrant Aid Company party and the New York City contingent which joined it at Albany, the Albany Kansas League was organized.[48] This association co-operated with the Emigrant Aid Company by making arrangements for the accommodation of its parties on their overnight stops at Albany, and by recruiting settlers to join these parties. The League ceased to be mentioned in the newspapers after the fall of 1854, but it was revived early in the spring of 1856 and soon merged into the New York State Kansas Committee, which worked in close co-operation with the Emigrant Aid Company during the remainder of 1856.

At a meeting held on August 21, 1854, at Oberlin, Ohio, there was organized the Kansas Emigration Aid Association of Northern Ohio, with Professor J. H. Fairchild of Oberlin College as president.[49] There is reason to believe that the idea was suggested by reports of the formation of the Emigrant Aid Company in Boston.* Early in September the Association sent an agent, Samuel Plumb, to Boston to try to arrange a plan of co-operation, but he returned empty-handed.[50] Shortly after this Plumb and two or three others were sent to Kansas to prospect and to prepare the

---

*Suggested by quotations from Thayer's speeches in newspaper reports of the organization. Clayton S. Ellsworth, who has made a careful study of the Oberlin organization, states that its formation was presumably prompted by the example of the Emigrant Aid Company. See note 52.

way for a party of settlers. This party, about fifty strong, left for Kansas on or about October 23, under the direction of J. H. Howe. When the group arrived in Kansas they were sorely disappointed by the lack of preparations for their reception, and most of them returned at once. Howe gave out a report, published in a number of papers, denouncing the aid associations for deceiving and defrauding settlers.[51] The Northern Ohio Association operated in a hit-and-miss fashion until 1857, sending out seven parties in all. Among those who came in its parties were several men who were prominent in early Kansas, including S. N. Wood and Preston B. Plumb. At first it refused to give any direct pecuniary aid to settlers, but in 1856 it changed its policy and supplied them with weapons and, in some cases apparently, with cash.[52]

Two emigrant aid organizations were launched in Cincinnati in the fall of 1854. One was a German society called the *Kansas Anseidlungsverein*. No information regarding its activities has come to light.[53] The other, the Cincinnati Kansas League, joined with the American Reform Tract and Book Society in sending out the Rev. Charles Boynton and T. B. Mason as an exploring party in September, 1854.[54] The following April this organization joined with the Kentucky Kansas Association of Covington, just across the Ohio River, in sending out a colony of about sixty persons who founded the town of Ashland, near Manhattan. Franklin G. Adams, later prominent in Kansas, was president of the League.[55] There are some rather vague newspaper references to some sort of organization in Pittsburgh, Pennsylvania, but little is known about it.

Of course the emigrant aid movement had its lunatic fringe, and the various freak projects that it evoked are best typified by a pair of twin organizations launched in New York City by Henry S. Clubb, a prominent temperance worker of the day. The Vegetarian Settlement Company was formed in the summer of 1855 with Charles H. De Wolfe of Philadelphia as president, Dr. John McLauren as secretary, and Clubb as treasurer. It was proposed to form a settlement of vegetarians on the fantastic "octagon plan," whereby tracts two miles square were to be cut up into sixteen triangular farms, forming an octagon, with a village in the center, and the corner triangles used as common pasture and timber land.[56] The Octagon Settlement Company, formed a few months later with the same officers, had identical plans except that its colony was not limited to vegetarians.[57] The twin organizations were of the non-corporate joint-stock type with the stock in five-dollar shares. Like the American Settlement Company they required each settler to be a stockholder, each share entitling him to an acre in the settlement. Each member paid an initial fee of ten dollars and was assessed fifty cents on each share. On paper the plans were similar to those of the Emigrant Aid Company, calling for mills, hotels, and other improvements; but none of these things got beyond the paper stage.[58] A colony of about a hundred was sent out in the spring of 1856 and located on the Neosho River about six miles south of present Humboldt, but one disaster after another overtook the settlers and in a few months the settlement was abandoned. The colonists believed that Clubb had deliberately swindled them out of their money,* but a recent student of the subject is convinced that the failure of the venture was due to mismanagement.[59]

The actual accomplishment of these various organizations in the settlement of Kansas and the shaping of its destiny was slight. Their significance in the history of the Emigrant Aid Company lies in two directions. In the first place, the fact that the Company was so widely imitated in the early months of its activity gives some inkling of the appeal it made to popular imagination in the North. In the second place, the fact that on the frontier the all-embracing term, "Emigrant Aid Society," was applied indiscriminately to the Boston company and to all this motley array of imitators meant that anything that any of them did was laid at the door of the New England Emigrant Aid Company.

---

* Mrs. Colt insists throughout her book *Went to Kansas* that the whole scheme was a swindle.

So during the summer and early fall of 1854, while it was still grappling with problems of organization, the Emigrant Aid Company was launching the Kansas crusade and setting up the machinery for carrying on its work. Seen in perspective, the prospect was not bright. The actual opposition on the frontier had not yet developed, but the difficulty of carrying on operations fifteen hundred miles from the base was already apparent. The agents on whom the company had to rely were never quite satisfactory, and the financial difficulties seemed insuperable. The host of imitators that flocked into the field and sought to tie themselves to the apron strings of the parent enterprise only complicated the problem. Yet it never occurred to any of the organizers to admit defeat and not one of them ever proposed to abandon the project. They had sounded the battle cry of freedom for Kansas and they were determined to struggle on until the battle should be won.

CHAPTER V

Driving Down the Stakes

THE KANSAS-NEBRASKA ACT had scarcely become a law when the "squatters" began to pour into Kansas. Technically the land was not yet open to settlement. The first of the treaties extinguishing Indian titles was not ratified until May 15, 1854, and the Pre-emption Act was not extended to Kansas until July 22. Yet a settler who arrived as early as May 8 reported that, although no land was open, there was already an influx of "sooners"; he found no actual settlers on the Delaware and Shawnee lands, but everywhere claims were "staked" by writing the claimant's name on a board driven into the ground or on the blaze of a tree. Here and there was a "foundation" of a house, consisting of four logs notched and laid on the ground in the form of a rectangle.[1] George W. Manypenny, Commissioner of Indian Affairs, had visited the region during the preceding August, and had negotiated treaties to reduce the size of Indian reservations, thus clearing the way for white settlers.[2]

Some of these first land-seekers came from the states of the Ohio valley, but naturally the greater number of the early arrivals were men from the Platte Purchase district of Missouri. These men had long coveted the desirable lands of the Delawares, Kickapoos, and Iowas just across the Missouri River, and as soon as word arrived that the country was to be opened to settlement, they ferried across the river in great numbers and located claims. Despite the assertion of many historians that the early inrush of Missourians represented a conspiracy to fasten slavery upon the new territory, there is every indication that these first comers, real frontiersmen as they were, were prompted only by land hunger. Many of them, to be sure, did not settle on their claims at once; it was past the planting season and so was a poor time to start opening up a new farm. Some of them evidently intended to move to the land at some future time, but many, undoubtedly, were attempting merely to establish priority rights for the purpose of speculation, hoping to sell out to later comers. Since the land had not yet been surveyed,* the rule followed was to consider any attempt to locate within one-half mile of a claim stake as "claim jumping."[3] To protect these "squatter rights" against later arrivals, squatters' associations were organized, with registrars to record claims and judges to settle disputes. The first of these was the Squatters Claim Association, formed on June 10, 1854, at a meeting held in the Salt Creek valley near Fort Leavenworth. A group of resolutions were adopted forming a sort of constitution:[4] among these was a resolution declaring that no protection would be afforded to abolitionists, as well as another urging slaveholders to move in with their slaves.[5] In August there was formed in the Lawrence neighborhood the Actual Settlers Association, in which both free-soil men from the Ohio Valley and squatters from Missouri participated; John A. Wakefield was judge and S. N. Wood, clerk.[6] Several other such associations were formed during the summer in various parts of the territory.

Close on the heels of the absentee claimants from Missouri came the actual settlers. Hundreds came from Missouri during the first year. Others came from Kentucky and Tennessee, and not a few from Virginia and the states of the deep South. But by far the greatest number came from the Old Northwest: Illinois, Indiana, and Ohio. Some came by steamboat down the Ohio and up the Missouri; but, according to the tales of old settlers, the great influx from the Ohio River states came overland, bringing their families and household effects with their few farm implements in covered wagons, and driving their cattle before them. These, declared Colonel S. N. Wood,* one of their number, "were the real pioneers of Kansas," and he added that when

---

*John Calhoun, who had once been Abraham Lincoln's employer in Illinois, was commissioned Surveyor General for Kansas and Nebraska August 4, 1854. On November 8, 1855, he reported that the guide meridian, three parallels, and fifty township lines had been completed, and that the first section lines (in a hundred townships) would be completed about February, 1856 (34 Cong., 1 Sess., *Executive Documents,* I, Part I, 308-18).

[73]

many of them left their old homes "we had never heard of the New England Emigrant Aid Society."[7]

There can be no doubt that the primary motive that impelled these pioneers to move to Kansas was the hope of bettering their economic condition by securing new homes on the public domain.[8] A few went in the interest of their health; some went for sheer adventure; some, like James H. Lane, went to make or rebuild their political fortunes; but most of them went to get farms. Yet, insisted Colonel Wood, they went for something more.[9] Practically all from the northern states, and many from Missouri and the South, were opposed on principle to the extension of slavery and had been aroused by the passage of the Kansas-Nebraska bill. They did not go to fight a civil war, but they did expect by their presence and their votes to check the ingress of slavery into the territory. Somewhat crude in speech and uncouth in manners, these people were from regions that were still largely frontier in character, and they were fully qualified to endure the hardships and privations of pioneering. Most of those from Missouri and the South were pro-slavery in sentiment, but except when they were aroused by the politicians or were caught in the mob spirit they were content to live in peace with their free-soil neighbors. Indeed, a number of them changed their views and became free-state men. One of these, who first went to Kansas to vote in the famous "bogus election" of March 30, 1855, later told an interesting story of how he became so interested in locating a claim that he neglected to vote and, having moved his family to his claim a few weeks later, became an active free-state man, "helping to undo what the Pro-Slavery invasion, of which I had been in some measure a part, had accomplished at that election."[10]

As previously noted, the first party of settlers to migrate to Kansas under the auspices of the Emigrant Aid Company, the

---

* Colonel Wood left his home in northern Ohio for Kansas just a week after the signing of the Kansas-Nebraska Act. He became one of the foremost leaders of the free-state movement.

DRIVING DOWN THE STAKES

much-discussed pioneer party, twenty-nine strong, reached the site of Lawrence August 1, 1854. There were already, according to Colonel Wood, approximately a hundred settlers in the vicinity.[11] On September 12 the advance contingent of the second party arrived, to be joined three days later by the main body, eighty-five in all.* These groups merged and founded Lawrence. Four other parties were sent during the fall of 1854, on September 26, October 17, November 7, and November 21. Most of these colonists settled in the vicinity of Lawrence. It is probable that, counting accessions en route, the six fall parties numbered around 650.† Three hundred and eighty-nine left Boston in the parties.[12] The records show 528 tickets sold at the Boston office and through branch Kansas Leagues.[13] Accessions to the parties along the way were considerable, probably averaging around a fourth of the original strength. The second party grew from sixty-six to eighty-five; the sixth, from twenty-two to thirty. The third and fourth increased to such an extent that the Missouri River steamboats, engaged on the basis of the number of tickets sold, could not accommodate them.[14] Thayer claimed that the parties often doubled and sometimes quadrupled, but allowances must be made for his habit of exaggeration.[15] The newspaper accounts of the parties greatly magnified their size.‡

The first spring party of 1855 left Boston on March 6. From that date to and including May 8 a party left each Tuesday. A small party is mentioned as leaving June 19 and another September 11. There may have been others, especially privately organized parties which secured tickets through the Emigrant Aid Company§. According to the figures that Dr. Webb reported to

---

* This party numbered sixty-six when it left Boston. About fifteen from New York City joined it at Albany. Four or five others must have joined somewhere along the route.

† The *Directors' History* gives 750 as the number. Miss Barry estimated the number at 670 (Louise Barry, "The Emigrant Aid Company Parties of 1854," *Kansas Historical Quarterly*, XII, May, 1943, 115-55).

‡ The *Albany Journal*, August 30, 1854, reported the second party as numbering 300 (copied in *New York Daily Times*, August 31, 1854).

§ One such "private" party known to have traveled on Aid Company tickets in 1855 was the Hampden colony. This estimate cannot be checked against ticket sales, as was done for 1854, because Emigrant Books covering the period from April 17, 1855, to May

the Executive Committee, the twelve parties numbered 835 when they left Boston.[16] If allowance be made for accessions from the branch societies and along the route, the Company migration for 1855 must have amounted to around a thousand.

These parties consisted mostly of men, but, Thayer's statement to the contrary notwithstanding,[17] they included considerable numbers of women and children. Fifteen women are listed in the second party, and each of the remaining fall parties of 1854 contained several women and children. On the eve of the departure of the fourth party, Dr. Webb wrote to Pomeroy regretting that, despite his efforts to discourage the migration of women and children at that season of the year, the party about to leave would include a large number of children.[18]

These Yankees, as Westerners always called them, were of a different breed from the Western frontiersmen. Most of them were relatively well educated and many had attended college, whereas the frontiersmen were a step removed, at best, from actual illiteracy. The New Englander's language was different: his speech was precise and relatively grammatical, to Western ears sounding affected; the Westerner broadened his vowels, took unspeakable liberties with inflections and syntax, and spoke with a harsh drawl. The Easterner was fastidious in his tastes and found it difficult to adapt himself to the barren life of the frontier which the Western man took as a matter of course. The people from New England were usually temperate in their habits and felt the need of the regular ministrations of organized religion; the Western pioneers were apt to be hard drinkers and, as one writer puts it, "got religion as they got the measles." It is true, of course, that the bulk of the Aid Company settlers migrated, as did the Westerners, with a view to bettering their economic condition, but to a far greater extent they were motivated by the emotional urge of the antislavery crusade. A disappointingly small

---

6, 1856, are lost. For additional detail on the parties of 1855, see Louise Barry, "The New England Emigrant Aid Company Parties of 1855," *Kansas Historical Quarterly,* XII, August, 1943, 227-68.

number of them were farmers; although many of those who had been urban mechanics or tradesmen at home were able to adjust themselves to the strange life on the quarter-sections, many others, going to Kansas with the expectation of finding remunerative employment in their accustomed vocations, were utterly unable to care for themselves when this expectation was disappointed.

Naturally such people found it difficult to fit themselves into the life of a frontier community. They were usually unpopular with the Westerners. Their natural preference for the company of people of their own kind and their efforts to preserve their own manners and customs were regarded as clannishness and an assumption of superiority. The *Kansas Free State,* edited by Western men, never ceased to rail at the Yankees and at the Emigrant Aid Company which had sent them, insisting that they were hindering rather than helping the free-state cause.* It was inevitable that many of these people, baffled by the conditions they found, should become discouraged and return to their old homes. The Reverend Richard Cordley, who was well disposed toward the Emigrant Aid Company, tells in his *History of Lawrence* how "several of those who came in these parties became disgusted when they saw the true situation. This was especially true of the third party who arrived in October. The movement by this time had attracted wide attention, and the colonists had sent back glowing accounts of the country. These accounts were interpreted by a vivid imagination, and a number of soft-slippered people, such as they would call tenderfeet in Colorado, enlisted, who expected to find an earthly paradise. When they came and found only a few tents and a few thatched hovels, their disgust knew no bounds. They were looking for hotels with all the modern conveniences, and expecting to find good positions waiting for

---

*Connelley quotes a long excerpt from an editorial in the *Kansas Free State* of February 7, 1855, charging the Yankees with clannishness and with trying to impose on Westerners a "model New England State." The editorial goes on to warn Easterners that Kansas is being settled mainly by Westerners and that "they may as well make up their minds to regard Western men as human beings and conclude to associate with them" (Connelley, *Appeal to the Record,* 123).

them in large business establishments. After exhausting their vocabulary in denouncing the leaders who had 'deceived them' and induced them to come to such a barbarous place, and the people of Lawrence for not providing for them in a more appropriate way, they turned on their heels and 'went back to their folks.'" He adds, however, that "most of those who came were of different stuff, and were prepared to 'endure hardships as good soldiers.'"[19]

Those who did return must have been numerous. The newspapers of the time were replete with allusions to them, as well as with their complaints. More than a dozen persons testified before the Howard Committee that they had seen Eastern "emigrants" returning.[20] The Emigrant Aid Company admitted in an official document, "A few of those who went out without a sufficient acquaintance with the difficulties and hardships incident to pioneer life, became discouraged and wished to return." But the same document insists, "The number of these is small compared with those who remain as permanent settlers of the Territory."[21] Dr. Webb lamented these desertions in his letters, insisting that he had warned all inquirers of the difficulties they would encounter and had done all he could to discourage those who were without financial means or who appeared unable to comprehend the hardships of pioneering.[22] Much was made of this situation by opponents of the Company. Western free-state men insisted that this backflow of Eastern colonists discredited their cause, while proslavery spokesmen used it as proof that the Emigrant Aid Company was sending men merely to vote and return.

Just how extensive this outflow of Easterners was it is impossible to say. One contemporary newspaper correspondent estimated it at 25 to 50 per cent of those who went out.[23] Of course not all the settlers who became discouraged and abandoned the territory had migrated under the auspices of the Emigrant Aid Company, but in view of the extra strain which frontier conditions put upon city dwellers from the East, it is safe to assume that a disproportionate number of those who left the territory were New Englanders. To be sure, not all who returned East were abandoning the territory. Some returned temporarily on private business; others went for their families; still others, who went out in the earlier parties only to look over the ground, came home for the winter and went back to Kansas as real settlers in the following spring. But after all is said, it remains a fact that too large a share of the Emigrant Aid Company "emigrants" did not become permanent inhabitants of Kansas.

But in spite of all their handicaps and difficulties, the Aid Company settlers played an important part in the making of Kansas, and not the least of their contributions was the launching of those towns which served as centers of free-state activity. The first-born of these towns was, of course, Lawrence. On September 18, 1854, the members of the first two Aid Company parties held a meeting on the site and organized the Lawrence Association. Two days later officers were elected. A. D. Searle was appointed surveyor and at once began to lay out the townsite.[24] The original plan called for the occupancy of two square miles, although only a half-section could be pre-empted; one-half of the lots were to be assigned to members of the Association and one-fourth to the Emigrant Aid Company, the remainder being reserved for persons who would make improvements.[25] A squatter, Clark Stearns, who occupied a part of the site, was bought out by Robinson and Pomeroy on behalf of the Emigrant Aid Company for five hundred dollars. On October 1 the Association voted to adopt and confer upon the settlement the name of "Lawrence," in honor of Amos A. Lawrence.[26] Before that time the place had been called Wakarusa. About the same time there appeared four men, John Baldwin, William Baldwin, William Lykins, and J. N. O. P. Wood, with C. W. Babcock as their attorney, who laid claim to parts of the townsite and threatened to expel the New Englanders by force. Threats were exchanged and weapons drawn, but no actual violence occurred. Whether these men were bona fide squatters or only claim jumpers, as Robinson asserted, cannot be determined. At any rate, the dispute dragged on with rival "indignation meetings" and denunciatory resolutions until the following February, when, in the absence of Robinson, Pomeroy agreed to a compromise. By the terms of this agreement these later claimants were admitted to the town association. The townsite was now limited to 640 acres to be secured by a Wyandotte float belonging to Lykins,* and its ownership was to be divided into 220 shares. Of these, 100 were assigned to Lykins, Wood, and the Baldwins, 110 to the original Association, and eight to the Emigrant Aid Company, two being reserved for school purposes.[27] Dr. Webb regretted that the arrangement had reduced the holdings of the Company, fearing that it would retard the raising of funds and weaken the desire of the Executive Committee to make improvements in Lawrence.[28]

This dispute was, in many ways, typical of the land disputes with which the early history of Kansas abounds. Actually it had no political significance whatever, but in the writing of the time it was played up as an attempt of Border Ruffians to drive out free-state men.[29] As a matter of fact, with the possible exception of Lykins, who was a Southern man, all of the group who contested the right of the Emigrant Aid Company settlers to the site were free-state in sympathy, as were Josiah Miller and R. G. Elliott, editors of the *Kansas Free State,* who helped to bring about the compromise. The episode was significant, too, as indicating the attitude of the settlers from the West toward New Englanders.

But in spite of all difficulties Lawrence grew rapidly. By February, 1855, a newspaper correspondent estimated that there were around 400 inhabitants, including over a hundred women and girls. Only about a hundred of these people were from New Eng-

---

* By the terms of the Manypenny treaty with the Wyandotte Indians, certain members of the tribe were each given a transferable right to locate and acquire in fee simple a tract of 640 acres anywhere in the public domain. These rights, bought and sold freely, were known as "Wyandotte floats."

land, most of the others having migrated from the western states.[30] At first the people dwelt in tents furnished by the Emigrant Aid Company. As the fall wore into winter, a mild one fortunately, the tents gave way to rude shanties of thatch and turf (hay tents, the settlers called them) and log cabins. There was no end of complaint from travelers and disappointed "emigrants" that the St. Nicholas Hotel was only a mud hut, that the boarding house was but a "hay tent," and that the fare, chiefly the "hog and hominy" so typical of the frontier, was unspeakable.[31] But for all that, the colony took root and remained the chief center of the free-state movement throughout the period of the conflict.

The second town to be founded largely through the efforts of Emigrant Aid Company agents and settlers was Topeka. On October 30, 1854, Dr. Webb wrote to Pomeroy suggesting the formation of a second settlement in order to disperse the New England leaven as widely as possible.[32] By a singular coincidence, Pomeroy wrote to Webb the same day asking if the trustees would approve a second town.[33] The location was selected by a committee of the fourth Aid Company party accompanied by Robinson on November 29, 1854. A few days later a few members of the fifth and sixth parties joined them.[34] On December 5 nine men, seven of them New Englanders, met in the cabin of M. C. Dickey at what is now First Street and Kansas Avenue in Topeka, organized themselves into a town association, and signed an agreement to lay out a town on a section of land to be preempted by four of their number. The ownership of the town was to be divided into fifty shares, one-sixth of which were assigned to the Emigrant Aid Company on the condition that it install a mill, erect a receiving house, and build a schoolhouse. Robinson, who was present, accepted the conditions on behalf of the Company. C. K. Holliday was chosen chairman of the association. The name "Topeka," selected some time later, was suggested by the Reverend S. Y. Lum, of Lawrence; it was a Kaw Indian word

[81]

signifying a place where wild potatoes grow.[35] The Emigrant Aid Company took a less active interest in Topeka than it did in Lawrence, but its agents continued to direct settlers thither and the Company made some improvements. Topeka ranked second only to Lawrence as a center of free-state activity, and became famous for the "Topeka Constitution."

The third free-state settlement to which the Emigrant Aid Company may lay some claim was Osawatomie, indelibly associated with the career of John Brown. The location, at the point where the Marais des Cygnes and Pottawatomie Creek join to form the Osage River, was first settled by a party of New Yorkers who went to Kansas under the auspices of the New York League. Arriving at Kansas City on October 15, 1854, and failing to find the agent of the League who was supposed to receive them, they divided into two groups and set out for themselves. One group of twenty-six, headed by Orville C. Brown, the original "Osawatomie Brown," settled at the head of the Osage River and named their settlement *Osawatomie* from *Osage* and *Pottawatomie.*[36] Whether or not the Emigrant Aid Company agents had a hand in the selection of the site is not clear.* Anyhow a town company was formed in December, 1854, or January, 1855, consisting of O. C. Brown, William Ward of New York, and S. C. Pomeroy as trustee for the Emigrant Aid Company, each holding a one-third interest. The townsite was surveyed in February, 1855, by A. D. Searle of Lawrence. The town grew slowly, being far removed from the regular emigrant routes and being located in territory that was settled mainly by pro-slavery men from Missouri. The Emigrant Aid Company, although it was a one-third owner, did little to develop the settlement except to locate a mill. So far as can be determined, no appreciable number of New Englanders ever settled there. Osawatomie was never so important as a free-state center as were Lawrence and Topeka, but at-

---

* D. W. Wilder asserted that the site was selected by agents of the Emigrant Aid Company, but no contemporary evidence on the question has come to light (D. W. Wilder, *The Annals of Kansas* [Topeka, 1875], 615).

tention was attracted to it by the operations of John Brown and by the two raids made on the place in the summer of 1856.

The leader of the Emigrant Aid Company's first spring party of 1855 was Isaac T. Goodnow, who, according to his own story, had just resigned the principalship of the East Greenwich, Rhode Island, Academy to migrate to Kansas. Proceeding ahead of the party with a few companions, Goodnow was directed by Pomeroy to the mouth of the Big Blue River. Five or six squatters on the site were induced to join these Aid Company settlers in the organization of a town company and the founding of the town of Boston.[37] A rival claimant, a pro-slavery man named Osborne, was forcibly expelled.[38] One-tenth of the townsite or nine quarter sections, later defined as ninety-five shares, was assigned to the Emigrant Aid Company on condition that the Company locate a mill in the community. About a month later, June 3, 1855, the steamboat *Hartford,* bearing a party of seventy-five colonists from Ohio who called themselves the Cincinnati and Kansas Land Company, grounded on a sandbar near the mouth of the Big Blue, and this group accepted the offer of the founders of Boston to join the settlement. However, since the Ohio people were being financed by some New York men who had pledged them to call their community "Manhattan," it was necessary to change the name of the town. On the way back down the Kansas River the *Hartford* was burned, and the Emigrant Aid Company bought one of its boilers to run the Lawrence sawmill.[39]

As was usual in such situations, the title to the townsite continued to be questioned. In 1856, the Executive Committee of the Emigrant Aid Company having declined to purchase a Wyandotte float to quiet title, Dr. Webb gave one for that purpose on condition that the Manhattan Town Association should refrain from taxing his holdings in the town as long as he should own them.[40] The Emigrant Aid Company took an active interest in Manhattan. Its agents directed a large number of settlers to the vicinity. The Company located one of its best mills there, and later contributed extensively to local improvements. Manhattan was one of the staunchest of the free-state centers, but being located some distance from the theater of conflict, it played no spectacular part.

Settlers who migrated to Kansas under the auspices of the Emigrant Aid Company founded several other towns, but these failed to achieve importance in the Kansas struggle. Most of them never developed beyond the village stage. Two of them, Hampden and Wabaunsee, started out with great promise and for a time attracted wide attention. Hampden, located directly across the Neosho River from the present Burlington, was settled on April 27, 1855, by a party of about ninety colonists from Hampden County, Massachusetts.* The site was selected by Pomeroy.[41] There were considerable accessions to the colony during the first few months, but these were offset by the return of many members of the original party who became discouraged by the difficulty of breaking prairie.[42] The agricultural community survived, but the town failed to take root. Even the location of a mill by the Aid Company did not save it, and it was gradually absorbed into Burlington, founded about a year later by men from Lawrence. The site was definitely abandoned in 1866.

The beginning of the settlement of Wabaunsee (originally spelled Wabonsá) was made by a portion of the fourth party of Aid Company emigrants in November, 1854. The site was selected by James Blood, acting on behalf of the Company,† and the name was chosen at the suggestion of the Reverend Johnston Lykins, a missionary to the Pottawatomie Indians in the vicinity. By the spring of 1856 the village had about twenty-five or thirty inhabitants.[43] Wabaunsee's chief claim to fame lay in the fact that it was the place of settlement of the famous "Beecher's

---

* There were seventy men, of whom ten brought wives or families.

† James Blood, a lawyer by profession, was sent to Kansas by Amos A. Lawrence in the summer of 1854 to assist in explorations. He helped select the site of Lawrence. In the fall he was employed by Robinson and Pomeroy as legal adviser, and acted as a sort of subagent of the Company in various matters. Later he served as mayor of Lawrence, and was commissioned a colonel in the free-state militia.

Bible Rifle" colony, which will be discussed more fully later. This party, numbering forty-nine men, reached Wabaunsee April 28, 1856. As in the case of Hampden, later accessions were offset by the return of earlier settlers, so that Wabaunsee never became more than a hamlet. The Emigrant Aid Company placed a mill there, for which the town association assigned the Company ten lots. New Englanders, partly through the efforts of Dr. Webb, raised funds for the erection of a small church building that is still in use, being known as the "Beecher's Bible Rifle Church." During the period of the Kansas conflict Wabaunsee was widely known as the headquarters of the "Beecher's Bible Rifle Company," a unit of the free-state militia.

During the boom period of 1856-57 settlers who had been assisted more or less by the Emigrant Aid Company established Zeandale, near Manhattan, and the German colony of Humboldt. Lawrence men, who had migrated originally as Company settlers, were active in promoting Burlington, Emporia, and Wyandotte, as well as several other places that failed to attain importance. The Company took a hand directly in the launching of Claflin (Mapleton) and Batcheller (Milford), and also acquired extensive interests in Atchison and Quindaro.

The only free-state settlement of any consequence whose founding was entirely independent of the Emigrant Aid Company was Council City. The place was settled in November, 1854, by a party from Pennsylvania under the auspices of the American Settlement Company. Only nineteen of the original party remained through the winter, but new settlers came in the spring of 1855. A large double log cabin, called the Council House, was built by the Settlement Company and was used as a boarding house. The town led a precarious existence. The site was shifted several times. In the spring of 1856 the American Settlement Company collapsed and its agent, J. M. Winchell, undertook to organize a new town to be called Frémont, but he failed in the venture. About the same time Dr. Webb and Thayer assisted Philip Schuyler, one of the Council City settlers who had returned East for the purpose, to raise funds for the purchase of a combination saw and grist mill for the place.[44] Finally in the spring of 1857 Schuyler and a few others organized a third town association and founded the town of Burlingame on the site, naming it in honor of Anson Burlingame, a personal friend of Schuyler. The principal importance of Council City during the Kansas conflict, besides its being known as a free-state town, was that it was the home of Philip Schuyler, a descendant of General Philip Schuyler of Revolutionary War fame and one of the most active of the free-state leaders.

While the Emigrant Aid Company settlers and others were founding the centers of free-state activity, Westerners, mostly from Missouri, were launching as pro-slavery centers Leavenworth, Atchison, Lecompton, and Franklin, not to mention at least a score of less important places, such as Iowa Point, Doniphan, Kickapoo, Tecumseh, and Juniata. With scarcely an exception, all the towns founded or projected in territorial Kansas were primarily speculative ventures. Although many of them came to be identified with either the free-state or the pro-slavery cause, there were many, perhaps a majority, such as Paola, Grasshopper Falls (later Valley Falls), Palmyra (Baldwin), and Millard (Junction City), whose founding had no political significance whatever. Pawnee, on the Fort Riley military reservation, the first place designated as territorial capital, was largely a private venture of Governor Reeder, projected for speculative purposes.

During these formative days the Emigrant Aid Company was doing its best to care for the needs of its colonists, although this may have been a poor best if one may judge from the numerous complaints appearing in the Eastern newspapers. In September, 1854, Robinson and Pomeroy purchased for the Company the Gillis Hotel in Kansas City for $10,000.[45] The hotel was operated by a lessee, a Mr. Hoad at first and later S. W. Eldridge, for the accommodation of settlers and travelers of free-state sentiments. The regular rates were $1.25 a day, $4.50 a week, American plan, but members of Emigrant Aid Company parties were accommodated at seventy-five cents a day or $3.50 a week.[46] The American Hotel, as it was renamed, became free-state headquarters in Kansas City and was usually patronized by settlers from the free states, although there was some complaint about the manner in which it was conducted until Eldridge took it over in the spring of 1855.

Almost at once the agents of the Emigrant Aid Company began the building of a large stone hotel in Lawrence on the site of the present Hotel Eldridge. Work proceeded slowly because of lack of funds, at times having to be stopped entirely, so that the hotel was just ready to be opened to the public when it was destroyed in the sack of Lawrence on May 21, 1856. Pending the completion of this Free State Hotel, the Company undertook to provide temporary accommodations for new arrivals. At the time of the departure of the pioneer party fifty tents were purchased, at a cost of eight dollars each, to be used by the settlers until cabins could be built.[47] Soon after the second party reached Lawrence the agents had temporary shacks put up to serve as a "receiving house," or dormitory for transients, and a boarding house. Within a few weeks they began the erection of a frame building to serve as church, schoolhouse, and town hall.[48] This building, known when completed as the "Emigrant Aid Company Building," was used for all these purposes and also housed the Company's Lawrence office. The Reverend S. Y. Lum, employed by the Home Missionary Society of the Congregational Church, accompanied the second Emigrant Aid Company party. On October 15, a month after this party reached Lawrence, the Plymouth Congregational Church was organized in the "hay tent" that had just been built for a boarding house. Pomeroy acted as secretary of the meeting.[49] The congregation continued to meet in the "Pioneer Boarding House" until the Company building was completed, when it used the assembly hall in that building. During 1855 and the first months of 1856 funds were raised in New England for the erection of a permanent edifice for the congregation. Lawrence and Webb took an active part in raising the money and Lawrence contributed a thousand dollars personally. In 1855 Robinson helped to organize the Unitarian Church in Lawrence. In 1857 Amos A. Lawrence contributed funds for the erection of an Episcopal Church in the town of Lawrence, and the Emigrant Aid Company donated a lot for it.[50]

In the fall of 1854 Dr. Webb began soliciting and collecting books for a library, or Atheneum, as he called it, for Lawrence. He sent the first package of books with the fourth fall party in October. He continued to send books from time to time for the next two years,[51] and included in his *Information* pamphlet a paragraph soliciting the contribution of books.[52] After Topeka and Manhattan were founded he sent books to them also. So accustomed were the forwarding agents to handling boxes of books directed to the agents of the Emigrant Aid Company that when, in the fall of 1855, boxes of rifles marked "Books" arrived, no suspicions were aroused.

In various other ways the Company, its officers, and its agents endeavored to look after the welfare of the settlers. Soon after the departure of the second party in September, 1854, Lawrence wrote to Pomeroy directing him to make provision for their medical care during Robinson's absences and asking for a list of common medicines needed.[53] A few weeks later Webb wrote to Pomeroy to make the best arrangements he could for the women and children, and added, "And we trust that our agents will always be prompt to administer to the wants of the distressed, assuage the suffering of the sick, and guard, for those concerned, the interests of the departed."[54] In November Pomeroy was directed to lay out a cemetery.[55] The following spring garden seeds were sent to be distributed to the settlers, and Webb wrote, "I wish to learn what the wants now are at the various actual or contemplated

[88]

settlements."[56] Although the Company appeared less solicitous of the welfare of the colonists in other localities than in Lawrence, considerable effort was made in other settlements also.

One of the greatest needs of any frontier community was mills to provide lumber for building and to grind grain for food. Their establishment in Kansas Territory was the activity toward which the Emigrant Aid Company directed its greatest effort. A full discussion of the work of the Company in this direction must be reserved for subsequent chapters. Suffice it at this point to remark that some of the earliest expenditures of the Company were for mill machinery and that during the fall of 1854 and the spring of 1855 five sawmills were purchased and shipped to Kansas, to be located at Lawrence, Topeka, Osawatomie, Manhattan, and Hampden. The first two set up, at Lawrence and Topeka, proved to be too small and defective to meet the needs of these communities, but at least a beginning had been made.

During the first few months of Emigrant Aid Company activity in Kansas, the foothold of the Company was further strengthened by the establishment of a newspaper which, though privately owned and published, was virtually a Company organ. This was the *Herald of Freedom,* published at Lawrence by George Washington Brown of Connaughtville, Pennsylvania. A preliminary number of the paper, dated "Wakarusa, Kansas Territory, October 21, 1854," was printed at Connaughtville; the first issue in Kansas appeared in January, 1855. At almost exactly the same time two other papers were launched in Lawrence: the *Kansas Free State,* already mentioned, and the *Kansas Tribune,* edited by John Speer from Medina, Ohio. Both these papers, while free-state in sentiment, were bitterly hostile toward the *Herald of Freedom* and ill-disposed toward the Emigrant Aid Company.

In September, 1854, G. W. Brown, having read an item about the Emigrant Aid Company in the *New York Tribune,* wrote to Thayer soliciting a loan of two thousand dollars to establish his paper in Kansas.[57] Thayer turned the request over to the trustees of the Emigrant Aid Company, who decided that the state of the treasury would not permit the Company to make the loan, but who agreed to make it personally, taking a bill of sale of Brown's press as security. Thayer was to be responsible for one thousand dollars; Lawrence and Williams for five hundred each. The money was forwarded to Brown, who at once sent back the bill of sale to the three trustees.[58] It soon developed, however, that Thayer had either misunderstood the arrangement or had deliberately disregarded it, for he had advanced only two hundred dollars of the amount himself. The other eight hundred dollars came from funds which had been collected by the Worcester County Kansas League for the Emigrant Aid Company, which Thayer had persuaded W. W. Rice, secretary of the League, to turn over to him for Brown. Lawrence was furious and wrote Hale a scathing letter in which he complained bitterly of the lax way in which business was done in Worcester, declaring, "I might as well have used the Boston subscriptions to pay my own or my friends' debts."[59] In March, 1855, at the suggestion of Lawrence, the Company assumed the loan and refunded to the former trustees the amounts they had advanced, they in turn assigning their bill of sale of the press to the Company.[60] In April Lawrence wrote to Pomeroy, "Brown's steam press . . . now belongs to the Emigrant Aid Company, and you are its keeper."[61]

Until the destruction of his plant in the sack of Lawrence, on May 21, 1856, Brown ran the *Herald of Freedom* in close co-operation with the Emigrant Aid Company. Although the Company paid for all copies of the paper used, the Boston office distributed the *Herald* widely as propaganda and acted as a subscription agency for New England. The paper was not held in very high esteem by Kansas settlers generally; Brown was too narrowly partisan and too violent and indiscreet in his writing. But it was the only territorial newspaper that circulated widely in the North and was quoted extensively in the Northern press. Outside Kansas, it was regarded as the voice of the Free State party. Thus it was a powerful propaganda agent in the hands of the Emigrant Aid Company.

And so, in these various ways, the Company "staked its claim" in Kansas. There was never a time, so far as can be determined, when its colonists constituted a majority of the population, but they were largely concentrated in centers of free-state activity, which gave them a disproportionate influence. The Company's property holdings and benevolences gained for it an influence even with those Western squatters who resented its intrusion. Its control of the *Herald of Freedom* and the position of its agents as leaders of the free-state movement gave it a voice that carried to every nook and cranny of the North and East. Thus the outbreak of the Kansas conflict found the Emigrant Aid Company on the ground ready to play a part which, if not decisive, was by no means negligible.

CHAPTER VI

Drawing the Battle Lines

WHILE THE EMIGRANT AID COMPANY was launching its Kansas crusade and establishing its foothold in Kansas, the forces of opposition were drawing up their lines of battle. The factors that combined to set the stage for the civil war on the Kansas border were numerous and varied. It would be wandering too far afield to undertake a thorough analysis of the causes of the Kansas conflict, but in order to clarify the relation of the Emigrant Aid Company to that struggle it is necessary to take a peek at one of the major factors: the course of politics in the state of Missouri.

For the first quarter-century after the admission of Missouri, the ever victorious Democratic Party in that state had been dominated by Thomas Hart Benton, an old-school "Jacksonian" or "Union" Democrat. During the 1840's, when sectionalism was beginning to tell in American politics, there arose in Missouri an element within the Democratic party which rejected Benton's leadership and looked more and more to the particularist statesmen of the South. In some measure this rift grew out of resentment of Benton's domineering character and the jealousy of local politicians over patronage matters, but it was largely the expression of a growing local sectionalism within the state which reflected the wider sectionalism that was developing in the nation as a whole.[1] The schism was brought to a crisis by the controversy aroused by the Congressional debates that led up to the Compromise of 1850. Benton was opposed on principle to the extension of slavery into the territories, had no sympathy with Calhoun's "State Rights" philosophy, and was much interested in the central route (westward from St. Louis, his home) for the proposed Pacific Railway. In January, 1849, while the sectional questions then facing Congress were being widely discussed, Claiborne F. Jackson introduced into the legislature of Missouri a series of resolutions based upon those previously presented to the United States Senate by John C. Calhoun. They set forth the familiar doctrine of "non-intervention," denying the right of Congress to interfere with slavery in the territories, called for co-operation with the other slave-holding states, and contained a threat of disunion. They were carried over the opposition of Benton's supporters in the legislature.[2] These resolutions were intended as instructions to Missouri's United States Senators. David R. Atchison, Benton's colleague in the Senate, who had already shown leanings toward the Southern point of view and who apparently aspired to replace Benton as the Democratic "boss" of Missouri, accepted the resolutions and presented them in the United States Senate. Benton denounced the move as disloyal and disunionist, and threw all the weight of his influence against concessions to the South in the pending compromise legislation.[3] From that moment the split in the ranks of the Missouri Democrats was complete, and for the next six years "Bentonite" and "Anti-Bentonite" were virtually rival political parties.

In January, 1851, Benton, who was completing his fifth consecutive term as Senator, was again before the legislature for re-election. The Anti-Bentonite Democrats placed in nomination B. F. Stringfellow, later prominent in the Kansas struggle, but, after a long deadlock, enough of them switched to the Whig candidate, H. S. Geyer, to elect him.

Early in the summer of 1854 the Kansas question and senatorial politics began to stir simultaneously in western Missouri, and the Bentonite newspapers in St. Louis pointed out that there was more than casual connection between them. Atchison's term as Senator would expire the following spring. In January he would stand before the legislature for re-election, so it was highly important that the right legislators be chosen in November. As early as June, 1854, a correspondent of the *New York Tribune* was writing to his paper that a meeting recently held in Westport, "ostensibly for the purpose of protecting the slavocrats," was "really for the purpose of adding capital to the small stock in trade of a few political demagogues of the anti-Benton stripe, for use in the coming elction."[4] Another correspondent, describing the same meeting, declared that, while there could be no doubt as to sentiment in Westport in regard to the desirability of introducing slavery into Kansas, it was obvious from the whole proceedings of the meeting "that party politics have sought a place in them." Although the name of Colonel Benton was not mentioned, he continued, "still the praise so lavishly bestowed upon his enemies is more than silent censure of himself, and very clearly indicates the quarter in which the movement had its inception."[5]

But the politicians had a fertile field in which to work. The land hunger of the frontier farmer was proverbial, and for years the men of the Platte Purchase had cast longing eyes across the Missouri River, which separated them from the alluring valleys and plains of the Indian country. In the summer of 1854 that land appetite was whetted by a general failure of the corn crop in northwestern Missouri.[6] As indicated in the last chapter, hundreds of these pioneer farmers, at the first news of the passage of the Kansas-Nebraska Act, had rushed across the river to possess the land which, by an unwritten law of the frontier, they regarded as rightfully their own. They assumed, possibly at the prompting of their politicians, that the Kansas-Nebraska Act was in the nature of a compromise, intended to consign Kansas to slavery, Nebraska to freedom. Then reports began to reach the border of the formation by Eastern abolitionists of a giant corporation with five million dollars capital, an enormous sum for that day, a corporation which proposed to use its vast resources to send immediately twenty thousand men to seize the lands of Kansas and to drive out all advocates of slavery. Many of these farmers of western Missouri owned a few slaves; all, or nearly all, took slavery for granted and hoped to own slaves. Small wonder, then,

[94]

that the borderers were seized with panic at the thought of being driven from their heritage by abolitionist fanatics, and that their early squatters' associations declared that they would afford no protection to abolitionists.

The source of these rumors is not far to seek. The "Plan of Operations" which Thayer and Hale had written, which Amos A. Lawrence once referred to as "a harum-scarum paper of Thayer's" had, as already noted, announced the incorporation of the Massachusetts Emigrant Aid Company with an authorized capitalization of five million dollars and had recommended making arrangements for the transportation of twenty thousand emigrants. This document had been published widely and had been carried to the frontier by the weekly edition of Greeley's *New York Tribune*. As the Westerner read it, the five million dollars was actually on hand and the twenty thousand emigrants were already recruited and ready to start. It was natural for the frontier farmer to assume that the project was the work of radical abolitionists and that the emigrants were hired to go to Kansas to vote. The proposal in the "Plan" that the Emigrant Aid Company, when Kansas should become a free state, should dispose of its holdings there and seek another field of operations was construed to mean that these selfsame emigrants, once they had voted slavery out of Kansas, would be transported elsewhere to repeat the operation. A chance remark in one of Greeley's editorials about carrying the war into Africa was interpreted to mean that the Company intended to extend its operations into Missouri.[7]

With this state of mind prevailing in border counties, Atchison's strategy was marked out for him. He would play upon these fears and arouse the frontiersmen to the belief that their interests, their institutions, and even their homes were imperiled by the aggression of Eastern abolitionist fanatics. He would then lead a movement to resist the aggression, and so become the hero of the slaveholding agricultural elements in the state. These should be able to outvote the St. Louis commercial interests that supported Benton and his ideas, and so secure the senatorship.[8]

That the hand of Atchison was moving stealthily in the West-port meeting of June 3 seems likely. Late in July he joined the Stringfellow brothers and several others in issuing a call for a meeting, held at Weston, Missouri, July 29, which organized the Platte County Self-Defensive Association.[9] The meeting adopted a series of resolutions, known from their author as the "Bayless Resolutions," one of which was: "That this association will, whenever called upon by any of the citizens of Kansas Territory, hold itself in readiness to go there to assist in removing any and all emigrants who go there under the auspices of Northern Emi-grant Aid Societies." The Association proposed also to expel all "abolitionists" from the vicinity and to boycott all merchants who did not purchase their goods in the slaveholding states.[10] Accord-ing to one historian of early Kansas, the Platte County Self-De-fensive Association was composed chiefly of "Pukes," the "poor white" riffraff who gravitated to the frontier, infested its saloons and disreputable places, and were always available for any mob enterprise.[11] Certainly, a protest meeting, attended apparently by merchants who hoped to find customers in the Kansas settlers from farther east, and bearing a distinct Bentonite tinge, was held in Weston on September 1. This meeting, asserting in its resolutions that "we love the South much, but we love the Union better," denounced the proceedings and program of the Self-Defensive Association.[12] At all events the Self-Defensives, under the guidance of Atchison, B. F. Stringfellow, and a few local politicians, were able to keep the excitement alive, and soon the virus began to infect the more substantial citizenry.

On November 6, 1854, after the Emigrant Aid Company set-tlers had begun to reach the border, Atchison delivered a speech in Liberty, Missouri. He complained that the natural course of emigration along parallels of latitude was being interfered with and that the abolitionists of the North were spending vast sums of money and exerting every influence to turn the North to the South, to "abolitionize" all the territories, and ultimately to assail Missouri, Arkansas, and Texas. Success of the abolitionists in Kansas would, he asserted, mean the ruin of Missouri. "Now," he thundered, "if a set of fanatics and demagogues a thousand miles off can afford to advance their money and exert every nerve to abolitionize the Territory and exclude the slaveholder, when they have not the least personal interest, what is your duty? When you reside in one day's journey of the Territory, and when your peace, your quiet and your property depend upon your action, you can, without an exertion, send five hundred of your young men who will vote in favor of your institutions."[13]

About the same time the Bentonite St. Louis *Intelligencer* sounded a warning. After observing that Senator Atchison was not returning to Washington for the short session of Congress, ostensibly because he wanted to be in Jefferson City to look after his political fortunes, the *Intelligencer* reported: "Rumors have lately been leaking out, both in Missouri and in the East, connecting Senator Atchison with a secret filibuster scheme to make a foray into Kansas Territory, carrying the banner 'Slavery or Banishment,' and forcibly dispossessing and expelling every man in that Territory who will not bow the knee to the behests of the intolerant invaders . . . . The leading feature of the plan would probably be to transport a force from Missouri, when the time comes, sufficient to accomplish the end desired."[14]

While Atchison was thus coming out into the open with his scheme for intervention in Kansas, secret organizations were being formed in western Missouri to carry out his purpose. These were known variously as "Friendly Societies," "Social Bands," "Blue Lodges," and "Sons of the South." There has been some little controversy as to when these organizations appeared, the Emigrant Aid Company contending that they antedated its own formation.[15] A number of Missourians stated in their testimony before the Howard Committee that such societies were first organized in the fall of 1854, and that their purpose was to counteract the activities of the Emigrant Aid Societies.[16] One of the first

[97]

of them, so far as now appears, and the one with which Atchison was most directly connected, was a sort of inner circle of the Self-Defensives called the Platte County Regulators.

Governor Reeder set November 29 as the date for an election to choose a territorial delegate for the remainder of the thirty-third Congress. The candidates were John W. Whitfield, Pro-slavery; R. P. Flenniken, Democrat; and John A. Wakefield, Free State. There was really little at stake, since the successful candidate would serve only until the following March 4, and many settlers did not take the trouble to vote. In all probability Whitfield would have won in any case, even if the free-state men had not divided their strength between Wakefield and Flenniken, and if no fraudulent votes had been cast. Nevertheless the "Blue Lodges" crossed over in force and voted. Dr. Robinson estimated that 1,729 illegal votes were cast.[17] The only effect of the illegal voting was to show the hand of the Atchison party and to arouse the free-state men in Kansas and throughout the North to greater effort.

On January 5, 1855, the two houses of the Missouri legislature met in joint session to elect a senator. Against Atchison were pitted the veteran Benton and Colonel A. W. Doniphan, Whig. No one of the three could get the necessary majority. On the twenty-fifth ballot the name of Atchison was withdrawn and that of William Scott substituted, but there was no change. Two more ballots, and the name of Governor Sterling Price replaced that of Scott. After a week of futile balloting, the name of Atchison was again presented. But the deadlock was hopeless, and after forty-one ballots the legislature adjourned without electing a senator.[18] Had Atchison been elected, the history of the next two years in Kansas might have been quite different. As it was, his political future was still at stake. It was apparent that he had not yet made himself master of the slavery-extensionist element in Missouri, but that, in the words of one newspaper reporter, the politicians of the legislature had only been using him "to play

[98]

horse with Benton."[19] In consequence, he redoubled his efforts on
the Kansas border. One cannot now decide whether his aim for
the next year and a half was, as generally believed in Bentonite
circles, "to try to reconcile the Doniphan Know-Nothings" (the
ex-Whigs), and so regain his senatorship at the next meeting of
the legislature;[20] or, as asserted by the *St. Louis Evening News,*
to force the admission of Kansas as a slave state in order to secure
a senatorship there "in lieu of the one he lost in Missouri."[21] He
may have been thinking of both possibilities.

While the Missouri senatorship was slipping from Atchison's
grasp, Governor A. H. Reeder of Kansas* was dividing the territory into election districts and having a census taken preparatory to the calling of an election for a territorial legislature. This
census, taken during February, 1855, registered 8,601 inhabitants,
2,905 voters.[22] As soon as the census was completed and the returns were tabulated, the governor called the election for March
30, 1855.[23]

As the time approached, rumors flew thick along the border
that the governor had given to the Emigrant Aid Company advance information of the date of the election and had delayed
the date until the thawing of the Missouri River should make it
possible for Easterners to arrive in overwhelming numbers. It
was reported that the Company was shipping paupers to Kansas
by the thousands to vote slavery out of the territory and that the
river was crowded with boats bringing these "armies of hirelings."[24] Meetings were held in practically all the slaveholding
counties of western Missouri, in which Reeder was denounced
for betraying the people to the "abolitionists," and the Emigrant
Aid "Society" for violating the spirit of the Kansas-Nebraska

---

* Andrew H. Reeder, an administration Democrat from Pennsylvania, was appointed
Governor of Kansas Territory on July 7, 1854. He reached Fort Leavenworth on October
7, and at once began a tour of inspection through the settled portions of the territory. Immediately upon his return from this trip he called the election for a delegate to Congress,
discussed above. He attempted to safeguard the election by issuing a proclamation which
defined a voter as an actual resident of the Territory who intended to remain permanently,
but the Missourians disregarded the proclamation. See J. N. Holloway, *History of Kansas*
(Lafayette, Indiana, 1868), 131-37.

Act by sending "Hessian mercenaries" to "abolitionize" Kansas.[25] Atchison, B. F. Stringfellow, and others made speeches in which they assured their fellow Missourians that they had as much right to go into Kansas on election day and vote as did the "military colonies" sent out by the Emigrant Aid "Society," and that the only test for voters contemplated in the organic law of the territory (the Kansas-Nebraska Act) was American citizenship and presence at the polls.* As far east as Howard County young men were recruited and organized into companies. Transportation, food, and liquor were provided by popular subscription, and, at least in some instances, a cash consideration was offered as an inducement to go over to the election.† In the territory both factions were active. Though neither group perfected a true party organization prior to the election of March 30, both held conventions and nominated candidates, and each side carried on a rudimentary sort of political campaign.

The charge that Governor Reeder had given the Emigrant Aid Company advance information of the date of the election and had delayed that date to accommodate the Company rests upon little more than hearsay, and may have originated with Atchison or his friends. The officers of the Company undoubtedly sought to discover the date of the election as early as they could and hoped that it might be put late enough in the spring to permit the arrival of their emigrants. In fact, Lawrence wrote John Carter ·Brown on March 16 that Pomeroy had an appointment for a conference with Governor Reeder and that "this interview was, without doubt, in regard to locating the capital and to fixing the time for the election."[26] Nevertheless, all the evidence indicates

---

* Dr. G. A. Cutler, a Free State candidate for the legislature (he was a native of Tennessee and had moved to Kansas from Missouri), told the Howard Committee that, although the Emigrant Aid Company was made a pretext, the real reason for the fraudulent voting was that Atchison had told the Missourians they had a right to vote (*Howard Report*, 358). Holloway quotes a speech of B. F. Stringfellow asserting the right of the Missourians to vote (Holloway, 140-41).

† April 10, the *New York Times* printed a letter from a correspondent on the border, written before the election, which stated, "Funds have been raised in Missouri and men hired by thousands, to come over into the Territory and do all the voting."

that the Boston office had no knowledge of the date in advance of the public proclamation. A few days after the election Dr. Webb wrote to Senator Charles Sumner specifically denying the charge and asserting that it originated with the *St. Louis Republican,* an anti-Benton paper favorable to Atchison.[27]

Although there is not one shred of valid evidence that the Emigrant Aid Company ever sent anyone to Kansas merely to vote—indeed the evidence to the contrary may be accepted as conclusive—Dr. Webb did try to get the first spring parties there in time for the election. On March 12 he wrote to Pomeroy that he expected to send a party each Tuesday, "and if there is a probability of getting them there in time for the election by so doing, I shall forward extra parties on Fridays."[28] On March 20 he wrote to Slater, the St. Louis forwarding agent, "It has occurred to me that if the party [leaving Boston that day] seasonably reaches St. Louis to go up on Saturday afternoon, and by so doing there is a probability of their reaching the Territory in season to vote, it will be best to forward them at once, they desiring it, instead of waiting, as we generally prefer they should do, until Monday."[29]

When March 30 arrived, Missourians swarmed across the border and distributed themselves to the various polling places. In some instances they blandly swore that they were residents of the territory; in others they deposed the election judges by threats of violence and took possession of the polls. When the ballots were counted, the Pro-slavery candidates had carried every election district but one. Of the 6,318 votes cast, the Howard Committee declared 4,908 had been fraudulent.[30]

A year later, in the Howard investigation, almost every Missourian questioned insisted that he and his fellows had gone into Kansas to counteract the influence of the Emigrant Aid Societies. Many stressed the fact that Eastern antislavery men, as well as pro-slavery men from Missouri, had arrived in Kansas on the eve of the election, had voted, and had then returned to their homes. In fact, two Emigrant Aid Company parties had arrived in the territory in the spring of 1855 before the election. One of these, the party that settled Manhattan, reached the site of their settlement three days before the election and all voted. Together with a party of Pennsylvanians who had just settled Pawnee, probably with a foreknowledge of Governor Reeder's intention of locating the capital there,* the Manhattan colonists were able to outvote the small pro-slavery delegation sent out to carry the district and so elect the only free-state members in the territorial legislature.[31] After the election some of the Pennsylvania men returned; most of the Manhattan settlers stayed. Another Company party, piloted by Dr. Robinson, reached Lawrence the evening before the election. According to Dr. Webb, the party contained 126 men (besides about sixty women and children) of whom the poll books showed thirty-seven to have voted.[32] There were probably also instances of voting by other newly arrived Easterners who were in no way connected with the Emigrant Aid Company.

From the point of view of free-state men, this voting by recent arrivals was very different from the Missouri incursion, since these men had come as bona fide settlers. Still the circumstances gave the Missourians a peg on which to hang their excuses. Indeed, many cited it as proof that the Emigrant Aid Company was hiring voters, and also cited as further evidence the fact that many Easterners were seen returning shortly after the election.†

Naturally the free-state men were embittered by this "bogus" election; they began to denounce all Missourians as "border ruffians," and demanded that Governor Reeder set aside the whole election as a fraud. At first he expressed a willingness to do so, even though pro-slavery leaders threatened his life if he should

---

* About a dozen persons testified that they knew of a group from Pennsylvania (the number mentioned varied from fifteen to 150) who had come to Pawnee under Reeder's influence, at least a part of whom returned after the election. Governor Reeder admitted "lending" money to two or three (*Howard Report*, 263-64, 267-69, 271-77, 279, 856, 863, 865, 948-49, 1181). The *New York Tribune*, February 28, 1855, mentioned a party of thirty leaving Easton (Reeder's home town) February 24.

† A large number of persons testified that they had seen Easterners returning after the election, but, on cross-examination, most of them admitted that these men had said they were returning because they were disappointed in the country or had failed to find employment. (*Howard Report*, 216, 252, 262, 366, 846, 849-50, 851-52, 863, 1144-46.)

yield to the demand. But when only six of the eighteen electoral districts filed official protests, the governor felt that he could not, without an appearance of illegality, do more than annul the election in these six districts. This he did and called a supplementary election for May 22. At that time free-state men were elected in all the protesting districts except Leavenworth, where there was again fraudulent voting.* When the "Bogus Legislature," as the free-state people called it, met on July 2 at Pawnee, its first act was to expel the free-state members chosen at the supplementary election and to seat their pro-slavery opponents. Its next act was to adjourn, in the face of the governor's veto, to Shawnee Mission on the Missouri border. There it enacted, again over the governor's veto, the notorious "bogus laws,"—an excessively severe slave code and an election law which acknowledged as a voter any man, who, being present at the polls on election day, would pay a poll tax of one dollar and swear to support the Fugitive Slave Law. At that juncture Governor Reeder repudiated the legislature as an illegal body, and was forthwith removed by President Pierce, ostensibly because he had speculated in Indian lands.

Prior to the election of March 30 there was little coherence among the free-state settlers. Most of the actual settlers, especially those from the Ohio River states, were concerned chiefly with their farms and were only passively interested, if that, in the question of slavery. Political free-statism was limited almost entirely to the Lawrence Association, composed chiefly of Emigrant Aid Company settlers and dominated largely by Robinson.[33] The conduct of that election, even more than its outcome, had the effect of galvanizing this nascent sentiment into a fervor, and Robinson set about to whip it into activity. As to his motives, one may only guess. One guess might be that, as agent of the Emigrant Aid Company, he felt that the interests of the Company could best be served by striking a blow for freedom; that Northern settlers

---

* Several hundred Missourians crossed over and voted, while the Free State candidate (Gould) brought ashore the crew of a river steamer to vote for him (*ibid.*, 417, 527, 531).

would cease to come to the territory if it were tamely surrendered to the forces of slavery. The conventional explanation is, of course, that he was a zealot in the cause of freedom and could not stand idly by and see the cause lost. Perhaps there is truth in both of these theories, but the most likely guess as to his dominant motive would seem to be that he, too, like Atchison and Stringfellow, had political ambitions of his own which he could best advance by arousing his fellow settlers to resist the Missouri usurpation. Whatever the explanation, he set to work at once to organize resistance. Within three days after the election he had organized the men of Lawrence into military companies and had written a letter to Thayer pleading for two hundred Sharps rifles.[34]

Whether he originated the idea or not, Robinson at once began to preach repudiation of the territorial government and the launching of a movement for a state constitution. His own explanation is worth quoting:

When it became evident that the [Bogus] Legislature would be endorsed by the territorial judiciary and the President, and that there would be no escape by election for at least two years, it was equally evident that some means must be devised to keep the settlers from abandoning the fight. While the majority of the Free State party were anti-slavery from conviction, and would stand out against a slave state to the bitter end, a large minority were indifferent to the question of slavery, and had been driven to act with the Free State party because of the invasion of their civil and political rights. Under the circumstances it was deemed expedient to agitate the question of a state constitution. Such a movement would serve to occupy the minds of the people, attract the attention of ambitious politicians, become a rallying point for all opposed to the usurpation, and, in case of necessity, when all other means of self-preservation should fail, be used as a *de facto* government, even though not recognized by Congress.[35]

This statement would certainly confirm the suspicion that the free-state movement, instead of being the spontaneous uprising that is usually pictured, may have been largely the work of

local politicians who forced the issue to make a place for themselves. Robinson himself, in discussing the Topeka constitutional
convention, stressed the fact that many of the leaders of the
movement were self-seeking politicians, but he naturally excepts
himself as one actuated solely by principle.[36] If such a program
were to be carried out, the first objective must be the formation
of a party organization through which to operate. To achieve
such an organization it was necessary to reconcile the divergent
views among prominent free-state men, and to pump up a high
degree of indignation against the Missouri invasion. This latter
purpose was to be accomplished by playing up the horror of the
"bogus" election and the overzealousness of the pro-slavery leaders and of the legislature, much as Atchison and Stringfellow had
played upon the rumors about the Emigrant Aid Company. Had
the territorial legislature been more moderate and circumspect
in its actions, the free-state politicians might have lacked a ful-
crum on which to rest their lever; the blunders of that body
furnished the fuel for the fire that Robinson and his associates
sought to kindle.

The obvious place to begin such an agitation was in Lawrence, where the Yankees were more susceptible to political and
emotional appeal than were the squatters on the quarter-sections.
But before the movement could be begun even in Lawrence, the
timid must be given a sense of security; this was probably the real
reason for the call for Sharps rifles. Shortly after the first rifles
arrived, an open meeting or "mass convention" was held in Lawrence on June 8, in response to a call signed by "sundry citizens."
This meeting issued a call for a delegate convention, five from
each representative district, to meet in Lawrence on June 25.
This delegate convention formally launched the free-state movement by declaring that all issues but freedom in Kansas
should be put aside, by proclaiming that Kansans were not
bound by any acts which the legislature about to assemble
might pass, and by providing for the appointment of a Free

State Central Committee. On July 11 a meeting was held in Lawrence attended by the expelled free-state members of the territorial legislature. This meeting, unable to agree as to the feasibility of starting a project for a state constitution, called yet another meeting for the second Tuesday in August. This gathering of August 14-15, considered to be the first regularly called mass convention, definitely repudiated the legislature, then in session at Shawnee Mission, and declared for a state constitution. It decided upon a permanent organization for the Free State party and called a delegate convention to meet at Big Springs on September 5 to perfect such an organization. Immediately after the adjournment of the called convention, the same persons reassembled as a mass meeting and issued a call for a delegate convention to meet in Topeka on September 19 to settle finally the question of a state constitution.[37]

This long procession of meetings and conventions was necessary to generate the degree of sentiment requisite to support a party organization. On July 4 the movement was given a boost by the holding of a celebration in Lawrence at which Robinson delivered a fiery oration calling upon the people of Kansas to rally to the principles of the Declaration of Independence and to stand up against the tyranny of Missouri.[38] A further impetus was given to repudiation sentiment when the territorial legislature, having organized a number of counties, itself designated the county officers, all pro-slavery, of course, instead of providing for their election. This appeared to deny to the actual settlers even a modicum of self-government and was a powerful factor in rallying the Western squatters, who were steeped in the Jacksonian tradition, to the new Free State party.

By the time of the meeting of the Big Springs convention, both Ex-Governor Reeder and James H. Lane had been gathered into the free-state fold. Both had influence outside Kansas and would be useful in popularizing the free-state cause in the northern states, the more so inasmuch as both had gone to the territory as administration Democrats. Governor Reeder was enraged at his treatment by the federal administration and saw in the free-state organization an opportunity to strike back. It is not unlikely that he had foreknowledge that he would be rewarded with the nomination for territorial delegate to Congress and would later be in line for the Senate. Lane had been a member of Congress from Indiana and had voted for the Kansas-Nebraska bill. Failing of re-election in 1854, he went to Kansas shortly after the close of his term, arriving in April, 1855. Whether he went to rebuild his political fortunes as is usually assumed or, as asserted by his enemies, to escape private scandal, need not be discussed. It was widely believed in the territory that he had been sent by the administration to organize the Democratic party in Kansas; he himself gave some color to this suspicion by boasting that he enjoyed the confidence of President Pierce and Stephen A. Douglas. During his first summer in Kansas he did join with others in an effort to form a Democratic organization, but when it became apparent that the attempt was doomed to failure he cast in his lot with the free-state movement.[39] Robinson claimed that Lane was enticed with the promise of a senatorship.[40]

The Big Springs convention met September 5 and formally organized the Free State party with a permanent party central committee. It adopted a platform which, although it repudiated the territorial legislature as fraudulent and without authority, was in most respects conciliatory; it even included clauses denouncing any interference with slavery in the states where it existed, and opposing the admission of free Negroes into Kansas.* The convention renewed the call for a meeting at Topeka on September 19 to take steps toward the formation of a state constitution. Finally it nominated Governor Reeder as Free State candidate for delegate to Congress and called an election for the second Tuesday in October (a different date from that set by the territorial

---

* This "Black Law" clause was at first opposed by Robinson and most of the other Eastern delegates, but was finally acquiesced in by them as a matter of political expediency to win the support of non-slaveholding settlers from the slave states.

legislature) for the election of such a delegate.[41] The Big Springs convention may well be regarded as a turning point in the history of Kansas and of the nation. It committed the Free State party to the policy of nonrecognition of the territorial government and resistance to the territorial laws. Such a commitment, virtually a proclamation of revolution, made a struggle in Kansas and in Congress inevitable, and who can say but that, without the appeal of "Bleeding Kansas," the Republican party might have failed to materialize and the great Civil War might have been averted?

The convention called for September 19 met in Topeka on schedule and, not without incurring charges of "railroading" tactics, called a constitutional convention to meet at the same place October 23. On October 1 there occurred the election called by the territorial legislature for the choosing of a delegate to Congress. The free-state people, having now repudiated the Shawnee legislature and all its works, refused to participate in the election, so that J. W. Whitfield, the Pro-slavery candidate, was all but unanimously re-elected, receiving 2,721 of the 2,738 votes cast. On October 9 the free-state election was held. Reeder was unanimously elected delegate to Congress with 2,849 votes. At the same time, delegates to the constitutional convention were elected. When both Whitfield and Reeder presented themselves in Congress, the House of Representatives refused to seat either of them and appointed the Howard Committee to investigate the troubles in Kansas. The Kansas question had become a national issue.

The constitutional convention assembled in Topeka October 23 and remained in session nearly three weeks. After a good deal of factional squabbling, which again produced charges of "railroading," the convention produced a constitution which contained little that was distinctive except a prohibition of slavery. As a compromise, a general banking law and a provision for the exclusion of free Negroes from the state were to be voted upon

separately when the constitution was submitted for popular ratification. The convention also drafted a memorial to Congress
petitioning for the admission of Kansas under the constitution,
and created the Free State Executive Committee with Lane as
chairman to organize the state government when the constitution
should be ratified.[42] This ratification took place, and the exclusion of free Negroes was approved in an election held on December 15 at which, of course, only the free-state men voted; but
in the meantime the first blows of the Kansas struggle had been
struck in the so-called "Wakarusa War."

There has been much controversial discussion as to just what
purpose this "Topeka movement" was intended to serve. The
avowed theory was that, owing to the fraudulent character of the
March election, the territory was left without a legitimate government and that the people therefore should organize themselves and seek admission to statehood at the earliest possible moment. To the mass of free-state voters, and probably to most of the
actual participants in the movement, it was a bona fide attempt to
secure the immediate admission of Kansas as a state. But to the
instigators of the plan, the "insiders," as Professor F. H. Hodder
called them, it was merely a device to hold the Free State party
together by creating an issue about which to center political agitation until such time as the free-state men could obtain possession
of the territorial machinery.[43] It was essentially a revolution
against the *de facto* government of the territory.

On August 15, 1855, Wilson Shannon of Ohio was commissioned governor of Kansas Territory. He had been governor of
his state and minister to Mexico, and as a member of Congress
had voted for the Kansas-Nebraska bill. He reached Shawnee
Mission, the temporary capital, on September 3. Immediately he
made a speech in which he accepted the pro-slavery group as
"the people of Kansas," minimized the election frauds, declared
for "law and order," and announced his intention to enforce the
territorial laws. On November 14, three days after the adjourn-

ment of the Topeka constitutional convention, there assembled in Leavenworth a convention of "the friends of law and Order," which organized the "Law and Order party" or "State Rights party." It was composed almost exclusively of pro-slavery men, and was always called the Pro-slavery party. Governor Shannon, present as a "delegate from Douglas County," was chairman of the convention. The resolutions adopted praised law and order, branded the free-state activity as treason and rebellion, denounced the election of Reeder as delegate to Congress and the action of the Topeka conventions as illegal and void, and placed all the blame for the unsettled conditions in Kansas upon the Emigrant Aid Company.[44]

Thus the settlers of Kansas Territory were regimented into two armed camps supporting what were virtually rival governments, each branding the other as illegal and fraudulent. Almost any trifling incident, a drunken quarrel or a claim dispute, might set off the powder. The battle lines were drawn.

CHAPTER VII

The Sinews of War

WHILE THE FRIENDS and foes of the "peculiar institution" were marshaling their forces to do battle for the soil of Kansas, the Emigrant Aid Company was striving to set its house in order and to carry out its program of peopling that territory with advocates of freedom. Down to February, 1855, while the Company was leading a makeshift existence under the "voluntary association," Dr. Webb maintained a temporary office in the quarters of the Massachusetts Historical Society. This evidently proved to be an annoyance to the sedate Bostonians who frequented that seat of erudition, for the officers of the Society bombarded Amos A. Lawrence for weeks on end with pleas to get rid of Dr. Webb, even threatening to throw him out bodily. They complained that their rooms were constantly filled with rough men who smoked tobacco and otherwise made themselves a nuisance.[1] Finally, during the third week of February, about the same time that the second Massachusetts charter was granted, Dr. Webb yielded to the pressure and, acting on authority granted to him weeks before by the trustees, rented three rooms at No. 3 Winter Street and moved the office into the new location.[2] During the following two weeks the Company reorganized itself under the new charter as the New England Emigrant Aid Company. Direction of the concern now passed from the three trustees to the newly created Executive Committee of seven members which held weekly meetings in the Company office.*

The great problem facing the Company at the time of this reorganization was finance. The trustees had authorized a number of projects which called for extensive outlays of cash. Among these, some of which have already been mentioned, were: the

---

* For details of this reorganization, see chap. II.

[111]

purchase, transportation, and erection of three sawmills; the purchase of the Gillis Hotel in Kansas City; the purchase of such Wyandotte floats as might be necessary to quiet title to townsites; the erection of temporary boarding and lodging shacks in Lawrence; the erection of a combination hall and schoolhouse in that settlement, and preliminary work on the Free State Hotel. The agents on the ground plunged merrily ahead on all these ventures, and scarcely a week passed that Pomeroy's drafts were not presented to the treasurer, but the treasury bore a striking resemblance to Old Mother Hubbard's cupboard. By the time of reorganization $37,220 had been subscribed, but, as during the previous fall, the greatest difficulty was experienced in making collections. On January 19 Lawrence observed in a letter that almost nothing was being paid on the stock and that he feared it would be necessary to resort to sales of property in Kansas City and in the territory.[3] On February 20 the Company was still overdrawn $6,000, and Lawrence was beginning to wonder if enough would ever be collected to repay his advances.[4] During the next few weeks an effort was made to secure bankable notes from the larger subscribers in lieu of cash. Still money came in less rapidly than the drafts. On March 2 Lawrence wrote to Williams: "A crisis has arrived in the affairs of the Emigrant Aid Company, and the whole fabric must come down with a crash that will be heard over the whole country and will change the face of Kansas more than anything [else] that can happen, unless we have the energy to avert it. The time has come when our agent, Mr. Pomeroy, must be instructed to suspend all operations and discharge the workmen, or we must send him money to carry them on. I have advanced now $7,000, borrowed money, and see no advantage in going on unless I am prepared to carry the thing through with $30,000 to $50,000, which is out of the question."[5]

At the reorganization meeting March 5 Lawrence reported that he had received $17,903 (the $903 in outright donations), had paid out $23,623.73, and so was carrying an overdraft of

$5,720.73. There was due from unpaid stock subscriptions $10,750.[6] Practically all the money received had been collected in Boston, where all the larger subscriptions and most of the smaller ones had been paid. Subscriptions outside Boston were being obtained slowly and in small amounts, and they were scattered all over New England.[7] E. B. Whitman,* who had been traveling about as subscription and collection agent since the past October,[8] was able to collect on these "country" subscriptions only about enough to pay his own salary and expenses.[9] By the middle of March, Lawrence was becoming so disheartened that he considered resigning as treasurer to avoid the odium of having to dishonor drafts. But affairs took a slight turn for the better. John Carter Brown sent in a check for $1,500; Dr. Cabot went to work getting subscriptions and making collections; Williams made cash advances. By March 17 Lawrence was able to announce to the Executive Committee "that by a great effort during the past week, the balance of overdrafts has been reduced from $8,000 to $3,700."[10] Under Lawrence's chiding, Thayer began to plead in his lectures for stock subscriptions as well as recruits. For the next few weeks, although Lawrence continued to complain that money was coming in slowly, conditions improved somewhat. On April 19 Lawrence was so encouraged that he authorized Pomeroy to draw for an additional $5,000, venturing the opinion that the recent fraudulent election would help the Company in its financial efforts.[11]

But this flare of prosperity did not last long. Within a month the Company was again in severe straits, and Pomeroy was called back from Kansas to try his hand at money-raising. For two months he spent much of his time traveling about New York and New England, addressing Kansas meetings and pleading for

* E. B. Whitman was employed by the trustees, September 30, 1854 (Aid Company Records, Book I, 25). He was dismissed sometime around the middle of April, 1855, and migrated to Kansas, where he caused trouble by fraudulently posing as an agent of the Emigrant Aid Company.

financial support for the Emigrant Aid Company.* Early in June someone revived Lawrence's idea of the previous autumn of making an appeal to the clergymen of New England.† The plan was to ask each of the three thousand ministers who had signed a protest to Congress against the repeal of the Missouri Compromise to urge his congregation to raise a sum of twenty dollars or more to be contributed to the Emigrant Aid Company, in return for which the minister would be made a "life member" of the Company—in other words, would receive a share of stock. Edward Everett Hale was put in charge of the project. He at once prepared and had printed a form letter which, under date of July 2, 1855, was sent to practically every clergyman in New England. This epistle flew at its masthead, in half-inch block letters, the slogan, "Education, Temperance, Freedom, Religion in Kansas," and was signed by eighteen ministers, among them Hale, Lyman Beecher, Calvin E. Stowe, and Horace Bushnell. After expounding in glowing terms, with some interesting half-truths and exaggerations, the first year's achievement of the Emigrant Aid Company in each of these fields, and announcing that to carry on this good work the Company needed $150,000, the letter urged the recipient to procure in his congregation a subscription of twenty dollars, in return for which a share would be purchased in his name free from all liability beyond the original investment.[12] The effort was carried on through the fall and into the winter. The circular letter was reinforced by articles in the various newspapers and magazines for which Hale wrote regularly, particularly the *Christian Register*. On September 1 a meeting

---

* Vol. IV of the Webb Scrap Books contains numerous clippings giving accounts of these meetings. Although they appear under various date lines and are taken from different papers, these accounts are so much alike that they suggest not only that Pomeroy made the same speech everywhere, but that he furnished the papers with a prepared "write-up." These meetings were discussed by the Executive Committee June 6, 1855 (Aid Company Records, Book I, 146). On July 10, Lawrence wrote to Robinson that Pomeroy and Dr. Webb were starting for Connecticut to try to raise some money (Lawrence Letters, 80).

† The minutes of the Executive Committee (Aid Company Records, Book I, 146) create the impression that the idea was Thayer's but Thayer gives the credit to Hale (*Kansas Crusade*, 125). In a contemporary article in the *Christian Register*, Hale assigns the origin of the movement to "several clergymen."

was held in Boston, called by the same clergymen who had signed
the original plea, at which committees and secretaries were appointed to carry on the campaign more actively.[13] Several hundred ministers responded, but only about one in six or seven sent
the requested twenty dollars. Some sent less; a few, more. Nearly
all expressed sympathy with the plan, but many pleaded the
smallness of their congregation or the poverty of their parishion-
ers.[14] As nearly as can be determined from the incomplete records, ninety ministers took 105 shares ($2,100), and contribu-
tions of less than twenty dollars each aggregated $248.53, so that
the move netted the company around two thousand dollars—
$2,348.53 less expenses of the campaign.[15] One other gain, of
course, was that the ministers and church people were mobilized
in moral support of the Emigrant Aid Company, and this may
have been a factor in securing individual subscriptions.

But in spite of Pomeroy's speech-making, Thayer's intermit-
tent efforts, and Hale's appeal to the clergy, the overdrafts were
soon creeping up again. Lawrence grumbled about having to advance money that he could not spare, and scolded the Executive
Committee for voting to authorize drafts when there was no
money in the treasury; but he continued to pay. Finally, on August 4, he delivered his ultimatum: he would advance no more
money. The Executive Committee, which had been dallying for
weeks in an attempt to find a suitable subscription agent, now
decided to employ two: Bartholomew Wood and the Reverend
H. A. Wilcox.[16] Apparently, however, neither was much more
successful than Whitman had been, for on September 26, Lawrence announced his intention to resign as treasurer. He objected
to being compelled to borrow money to meet overdrafts, he declared that the work was taking more time than he could give to
it, and he was more fully convinced than ever that the stock
plan of financing the company was wrong and could never succeed.[17] When John Carter Brown wrote that if Lawrence should
resign he would do likewise, Lawrence agreed to retain the office

temporarily until Dr. Webb could return from Kansas.[18] Nevertheless, this double threat of the president and the treasurer to abandon the Company appears to have been just the jolt that the Executive Committee needed. Thayer went to work in earnest. Williams and Webb (who returned from Kansas the middle of November) made a trip to Providence and joined with John Carter Brown in launching a campaign there.[19] Dr. Le Baron Russell and Dr. Samuel Cabot, as finance committee, persuaded Hale to take a two months' vacation from his church and devote all his time to the Company.[20] He worked in Connecticut and Rhode Island, sometimes alone and sometimes with Thayer. As a result of these activities the country directors began to bestir themselves. Seth Paddleford in Providence, R. A. Chapman in Springfield, Professor A. C. Twining in New Haven, J. P. Williston in Northampton, and still others were soon sending in subscriptions and collections that ran up into thousands.[21] This sudden wave of interest may have been stimulated in part by the developments in Kansas, particularly the move for a free-state constitution; at least these developements gave the campaigners something to talk about. As the year 1855 came to a close the financial condition of the Company was better than it had been at any time before.

There is no specific mention either in Lawrence's letters or in the minutes of the Executive Committee of his formal withdrawal of his resignation, but after the middle of October no further mention was made of it. Lawrence undoubtedly was encouraged by the success of the financial drive and by the glowing reports brought back from Kansas by Webb and Williams, and another development that probably helped him decide to remain at his post was the decision of the Executive Committee to employ a full-time assistant treasurer. Lawrence had been authorized at the first meeting of the trustees in July, 1854, to employ a part-time clerk,[22] and apparently had assigned one of the employees of Mason and Lawrence to this duty. By the middle of April,

[116]

1855, the work of the treasury had grown so heavy that Lawrence complained that it was taking all the clerk's time and most of his, and so he engaged a Mr. Blanchard as part-time assistant treasurer.[23] At that time Lawrence reported: "The labor [of being treasurer] is much greater than you would suppose,—fully as much as to be treasurer of a manufacturing corporation with a capital of $1,500,000. For the past week I have done little else of business than to work at this. The collection of assessments alone will employ one man, but Mr. Blanchard will render great assistance in this."[24] But Mr. Blanchard proved to be an unfortunate choice. Le Baron Russell later wrote of him: "Mr. Blanchard was incapable of ever getting a clear view of anything, and made shocking mistakes in his figures."[25] The work of the office continued to pile up. When, in September, Lawrence sought to resign, he gave as one of his reasons that "the duties of the office require the whole time and attention of a competent person. They are now performed by three, all of whom devote to it a part of every day; and, as you know, some errors have been made." As a consequence of this condition, the special committee appointed to dissuade Lawrence from resigning proposed the employment of a full-time assistant treasurer, and J. M. S. Williams undertook to be personally responsible for his salary for three months.[26] Anson J. Stone was appointed to this position at an annual salary of $800,[27] and for the next three years he did practically all of the routine work of the treasurer's office, including the keeping of books.

During the first part of the year, at least, while Lawrence and the Executive Committee were struggling with problems of finance, Thayer was recruiting emigrants and Webb was contending with the numerous problems of emigration. As mentioned in Chapter V, parties were sent regularly each Tuesday from March 6 to May 8.[28] As Dr. Webb reported them to the Executive Committee, the numbers of these parties were: March 6, 75; March 13, 182; March 20, 157; March 27, 84; April 3, 115; April

10, 80; April 17, 64; April 24, 8; May 1, 17; May 8, 15.* This decline in numbers during May was not limited to Emigrant Aid Company parties; a newspaper correspondent wrote from Kansas May 19 that migration was much checked by the unprecedented low stage of the Missouri River, by exaggerated rumors of cholera, and by the outrageous conduct of the Missourians culminating in the destruction of the office of the *Parkville Luminary*.[29] On April 29 this Bentonite newspaper, whose editor, George S. Park, had already shown friendliness toward the Emigrant Aid Company, was attacked by a mob, and its press was thrown into the Missouri River because it had protested against the voting by Missourians in the Kansas election of March 30.[30] Early in May, William Philips, a free-state lawyer of Leavenworth, was tarred, feathered, and ridden on a rail, probably because he talked too much but ostensibly because he was believed to have been involved in a shooting scrape in which a friend of his had killed a pro-slavery man.[31] These and other acts of violence were published widely in the North as "Border Ruffian" atrocities, and probably frightened away some prospective free-state settlers. About this same time Dr. Webb wrote to Pomeroy, "Owing to the low state of the river, the uncertain price on board the boats, the prevalence of disease, the deficiency of mills, the dearth of building materials, the scarcity of provisions, and the increased charge on railroads, I think it best to cease sending parties for the present, so as to find time to obviate and remove some of the hindrances."[32]

But long as this list of difficulties appears to be, Dr. Webb scarcely hinted at his troubles with the emigrant business. For one thing, he was constantly having friction with B. Slater, the St. Louis forwarding agent. Slater insisted on retaining for himself the bonuses which the steamboat owners refunded for the

---

* Manuscript lists of seven of these parties, prepared, presumably, for the conducting agents, show slightly smaller numbers. Probably these were prepared ahead from advance ticket sales, and the difference represents the number who appeared at the last minute (Aid Company Papers).

sale of tickets in quantity, and then asked for additional pay for the forwarding of passengers. Webb demanded that this bonus money be paid over to the Company, and contended that the extra commissions which Slater received for forwarding Company freight and baggage were ample compensation for his work in handling passengers.[33] Then, too, Slater, in violation of his instructions, kept drawing on Lawrence instead of Webb for boat fares. Since Lawrence did not handle the ticket money and had authority to accept drafts only from Pomeroy and Robinson, he dishonored all such drafts and Webb had to run them down and pay protest fees.[34] Another problem was created by accessions to the parties along the route. When a party left Boston, Webb would telegraph the number to Slater, who would make steamboat reservations accordingly. Then frequently the party would reach St. Louis increased considerably in size. Some who had joined the party en route would contrive to get the reserved staterooms, thus forcing an equal number of the original party to take second-class accommodations or wait for a later boat; invariably, those who were thus inconvenienced would write back to their New England friends, and often to the newspapers, that the Emigrant Aid Company had deceived them. Dr. Webb tried to remedy this situation by issuing to members of the original party tickets of a distinctive color, and instructing Slater to accommodate first those bearing the colored tickets signed by himself or Branscomb.[35]

The most frequent complaint of emigrants against the Company was that they were overcharged. Often these excess charges were made by railroads, hotel keepers, or steamboat captains for "extras" which the emigrant had presumed were included in his ticket. Dr. Webb battled continually against this practice, and at the same time endeavored to absolve the Company for any responsibility for it. Perhaps the conducting agents were to blame in part. One of Hale's Western friends wrote to him: "For Heaven's sake, do something to prevent the fleecing of your emigrants

[119]

through the inexperience of their leaders. You must listen to experienced Western men if you do not want to pay two prices. The agents of the Emigrant Aid Company have, so far, been as green as grass, and the emigrants have suffered accordingly."[36]

Complaints of overcharges arose, too, out of the fact that freight rates on the Missouri River fluctuated with the stage of the river. Hence, rates were sometimes increased after a party had started, so that its members had to pay more for their excess baggage than they had expected. One such instance, typical of many, arose in connection with the party that left Boston on April 3. A few hours after the party had gone Webb received a telegram from Slater that the river was falling and that rates would be increased accordingly. Webb at once wrote to Pomeroy regretting that he had not learned of the increase in time to do anything about it, and instructed Pomeroy that if any of the party should complain after the circumstances were explained to them, he should refund the excess charge and draw upon him (Webb) for the amount, "although it must come out of my own pocket, and I can ill afford to lose it."[37] Not only does the incident afford an insight into Dr. Webb's attitude toward all legitimate complaints by emigrants, but it probably explains some of Pomeroy's payments to them that were reported to the Howard Committee as proof that the Emigrant Aid Company was hiring men to go to Kansas.

Besides the matter of overcharges there were literally dozens of subjects for emigrants' complaints, some inevitable, others justifiable. Parties sometimes missed rail connections, or their baggage was missent, and the blame fell on the Emigrant Aid Company. Many complained of the accommodations at Kansas City and at Lawrence. Others who, in spite of Webb's warnings, had gone out without funds, wailed to high Heaven because the agents of the Company would not advance them money, or declared that the Company had deceived them because they failed to find lucrative work in their accustomed vocations. Some objected that the agents left them to drift in the territory; apparently they expected the agents to transfer them to claims already pre-empted for their benefit, with dwellings ready for occupancy. Still others blamed the Company because the mills provided were inadequate and the cost of lumber and provisions was too high. These are but samples. Yet all these complaints and many more found their way into Eastern newspapers,[38] and tended not only to retard migration but to hamper the Company most severely in its efforts to raise funds for its work in Kansas.

Throughout the year 1855 the Executive Committee did what it could to fulfill the all too lavish promises to develop the Kansas settlements through the investment of capital, but the financial difficulties seriously retarded the effort. Work on the Free State Hotel proceeded at a halting pace, and the end of the year found only the masonry completed.[39] In the main, the energies of the Company during this year were devoted to furnishing sawmills to the settlements. The original instructions to Pomeroy had authorized him to purchase, with the consent of one other agent, not more than six sawmills.[40] On the way to Kansas in September, 1854, he and Robinson had bought in Rochester, New York, a mill and steam engine intended for the first settlement. The shipment of this mill was delayed; so after waiting several weeks for it, Pomeroy purchased an old sawmill in Westport and as soon as possible set it up in Lawrence. The Rochester mill reached Kansas City sometime in November. After some correspondence with the home office as to where best to locate it, Pomeroy and Robinson assigned this mill to the new settlement of Topeka. Its transportation by wagon was a difficult and tedious process. The mill and engine had to be hauled seventy miles through hilly country, much of it timbered, with no roads worthy of the name. The greatest difficulty was in transporting the boiler, for which a special vehicle had to be improvised. In the early summer it could have been taken by steamboat, but at that season the Kansas River was not navigable. At length the task was

[121]

accomplished, and about May 1 the mill was put into operation.[42] Neither of these mills proved adequate for the needs of the settlement it was to serve. The Lawrence mill was old and worn, and was out of order much of the time. The Topeka mill was too small and its engine of insufficient horsepower to cut the type of timber that was available. Of course the settlers, especially those from the West, blamed the Emigrant Aid Company. The *Kansas Free State,* which served as a sort of mouthpiece for the Ohio valley squatters, went so far as to assert that the Company mills were actually a drawback to the settlements, since, although they did no good, their presence prevented individuals from erecting adequate mills.[43] Still, it is apparent that both the Executive Committee and the agents were doing the best they could, poor as that best may have been.

In May, 1855, an agreement was made with one Nathan Haskins, a machinist, to assemble three twenty-five horsepower mills to be shipped to Kansas, located by Pomeroy, and owned jointly by Haskins and the Company. For its share of the cost, the Company was to pay three-fourths in cash and one-fourth in stock. Either partner was to have the privilege of buying out the other.[44] The mills were shipped in July and the Company paid Haskins $2,219.18 in cash and issued him thirty-seven shares of stock for its half interest.[45] Freight and storage charges, one-half of which were to be paid by the Company, amounted to $1,900.[46] This exhausted the treasury, so that nearly two months elapsed before funds were available to move the mills from Kansas City where they were in storage. Finally, about the middle of September, Pomeroy was able to have two of them hauled to Osawatomie and Manhattan respectively, agreeing to pay the charges half in cash and half in sawing.[47] Still further delays were experienced because some parts were missing, so that it was the end of December before the mills were ready for operation. The following spring the Company bought out Haskins's interest for $1,000 and the release of Haskins from some damage claims.[48]

[122]

In July the Executive Committee sent Dr. Webb to Kansas to look over the situation and report conditions.[49] As previously mentioned, he returned about the middle of November. While in Kansas he visited the various settlements in which the Company had an interest, and in September he went to Manhattan to arrange for the location of the sawmill. He was so impressed by the need of that settlement for a grist mill that he undertook personally the responsibility of supplying one to be operated in connection with the sawmill. Accordingly, Pomeroy purchased a "corn mill" for $235.75 and drew on Webb for the price. When the draft reached Boston, however, Company finances had begun to improve, so that the Executive Committee voted to pay the draft and take over the mill.[50] This was the first grist mill placed in Kansas by the Emigrant Aid Company and, so far as can now be discovered, the first one in the territory except those at military posts and Indian missions. Subsequently the Company sent out several others to be operated in connection with its sawmills.

That mills, both for sawing and for grinding, were needed in Kansas during the summer of 1855 is beyond doubt, but as soon as the "bogus" election of March 30 had aroused the indignation of the free-state settlers, appeals were sent out for another kind of "material aid." At the time of the supplementary election in May, the *New York Times* carried a significant editorial. After commenting at some length on the exasperation of Northern settlers at the shameless conduct of the earlier election, the editorial continued: "We do not wonder at what is now generally known, we suppose, that some hundreds of Sharpe's rifles have been sent out from Massachusetts at the request of the new immigrants to *assist* in the election. With this, we understand, the Aid Association had nothing to do; it was entirely an individual affair. But we are not surprised at it."[51] This arming of the free-state settlers with what, at the time, was probably the deadliest weapon in existence,* marked a turning point in the history of Kansas, and gave

---

* The Sharps rifle, one of the earliest breechloaders, had a firing rate of ten shots a minute and a much greater range than most other firearms of the time. There was con-

[123]

rise to one of the bitterest controversies in the history of the Emigrant Aid Company.

It was frequently assumed on the border and among administration supporters generally that the Emigrant Aid Company had supplied the weapons, and it was this assumption, much more than its colonization activities, that stirred the pro-slavery people to such a violent rage against the Company. Officers of the Company, on the other hand, declared repeatedly, under oath and otherwise, that the Emigrant Aid Company had never spent a dollar for arms or munitions.* The "inside story" would run something like this:[52]

On April 2, 1855, three days after the "bogus" election, Robinson wrote a letter to Thayer stating that the settlers of Lawrence had organized military companies, and asking for two hundred Sharps rifles and two field guns. A week later he dispatched an almost identical letter to Hale.[53] A few days later he sent George W. Dietzler as a personal envoy to reinforce the application. Dietzler presented himself to Thayer, who sent him, with a letter of introduction, to the Executive Committee of the Emigrant Aid Company. Dietzler described the next move thus: "Within an hour after our arrival in Boston, the executive committee of the Emigrant Aid Society held a meeting and delivered to me an order for one hundred Sharps rifles."[54] Dr. Webb described the incident in a letter to Robinson, dated May 8, 1855: "Mr. Dietzler presented himself at this office on Wednesday last with a letter from Mr. Thayer relative to certain business entrusted to him, no one in this village having received any advice. We are busily occupied getting ready for special meeting No. 2 . . . to see if we could raise funds for more mills; still, considering the exigencies of the case, we ventured to lend a helping hand to help forward the new movement, although by so doing we crushed out

siderable confusion as to the spelling of the name, but "Sharps" is correct. A circular of the Sharps Rifle Manufacturing Company is preserved among the William Barnes Papers, Kansas State Historical Society, Topeka.

* These charges and denials are discussed at length in a subsequent chapter.

for the time being, as we apprehended would be the case, our legitimate business. I eventually arranged, with the aid of Dr. Cabot mainly, so as to take the risk of ordering, in all, one hundred machines, at a cost of about three thousand dollars, taking our chances hereafter to raise the money."[55]

This conference took place in the Emigrant Aid Company office on May 2. Several members of the Executive Committee were present, but they did not officially hold a meeting; no minutes appear in the record books under that date. It is apparent from scattered allusions that they discussed the question of furnishing rifles and decided that the Company as such must take no action, but that those of its officers who cared to do so might furnish the weapons, acting in their individual capacities. Webb and Cabot assumed the responsibility and gave Dietzler an order on the Sharps Rifle Company. Webb, perhaps to obtain the necessary credit with the rifle company, evidently signed the order as "Secretary of the New England Emigrant Aid Company," for the invoice, dated May 7, 1855, was addressed to him with that title.[56] The cost of the rifles with ammunition was $2,670. Apparently Webb and Cabot offered their personal note in payment; when the rifle company declined to accept it, Lawrence gave his note for the amount,* Dr. Cabot undertaking to raise the money by subscription before the note should become due. As the date of maturity of the note approached, Lawrence seemingly began to fear that he would have to pay the entire amount; on July 24 he wrote to Dr. Cabot offering to guarantee a thousand dollars if Cabot could raise the balance.[57] It appears that Dr. Cabot raised the balance from about a dozen subscribers, among whom, in addi-

---

* On February 6, 1856, Dr. Webb wrote to Nicholas Brown, Providence: "When the first hundred rifles were solicited, people shrank with a kind of holy horror at the idea of sending such murderous weapons; I felt the importance of so doing, and assumed the risk of the indebtedness, for $2,500, and had them sent. When the second hundred were asked for, Dr. Cabot took the risk. Neither of us has got back the whole amount advanced" (Aid Company Letters, Book A, 248). On May 25, 1856, Lawrence wrote to an uncle in Ohio: "I gave my note for $2,700 for the first lot of Sharps rifles which were sent out. . . . The reason for this was that the rifle manufacturer would not take the note of others who would willingly have given it" (original letter, Kansas State Historical Society, Miscellaneous Papers).

[125]

tion to Cabot himself, were the following: Dr. William R. Lawrence (brother of Amos A.), J. M. Forbes, Wendell Phillips, Gerrit Smith, John Bertram, Samuel Hoar, and E. Rockwood Hoar.[58] The other names were of less prominent men. Of the entire list of subscribers, only Amos A. Lawrence, Cabot, Forbes, and Bertram were stockholders of the Emigrant Aid Company, and only the first two of these were active in its councils. Nevertheless the transaction was handled through the Company office, the work of ordering the rifles and raising the money was done by its officers, and the guns were consigned to and distributed by the Company's agents in Kansas.

Within two months after the first hundred rifles had been dispatched, Lawrence, probably at the prompting of Robinson, was concerning himself about more weapons. On July 14 he wrote to Professor Packard that the settlers must arm themselves "and we must help them."[59] On July 20 he instructed Dr. Webb to "write to Hartford and get their terms for 100 more Sharps rifles at once."[60] The same day he wrote to Robinson: "But you must have arms, or your courage will not avail. We must stir ourselves here tomorrow and see what can be done."[61] That this letter could have reached Robinson in Lawrence, Kansas, within six days seems unlikely, but on July 26 Robinson sent James B. Abbott to the East with a letter of introduction addressed to Thayer.[62] Abbott reached Boston on August 10. That very day Branscomb, acting as secretary of the Emigrant Aid Company while Webb was absent in Kansas, inscribed on Abbott's letter of introduction the following endorsement, signed in his official capacity as Secretary, *pro tem.,* of the New England Emigrant Aid Company: "Dr. Charles Robinson, within mentioned, is an agent of the Emigrant Aid Company, and is worthy of implicit confidence. We cheerfully recommend Mr. Abbott to the public."[63]

The next day A. A. Lawrence gave Abbott an order to J. C. Palmer, president of the Sharps Rifle Manufacturing Company, for a hundred rifles, agreeing to pay for them "according to the

[126]

terms agreed on between him [Palmer] and Dr. Webb."[64] Lawrence also gave Abbott a letter of introduction to his business partner, William Stone, in New York.[65] Equipped with this letter and Branscomb's endorsement, Abbott visited Hartford, Providence, and New York, in which places he raised money enough to buy seventeen more rifles. In New York he was assisted by Frederick Law Olmsted, Horace Greeley, and others. Olmsted himself raised about four hundred dollars with which he purchased a brass howitzer that was destined to play a large part in Kansas territorial affairs.[66] Again Lawrence agreed to pay one thousand dollars toward the rifles and to assume liability for the balance, which Dr. Cabot agreed to raise by subscription and to repay to him.

For the next year Dr. Cabot was treasurer of the rifle fund, and continued to raise money and purchase arms. Officers of the Emigrant Aid Company insisted then and later that this did not constitute a Company activity and could not properly be charged to the Company. Perhaps this is a matter of opinion. At all events, Dr. Cabot worked in close co-operation with the officers and Executive Committee of the Emigrant Aid Company. Dr. Webb, over his official signature as secretary, continued to negotiate purchases of rifles and to solicit funds for that purpose. Lawrence wrote a number of letters asking for contributions for the defense of the settlers. Arms continued to be shipped to Company agents in Kansas to be distributed by them, and later, in 1856, Dr. Cabot placed arms in the hands of men migrating to Kansas under the auspices of the Emigrant Aid Company. It is virtually certain, despite some opinions to the contrary,[67] that no money received from the sale of stock was ever diverted into the rifle fund, but there is positive evidence that contributions sent to the Company, the purpose of which was not designated by the donor, were so used.* All told, about $12,500 passed through Dr. Cabot's

* On February 21, 1856, Lawrence wrote to Samuel Hoar that his $50 contribution had been turned over to Dr. Cabot, who had charge of providing the settlers with means of defense (Lawrence Letters, 134). On February 24, he reported to Gerrit Smith that his

hands, which, after deductions for refunds to Lawrence on the earlier account, $2,500 drawn by Pomeroy, presumably to pay freights on rifles, and known expenditures for revolvers, ammunition, etc., would, according to Iseley, account for about 325 Sharps rifles.[68] Certainly the popular impression among friends and foes alike was that the Emigrant Aid Company was arming the free-state settlers, but spokesmen of the Company invariably insisted that the weapons were furnished by individuals.

The reason for this evasiveness is obvious. With the charges flying thick and fast that the Emigrant Aid Company was responsible for all the troubles in Kansas and that it was inspiring and directing the free-state movement, which was proclaiming resistance to the territorial laws and was suspected of plotting to resist the United States government itself, the officers of the Company felt it to be imperative that they should be able to deny, under oath if necessary, that the Emigrant Aid Company had taken part in any activity which tended to foster rebellion or lawlessness. There is no reason to question the sincerity of these men or to charge them with dissimulation. It is easy to agree with the Kansas historian who insists that the assertion that the arms were furnished by individuals and not by the Company is "a distinction without a difference," but it is impossible to go along with him when he adds that it is "a contemptible pretense."[69] A man like Amos A. Lawrence would not stoop to pretense. He and his associates believed honestly that they were entirely free to do as individuals things that would have been grossly improper in an organization like the Emigrant Aid Company.

While the Company in its corporate capacity was straining every nerve to provide the Kansas settlers with mills and other accommodations, and while its most active managers were exerting themselves to an almost equal degree, partly, at least, through Company channels, to arm these same settlers for possible military action, the free-state movement in Kansas was advancing

$250 gift had been similarly used (*ibid.*, 135). Earlier correspondence makes it clear that neither Hoar nor Smith had designated the purpose of his gift.

rapidly to the stage of open revolution.* It was widely believed at the time by both friends and enemies of the free-state cause that the whole movement was inspired, directed, and financed by the Emigrant Aid Company. The facts in this matter appear to run rather closely parallel to the facts about the rifles. Prior to February, 1856, when the Aid Company office in Boston became the rendezvous of members of the Topeka government, who went east on political missions, free-state activities are scarcely mentioned in the minutes of the Executive Committee. But the preserved correspondence makes it clear that Lawrence particularly, and to a lesser extent other officers and directors of the Company, took an active interest in territorial politics from the start. Writing to Robinson in December, 1855, when the pot was boiling most violently in Kansas, Lawrence summed up the situation by saying: "They [the Emigrant Aid Company officers] do not act corporately as they would as individuals. You and Pomeroy should not be allowed to spend your little property in these [political] expenses."[70]

There is nothing to support the view that the free-state movement was inspired by the managers of the Emigrant Aid Company unless the sending and encouraging of Robinson constituted such inspiration, for there can be little doubt that the scheme was Robinson's idea. It is clear, however, that Lawrence, at least, expected Robinson not only to look after Company business but to lead the free-state political activity as well. As early as the middle of October, 1854, in anticipation of the election of a territorial delegate, Lawrence sent Robinson one hundred and fifty dollars "to assist in the plan of bringing out the whole force of the free voters in Kansas."[71] A month later, after the election, he wrote Robinson that the latter must go on and complete the political organization, adding: "If more money is wanted, you must have it. I will confer with Mr. Pomeroy and authorize him to furnish it."[72] The letters of Dr. Webb reveal the fact that he too expected

---

* For details see chap. VI.

the Company agents to assume political leadership. Before the election of November 10, 1854, he wrote separately to Pomeroy and Robinson to be sure to be on hand at the time of the election.[73] After the election he lectured Robinson because the antislavery forces had not concentrated on Flenniken.[74] The next spring, as previously observed, Webb tried to get his first spring parties to Kansas in time to vote, and just before the election he admonished Pomeroy to see that the free-state people put up a united front.[75] After the election, both Lawrence and Webb at first put their trust in Governor Reeder. In April Lawrence wrote to President Pierce, to whom he was related by marriage, defending Reeder against the denunciations of the Missouri politicians and urging that the federal government should support him.[76] When Reeder was called to Washington for a conference in June, Lawrence made a trip to Washington and talked with both Reeder and the President; he returned home believing that he had Pierce's promise to sustain Reeder.[77] But by the middle of July he was convinced that no dependence could be placed in the administration, and that the settlers must prepare to defend themselves by force of arms; thus he wrote to his friend Professor Packard of Bowdoin College,[78] and thus he wrote to President Pierce, admitting to the President that he had helped to furnish the settlers the means of defense.[79] A few days later, in the same note in which he instructed Dr. Webb to get terms on another hundred rifles, he said: "That a revolution must take place in Kansas is certain, if that can be called a revolution which is only an overthrow of usurpation. If Pomeroy were there now to wake up the energy of the people [Pomeroy was in the East campaigning for funds] and prepare them for resistance to Missouri rule, with Robinson to lead the advance guard when the time for action comes, then we might expect to see the free state banner waving over the territory before long."[80]

During the summer letters streamed back and forth between Lawrence and Robinson. On July 20, Lawrence wrote: "You are on the eve of stirring times. I wish Pomeroy was with you. I wish we all were there if we could stand up like men to the work in hand."[81] Three days later he was praising Robinson's Fourth of July speech (a copy of which apparently had just reached him) and commenting: "Considering your provocations, you have been very forbearing thus far; but your people have been weak and few, and they are not strong now. Therefore, and the cause is just, this is the true policy to continue. Meanwhile, you gain strength in numbers and the pent up fire burns; but before action comes organization, thorough and binding."[82] One wonders to what extent Robinson was influenced by this advice in his decision to proceed slowly and deliberately with the perfection of a free-state organization! When Abbott reached Boston on his rifle mission and reported that it had been decided to repudiate the territorial legislature entirely and to resist its enactments, Lawrence wrote to Robinson approving the course, but warning against any resistance to federal authority.[83] A week later, having received a letter from Robinson relative to the feasibility of setting up a free-state government, Lawrence replied that the plan was novel and at first thought appeared to be just the thing. He thought it would take well with the people of the North. But since he feared that the setting up of a *de facto* government might lead to a clash with the United States, he suggested instead that the people hold a convention and assert their purpose to set up such a government when numbers should warrant. This, he felt, would serve to rally the country and might force the hand of Congress. "Prudence, Doctor, forbearance and decision," he warned, "are the qualities which will be most in requisition."[84]

Early in September, when the free-state movement in Kansas was well under way and the time was approaching for the election of a territorial delegate, Lawrence and John Carter Brown discussed the wisdom of sending to Kansas a political agent, who "should stump the Territory of Kansas, taking his plan from our agents there, but not being recognized as under our auspices."

[131]

The expense was to be borne in part by the Company and in part by individuals.[85] So far as can be determined, no such agent was sent, but the fact that such a step was considered is significant. During September, Pomeroy sent letters to Branscomb (acting secretary at the time), J. M. S. Williams, Lawrence, and possibly other of the Company leaders asking "for your opinion and advice about our political matters."[86] In his letter to Branscomb he reported that he was touring the settlements speaking for "Reeder and Freedom," and asked Branscomb to "talk the matter over with Dr. Cabot, Mr. Williams, Spooner, and all our friends who come into the office, and write me their opinions." By this time Lawrence was ready to approve the election of Reeder in a separate election and the setting up of a state constitution; in all probability the others were too, but their replies are not preserved. Judging from the practice Dr. Webb is known to have followed in such matters, Branscomb probably replied "unofficially" and did not enter the letter in the letter book. During the Reeder campaign, Robinson, in writing to Lawrence for money for campaign expenses, reported that Dr. Webb, then in Kansas, had "promised to get us some money for the campaign."[87]

Thus, it is apparent that, while it can scarcely be said that the Emigrant Aid Company or its officers inspired the free-state movement or directed it, the Company officials kept in close touch with political developments in Kansas, sanctioned what was being done, and aided with advice and money. The Company itself gave at least tacit consent to its agents' engaging actively in territorial politics; the Executive Committee knew that they were doing it, but offered never a word of reproof. It is more than likely that these matters were discussed and that decisions were reached in meetings of the Executive Committee itself, as undoubtedly happened in the case of the rifles; but such action would, of course, be regarded as "unofficial," so that no mention of it crept into the minute books. The evidence here cited would seem to indicate quite definitely that the Emigrant Aid Company personnel, if not the corporation as such, had a very real, even if somewhat hazy, connection with the free-state movement in Kansas.

Thus during the summer and fall of 1855, while the situation in Kansas was developing rapidly in the direction of violent conflict, the Emigrant Aid Company and its officers were striving to provide the cohorts of freedom with the sinews of war. The Company as a corporation, in the face of crushing financial difficulties, was sending recruits to swell the ranks and mills to sustain the settlements, while its agents in the territory were assuming the active leadership of the free-state cause. The officers of the Company, with some outside assistance, were giving advice and money to the free-state organization, and unofficially—today one might say "off the record"—they were even furnishing the arms and munitions to fight the battles, if battles must be fought. In the very nature of the case, the officers of the Company and members of the Executive Committee could not march forth to face the muskets in the Kansas struggle, but at least they were enlisted in the service of supply.

CHAPTER VIII

War to the Knife

FEELING WAS TENSE on both sides of the Kansas-Missouri border all during the summer and fall of 1855. Almost immediately after the election of March 30, as soon as it was apparent that the free-state element in Kansas was aroused to action by the huge fraud that Atchison and his followers had perpetrated, activity began in western Missouri to keep the agitation alive and to see that none of the momentum generated preparatory to the incursion into Kansas should be lost. During May and June mass meetings were held in various communities to send delegates to county conventions. These meetings, held in all the western counties, denounced all interference in Kansas by Congress or emigrant aid societies, demanded that those opposed to slavery should settle in Nebraska, and chose delegates to a general convention to be held at Lexington on July 12.[1] This convention was reported to have contained delegates from twenty-six counties. Its principal achievement consisted of a series of resolutions, published in the form of an "Address to the People of the United States," which declared slavery to be "exclusively a matter of state jurisdiction," and denounced the free-soil resolutions of some of the northern states as a dangerous threat. After approving the Kansas-Nebraska Act and the Fugitive Slave Law, and asserting that the maintenance of an equilibrium of free and slave states constituted the only guarantee against aggression, this manifesto proclaimed "that the incorporation of moneyed associations under the patronage of sovereign States, for the avowed purpose of recruiting and colonizing large armies of abolitionists upon the Territory of Kansas, and for the avowed purpose of destroying the value and existence of slave property in that Territory, in despite of the wishes of the *bona fide* independent settlers thereof, and the purpose, equally plain and obvious, whether

[134]

avowed or not, of ultimately abolishing slavery in Missouri," was an attempt to thwart the purpose of the Kansas-Nebraska Law by state legislation. The pronouncement went on to assert "that these organized bands of colonists, shipped from Massachusetts and other quarters under state patronage, and resembling in their essential features the military colonies planted by the Roman Emperors upon their conquered provinces, . . . authorize apprehension of an intent of exclusive occupancy and will necessarily lead to organized resistance upon the part of those who, under the constitution and laws of the United States, have equal rights to possession." While promising that independent settlers would not be interfered with, the declaration asserted that slave property in Missouri worth $25,000,000 was threatened "if Kansas is made the abode of an army of hired fanatics, recruited, transported, armed and paid for the special and sole purpose of abolitionizing Kansas and Missouri," and that Missouri must protect herself against "such disastrous consequences."[2]

One wonders to what extent, if at all, this bombastic pronunciamento was inspired by Robinson's Fourth of July address of a week before. Indeed, one wonders to what extent the whole proceeding was in response to the incipient free-state movement in Kansas and to what extent it was merely a matter of internal politics in Missouri, an attempt to attract the "Doniphan Know-Nothings" over to the Anti-Benton Democrats for the sake of the vacant senatorship. At any rate, here was a virtual declaration of war by the pro-slavery element in Missouri against the free-state element in Kansas, and the *casus belli* was found in the real or imagined activities of the Emigrant Aid Company.

The Company sought to correct the allegations contained in the Lexington resolutions by issuing an "Address to the People of Missouri." This paper, about a thousand words in length, was written by Edward Everett Hale at the direction of the Executive Committee and was signed by a large number of the directors.[3] It undertook to refute, point by point, the assertions of the Lexington resolutions and to set forth the actual program of the Company. The only false note in the address was the implication that the organization of the Emigrant Aid Company was suggested by the large volume of emigration from New England to Kansas that had already set in before its formation.[4] This address was distributed widely as a circular, and was printed extensively in newspapers favorable to the Company. It was good propaganda in the northern states, but, as was to be expected, its influence on the people of Missouri was negligible, if not negative. Indeed, Senator Geyer of that state, suppressing some significant passages, used the address as a text for a tirade against the Emigrant Aid Company in the United States Senate.[5]

As the free-state movement gradually took form during the summer and fall of 1855, the pro-slavery press of Kansas and western Missouri shrieked forth denunciation and threats of violence. There was incessant talk about driving out "nigger thieves" and hanging traitors. According to free-state accounts, this bluster was reinforced with constant nagging of free-state men, at times going to the length of bodily harm, in an effort to prod them into some overt act which could be construed as resistance to the territorial laws, and so give a pretext for an open armed attack which the free-state leaders believed, or professed to believe, was being planned by the "Border Ruffians."[6] This threatening attitude of their opponents convinced the free-state leaders (or did they only use it as an excuse?) that their followers must be prepared for defense. Military companies were formed in all the free-state settlements and, as discussed in the last chapter, J. B. Abbott was sent east to procure more arms. At the same time there was formed a secret military organization, supposed to have been modeled on the Missouri "Blue Lodges," called the Kansas Legion, with grips, passwords, and oath-bound obligations of secrecy.[7] Nothing came of the organization and it soon disintegrated. It would be too unimportant to deserve mention but for the fact that it was played up in Congress and in the border press

as a justification for pro-slavery excesses and as proof of the traitorous character of the whole free-state movement and of the
Emigrant Aid Company, which was supposed to be its sponsor.

During the summer several incidents occurred that were indicative of the growing tension and intolerance. Those in which
free-state men figured as victims were published widely in the
northern newspapers with correspondents in Kansas. The one
that was advertised most extensively as a pro-slavery atrocity was
the mobbing of the Reverend Pardee Butler in Atchison on August 17. Butler had proclaimed his free-soil views somewhat de-
fiantly in this overwhelmingly pro-slavery community and in consequence was asked to sign a resolution, adopted a few days previously in a local mass meeting, which approved a beating given
to a free-soiler by a pro-slavery man and alluded disparagingly to
"emissaries of this Aid Society." Upon his refusal to sign or to
promise to keep his views to himself, he was tormented for a
while with threats of hanging and was finally placed on a small
raft, with a flag bearing the legend "Emigrant Aid Express," and
was set adrift down the Missouri River.

As the free-state movement took on ever more tangible shape
and the repudiation of the territorial laws became more open and
definite, the situation grew more and more tense, and the pro-
slavery press talked more glibly about silencing abolitionists and
alluded obliquely to the use of hemp. Free-state men alleged and
apparently believed that the Missouri politicians, having despaired
of legislating them out of Kansas, were determined to drive them
out, and only awaited the slightest indiscretion on their part to
invade Kansas in force. The more cautious of the free-state leaders
such as Robinson exhorted their fellow partisans that, while they
should in no wise recognize the "bogus" laws, they must not
make any gesture in open resistance to them; and that, above all,
under no circumstances must they resist federal authority. There
may or may not have been truth in the assertion that the Missouri
leaders were trying deliberately to trap the free-state men by

goading them into some act of resistance, but there can be no doubt that in such a surcharged atmosphere any spark might set off an explosion.

The spark was struck by a killing over a claim dispute. Claim disputes were frequent in territorial Kansas, as they were on every other frontier settled under the pre-emption law. It was not at all uncommon for them to culminate in physical violence, and occasionally they resulted in homicide. When the contestants chanced to hold opposite views on the slavery question, such a dispute took on the semblance of a political issue and divided the community into warring factions, each charging that the other was merely trying to drive men out for their political opinions.

At a settlement called Hickory Point, some twelve miles south of Lawrence, a pro-slavery squatter named Coleman shot and killed a free-state settler named Dow in a quarrel over the boundary between their claims. Coleman fled to Westport and gave himself up to Samuel J. Jones, who, although acting postmaster of Westport, Missouri, had been appointed sheriff of Douglas County (in which Lawrence is located) by the territorial legislature. The Hickory Point community made an issue of the killing. The free-state men, who were in the majority, held an indignation meeting, made threats, and burned the cabins of some of their pro-slavery neighbors, most of whom fled in terror of their lives. Prominent among these avengers was old Jacob Branson, with whom Dow had lived. Just what threats Branson may have made can never be known, but one pro-slavery man named Buckley, asserting that his life had been threatened, swore out a peace warrant for Branson's arrest, and the warrant was placed in the hands of Sheriff Jones. Jones reached Hickory Point with a posse of fifteen men late at night on November 27, arrested Branson, who had gone to bed, and at once started for Lecompton, the county seat, by way of Lawrence. At Blanton's crossing of the Wakarusa Creek, four miles south of Lawrence, Jones and his party were intercepted by a party of free-state men, led by S. N. Wood and J. B. Abbott, and the prisoner was rescued.[8]

Jones hastened into Franklin, a pro-slavery hamlet four miles southeast of Lawrence, whence he forwarded a dispatch to Governor Shannon reporting "open rebellion as having already commenced," and calling for three thousand men "to carry out the laws."[9] It was rumored in free-state circles that, even before he sent his report to the governor, Jones sent a messenger to Colonel Boone of Westport with a plea that he rally the borderers. Governor Shannon immediately issued orders to Richardson and Strickler, the "Major Generals of Militia" designated by the territorial legislature, "to collect together as large a force as you can in your division, and repair without delay to Lecompton, and report yourself to S. J. Jones, Sheriff of Douglas County."[10] Two days later, on November 29, Shannon issued a proclamation, posted in all the pro-slavery settlements, which recited Jones's version of the rescue and called upon "all well disposed citizens of this Territory to rally to the support of the laws of their country, and...to assist the said Sheriff and his deputies in recapturing the above named prisoner, and to aid and assist him in the execution of all legal processes in his hands."[11] Again, free-state rumor asserted that Daniel Woodson, Secretary of the Territory, wrote to "General" Lucine J. Easton of Leavenworth (some versions of the rumor had the letter addressed to Senator Atchison) to call out the Platte County (Missouri) rifle company, adding, "Do not implicate the Governor, whatever you do."*

In the meantime the rescue party made its way into Lawrence and reported to Dr. Robinson. At his suggestion, a town meeting was called at once. In this meeting, which appears to have been dominated by Robinson, it was agreed that, since the rescue would probably be made a pretext for an attack upon Lawrence, the town must be put in a state of defense, while every precaution must be taken to avoid any appearance of resistance to the terri-

---

*The alleged letter is reproduced in *Kansas Historical Collections*, V, 243. Holloway, who also quotes it, states: "It is doubtful whether the Secretary ever wrote this, but it was penned by somebody, sent to Platte City and read to a large public meeting, and it had the effect to bring over the Platte County Riflemen, with their distinguished leader" (Holloway, 225).

torial laws or to legal processes issued under them. Accordingly, it was decided that Branson and his rescuers, only two of whom were Lawrence men, should seek refuge elsewhere, so that if Jones should appear in the town with warrants for their arrest there might be no occasion for resistance. The meeting gave no approval of the rescue, but disavowed all responsibility for it. A committee of public safety was created, and the citizens were organized into a home guard, with Robinson as commander-in-chief and Lane as second in command. Within a few days pro-slavery "militia," which by Governor Shannon's own admission consisted chiefly of inhabitants of Missouri,[12] began to gather at Lecompton and Franklin. Thereupon, on December 4, the Committee of Safety issued a proclamation calling upon their (free-state) "Fellow Citizens" to come to their aid "fully prepared for any emergency."[13] On the same day they sent memorials to President Pierce and to Congress stating their position, and a letter to Colonel Sumner, commandant at Fort Leavenworth, requesting him to send troops for their defense. About this same time the second contingent of Sharps rifles and the Abbott howitzer arrived, having been literally "smuggled through the enemy's lines" from Kansas City. In a day or two, parties of men began to arrive from all the free-state settlements, armed with such weapons as they happened to possess. All were formed into companies and were set to work drilling and constructing earthen defenses at strategic points about Lawrence. The Emigrant Aid Company's unfinished Free State Hotel was pressed into service as barracks, and the people of the community fed and equipped the "soldiers" as best they could.

Governor Shannon also called upon Colonel Sumner for federal troops, but that officer refused to move without orders from Washington. Over the protest of Sheriff Jones and the militia generals (who apparently feared that the presence of federal troops would avert the hostilities which they seemed anxious to force), the governor then telegraphed President Pierce asking that the necessary order might be sent to Colonel Sumner. The President replied that the order would be sent, but it never arrived —possibly because the President's advisers persuaded him that the appearance of federal coercion would place the administration in an unfavorable light before Northern voters.[14]

The free-state people were ready for a fight if it had to come. They were confident that their Sharps rifles and their defensive position would offset any advantage their opponents might have in numbers. But they were anxious to avoid a battle if it could be done without complete surrender. It was certain that if they should fire upon the sheriff's "posse" the act would be advertised by the federal administration as armed rebellion and resistance to law. This would tend to discredit them with the people of the North, upon whom they were dependent for moral, political, and financial support, and in all probability it would be used by the administration as justification for suppressing by force, as being revolutionary and seditious, the provisional government that they were about to set up under the Topeka constitution. At least it would shatter any faint hope that might exist of securing admission to the Union under the Topeka constitution, and even those leaders who had no hope of such admission were unwilling to forfeit the hold on their followers which the Topeka movement gave them. Therefore, the Committee of Safety determined to make a final appeal to Governor Shannon. G. P. Lowrey and C. W. Babcock, members of the Committee, were selected to carry the message. Making their way with difficulty through the besiegers' sentry lines, they reached Shawnee Mission on December 5 and presented the case of the free-state men to the governor, finally persuading him to visit the front in person.

Governor Shannon reached General Strickler's camp on Wakarusa Creek near Franklin on the morning of December 6. He was convinced at once that he had been deceived. He found upwards of a thousand men encamped, most of them from Missouri. The Clay County contingent had raided the United States arsenal

[141]

at Liberty and had seized three cannons, along with a supply of rifles and side arms. The Platte County Rifles were there in force, with D. R. Atchison in their midst. The men were clamoring to attack Lawrence at once, while Atchison and Strickler were straining every nerve to hold them in check. Atchison was reported to have said on the occasion that an attack would ruin the Democratic party. "I found," wrote Governor Shannon to President Pierce a few days later, ". . . a fixed determination to attack that place [Lawrence] and demolish it and the presses, and take possession of their arms."[15] So far as Jones and the militia were concerned, it was war to the knife.

The governor grasped the situation instantly. If the free-state men could be awed into submission, or if they could be made to appear the aggressors, that was one thing; but if the clash should occur under circumstances which would make it appear to the country as a wanton attack by Missourians, that was another matter. The rising Republican party could ask for no better political ammunition in the approaching campaign. The battle must be prevented at all cost. Shannon wrote frantically to Colonel Sumner pleading with him, orders or no orders, to come with his troops and save the situation. The men, he wrote, "are beyond my power, or at least soon will be . . . . It is peace, not war, that we want, and you have the power to secure peace. Time is precious,— fear not [but] that you will be sustained."[16]

But Governor Shannon dared not depend on Colonel Sumner now. The following morning he entered Lawrence and, after conversation with the leaders, was satisfied that the community had violated no law and had presented no obstacle to the service of any writ. He thereupon signed an agreement with Robinson and Lane, commonly referred to as the Treaty of Lawrence. In this document, couched in somewhat evasive language, the free-state men denied all responsibility for the Branson rescue, disclaimed knowledge of any organization to resist the laws, and agreed, "when called upon by the proper authority," to aid in

[142]

the execution of the laws and to furnish a posse for the service of any legal process. But they added a codicil that "we wish it understood that we do not express any opinion as to the validity of the enactments of the Territorial Legislature." Governor Shannon, on his part, denied that he had called upon the citizens of any other state to aid in the execution of the laws and promised that he would not do so in the future.[17]

The governor at once issued orders to his militia generals to withdraw their forces from the vicinity of Lawrence and disband them. Many of the men were reluctant to leave without a fight, but the order was reinforced by a sudden change in the weather— a prairie blizzard struck with driving sleet and sub-zero temperature—and the "army" melted away. The crisis had passed, but men on both sides realized that the real struggle had only begun. The principal effect of this "Wakarusa War" was to focus the attention of the entire nation on Kansas. The free-state men had a breathing spell in which to perfect their Topeka government and to advertise it to the North. The Republicans saw the possibilities of "Bleeding Kansas" as political capital and adopted the free-state movement as a national issue. To checkmate this bit of strategy on the part of the opposition, the administration forces threw the Kansas question into Congress and attempted to put the entire blame for all the troubles in Kansas on the Emigrant Aid Company. "The whole atrocity in Kansas," wrote Senator Charles Sumner a few months later, "is now vindicated as a natural counter movement to the Emigrant Aid Company, and the Company is gibbeted before the country as a criminal."[18]

During the week of the "war," several incidents occurred which, while somewhat extraneous to the story of the Emigrant Aid Company, are deserving of passing mention as a part of the Kansas conflict. On December 6 Thomas W. Barber, a young free-state squatter who had gone into Lawrence and enrolled in its defense force, was riding out to his claim, five miles from the village, accompanied by his brother and another man. About two

[143]

miles from Lawrence the little party was stopped by a pro-slavery patrol of several times its number, among them "General" W. P. Richardson, Judge Cato, a federal judge of the territory, and G. W. Clark, a federal Indian agent, destined to create much trouble later in the border wars around Fort Scott. After a brief parley, one of the patrol, generally believed to have been Clark, shot Barber, who died a few minutes later. This was the only free-state casualty of the "war." The body was shown to Governor Shannon when he visited Lawrence the next day, and may have been a factor in persuading him that "law enforcement" was going too far. In the subsequent Congressional debates, much was made of cold-blooded murder of the free-state men by officers of the administration.*

It was about the same time that John Brown made his first appearance on the Kansas scene. Arriving in Lawrence while defense preparations were in progress, he was commissioned a captain by the Committee of Safety. It was from this fact that he was known ever after as "Captain" John Brown. When the "treaty" with the governor was made public, Brown began a street speech, which he was not permitted to finish, in which he denounced the treaty and urged an immediate attack upon the besiegers.* Had his rash advice been followed, it would have been an act of open rebellion which would have seriously compromised, if not entirely ruined, the free-state cause.

Just a week after the signing of the treaty of Lawrence and while the excitement was still running high, the election was held for the ratification of the Topeka constitution. No attempt was made to hold elections in Atchison and certain other pro-slavery centers. At Leavenworth the election was broken up by a pro-slavery mob, and a few days later the office of the *Territorial Reg-*

---

* In free-state circles the killing of Barber was always rated as cold-blooded murder. It may have been an impulsive act under the excitement of the moment, or it may have been the culmination of a personal quarrel. The latter view was held by Professor F. H. Hodder.

* The authenticity of this incident is questioned by some historians. See James C. Malin, *John Brown and the Legend of Fifty-Six* (Philadelphia, 1942), 19-21.

ister, published by Mark W. Delahay, one of the most conservative and moderate of the free-state men, was wrecked and the printing press thrown into the Missouri River. Only forty-six votes were cast against the adoption of the constitution, but of course pro-slavery men took no part in the election.

A week after this election a convention met in Lawrence and nominated a full slate of state officers. In each district, nominations were made for members of the state legislature. Some of the more conservative of the free-state men bolted the Lawrence convention and nominated an "Anti-Abolition" ticket, feeling that to give the whole movement the brand of conservatism might secure more favorable action in Congress. On January 15 the election was held for state officers and members of the state legislature under the Topeka constitution. Again no attempt was made to open polls in the pro-slavery centers. At Leavenworth, where a large sprinkling of the citizenry were free-staters, a sub-rosa unofficial election was held, but this was not recognized by the state legislature when it met. In general, pro-slavery men simply ignored the election, declaring it to be illegal and void, but at Easton, near Leavenworth, threats were made that the polls would be broken up. Accordingly a free-state "militia" company, captained by R. P. Brown, went from the neighborhood of Leavenworth to guard the polls. The election was carried out, but a clash occurred in which one pro-slavery man was killed. In retaliation, Brown was set upon the next day by a pro-slavery military company called the "Kickapoo Rangers," and in spite of the efforts of their captain, J. W. Martin, to save him, was killed in a most revolting manner. Another "atrocity" for the politicians! The full roster of the Lawrence convention was elected, with Dr. Robinson heading the roll as governor.

The state legislature met at Topeka on March 4, organized, inaugurated the state officers, elected Reeder and Lane United States Senators-designate, adopted a memorial to Congress petitioning for the admission of Kansas to the Union under the To-

[145]

peka constitution, received the final report and resignation of the Territorial Executive Committee, and adjourned to July 4. But in the meantime President Pierce and his spokesmen in Congress had transferred the Kansas conflict to the national stage.

During the five and a half months of its existence, the Territorial Executive Committee, under the chairmanship of Lane, had had, nominally at least, complete direction of the free-state movement. They had held all the various elections and had certified the results. They had sent one of their number, Marcus J. Parrott, to Washington to lobby for the admission of Kansas. They had, in February, sent a delegation of six to tour the eastern states and arouse interest in the free-state cause. But to finance all these activities, no means were available, and so the committee fell back upon the issue of scrip. They issued, in all, $15,265.90,[19] which netted them about $11,000. A small portion of this was expended in Kansas at face value, particularly in financing the defense of Lawrence in the Wakarusa War, but most of it was sold at varying discounts to sympathizers in the East. Amos A. Lawrence was much perturbed at the issue of the scrip, fearing, as was the fact, that it was Lane's idea. He felt that the necessary funds should have been provided by New England philanthropy.[20] Nevertheless, Lawrence and several other officers of the Emigrant Aid Company got behind the move and helped to sell the scrip, taking considerable sums themselves. Even Dr. Webb wrote several letters to directors of the Company soliciting their aid in marketing the scrip, although the official attitude of the Company was to take no cognizance of the matter.

When the free-state propaganda delegation went East in February, 1856, they made their headquarters at the office of the Emigrant Aid Company in Boston. Indeed, the office appears to have acted as a sort of booking agency for them, arranging their speaking dates and mapping their itinerary.[21] In several instances funds raised in the communities where they had spoken, "for the use of the Free State Party in the Territory of Kansas,"[22] were

[146]

sent to the Company office to be forwarded to the Territorial Executive Committee in Kansas. At the same time, Lawrence continued to write letters to Robinson urging the continuation of what he called the Fabian policy and the avoidance of all resistance to federal authority, and Dr. Cabot kept up his efforts in behalf of the rifle fund.[23]

In his annual message to Congress on December 31, 1855, President Pierce stated that, although there had been acts prejudicial to good order in Kansas, nothing had occurred to justify the interposition of the Federal Executive.[24] On January 24, when there had been no new development of any consequence in Kansas except the election of officers under the Topeka constitution, the President sent a special message on Kansas in which he blamed Reeder for all the irregularities in the territorial elections, denounced the free-state movement and the formation of the Topeka constitution as being "of revolutionary character," asserted his intention "to exert the whole power of the Federal Executive to support public order in the Territory; to vindicate its laws, whether Federal or local, against all attempts of organized resistance," and recommended the passage by Congress of an enabling act to authorize the territorial authorities to call a constitutional convention. In his message he stated that the parties opposed to the Kansas-Nebraska Act, having failed to defeat it in Congress, "then had recourse . . . to the extraordinary measure of propagandist colonization of the Territory of Kansas, to prevent the free and natural action of its inhabitants in its internal organization, and thus to anticipate or force the determination of that question [slavery] in that inchoate State," and he implied very clearly that the formation of associations for this purpose in some of the states furnished the explanation, though no sufficient justification, for the "illegal and reprehensible countermovements which ensued."[25]

Just three days before the appearance of this message, on January 21, the free-state leaders in Kansas, growing alarmed at the repeated threats from pro-slavery sources, had sent a letter to President Pierce, signed by Lane as chairman of the Territorial Executive Committee, and Robinson as chairman of the Committee of Safety, in which they informed him that they were threatened with invasion and asked that the commandant of the federal troops be instructed to intervene to prevent it.[26] Two days later they sent a second letter requesting that he issue a proclamation forbidding such invasion.[27] Whether prompted by these requests or by his conference with Governor Shannon, who visited Washington at about this time, or by both, the President, on February 11, issued his proclamation, but it was directed equally against "combinations . . . formed therein to resist the execution of the Territorial laws," and against "persons residing without the Territory, but near its borders, [who] contemplate armed intervention in the affairs thereof." The proclamation commanded "all persons engaged in unlawful combinations against the constituted authority" to disperse and warned them that "any attempted insurrection in the said Territory or aggressive intrusion into the same" would be resisted by the federal troops. It called upon "citizens both of adjoining and of distant States, to abstain from unauthorized intermeddling in the local concerns of the Territory," and it invoked "all good citizens to promote order by rendering obedience to the law. . . ."[28] At the same time Governor Shannon was authorized to call upon Colonel Sumner for federal troops "for the suppression of insurrectionary combinations or armed resistance to the execution of the law."[29]

It was not long before the territorial authorities made use of the President's proclamation, or a one-sided interpretation of it, to strike what was expected to be a telling blow against their antagonists. But in the meantime, the battle was transferred to Congress. When Reeder presented himself to dispute the right of Whitfield to sit as delegate of the territory the proposal was made that the House undertake an investigation.* The proposition was

---

*The original proposal was to authorize the Committee on Territories to send for persons and papers. This was subsequently changed to the appointment of a special com-

debated intermittently for several weeks, and culminated on March 19 in the appointment of the notable Howard Committee. On March 7, in the course of a speech opposing the investigation, Mordecai Oliver, Representative of the border district of Missouri, delivered a philippic against the Emigrant Aid Company, charging that it was pouring armed men into Kansas to control the elections, and urging this as justification for the inroad of Missourians on election day "to aid in preserving the laws of the Territory and the purity of the ballot box." He averred that *if* any of the Missourians voted, it was "to prevent the effects which would otherwise have resulted from this unusual and extraordinary intermeddling with the local interests and domestic institutions of that Territory by those who reached it under the auspices of the emigrant aid society."[30] In the course of the debate several other representatives of the administration party echoed the same sentiments. Kunkel of Pennsylvania replied to Oliver, arguing that whatever the emigrant aid societies might have done was no justification for interference with the rights of free-state settlers generally.[31] Mark Trafton, on March 12,[32] and W. S. Damrell, on March 18,[33] both of Massachusetts, made spirited defenses of the Emigrant Aid Company against Oliver's allegations. They denied that the organization was composed of abolitionists or that it had any such capital as alleged. They maintained that it had sent only bona fide settlers, that it had never furnished arms, and that it had sent no one merely to vote. Above all, they insisted that its activities were strictly legal and ethical. Barbour of Indiana pointed out very significantly, on March 18, that while the accusers of the emigrant aid societies bitterly opposed a full and free investigation, their defenders not only welcomed such an investigation, but demanded it.[34] Finally, on April 30, Meachem of Vermont, while introducing a bill for the admission of Kansas

---

mittee to conduct investigations wherever it might see fit. Such a committee, consisting of William A. Howard of Michigan, Chairman, John Sherman of Ohio, and Mordecai Oliver of Missouri, was appointed March 19, and proceeded to Kansas. (Their report is cited extensively in the notes as *Howard Report*.)

under the Topeka constitution, defended the Emigrant Aid Company and charged that the President and all his spokesmen were merely using it to play politics. "They do not care a fig about these emigrant aid societies," he declared. "It is only a blind."[35]

But the battle royal came in the Senate. On January 3 Henry Wilson of Massachusetts introduced a resolution calling upon the President for any information he might have regarding the disturbances in Kansas, so worded as to insinuate that the incursion of armed men from Missouri constituted the essence of the trouble. On February 14 the resolution came up on the calendar. In the debate which ensued, Fessenden of Maine was the chief defender of the resolution. In the course of his remarks objecting to the resolution as one-sided, Geyer of Missouri asserted that "those disorders originated, not on the border, but they are to be attributed to an extraordinary organization, unprecedented I believe, of what is called an 'Emigrant Aid Society'—the first attempt in the history of this country to take possession of an organized Territory, and exclude from it the inhabitants of other portions of the Union."[36]

This set off the fireworks. Four days later Henry Wilson delivered a speech in denunciation of the Missouri invasions in which he quoted extensively from a memorial of S. C. Pomeroy. He defied the President, the administration organs, and Senator Geyer to show that the directors of the Emigrant Aid Company had ever authorized an unlawful act. He stated that all the Company had done was to organize settlers into parties for travel at reduced fares, to build a hotel, to send some sawmills, and to aid in the establishing of schools and churches. In contrast he observed that, weeks before the first Emigrant Aid Company settlers arrived, the Platte County Self-Defensive Association had "proclaimed to the world its readiness to cross into Kansas and remove actual settlers from their homes."[37] A week later, on February 25, J. C. Jones of Tennessee replied to Wilson in a sarcastic speech in which he repeated the assertion that the Emigrant Aid "Society" was the cause of the Kansas trouble, and sought to link it with the free-soil politicians. He ridiculed the whole idea of an emigrant aid society and undertook to prove that the Massachusetts organization was a money-making concern with the political aim of making Kansas a free state. To climax his arraignment he quoted the constitution of the Kansas Legion, which he treated as a mere auxiliary of the Emigrant Aid Company, to prove the traitorous objective of the whole movement.[38] This outburst provoked a reply from John P. Hale of New Hampshire. On February 28 Hale, on behalf of the Emigrant Aid Company and the free-state settlers in Kansas, pleaded guilty "to everything charged upon them by the Senator from Tennessee" —except responsibility for the troubles. He said that Jones had made no startling discovery as to the aims of the Emigrant Aid Company; the Company had published to the world that its goal was a free state in Kansas and a pecuniary return. Nor was there anything new about it; most of the original colonies had been founded by similar corporations.[39]

The high point of senatorial denunciation of the Emigrant Aid Company came in a report presented to the Senate on March 12 by Stephen A. Douglas on behalf of the Committee on Territories, and a speech by Douglas on March 20 in support of this report. In the report Douglas asserted that, although it was not avowed in the charter, it was the obvious purpose of the Emigrant Aid Company to force Kansas into the Union as a free state, "regardless of the rights and wishes of the people as guaranteed by the Constitution of the United States." He conceded the right of persons from any part of the country to go to Kansas independently, but declared it to be "a very different thing where a State creates a vast moneyed corporation for the purpose of controlling the domestic institutions of a distinct political community fifteen hundred miles distant, and sends out emigrants only as a means of accomplishing its paramount political objects." He referred to the Emigrant Aid Company as a "powerful corporation, with a capital of $5,000,000 invested in houses and lands, in merchandise and mills, in cannon and rifles, in powder and lead, in all the implements of art, agriculture and war, and employing a correspondng number of men, all under the management and control of non-resident directors and stockholders. . . ." The passage of large numbers of Company emigrants through Missouri, the violence of their language, and their hostility to the domestic institutions of that state, aroused apprehensions, the natural consequence of which was the organization of societies in western Missouri to counteract such efforts by similar activities, which differed only in being defensive in character.[40] In his speech a week later Douglas reiterated at greater length the allegations of the report and his defense of the Missouri activities, denied the right of "any State of this Union to pass any law or do any act with a view to changing the domestic institutions of any other State or Territory," and summed up his position in the sweeping indictment that "the whole responsibility of all the disturbances in Kansas rests upon the Massachusetts Emigrant Aid Company and its affiliated societies."[41] Evidently Douglas had been reading the unused first Massachusetts charter of the Emigrant Aid Company and Thayer's abortive "Plan of Operations," and coupling these with the wild tales from the Missouri border he constructed a pattern of the Company and its activities that suited the purpose of the administration forces.

Two days after Douglas's report was read to the Senate, his colleague from Illinois, Lyman Trumbull, spoke in refutation. He analyzed the report to show that it implied what it dared not charge directly, and then defended the Emigrant Aid Company against the implications.[42] On April 3 Collamer of Vermont, minority member of the Committee on Territories, attacked Douglas's majority report. "I consider that the scolding about the emigrant aid society," he said, "is for the purpose of diverting public attention from the violence and usurpation which has taken place in Kansas by the Missouri invasion." He reviewed the real activities of the Emigrant Aid Company and avowed that these opera-

[152]

tions had nothing to do with the question before Congress,—
the question "whether the settlers and inhabitants have been in-
jured and abused in such a manner as to call for redress at our
hands."[43] The next day Douglas replied to Collamer, attempting
to explain away the Missouri invasion, charging collusion between the Emigrant Aid Company and Governor Reeder, and
presenting the Kansas conflict, "not as a question between free
State men and pro-slavery men, but between the Abolitionists
and Free Soilers, rallying under the banner of emigrant aid societies, on the one hand, and advocates of non-intervention and
the principles of self government according to the Nebraska bill,
on the other."[44] Three days later Geyer again spoke on the Kansas controversy, repeating much of Douglas's argument. He ridiculed the Emigrant Aid Company's "Address to the People of
Missouri," and argued that the Company was really a political
organization under the control of the Republican party, undertaking to do with money what the antislavery congressmen
had failed to do in their attempt to defeat the Kansas-Nebraska
bill: to exclude Southern people from the Territory. He maintained, as Douglas had, that the supposed Missourians who had
flocked into Kansas to vote in the election of March 30, 1855, were
really bona fide settlers who had returned to their former homes
or to neighboring states for the winter and were then returning
to their claims.[45]

On April 9 William H. Seward of New York spoke in reply
to both the President's special message and Douglas's report and
speeches, defending the Emigrant Aid Company against all their
allegations.[46] But the climax came in Charles Sumner's famous
speech on "The Crime against Kansas," on May 19 and 20,—
the speech that cost Sumner the severe clubbing at the hands of
Representative Brooks of South Carolina two days later. Sumner
had written to Dr. Webb and had received from him a first-hand
statement of the program and activities of the Emigrant Aid
Company.[47] In his vitriolic speech, which occupied the greater

[153]

part of two days, Sumner devoted a large share of his time to a defense of the Aid Company. He explained in detail the operations of the Company and answered or denied every charge that had been brought against it. The Emigrant Aid Company, he declared, while utterly blameless, had been made a pretext for an unpardonable crime, the subjugation of Kansas, and now it was being made a scapegoat at the behest of the administration.[48]

The strategy of the administration forces in this battle of words is perfectly transparent, and was not lost on the opposition. The federal administration, under the guiding hand of Jefferson Davis, Secretary of War and a power behind the throne, had consistently supported the Pro-slavery party. When the widely publicized Wakarusa War began to rally Northern sentiment in support of the Free State party in Kansas, and the Republican politicians began to arrogate to themselves the sponsorship of the free-state movement, it looked like breakers ahead for the Democratic party. Under the circumstances it appeared to be a clever move to throw the onus of the Kansas trouble on the Emigrant Aid Company. Such a move promised not only to embarrass the Republicans in the Middle West, where they were making the greatest headway, and where the Company was mistrusted, but also to play the Middle West against New England, and so divide the opposition. But the trick backfired. Northerners generally refused to take the bait, while their representatives in Congress stripped the ruse so bare that it appeared ridiculous. The Emigrant Aid Company emerged stronger than ever from the pummeling, and its stock subscriptions shot forward as by a miracle. But what was most important, the attack gave the heterogeneous opposition in Congress a common rallying ground. Political parties had been in a state of flux when the thirty-fourth Congress was elected, so that party designation meant almost nothing. Most of the pro-slavery Whigs rallied to the support of the administration, but standing in opposition on one question or another were, besides Republicans, Free Soilers, Antislavery Whigs, Know-

Nothings, and Anti-Nebraska Democrats. So hopelessly divided among themselves were these factions that, in the House of Representatives, where collectively they constituted a majority, it required two months to elect a speaker. But now members of all these groups sprang to the defense of the Emigrant Aid Company, and when the smoke had cleared most of them were ready to avow themselves Republicans.

But while the attack by the friends of the "peculiar institution" in Congress was bogging down, the more lethal attack on the soil of Kansas was more successful. While Sumner was speaking, the hosts of destruction, in the guise of a United States marshal's posse, were gathering about Lawrence. The next day, on May 21, the blow fell.

Ever since his rebuff in the Wakarusa War, Sheriff Jones had been watching for an opportunity to avenge himself on the hated town of Lawrence. The whole Pro-slavery party, as evidenced by its press, clamored for the destruction of that village, which it regarded as the hotbed of abolitionism and the especial stronghold of the detested Emigrant Aid "Society." The Free State Hotel was particularly an object of execration, not only, as in the case of the American Hotel at Kansas City,* because it was the property of the Emigrant Aid Company, but also because it was generally believed in pro-slavery circles to have been built and equipped as a fort.[49] If an instance of resistance to law could be fastened upon the people of Lawrence, it was practically certain that the place would be invested by another "posse" like that of the Wakarusa War, and with feelings as intense as they were in the spring of 1856, it was more than doubtful if such a posse could be restrained from destroying the town.

---

*"When the border troubles were at their worst, it was feared that the property [the American Hotel] would be destroyed in some outbreak of the Missourians, and it was leased to H. W. Chiles, a strong pro-slavery partisan" (Theo. S. Case [ed.], *History of Kansas City, Missouri* [Syracuse, New York, 1888], 55). Alexander Gilham of Kansas City testified before the Howard Committee that many people in Jackson County desired the destruction of the American Hotel because it was reported to belong to the Emigrant Aid Company (*Howard Report*, 850). J. M. Winchell testified that it was threatened with destruction at the time of the Wakarusa War (*ibid.*, 1092-93).

S. N. Wood, the leader of the Branson rescue, had left Kansas immediately after that episode and returned to his old home in Ohio. He spent the winter lecturing, raising funds for war supplies and, in conjunction with the Emigration Aid Association of Northern Ohio, recruiting a party of about a hundred prospective settlers with whom he returned to Lawrence in April. On April 19, Sheriff Jones appeared in Lawrence with a warrant for the arrest of Wood on the Branson rescue charge. Wood at first submitted and then escaped. The next day, Sunday, Jones returned to Lawrence and sought to recruit a *posse comitatus* among the citizens to aid in the arrest, but not a man approached would serve. The same day Jones attempted to arrest S. F. Tappan, another of the Branson rescuers; Tappan struck the sheriff in the face and escaped. Here, surely, was resistance to law. Whether or not, as always alleged by free-state partisans, Jones deliberately sought to provoke resistance in order to have a pretext to sack the town, it is impossible to say. At all events he left in a rage, declaring that he would return with troops. Under the power recently conferred on him by the War Department, Governor Shannon immediately requisitioned a squad of soldiers, and with these Jones returned to Lawrence on April 23 with warrants for the arrest of all who had refused to serve in his posse. Remaining in town that night, he was shot and critically wounded by an irresponsible person.* It is easy to believe that the free-state people were as disturbed by the shooting as their opponents could possibly have been. It was directly contrary to their policy of avoiding any act of violence, and it was certain to arouse the border to a new outburst of fury. A mass meeting was held in Lawrence the next morning at which the act was disavowed and five hundred dollars offered for the apprehension of the criminal. But such feeble efforts could avail little. The pro-slavery press of the

---

* Jones's assailant was identified twenty-five years later as one J. F. Filer, a tramp printer. See Leverett W. Spring, *Kansas, The Prelude to the Civil War* (Boston and New York, 1907), 108-10.

border announced that Jones was dead and called loudly for avenging of the murder.

The United States District Court for the Territory of Kansas convened at Lecompton the first week in May. With or without instructions from Judge Samuel D. Lecompte,* the grand jury (all pro-slavery, of course) found indictments for treason against Andrew H. Reeder, Charles Robinson, James H. Lane, George W. Brown, George W. Dietzler, George W. Smith, S. N. Wood, and Gaius Jenkins.[50] According to Robinson, the purpose was to place in custody everyone connected with the free-state government and so prevent its going into operation.[51] Whether or not such a political purpose lay behind the indictments, and to what extent, if any, the action was prompted by the excitement over the shooting of Sheriff Jones, can only be conjectured. Warned in advance, Robinson, at the prompting of Howard and Sherman of the Congressional Committee, left the territory, ostensibly on an errand for the Free State party and to convey the testimony taken thus far by the Congressional Committee. He was intercepted at Lexington, Missouri, and brought back to Kansas. Reeder at first defied arrest on the ground of Congressional immunity, but soon fled the territory disguised as a woodchopper. Lane was already out of the territory.

Warrants for the arrest of the others were placed in the hands of United States Marshal J. B. Donaldson for service. Construing Reeder's defiance of Deputy Marshal William P. Fain on May 7, made in the presence of the Congressional Committee and all the persons attending its session, as resistance "by a large number of the people of Lawrence," Donaldson issued a proclamation com-

---

* Most free-state accounts quote supposed instructions of Judge Lecompte to the grand jury directing them to find bills for high treason against any who had actually resisted the Territorial laws, and bills for constructive treason against any "individuals of notoriety" who had conspired to resist them (e.g., Robinson, Kansas Conflict, 234). Judge Lecompte in later years denied that he had issued any such instructions (Kansas Historical Collections, VIII, 389-405). The records of the court are lost, so that the truth cannot be ascertained, but Professor F. H. Hodder was inclined to accept Judge Lecompte's defense at face value. See James C. Malin, "Judge Lecompte and the 'Sack of Lawrence,' May 21, 1856," Kansas Historical Quarterly, XX, August, 1953, 465-94 (especially 489-92).

manding "the law abiding citizens of the Territory . . . to be and appear at Lecompton as soon as practicable, and in sufficient numbers for the execution of the law."[52] About the same time, J. H. Stringfellow's *Squatter Sovereign* proclaimed "War to the knife, and knife to the hilt; neither asking quarter nor granting it."[53]

The people of Lawrence were thrown into a mental state bordering on panic. The same grand jury which had found the indictments for treason had "presented" the Free State Hotel, the *Herald of Freedom,* and the *Kansas Free State* as "nuisances," and although no court action was had on these presentments, there was little doubt that if the "posse" should enter the town, this action of the grand jury would be used as a pretext for a general sack. On May 11 a committee appealed to Governor Shannon for protection against the gathering bands by the troops at his disposal, but the governor refused to interfere unless the free-state men would agree to recognize the territorial laws.[54] There was confusion in the town. Some wanted to resist; others did not. Still others proposed to submit to the service of the warrants by the marshal, but to resist the mob. It was even suggested that a group of citizens go to Lecompton and offer themselves as a posse. A new Committee of Safety was chosen, headed by S. C. Pomeroy. Finally a policy of nonresistance was agreed upon, and last-minute appeals were sent to Donaldson and Colonel Sumner. Donaldson replied that he could not trust their pledges, and Sumner, as usual, refused to move without orders.[55]

On May 20 the marshal's "posse" in motley array began to converge upon Lawrence. It was estimated that there were about eight hundred men. Besides all the prominent pro-slavery leaders with their followings, there were present in the throng ex-Senator D. R. Atchison with the Platte County (Missouri) Rifles, Colonel Boone of Westport with another force of Missourians, Colonel Buford of Alabama with nearly a hundred of the men he had recently brought into the territory, Colonel Jackson of Georgia, Colonel Titus of Florida, and a company of about fifty South Carolinians who insisted on carrying a state flag. They had several pieces of artillery. At dawn on the twenty-first the attackers were drawn up on Mount Oread overlooking the town. After scouts had reconnoitered the village, Deputy Marshal Fain entered Lawrence with a small party, impressed a posse of citizens, and arrested Dietzler, Smith, and Jenkins without opposition. Fain and his party were entertained at dinner at the Free State Hotel, which the Eldridge brothers had leased, furnished, and provisioned, and were just ready to open to the public. The Committee of Safety handed Fain a note addressed to Donaldson in which they promised to "make no resistance to the execution of the laws, national or territorial," and begged for protection.[56]

But even this abject surrender, although it elicited from Fain a promise that the marshal's posse should not enter Lawrence, could not save the town. When Fain returned to the mob on the hill, Marshal Donaldson dismissed his posse, and they were at once re-enrolled en masse as the posse of Sheriff Jones of Douglas County. At the head of his forces, Jones entered the town about three in the afternoon. At his demand, Pomeroy surrendered the howitzer and a part of the Sharps rifles,* hoping to avert a greater calamity. But nothing could stop the mob. The two newspaper offices were entered and wrecked, their presses were shattered, and their type was thrown into the street. The Free State Hotel was reduced to a pile of smouldering ruins, and Dr. Robinson's house on Mount Oread was burned. According to free-state sources, there followed a general pillage of the town, but this is denied in pro-slavery accounts. Jones was reported to have shouted, "This is the happiest day of my life."

May 21, 1856, marks the lowest ebb in the fortunes of the free-state movement. The most important leaders were in prison or in exile. The citadel of Lawrence was in ruins, and its news-

---

* Pomeroy refused to surrender the rifles that were in the hands of individuals on the ground that they were private property.

papers silenced. The whole force of the national administration was arrayed against the Free State party and its friends. It was a dark day, too, for the Emigrant Aid Company. Twenty thousand dollars of its meager capital was wiped out. One of its agents was in prison charged with treason. And in Congress it was being advertised to the nation as the archcriminal responsible for all the trouble in Kansas.

CHAPTER IX

Behind the Lines

WHILE THESE EXCITING EVENTS were happening in Kansas and in Washington, the Emigrant Aid Company did not relax for an instant its efforts to supply the free-state people of Kansas the sinews of war. The Company as such continued its financial drives, its investments in Kansas, and its work of forwarding settlers, while Dr. Cabot kept up his exertions on behalf of the rifle fund, and Dr. Webb endeavored to raise funds for the relief of those who had suffered at the hands of pro-slavery marauders. On the whole, the Company profited from the excitement. The first four months of 1856 marked the zenith of the Company's success in its financial drives. The Wakarusa War and the movement to consolidate the Republican party for the approaching Presidential election focused attention upon Kansas and aroused a high pitch of excitement throughout the North. This excitement the Emigrant Aid Company was able to utilize in its campaigns for stock subscriptions and relief funds. Even the mission of the Territorial Executive Committee to the East in February, 1856, was turned to account, for while the Company office aided these free-state missionaries by arranging speaking engagements for them, it sent its own representatives to accompany them,* supplementing their pleas for support of the free-state cause with suggestions that the cause could be served to best advantage through the channel of the Emigrant Aid Company.

During the fall of 1854 and most of 1855, the Company had followed the plan of employing one or more subscription agents on salary or commission, or both. Several had been tried,—E. B. Whitman, Bartholomew Wood, H. A. Wilcox, and possibly others,

---

* Pomeroy and Williams on several occasions spoke at the same meetings with members of the Kansas delegation (Aid Company letters, Book A, 193 ff.; newspaper accounts of meetings in Webb Scrap Books, VIII-IX).

[161]

—with equally disappointing results. During October and November, 1855, as previously noted, Edward Everett Hale had devoted all his time for six weeks to solicitation for the Company at what for him was the merely nominal salary of twenty dollars a week. Thayer had given time intermittently to speech-making, appealing for stock-subscriptions at the same time that he sought to stimulate migration and to arouse interest in the cause in general. Sometimes he had paid his own expenses, sometimes they had been paid from the Company treasury, but at no time prior to December, 1855, had he received any compensation for his services. But on December 1, 1855, Thayer proposed to the Executive Committee that he be employed as stock-subscription agent, devoting all his time to the work, paying his own expenses, and receiving as compensation 10 per cent of all subscriptions collected in excess of $20,000.* At a special meeting on December 19 his offer was accepted,[1] and a contract was drawn.[2] Accompanied by Branscomb, who was delegated to assist him, Thayer left at once for New York and spent about three months working there and in Brooklyn. In New York he enlisted the active support of John Bigelow (then editor of the *Evening Post*), George W. Blunt, William Cullen Bryant, Horace B. Claflin, Simeon Draper, William M. Evarts, Parke Godwin, Moses H. Grinnell, Thaddeus Hyatt, and numerous other prominent men, including the group who had been active in the now defunct American Settlement Company.[3] Thayer's commissions for this work amounted to $5,158.00,[4] but because of the ambiguity of Thayer's contract it is impossible to say whether this represented 2,575 or 3,575 shares of stock.

Except for the employment of Thayer, the Company abandoned the subscription agent plan at the beginning of 1856 and turned to the services of volunteer workers.† The plan used was

---

* The minute of the transaction states that the commission was to be paid on "money collected in excess of $20,000." Thayer's contract read that 10 per cent was to be paid on "moneys collected, . . . no portion of the said percentage to be paid unless the subscription by him obtained and collected amount to the sum of Twenty Thousand Dollars." Therefore it is not clear whether or not Thayer received a commission on the first $20,000.

† Dr. Webb wrote, February 15, 1856, to an applicant for a position as subscription agent, "The plan of using temporary agents to solicit was not satisfactory; their salaries

to have a director or friend of the Company in each community call a meeting of the "friends of freedom." This meeting would be addressed by a representative of the Company, usually Pomeroy or Williams, or a member of the Kansas delegation, or both, who would plead for subscriptions to the stock of the Company for improvements in Kansas, donations for the relief of those who had suffered loss in the "invasion," and contributions to "put Kansas in a state of defense."[5] After the speaking a collection would be taken for the relief fund, and a committee would be appointed to canvass the town in the interest of all three objects.[6]

This plan met with notable success. Letters poured in from all parts of New England announcing the success of the local drives, and each week at the meeting of the Executive Committee the assistant treasurer reported thousands of dollars received by the treasury. At the same time the defense fund in the hands of Dr. Cabot and the relief fund administered by Dr. Webb prospered proportionately. Among the volunteer workers mentioned in the correspondence were many whose names would have appeared prominently in *Who's Who,* had there been such a thing in the 1850's.[7]

So successful were these efforts that the amount received from stock subscriptions, which had stood at $45,835 on November 24, 1855,[8] had jumped to $98,940 by the time of the annual stockholders' meeting on May 27, 1856,[9] making a net gain for the six months of $53,105. During these same months $449.17 was donated outright to the Company, in addition to the donations to the defense fund and relief fund, no account of which was rendered because money received for these purposes did not pass through the treasury and was not regarded as Company funds.

While Dr. Cabot was not only striving to secure contributions to supply the free-state forces war equipment, but also administering the fund by purchasing and dispensing weapons and muni-

---

ate up all they collected. The only plan that has worked satisfactorily has been to appoint committees in the towns, and have them thus thoroughly canvassed" (Aid Company Letters, Book A, 266).

tions, other officers of the Company were actively supporting him. Lawrence continued to contribute heavily from his own means and appealed to his brothers to do likewise.* Thayer appears also to have been making pleas for the defense fund. He later asserted that he had spent $4,500 of his own money for rifles and cannon.[10] Early in February Thayer and Pomeroy addressed a meeting in Worcester, in the course of which Thayer offered to pay for ten Sharps rifles at twenty-five dollars each if the citizens of Worcester would raise enough money to bring the total up to one hundred. In the same meeting Thayer was reported to have said that he was engaged in the manufacture of a new rifle, superior to the Sharps, and had undertaken to furnish a thousand for Kansas.[11] Dr. Webb, apparently in his official capacity, continued to interest himself in the problem of providing "means of defense." On December 28, 1855, he wrote to the editor of the Detroit *Evening Tribune* that he had seen in the paper that one of Detroit's wealthiest citizens had offered to contribute one thousand dollars toward supplying rifles to a company of two hundred in Kansas. "We," he continued,—and he entered the letter in the Company's letter book,— "are working to the same end, and hope for cooperation." He went on to quote Robinson's estimate of the defense needs of the Free State party and added that in Robinson's opinion the money for this purpose "should be raised, not by the Emigrant Aid Company as stock, but it should be a free contribution from the true patriots of the North."[12] On January 17, 1856, Webb wrote to R. A. Chapman that he had heard of a firm in New York which had five hundred Hall's rifles, as good as new, which he thought might be bought cheap, but since the owners were not free-soil men, they must be approached cautiously; he asked Chapman "to aid us in a quiet way."[13]

In February, 1856, David S. Hoyt was sent from Boston with

---

* Amos A. Lawrence wrote on February 12, 1856, to his brother James appealing for other members of the family to help supply rifles to save the town of Lawrence from destruction (Lawrence Letters, 131-32). Another brother, Dr. William Lawrence, was one of the heaviest contributors to the rifle fund (Lawrence, *Amos A. Lawrence*, 97).

one hundred rifles and two cannon, packed in nine tool chests. One hesitates to say that the Emigrant Aid Company sent these weapons,—there is no minute of it in the Company record books,—but Hoyt's offer to take them was addressed to Pomeroy and is endorsed on the outside in Dr. Webb's handwriting, "Answered in person, relative to taking charge of supplies for Kansas.[14] The "supplies" were paid for out of Dr. Cabot's special fund, and the arrangements were made, in part, by Amos A. Lawrence.* It was the original plan that Hoyt should haul his boxes across Missouri in a wagon, pretending to be bound for the Mormon settlement in Utah; but at St. Louis he changed his mind and took passage on the steamboat *Arabia,* having his "9 boxes of merchandise" billed as freight by the Emigrant Aid Company's forwarding agent.[15] Hoyt's mission and the nature of his freight were discovered,† and the rifles were seized and put ashore at Lexington. Fortunately, the locks of the guns had been sent by another route, so that the rifles were useless to the Missourians. Sometime later the value of the weapons was recovered in a lawsuit, and eventually, in 1859, the rifles themselves were restored to an agent of the Company and were used by Montgomery and his "Jayhawkers" in the later border troubles.[16]

Down to the time of the seizure of the Hoyt rifles, the Emigrant Aid Company office had consistently refused to take any hand in the arming of individuals intending to migrate under Company auspices. To every letter of inquiry Dr. Webb sent essentially the same reply: that the Emigrant Aid Company had nothing to do with arms, but that since arms for defense might be advantageous, he referred his correspondents to private dealers by whom they might be supplied.[17] After the loss of this shipment,

---

* Lawrence wrote to his uncle, Giles Richards, May 25, 1856, "As I have spoken of rifles, I will add that with my friend Dr. Cabot, I started off a man named Hoyt with $4,000 worth of that ware early in the spring . . . " (original letter, Kansas State Historical Society, Miscellaneous Papers).

† Lawrence said in the letter just quoted that a letter Hoyt was writing to his mother, in which he mentioned the nature of his baggage, was taken from his stateroom while he was at dinner.

however, he began referring all inquirers to Dr. Cabot. Typical of his letters on the subject during this period is one dated April 2, 1856, to Reverend B. Farrand, a prospective emigrant: "The Company does not deal in arms. Dr. Cabot of this city has kindly offered to aid those who desire it in selecting and purchasing Sharps rifles."[18] To some he volunteered the information that the weapon could be procured from Dr. Cabot for twenty-six dollars, "which is $4 less than the government wholesale price."[19] Dr. Cabot ordinarily sold the rifle to the emigrant outright, sometimes accepting part payment,[20] but when the individual pleaded his inability to pay a rifle was sometimes lent to him.[21]

Dr. Cabot offered, through Dr. Webb, to supply arms to several independent parties of settlers who proposed to migrate to Kansas in the spring of 1856.[22] Apparently, arms were furnished to the New Hampshire party, led by S. W. and D. D. Cone, which settled at Millard City (Junction City); to the Cutter party from Worcester which was captured on the Missouri River and sent back; and to the Stowell party, also from Worcester, which went to Kansas through Iowa and Nebraska as a part of "Lane's Army of the North." On May 30, 1856, Branscomb, who was again acting as secretary during a six weeks' illness of Dr. Webb, wrote to William Barnes, secretary of the New York State Kansas Committee: "Your letter of the 27th inst. to Dr. Webb is received. I answer by request of Dr. Cabot, who has charge of our arms department. We do not think it advisable to send any arms to Kansas at present except in the hands of persons who go,—they are said to be intercepted. We have here 150 rifles and we are trying to get up a company of 150, arming each man with a rifle, revolver and bowie knife. Can you not raise a company of 50, arming them in the same manner, and have them ready to join our party? If you send rifles by men, be sure to have it arranged so that the rifles shall not be carried away from the point of danger. Have the men agree to stay at the order of the commander."[23] Apparently, after the sack of Lawrence, the Emigrant Aid Company reached the point where it was all but ready to come out into the open in the matter of arming the Free State party.

But while the officers of the Company were straining every nerve to arm their friends in Kansas, they were not unmindful of the physical needs of the free-state settlers. They realized fully the force of the axiom that an army fights on its stomach. The day after the destruction of the Free State Hotel, Amos A. Lawrence wrote to J. M. Bunce of Hartford, "... if you are disposed to help on a good cause, there never has been a moment when you could do it with money as well as this, at this very time . . . . There are many brave hearts there, but they have got stomachs near them."[24]

Soon after the Wakarusa War, local committees began to spring up in various parts of the North and to group themselves into state organizations, to furnish relief for the free-state settlers who were reported to be unable, because of the border disturbances, to provide for themselves. By the middle of February, 1856, these committees were raising funds in considerable amounts and sending them to Kansas. Those in New England, and some as far west as Pennsylvania, usually sent their contributions to Dr. Webb, who sent the money to Robinson and the Reverend Ephraim Nute (Unitarian minister in Lawrence) for distribution. Although the Emigrant Aid Company steadfastly refused to render pecuniary aid to prospective settlers, the Executive Committee deemed it entirely proper to take a hand in the relieving of distress. Indeed, the Company may be considered a pioneer in this effort. As early as January 23, 1856, Dr. Webb wrote to Robinson describing the plans of the Company to raise relief funds, but stating that he was not very hopeful because of "an almost incessant call upon, and continued drain from those on whom we mainly rely on all occasions and for all purposes, for two years past." Nevertheless, he authorized Robinson to draw upon him for five hundred dollars for relief of the most urgent cases, in advance of any collections.[25] On February 6 he told Nicholas Brown: ". . . at the present time, besides the demand for rifles, comes a strong appeal for funds to relieve those who suffered much, and in several instances lost their all, during the recent troubles; for this, some thousands of dollars are requisite, and as the case is an urgent one, I have authorized Dr. (now Genl.) Robinson to draw on me for $1,500, trusting that the case will so commend itself to the beneficence of the community as to enable me to meet the draft."[26] A week later he wrote to Moses Emery, Saco, Maine, that the Company was still desirous of getting stock subscriptions, but that relief and defense were more urgent. The Company also desired a large spring migration, but for the moment it was more important to send money.[27] Similar letters went to volunteer workers in other parts of New England and New York.[28]

Mention has already been made of the inclusion of relief as one of the avowed objectives of the financial drives of February and March, 1856, and, to judge not only from letters of Dr. Webb just cited, but also from newspaper accounts of the meetings held,[29] this object appears to have received the major stress. On March 3 Webb wrote to Robinson that the response had been so gratifying that he was able to authorize drafts for an additional thousand dollars ($2,500 in all down to that date). In this same letter he named the towns that so far had sent in contributions and mentioned a number of individual contributors, among whom were A. A. Lawrence, J. M. S. Williams, C. J. Higginson, Edward Winslow, Francis Amory, Le Baron Russell, and R. A. Chapman,—all officers or stockholders of the Emigrant Aid Company.[30] Evidently "those on whom we mainly rely" were still willing to rise to the occasion.

It was the original intention to keep the relief work entirely separate from both the rifle fund and Company business, but as conditions in Kansas became more acute, first unearmarked donations and finally Company funds were diverted to this purpose. On April 21, 1856, Dr. Webb replied to a letter of William H.

Hewes, who had sent fifty dollars expressly for rifles and fifty-two dollars to be used for rifles "or any other way thought best," that he had turned the fifty dollars over to Dr. Cabot, but had decided to appropriate the other fifty-two to relief work.[31] Finally, just after the raid on Lawrence, Anson J. Stone wrote to Pomeroy, on behalf of Dr. Webb, who was ill: "Inasmuch as you will find it inconvenient to locate the mills at present, you are hereby authorized to draw on the undersigned and lend to the settlers from three to five thousand dollars. Money to aid the settlers will be raised at once in the States and sent to them. Be encouraged and you will have help."[32] There is nothing to show whether or not this money was later returned to the Company treasury from funds donated for relief purposes; certainly it was never returned by the settlers to whom it was lent. This relief work continued on into the summer and gradually merged into the National Kansas Relief Movement which will be discussed in a later chapter.

During these same months the Company was plodding along as best it could with its development projects in Kansas. As fast as money came in from stock sales, it was expended on the work in the territory, chiefly the completion of the Free State Hotel and the construction of buildings for the mills. In January the work on the hotel had come to almost a dead stop for lack of funds,* but as the financial drive began to meet with success, the construction was pushed ahead. As noted previously, the building was just completed and ready for its public opening when it was destroyed on the fateful twenty-first of May. During the winter it was looked upon as a citadel of defense by the people of Lawrence. In January, when an attack was expected daily, the hotel was garrisoned and used as military headquarters. One correspondent wrote to his paper: "Gen. Robinson does not sleep at his own house, but takes his quarters here in this fortress, and sleeps sometimes in my room, while a company of soldiers are

---

* On January 12, 1856, Robinson, who was in charge of the work on the hotel, wrote that he must stop work at once unless more money was forthcoming (Aid Company Records, Book II, 30-31).

quartered in another nearby. The roof of the building, three stories in height, has a parapet running all around it, pierced with loopholes from which, in a street fight, there could be poured a most destructive volley of rifle balls."[33] It is small wonder that pro-slavery men came to believe that the hotel had been built by the Emigrant Aid Company expressly as a fort, and to execrate it accordingly. Indeed, while it is virtually certain that no such purpose entered into the original plans or was ever intended by the Executive Committee, it falls well within the range of probability that Pomeroy and Robinson, who alternately directed the construction, may have modified some details of the original plan with a view of increasing the utility of the building for defense,—especially in the matter of the portholes in the parapet of the roof.

At the beginning of 1856 much needed to be done for the mills. The Manhattan mill was in operation under a temporary shelter,[34] but the Osawatomie mill could not be set to work because money was not available to purchase a smokestack and grates.[35] The mill assigned to Hampden had not even been assembled; a part of the machinery had been sent as far as Osawatomie, but the rest of it was still stored in Kansas City. About the first of January the boiler of the Lawrence mill burst, putting the mill out of commission. About two months later Pomeroy, on authorization of the Executive Committee, bought one of the boilers of the steamboat *Hartford,* which had burned near Manhattan, and installed it in the Lawrence mill.[36] Some time in February the Osawatomie mill was finally put into operation, but the Hampden mill, moved across the Neosho River to Burlington, did not get under way for another year. Much additional machinery had to be purchased for the mills. In February three hundred dollars' worth of saws were bought and paid for in stock.[37] There is frequent mention of the purchase of belting and other supplies. Early in April Pomeroy bought from Nathan Haskins (the same man who had furnished the Manhattan, Osawatomie, and Hampden mills) three additional mills.[38] One of these, a large mill of highest quality, designated "Class A," was intended for Lawrence to replace the old mill there that was constantly breaking down.[39] Of the two smaller, styled "Class B," one was intended for the C. B. Lines ("Beecher's Bible Rifle") colony, wherever it might settle, and the other was to be located by Pomeroy wherever he might see fit.[40] These mills were shipped to Kansas City,[41] but by the time they arrived there conditions in Kansas had become so chaotic that it was deemed inexpedient to attempt to set them up and, as already noted, the money intended for that purpose was used for relief activities.

The Company received numerous applications from individuals for aid in various ventures. E. B. Whitman, the former subscription agent, wanted the Company to enter into a sort of partnership arrangement with certain parties to erect sawmills in Kansas.[42] One C. C. Andrews besought the Company to sponsor the publication of his book, *Six Months in Kansas*.[43] Several applied for employment as lecturers on Kansas.[44] One man wanted to sell to the Emigrant Aid Company the Kansas and Nebraska rights to a new "wind engine" he had invented,[45] while another sought "pecuniary aid" to "bring into the lists against the Slavocracy" certain sawmill machinery he had invented or improved.[46] At least one man asked the Company to employ him as a teacher in Kansas,[47] and at least one other desired Dr. Webb's office to cash his Kansas scrip.[48] Any number asked for loans to go into business in Kansas, while two applied for loans to start free-state newspapers. Although the Company rejected all these applications, this did not indicate any hostility to private business in Kansas. Dr. Webb wrote to a man who was considering the establishment of a sawmill there strongly encouraging him,[49] and several letters to the agents instructed them to encourage individuals to make the local improvements desired by the settlers.

After the burning of the *Hartford*, whose owners had planned to put it into regular service between Manhattan and Kansas City,

[171]

pleas came in from several quarters for the Emigrant Aid Company to establish a steamboat line on the Kansas River. Some consideration was given to the plan of purchasing a boat outright.[50] Finally, at a special meeting of the Executive Committee on April 30, it was voted to authorize a loan of three thousand dollars to citizens of Kansas for the establishment of a boat line, provided ten thousand more could be secured elsewhere;[51] but when pandemonium broke loose in Kansas after the sack of Lawrence, the order was rescinded.[52]

During the first months of 1856 the Emigrant Aid Company appears to have made greater efforts than at any previous time to stimulate emigration to Kansas, and particularly to encourage the formation of emigrant parties in the various localities. The Company refused many requests to establish recruiting agencies or branch offices,[53] but Dr. Webb did a great deal of letter writing and sent out quantities of pamphlets. Letters of inquiry poured in by dozens, and for three weeks straight Webb reported to each weekly meeting of the executive Committee that he had received around sixty such letters during the preceding week.* He corresponded with a number of persons regarding the organizing of parties.[54] In each case he supplied them with pamphlets, and in several instances he arranged for public meetings to be addressed by Pomeroy or one of the free-state delegation.[55] Often it is impossible to tell whether or not these parties materialized but the evidence is fairly conclusive that at least half a dozen parties, which migrated to Kansas during the first six months of 1856, were organized with more or less assistance from persons connected directly with the Emigrant Aid Company, were supplied with tickets by Dr. Webb, and, in several instances, were

---

* The numbers reported were: March 22, 61; March 29, 64; April 5, 58 (Aid Company Records, Book II, 90, 93, 95). No doubt the letters continued to come in in comparable numbers, but during the six weeks of Dr. Webb's illness, from the middle of April until early in June, the minutes of the Executive Committee are very sketchy, and no correspondence of any kind is noted.

armed by Dr. Cabot.* The first of these of which anything definite is known was a small party of young men (the number is nowhere mentioned) organized at Worcester by Dr. Calvin Cutter, which accompanied David Starr Hoyt when he undertook to carry the rifles to Kansas. They reached Kansas early in March—minus the rifles.[56] The next was a party of about forty[57] from Exeter, New Hampshire, led by a Mr. Cole, which left Boston on April 2, intending to settle on Mill Creek near Wabaunsee.[58] They must have changed their plans and gone elsewhere, as there is no record of their having settled in that locality. The C. B. Lines colony from New Haven, forty-nine strong, started late in March or early April[59] and, as previously mentioned, reached Wabaunsee, their place of settlement, on April 28.[60] This party was always called the "Beecher's Bible Rifle Colony," because Henry Ward Beecher raised, in his congregation, the money to present each member of the party with a Bible and to pay a large share of the cost of equipping each of them with a Sharps rifle. It was from this incident that the Sharps rifle acquired its popular nickname of "Beecher's Bible." Lines had been assisted in the organization of his party by Thayer[61] and H. A. Wilcox, at the time a subscription agent of the Emigrant Aid Company, and had received much advice from Dr. Webb.[62] There was a great deal of correspondence with S. C. and D. D. Cone, who were organizing a party in New Hampshire to settle at Millard City (the present Junction City), where a settlement had already been begun by a group from Cincinnati.[63] Webb sent Emery of the Kansas delegation to assist with the recruiting,[64] and apparently furnished the tickets. The party was scheduled to leave on April 22, but the departure was postponed.[65] There is some indication that the party left Boston on May 6.[66] At all events, the Cones reached the territory and started a newspaper at Millard City.[67] The second party of Dr. Calvin Cutter, forty-two in number, which

---

* Much more definite information in regard to these parties, at least the number of tickets supplied them would be available if the Aid Company Emigrant Books, covering the period from April, 1855, to April, 1856, were not missing.

[173]

was disarmed and turned back on its way through Missouri, was ticketed by Dr. Webb,[68] as was Martin Stowell's "Worcester Party" of thirty-one which left Massachusetts on June 30, and entered Kansas through Iowa and Nebraska.[69]

In spite of all efforts to stimulate migration, the numbers who appeared for the regular Tuesday parties were disappointingly small—so small, indeed, that after the middle of April Dr. Webb ceased to send conductors with them, but merely sold individual tickets to such as appeared.[70] The first regular party left Boston on March 18.[71] The number is nowhere mentioned, but it must have been small, for two days later Webb wrote to Hale, "The cold weather dampens the ardor of settlers bound for Kansas at present. We shall not get under full headway before April."[72] For the next two months an effort was made to send a party each Tuesday. The group that left on March 25 must have been small also, since the weather continued cold, and Dr. Webb always reported the number to the Executive Committee when it was large. The party scheduled for April 1 was postponed a day to accommodate the delegation from New Hampshire; it numbered thirty-eight.[73] On April 8 twenty-six were sent.[74] The largest party of the season, numbering fifty-three when it left Boston, started on April 15. It received twelve accessions at Albany, sent by the New York State Kansas Committee, and several at Rochester, raised by D. R. Anthony.[75] The next week only four appeared.[76] As nearly as can be determined, the numbers for the rest of the spring season were: April 29, nine; May 6, four; May 13, fourteen; May 20, three; May 27, one.[77] On May 8 Dr. Webb wrote to Professor Silliman: "Emigration thus far this year is not so great as anticipated, and not nearly so great as for the same time last season. This is due in part, perhaps, to the backwardness of the season, but it is due mainly to rumors (from pro-slavery sources) of unsettled conditions in Kansas."[78] He was undoubtedly mistaken in assigning all the rumors to pro-slavery sources, but there can be little question that the stories that found

[174]

their way into New England newspapers telling of threatening war and of the hardships and disappointments of settlers had a depressing effect on migration.[79]

But the smallness of the emigrant parties was by no means Dr. Webb's only worry in connection with the passenger-forwarding business. He continued to have difficulties with the St. Louis forwarding agency. During the summer of 1855 B. Slater, who down to that time had handled the Company's business in St. Louis, joined the firm of F. A. Hunt & Co. as a partner, and Webb transferred the Emigrant Aid Company business to that firm. But as in his earlier relations with Slater, he was never able to reach a satisfactory agreement as to commissions.[80] In the spring of 1856, the partnership between Slater and Hunt was dissolved, and each, in an effort to get the Company business, wrote letters to Webb charging the other with dishonesty.[81] In April, Webb quarreled with Hunt about charging for negotiating drafts, and scolded him for addressing letters on Company business to Branscomb or Webb personally.[82] Hunt was unable to make the usual contracts with steamboat owners to carry Emigrant Aid Company parties at reduced fares, so that in March Branscomb was sent to St. Louis to negotiate such contracts. He returned about the middle of April, having failed in his mission.[83] In consequence, Dr. Webb was unable to sell tickets beyond St. Louis. About the time that Branscomb returned, Hunt wrote that he could no longer obtain from the steamboat captains the customary free passes for the conductors of parties. Dr. Webb insisted that, this being the case, Hunt & Co. should pay the fares of the conductors, since they received a bonus of fifty cents per passenger from the boat captains.[84] It is not recorded how this controversy was adjusted. This unwillingness of steamboat owners to make concessions was due in part to a scarcity of boats, caused by damage to many of them in the breaking up of the ice, but it may have been due in some measure to the growing "anti-abolitionist" feeling in the river counties of Missouri.[85]

[175]

Dr. Webb had trouble not only with the steamboat owners, but with the railway companies as well. In making agreements with the passenger agents he demanded, in addition to reduced fares for emigrants, a free conductor's pass out and back with each fifty tickets, free transportation for officers and permanent agents whenever on Company business, and the privilege of sending a trunk or package free at any time.[86] At the beginning of the season, the railways west of Buffalo met these conditions and granted a 25 per cent reduction to emigrant parties, but the eastern roads refused to grant even the customary reductions.[87] In attempting to secure such reductions on the eastern lines, Dr. Webb worked in close co-operation with William Barnes, secretary of the New York State Kansas Committee, who undertook to negotiate with the New York roads while Webb concentrated his efforts on those of New England.

This New York State Kansas Committee grew out of a local Kansas Aid Committee, appointed at a mass meeting in Albany, on February 18, 1856. This local commitee invited selected persons from all parts of the state to a meeting at Albany on March 13, at which time the Albany committee, with the addition of a few outside names, was transformed into the New York State Kansas Committee.[88] As originally organized, the officers were: Bradford R. Wood, president; H. H. Van Dyck and M. McGowan, vice presidents; William Barnes, secretary; and C. P. Williams, Treasurer.[89] An office was opened at once in Albany with Barnes in charge. A few weeks later a branch office was established in New York City in charge of I. L. Wilde, a member of the Committee, in conjunction with the New York Kansas League.[90] The plan of the Committee was to raise money by subscription for the relief and arming of the free-state settlers in Kansas, and to organize emigrant parties and secure for them reduced rates of transportation. Unlike the Emigrant Aid Company, it had no investment features.

Shortly after the formation of the Committee, Barnes wrote

[176]

to Dr. Webb requesting a supply of his pamphlet, *Information for Kansas Emigrants*. Receiving a favorable reply and a hundred pamphlets,[91] Barnes wrote again proposing active co-operation with the Emigrant Aid Company. To this Webb replied, on April 4, that since the two organizations had the same objects, the Emigrant Aid Company would be "happy at all times to co-operate," and asked Barnes to undertake the negotiations with the New York Central Railway.[92] From this time until the end of 1856, Webb and Barnes were in constant communication. Webb furnished Barnes with supplies of his pamphlet and with railway tickets, and frequently routed the Company parties via Albany to accommodate Barnes's recruits. It might almost be said that the office of the New York State Kansas Committee was a branch office of the Emigrant Aid Company. The New York Committee employed a number of local agents to recruit emigrants. A form receipt, issued by these local agents to their recruits when fares were collected, agreed to furnish the holder a ticket to Kansas City "under the direction of the New England Emigrant Aid Company."[93]

The annual stockholders' meeting of the Emigrant Aid Company occurred on May 27, 1856. The tone of the meeting was most optimistic. Although news of the destruction of the Free State Hotel had just reached Boston, no mention of this fact found its way into the minutes of the meeting. Indeed, but for incidental mention in one of the resolutions, there is nothing to suggest that the Company had suffered any reverses in Kansas. The treasurer's report showed $102,243.63 received to date ($98,-940.00 from stock subscriptions, $3,303.63 from donations), and $96,956.01 expended, leaving $5,287.62 cash on hand.[94] This report took no account of money received from the sale of tickets, nor of that which passed through the relief fund and the rifle fund. The same officers were re-elected: John Carter Brown, president; Williams and Thayer, vice presidents; Amos A. Lawrence, treasurer; Dr. Webb, secretary. Most of the members of the Board of

Directors were re-elected;[95] a few who had not taken an active interest in the affairs of the Company, or who declined to serve longer, were dropped, and enough were added to bring the total number up to thirty-seven. Among those added were: S. G. Howe, George B. Upton, and Patrick T. Jackson, all of Boston; Edward Everett Hale, Worcester; William Cullen Bryant and William M. Evarts, New York City; Horace B. Claflin, Brooklyn.[96] Resolutions were adopted expressing indignation at and denial of Stephen A. Douglas's report in the United States Senate; thanking Senators Charles Sumner and Henry Wilson and the various members of the House of Representatives for their defense of the Emigrant Aid Company in Congress; expressing sympathy for the free-state settlers in Kansas who had suffered from "the outrages of the slave power"; and declaring the intention of the Company to continue its efforts unaltered despite temporary reverses.[97]

At the quarterly meeting of the directors, held immediately upon the adjournment of the stockholders' meeting, the Executive Committee for the ensuing year was elected. Except for the substitution of William B. Spooner for John Lowell, who was dropped because of his unwillingness to sign the pending memorial to Congress, and the addition of Edward Everett Hale, the Committee was the same as for the previous year; it consisted of Williams, Spooner, Thayer, Cabot, Waters, Russell, Higginson, and Hale.[98]

As indicated by the resolutions of the annual meeting, everyone connected with the Emigrant Aid Company was deeply incensed by the aspersions cast upon the Company by President Pierce's Kansas message and by Douglas's report in the Senate. Shortly after the delivery of the President's message, R. A. Chapman of Springfield, a director of the Company,* in introducing Pomeroy to a mass meeting of his fellow townsmen, made a

---

* At this time, Chapman was a prominent lawyer of Springfield. During the Civil War he became an associate justice of the Massachusetts Supreme Court. Later he became its chief justice (*National Encyclopedia of America Biography*, VII, 507).

[178]

spirited defense of the Company which was published widely in the eastern newspapers.[99] The day after the presentation of Douglas's report in the Senate, Charles Sumner wrote a letter to Edward Everett Hale in which he suggested that the Emigrant Aid Company prepare a reply to Douglas's charges and present it to the Senate as a memorial.[100] On March 15 Hale presented this letter to the Executive Committee, and, since Chapman had already taken up the cudgel, they turned to him with a request that he prepare such a memorial.[101] About the first week in April he sent in a rough draft, and Dr. Webb and Dr. Russell were appointed a committee to put it into final form. When their draft was completed, a few copies were struck off and sent to various directors for suggestions.[102] Numerous alterations were suggested. For several weeks the Executive Committee devoted much time to discussion of the memorial and consideration of alternative proposals. At the time of the annual meeting, they had not yet agreed upon a final form. About the middle of June it was decided, at the suggestion of Dr. S. G. Howe, to use the Chapman-Russell draft as a basis, but to summarize its content in fewer words; Russell and Higginson were appointed a committee to effect this revision. Finally, on June 21, their draft was completed, signed by five members of the Executive Committee,* and sent to Pomeroy in Washington to be delivered to Senator Wilson and Representative Damrell.[103] On June 25, 1857, Wilson presented the memorial in the Senate. It replied point by point to the allegations of the Douglas report, denying or refuting each charge, and closed with a prayer to Congress to protect the property of the Company, and to compensate it for losses sustained because of the lack of federal protection.[104] At the same time that the final revision was decided

---

* All signed but Thayer, Waters, and Hale. Thayer refused to sign because an alternative draft, offered by him, had been rejected. Waters and Hale apparently were not in Boston and it was deemed inexpedient to delay longer until their signatures could be obtained. John Lowell, of the old Executive Committee, refused to sign because he was unwilling, as a Hunker Whig, to have his name published in conjunction with the names of men reputed to be radicals and abolitionists. A. A. Lawrence and John Carter Brown were also asked to sign, but, although they approved of the document, for a similar reason they objected to having their names on it (Lawrence Letters, 141-42).

upon, the Executive Committee voted to print the original Chapman-Russell document for distribution under the title, "Address to the People of the United States."[105] This "Address," printed as a four-page three-column circular, was distributed widely.[106] It was copied and quoted extensively in the newspapers, and was introduced as testimony in the Howard investigation.[107] It may be considered the official statement by the Emigrant Aid Company of its purposes and methods of operation.

Thus, during the trying months when "war to the knife" was breaking out in Kansas and in Congress, the Emigrant Aid Company stood behind the lines striving to act as a service of supply for those on the firing line; while in the national arena, with the whole power of the federal administration pitted against it, it stood at Armageddon and battled for the Lord.

CHAPTER X

Knife to the Hilt

T HE SACK OF LAWRENCE, on May 21, 1856, was the signal for the outbreak of a civil war in Kansas, which was to last intermittently for nearly four months, until Geary should bring peace. Judged by the number of men engaged and the number of casualties, it was petty warfare indeed; but judged by its consequences, it was far more important than many a conflict waged on a much grander scale. The strength of the "armies" was numbered in dozens, not thousands, and the "battles" were the merest skirmishes, often only minutes in duration. Yet this "border war" presented to the nation the phenomenon of "bleeding Kansas," which drove a wedge between the sections that could be extricated only on the greater and more sanguinary battlefields of the great Civil War. And, petty as it may appear, this was real war. The combatants grappled in deadly earnest. The tiny armies marched, entrenched, and battled in mortal combat; guerrillas plundered; towns were sacked; prisoners were taken and exchanged. During the preceding months there had been threatening, drilling, maneuvering for position; but now there was literally "war to the knife and knife to the hilt."

Deprived of their leaders and divided in council, the free-state men of Lawrence had submitted tamely enough to the "posse" of Marshal Donaldson, but this did not mean that they would submit with equal docility to bands of marauders who were equipped with federal authority. Indeed, while the ruins of the Free State Hotel were still smoking, there were formed in and about Lawrence bands of free-state guerrillas who were determined to have an eye for an eye and a tooth for a tooth—or, if possible, two eyes for an eye and a whole mouthful of teeth. Some who joined these predatory bands were, of course, mere unscrupulous adventurers who used the unsettled state of affairs as pretext for indiscriminate plunder. But many of them were young men of sincere purpose who had lost their cabins, their jobs, or their crops at the hands of the pro-slavery "posses" and were out for revenge; deprived of their livelihood, they were going to live off the enemy.[1] One of the most notable and most aggressive of these bands was led by a young man named Charles Lenhart, who had been a printer on the *Herald of Freedom* and who had lost his job because of the destruction of the printing plant in the Lawrence raid. Before all of the companies that had composed Donaldson's force had retired from the vicinity of Lawrence, some of them were "bushwhacked" by Lawrence guerrillas, a number of their horses being stolen. Throughout the summer, with some abatement during July, these bands roved the territory, "bushwhacking"* organized pro-slavery forces, robbing stores and homes of pro-slavery men, maltreating and sometimes murdering individuals, and committing miscellaneous acts of depredation.† It was inevitable that pro-slavery men should retaliate in kind. Within a few weeks the whole territory was in a state of anarchy, with no person or property safe.

But while the forays of these brigands of both parties formed the background of the war, its specific beginning is to be found in the episode commonly known as the Pottawatomie massacre, on May 24, 1856. There are several diverse and contradictory accounts of the affair, but the one now commonly accepted, based on the confession of one of the participants, is as follows:[2] On May 20, when Lawrence was threatened, the Pottawatomie Rifle Company, with John Brown, Jr., as captain, started from Osawatomie to aid in the defense of Lawrence. Reaching the site of Ottawa (then called "Ottawa" Jones's place) on the morning of the twenty-second, they heard that Lawrence had been destroyed,

---

* A term in common use on the border. It meant attacking from ambush and disappearing before the attacked could defend themselves.

† A little later, such bands operating in southeast Kansas were termed "Jayhawkers." Several explanations of the origin of the name have appeared, none of which can be authenticated.

[182]

and went into camp for the day, undecided whether to go on or return. During the day, Old John Brown, so called to distinguish him from his son of the same name, took four of his sons—Frederick, Owen, Watson, and Oliver—his son-in-law, Henry Thompson, Theodore Weiner, and James Townsley, and started for Pottawatomie Creek, telling his men that trouble was expected there. Reaching that locality the next day, Brown revealed his plan, which was to kill every pro-slavery man along the creek. He asked Townsley, who lived in the vicinity, to point out where each pro-slavery man lived; when Townsley, according to his own story, refused to do so, Brown said he would go where he knew there were pro-slavery men. That night, May 24, the party went along the creek and called from their cabins five men: James P. Doyle and his two sons, Allen Wilkinson, and William Sherman. John Brown shot Doyle through the head; the other four men were hacked to death with swords by Brown's sons. Two other men were sought for slaughter, but could not be found.[3] At the time, Brown was generally suspected of responsibility for the act; he denied participation in the affair, but said he approved of it. At first most of the free-state leaders were inclined to justify the killing as necessary, but later when the facts became known, nearly all of them denounced it as wanton murder.

Several theories have been advanced as to the purpose of the massacre. Many free-state people regarded it as an act of reprisal for the sack of Lawrence and the killing of free-state men. Those close to Brown explained that the men killed had been particularly aggressive in threatening the free-state settlers in the neighborhood, and were the center of a conspiracy to drive them all out of the territory; Brown's admirers have always claimed that the blow saved the free-state settlers in the locality from extermination. The most likely hypothesis is that it was an act of sheer terrorism, calculated to frighten all pro-slavery people of the region into quiescence, or even to scare them out of Kansas.

There has been a tendency in some quarters to hold the Emigrant Aid Company responsible for Brown's presence in Kansas, and hence indirectly for the massacre. Edward Everett Hale stated that Brown made the Company office his headquarters whenever he was in the East.[4] It was Amos A. Lawrence who paid his fare when he first went to Kansas,[5] and gave him a letter of introduction to Robinson.[6] Lawrence later corresponded with Brown extensively, gave him money on several occasions,[7] and presented him with a share of stock in the Emigrant Aid Company.[8] Thayer carried on an extensive correspondence with Brown, and arranged for him to speak at Kansas meetings.[9] Other officers of the Company contributed money to him from time

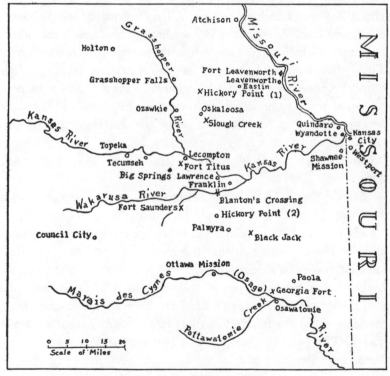

Scene of the Kansas Conflict

[184]

to time.[10] Still, Brown was never an employee of the Company, and its officers, who unwittingly aided him with money in the belief that he was just another antislavery crusader battling for the cause, had no knowledge of the insidious character of some of his activities.

Although Brown's apologists have consistently defended the Pottawatomie massacre as a telling blow for freedom, there can be little doubt that on the whole the consequences were unfortunate for the free-state cause. Certain it is that the act provoked reprisals on the part of pro-slavery men, and that harrowing accounts of it loomed large in the pro-slavery propaganda. Moreover the massacre sent a feeling of revulsion throughout the North which reflected unfavorably upon the whole Free State party, and served to counteract in a measure the effect produced on Northern feelings by Brooks's attack upon Senator Sumner, which occurred at about the same time.[11]

After the sack of Lawrence, Captain Henry Clay Pate and his company of territorial (pro-slavery) militia remained at Franklin, near Lawrence. When he heard of the Pottawatomie massacre, Pate started for Osawatomie to capture or kill "Old Brown." Failing to find Brown, he arrested two of his sons, John Brown, Jr., and Jason Brown, whom he sent in custody of United States dragoons to Lecompton. Returning north, Pate encamped on Black Jack Creek, six miles east of Palmyra (the present Baldwin), from which point detachments of his company raided the villages of Palmyra and Prairie City on Sunday, June 1, taking two or three prisoners. Later in the same day, John Brown appeared in Prairie City with ten men and, joined by Captain Samuel T. Shore's company of nineteen, started in search of Pate. The next morning about ten o'clock, they found and attacked his camp. After three hours of gun play, Pate surrendered with twenty-eight men, the rest of his company, variously estimated at from fifty to eighty, having escaped. Thus, instead of capturing or killing "Old Brown," Pate had been captured by him.

[185]

This "Battle of Black Jack" was the first open fight of the Kansas war.[12]

On the night of June 4-5, an attack was made by the "Stubbs" company from Lawrence on the blockhouse at Franklin. The plan had been for a concerted attack by the "Stubbs" and Captain Abbott's Wakarusa company,* but Abbott's men, having lost their way in the darkness, were unable to join in the fight and contented themselves with appropriating a wagon-load of provisions belonging to Buford's Alabama company. The object of the raid was to capture a brass cannon that was in possession of the pro-slavery men. This cannon, called "Old Sacramento" because it had been captured by Colonel Doniphan in the battle of Sacramento during the Mexican War, had been stolen from the United States arsenal at Liberty, Missouri, and had been used by Sheriff Jones in the sack of Lawrence. Having surrendered their "Abbott howitzer" on that fatal day two weeks before, the free-state men were entirely without artillery, and they took this means to attempt to recoup their loss. The assault began about midnight, and the firing was continued until dawn, when the attack was abandoned for fear of intervention by federal troops. Six of the defenders were wounded, one of them dying of his wounds. None of the attackers was hurt.[13]

"Old Sacramento," which the Lawrence men failed to capture until two months later, was desired for use in a much greater battle that was expected to take place soon in the vicinity of Palmyra. On hearing of the Pottawatomie massacre, J. W. Whitfield, the territorial delegate to Congress, who had just left the Howard Committee at Leavenworth, collected a force of two or three hundred men in the vicinity of Westport for the purpose of hunting down John Brown. He entered Kansas at about the time of "the Battle of Black Jack" and on June 3 encamped on

---

* This was the same James B. Abbott who had brought the rifles and howitzer from the East the fall preceding. He was captain of a small company of settlers living along the Wakarusa south of Lawrence. This company was armed with some of the rifles he had obtained in Boston.

Bull Creek, about twelve miles east of Palmyra. At once the free-state clans began to gather about Palmyra, and by June 5 some two hundred men had assembled to oppose Whitfield. On that date Whitfield moved his force to within two miles of the nearest free-state company, and a battle seemed imminent. At this juncture Colonel Sumner arrived on the scene with a regiment of federal dragoons, accompanied by Deputy Marshal Fain, and at once interposed his force between the opposing "armies." The day before, Governor Shannon, becoming alarmed, had issued a proclamation ordering all armed bands to disperse and, under the authority granted to him by the Secretary of War, had called out the federal troops to enforce the proclamation. Visiting each free-state company in turn, Colonel Sumner read the proclamation and ordered them to disperse; whereupon, in the words of the Andreas history, "they disbanded sufficiently to be invisible, if they did not go home."[14] John Brown surrendered his Black Jack prisoners to Colonel Sumner, who released them at once on their promise to disband. Going next to "General" Whitfield's camp, Sumner ordered the Missourians to disband and leave the territory. Whitfield promised to obey the order, and immediately broke camp.[15]

The battle had been averted, but there was a sequel to the story. Colonel Sumner, either trusting the promises of the leaders to disband or feeling that, having executed his orders, his responsibility was ended, left only a small detachment under Major Sedgwick in the vicinity, and returned to Fort Leavenworth. As Whitfield's force proceeded slowly toward the Missouri border, they took several prisoners in violation of the promise made to Colonel Sumner, at least one of whom, a man named Cantrel, was killed.[16] A portion of the troop detoured southward, and on the afternoon of June 6 surprised and raided the town of Osawatomie. Not expecting an attack and relying on Major Sedgwick's force for protection, the village was entirely defenseless. It is not certain whether or not Whitfield was with the raiders. Accounts

[187]

differ, too, as to the extent of the damage, some saying that houses were fired, others denying it. At least, stores and houses were looted and horses were taken. The Emigrant Aid Company's mill was saved by the miller, Charles Cranston, who persuaded the raiders that the mill belonged to him. It is impossible to say to what extent the raid was motivated by a mere desire for pillage, to what extent it was in retaliation for Brown's activities, or to what extent it was an act of war against the free-state element in general.[17]

For the next few weeks all strategic points were guarded by federal troops, and the excitement died down somewhat, although marauding bands of both pro-slavery and free-state guerrillas continued their depredations to whatever extent they were able to elude the federal soldiers. The Free State Legislature, elected under the Topeka constitution, was scheduled to meet in Topeka on July 4. It was the threat, and apparently the intention, of the pro-slavery leaders to attack the legislature and arrest its members. To defend it against such an attack the Free State party planned to mass about two thousand armed men in Topeka in the guise of a mass convention. But both plans miscarried. In the face of the approaching Presidential election, the federal administration felt constrained to take a hand. To permit the legislature to be broken up by mob violence, or to permit a major battle to be fought in its defense, would materially injure the Democratic prospects in the North. On the other hand, to permit it to meet under the protection of federal troops (for only the presence of troops could afford an adequate safeguard against mob attack) would appear in the South to be countenancing abolitionist revolution, and that was unthinkable. Accordingly, word seems to have been passed down to Governor Shannon to use the troops to prevent the meeting of the legislature, but to proceed without violence. The plan worked. When July 4 arrived, Sumner was on hand with a regiment of dragoons. The mass convention dwindled to a few hundred men, most of them unarmed.* At the appointed hour the House of Representatives convened, but failed to muster a quorum. Members of the Senate came together, but were not called to order. To each Colonel Sumner made a short speech regretting the necessity for his action, but declaring that they must disperse. There was no attempt at resistance and, apparently, no ill feeling.[18]

The events of July 4 led to a considerable feeling of exasperation on the part of free-state people generally, and this, according to Andreas, was a factor in their decision to renew the war.[19] Throughout the North, too, there was a feeling of revulsion against the Pierce administration. To counteract this sentiment, the authorities at Washington endeavored to throw the onus of the affair on Colonel Sumner. The act was disavowed; Colonel Sumner was reprimanded by Secretary of War Davis,[20] and almost immediately was superseded in the command of Fort Leavenworth.† It is not unlikely that this reaction to the dispersal of the Free State Legislature hastened the decision of the administration to send Geary to Kansas with instructions to restore peace at any price.

While the pro-slavery men in Kansas, reinforced by the recruits from across the border, were waging war in Kansas, their allies in Missouri were endeavoring to aid them by cutting the free-state line of communications along the Missouri River. The conventional accounts by free-state sympathizers all declare that the river was effectually blocked against all free-state immigrants and against all freight consigned to persons of known free-state views. Some persons, on the other hand, have held that the river was never really closed to free-state immigration and that, while

---

* The main reason the free-state force failed to materialize was the fixed determination of the more responsible leaders never to resist federal authority. Another reason was that, with their foremost leaders in prison or out of the Territory and their newspapers silenced, it was impossible to rally the Free State party in force.

† Some historians have concluded that Sumner was removed as a political scapegoat, but apparently the War Department had already determined to replace Sumner, for General Smith reached Fort Leavenworth July 7, and must have left St. Louis at least three weeks earlier.

[189]

a few blustering individuals may have been turned back, the blockade story was essentially a fabrication for propaganda purposes.* Although, as usual, the truth lies between the two extremes, the former view appears to be more nearly correct than the latter.

Since the spring of 1855, various pro-slavery meetings and conventions in Missouri had been protesting against the use of steamboats, owned by Missourians, in carrying the "hirelings" of the Emigrant Aid Company, and had urged the boycotting of boats and merchants who catered to "abolitionists"; but prior to May or June of 1856, this clamor had produced little, if any, effect. Just before the election of March 20, 1855, a few boats may have "flirted with sandbars" to delay their free-state passengers until after the election,[21] but in general the boats had competed lustily for the traffic. At times there were threats and bluster by pro-slavery passengers, matched, if not prompted, by the boasts and bluster of the free-staters; but except to make it a pretext for their doings in the territory, neither side appears to have taken this swagger very seriously before the spring of 1856. When it became known that arms were being sent out from the East, parties sometimes boarded the boats at Lexington and other strongly pro-slavery river towns and ransacked baggage in search of such "contraband"; but until the seizure of the Hoyt rifles in March, 1856, this had resulted in nothing more than annoyance to the free-state people. When the C. B. Lines party ascended the river in April, they reported that they were "threatened by the Border Ruffians" at Lexington and Kansas City, but they were not actually molested.[22]

But as the excitement in Kansas grew more intense during April and May, the Missourians along the river became more

---

* R. G. Elliot, himself a free-state man (editor of the *Kansas Free State*), but a severe critic of Robinson, G. W. Brown, and all others connected with the Emigrant Aid Company, ridiculed the idea of a blockade of the Missouri River, but virtually admitted that such a blockade was maintained during the war of 1856 (R. G. Elliott, *Foot Notes on Kansas History*, 9-13). Professors F. H. Hodder and J. C. Malin, of the University of Kansas, have expressed doubts as to whether the blockade was ever as complete as is represented.

and more threatening, laying violent hands on passengers and baggage with increasing frequency. Still, although some free-state settlers were driven from Kansas and some individuals were probably frightened into abandoning their trip up the river, there is no notice of the turning back of any organized party before the sack of Lawrence. On May 24, however, four days after the Lawrence raid, "eight families with twelve teams, from Illinois, were stopped in Platte [County] on their way to Kansas, and were sent to Clay [County] where they were provided with homes."[23] By the middle of June Dr. Webb had received so many reports of interference with emigrants on their way up the river that he was considering sending the Emigrant Aid Company parties through Iowa.[24] A week later he announced that the route had been established via Iowa City.[25]

After the raid on Lawrence the North burst into flame, and all over the country public meetings were held to raise men, money, and arms for the relief of the Kansas free-state cause. One such meeting, held in Chicago on May 31, was addressed by Lane; a large sum of money and five hundred men were pledged for the aid of Kansas. Flamboyant reports of this meeting and of Lane's speech gave rise on the border to rumors of a great "Army of the North" being recruited by Lane to march into Kansas, drive out all pro-slavery settlers, and set up the Topeka government by force. When, a few weeks later, a party of seventy-five armed men from Chicago, traveling under the auspices of a committee created by this meeting and regarded as the vanguard of Lane's "Army of the North," ascended the Missouri River on the steamboat *Star of the West,* the boat was boarded at Lexington by a large party led by Colonel Joe Shelby, and the Chicago men were disarmed. At Kansas City a bodyguard led by Atchison, B. F. Stringfellow, and Jefferson Buford took the Chicagoans in charge and remained with them until the boat reached its destination, Weston, whereupon, without being permitted to land, the party was sent back to Alton on the same boat.[26]

[191]

A few days later a party of forty-two from Worcester, Massachusetts, captained by Dr. Calvin Cutter, ascending the river on the steamboat *Sultan,* was similarly overhauled at Waverly, Missouri, and there disarmed and turned back.[27] On July 2, Dr. Webb wrote to Professor Twining in regard to these parties:

The surrender of the Chicago party is exceedingly vexatious, as they were strongly urged to avoid the river route, and told they would never be able to pass Lexington in safety. This I have from the adviser; but the advice was unheeded, and the result has proved as predicted. The capture of the second party, that of Dr. Cutter, is still more vexatious. He was directed to take the land route; was furnished with tickets and money accordingly; and yet, for some inexplicable reason, he turned off to Alton, which was bad enough, and then went down to St. Louis and took passage. Of course all this was telegraphed to Lexington, and the robbers and pirates were ready to waylay him. His proceedings in the East had been trumpeted by himself and others, and extensively blazoned abroad. Had he fired a few shots before surrendering I should have thought better of him.[28]

One other party is known to have been disarmed and sent back down the river about the first of July. This was a group of indeterminate size (one account says twenty-five, another fifty) from Ottawa, Illinois, led by "Captain" William Strawn.[29] Other parties may have been turned back, but there is no record of them. Some parties may have been permitted to pass up the river unmolested during July and August, but there is likewise no record of them. There is no way of knowing how many individuals were intercepted and how many got through. Dr. Webb was never convinced that the river was entirely blocked to Northern men, but he considered the route too dangerous for parties or freight. On July 14, he replied to the inquiry of a prospective emigrant that he would ticket him via St. Louis if he wanted to go that way, but that all *parties* were advised to take the land route.[30] On August 12, he answered another inquirer that he was sending all parties through Iowa, but that small groups of two or three could probably use the river route safely.[31] Apparently, there was never a time when an unarmed individual, if he used reasonable discretion, could not enter Kansas by the river route. But whether or not the blockade of the river was airtight, so hazardous was the route regarded that from the first of July until October, no organized party of which there is any record ventured to travel it.

Not only was the river route virtually, if not actually, closed to free-state passengers, but freight consigned to known free-state sympathizers was intercepted, and even the mail was tampered with, though it is likely that most of this was done by pro-slavery guerrillas between Kansas City and Lawrence, rather than on the river itself. From June to October, all Emigrant Aid Company freight and practically all supplies sent by the various relief agencies were sent by the overland route. Dr. Webb did not dare to address letters to the Emigrant Aid Company agents, but sent them to other persons to be turned over to the agents,[32] and even then he was so guarded in what he wrote that it is often difficult to understand the real import of his messages. The last of August, Philip Schuyler wrote William Barnes: "We are now entirely cut off from the frontier, and have only one communication with the States, up through Nebraska and so through Iowa. Our provisions are now entirely cut off. The strife has assumed the aspect of regular war."[33]

When the Chicago and Cutter parties were turned back on the Missouri River, they made their way to Iowa City with a view to entering Kansas by the land route.[34] Iowa City was then the western terminus of the railway in Iowa, and had become the rendezvous of parties planning to enter Kansas by the northern route. Since May, parties who had feared to traverse the Missouri River had been drifting into Iowa City, tarrying awhile, and then making their way across to Nebraska City, where the earlier groups awaited the arrival of later parties so that all might enter Kansas in a body for mutual protection. Late in July there had gathered in the vicinity of Nebraska City fourteen such parties

[193]

or "companies," each with a "captain" or conductor. Most of these parties were from Illinois, Ohio, and Wisconsin; one of them was the Milwaukee party from Wisconsin, captained by Edmund G. Ross, later famous as the United States Senator from Kansas who voted for the acquittal of Andrew Johnson.[35] Besides Dr. Cutter's party, there was another group from Worcester, Massachusetts, led by Martin Stowell, who had come as far as Iowa City on Emigrant Aid Company tickets. Samuel G. Howe and Thaddeus Hyatt, who inspected the assemblage on July 30 on behalf of the National Kansas Committee,* counted (or estimated) the number of individuals in all these parties as 396. Although these "emigrants" were heavily armed and had a semimilitary organization, as was common in all travel through unsettled country, there can be little doubt that the bulk of them were bona fide settlers, though many of them, having started for Kansas under strong excitement, fully expected to take an active part in the struggle. But James H. Lane was with the group and had assumed a sort of general direction of its movements. This fact, coupled with the rumors that had already reached the border, caused these emigrants to be identified in pro-slavery circles with the fabulous "Army of the North" which, a thousand strong, was supposed to be marching into Kansas to defend the Topeka legislature, rescue the prisoners accused of treason, and set up the free-state government by force.[36]

After the dispersal of the Topeka legislature, the pro-slavery people became panicky over the prospect of an invasion by Lane's army, and reports reached Dr. Robinson, in the prison camp near Lecompton, that the "territorial militia" were mustering to intercept Lane's entry into Kansas. Robinson apparently feared that there might ensue a general battle in which the federal troops would reinforce the pro-slavery militia, and so put the free-state men in the impossible position of fighting the United

---

* This National Kansas Committee was organized July 9, 1856, at a convention of emigrant aid organizations at Buffalo, New York. It will be discussed in the next chapter.

States Army. Not only would such an occurrence injure the free-state cause in the North, but it might well lead to the condemnation of the leaders of the Free State party, including Robinson himself, who were under indictment for treason.* Since Robinson was allowed by his jailor, Captain Sackett of the United States Army, to communicate freely with his friends, he at once sent for Samuel Walker, one of the most active leaders of the free-state fighting force, and dispatched him to Nebraska City to prevent the entry of the emigrants into Kansas as an organized body under Lane's command. Walker gathered fifteen men in Lawrence and about thirty more in Topeka and started north. Near the Nebraska line he met John Brown, on his way with a small following to pilot Lane's "army" into Kansas, and the two parties joined forces. At Nebraska City a council of war was held, in which Dr. Howe took an active part; Lane was across the river in Iowa. It was decided that, in view of the prevailing excitement and the stories about Lane's "army," Lane must not enter Kansas with the main body. Walker was able to dissuade Lane and offered to conduct him in ahead of the larger group. Accordingly, they started at once with about thirty men. Brown and his men dropped off just south of the territorial line to await the larger party and help pilot them to Topeka. Others gave out from exhaustion along the way, so that when Walker and Lane reached Topeka late at night on August 1, only four men accompanied them.† Lane rode on to Lawrence the same night, covering the entire 150 miles from Nebraska City in thirty hours.[37]

The main body of the "army" entered Kansas on August 7 under the leadership of M. C. Dickey of Topeka. Small groups separated from the party to found the towns of Plymouth (two miles south of the line), Lexington (near the present site of Sa-

---

* There may be some significance to the fact that Robinson does not mention the incident in his *Kansas Conflict*.

† Holloway, wishing to make the pro-slavery people appear ridiculous, wrote with much emphasis, "Let it be remembered, let it go down in history, that Lane's 'northern army,' which Secretary Woodson telegraphed the President numbered 1000 armed men, and which was so reported over the world, consisted only of six men in disguise" (Holloway, 414).

betha), and Holton. On reaching Topeka, about August 10, many scattered to take claims, though some, including Dr. Cutter and Henry J. Shombre (killed a week later in the fight at Fort Titus), hastened on to Lawrence to take part in the fighting that had broken out.³⁸ Such was Lane's famous "Army of the North," although this name was applied also to another large party that reached Kansas through Nebraska in September under the direction of S. W. Eldridge and Robert Morrow.³⁹

During July the brigandage and bushwhacking continued on both sides, though with less intensity than earlier in the season. In his first report to the Adjutant General, General Percifer F. Smith, who assumed command at Fort Leavenworth July 7, declared, "Lawless people from each [of the opposing parties] are spreading over the country, robbing, and even murdering, and nothing but the display of military force prevents the violent of both sides from resuming their organizations, when most lamentable collisions must follow."⁴⁰ Because, in part at least, of the fears aroused by Lane's approach, the pro-slavery people intensified their efforts to starve out their opponents, so that what at first had been mere irresponsible pillage became the settled policy of the party. Supply trains were raided with increasing regularity, and expeditions sent to the border for supplies by the free-state men were seized and the teamsters imprisoned.⁴¹ All appeals to the governor having proved futile, the free-state men sent a plea directly to General Smith, but he only referred them back to civil authorities.⁴² In fairness to General Smith, it should be stated that he was receiving so many conflicting and exaggerated reports from partisans of the two sides that he refused to credit any of them except such as came from well-authenticated sources; and he declined to use his troops except as requisitioned by the governor in accordance with his orders from Washington. Under the circumstances, the free-state people determined to take matters into their own hands and live off the enemy. On their side too, guerrilla bands were supplemented by regular foraging parties from the towns who raided pro-slavery settlements and robbed pro-slavery merchants.* Thus, by August 1, the irregular warfare had been resumed in all its vigor.

As "cities of refuge" against these free-state raids, and as bases of operations for their own depredations, the pro-slavery forces fortified several strong points in strategic locations. These "forts" consisted of "blockhouses," or large log houses built of heavy timbers with a view to defense, penetrated with apertures for rifle fire, and in some instances surrounded with earthworks. There were four of these that figured prominently in the operations during August. The oldest was the blockhouse at Franklin, which had been attacked unsuccessfully the first of June. Another, built after the raid on Osawatomie, on June 6, was located near that village, and was occupied by a company of Georgians; it was usually called the "Georgia Fort." A third, called "Fort Saunders," was located on Washington Creek, about twelve miles southwest of Lawrence, on the claim of J. P. Saunders; it was built sometime in July, and was garrisoned by a part of Buford's Alabama contingent. The fourth was the house of Henry T. Titus, near Lecompton. Titus was a pro-slavery "colonel" from Florida, and his fortified house was called "Fort Titus."

About August 1 the Free State Committee of Safety was ready to begin field operations. A plea having been received from settlers at Osawatomie for protection against the marauding of the Georgians, an expedition, led by Captain Joseph Cracklin of the Lawrence "Stubbs" company, was sent to attack the Georgia Fort. When the attackers reached the fort on August 5 they found that the garrison had abandoned the blockhouse, along with a considerable store of supplies. The supplies were appropriated and the house was burned.[43]

---

* At first these raids were limited to isolated cabins, farms, and small posts near Lawrence, but about the last of August two such raids were made on Tecumseh (Report of Lieutenant G. B. Anderson, U.S.A., *Kansas Historical Collections,* IV, 489) and in September the settlement around Neosho Rapids was raided (Flora R. Godsey, "The Early Settlement and Raids on the Upper Neosho," *ibid.,* XVI, 451-63).

But the ire of the Lawrence people was directed chiefly against Fort Saunders, from which as a base the farms of the Lawrence neighborhood were plundered, and traffic on the "California Road"* was constantly threatened. But before Fort Saunders could be attacked successfully it was necessary to procure a cannon, and it was desirable also to break up the pro-slavery base at Franklin in order that Lawrence might not suffer during the absence of her defenders. Therefore it was decided to make another midnight raid on Franklin in an effort to capture "Old Sacramento" and to scatter the garrison. On the night of August 12, Captain Cracklin's "Stubbs" company, armed with Sharps rifles, Captain Thomas Bickerton's artillery company, armed with such weapons as they could muster, and a few stray volunteers, eighty-one men in all, entered Franklin and began the attack on the blockhouse. Lane, calling himself "Captain Joe Cook," was present and assumed general command. After several hours of continuous firing, with little effect on either side, someone (Bickerton claimed the credit, and it was also claimed for Lane) hit upon the idea of moving a wagonload of hay up to the blockhouse and setting it afire. The scheme worked, and soon the defenders were crying for quarter. The firing ceased and the blazing hay was drawn aside before any serious damage was done; but before the attacking party could batter down the door and enter the building, most of the defenders had escaped through a connecting cabin operated as a hotel by "Squire" Samuel Crane, postmaster and owner of the blockhouse. Apparently Crane himself was the only prisoner captured, and he was released at once. Several on each side had been wounded. The attackers captured the cannon and eighty United States muskets that had been issued to the territorial militia. They plundered Crane's store and

---

* "The California Road," often mentioned in the writings of the time, was a branch of the Oregon Trail which left the Santa Fe Trail near the present site of Olathe and passed through Franklin, Lawrence, and Topeka on its way to Fort Riley, whence it followed the Republican River into Nebraska, joining the trail from Council Bluffs at Fort Kearney. It was the principal thoroughfare in territorial Kansas.

searched the postoffice, but, according to their own accounts, took nothing from it.[44] A few days later Crane had several of the attackers (all he could recognize) arrested on regular warrants; they were taken to Lecompton and placed in the custody of federal troops, but they were exchanged a day or so later after the capture of Fort Titus.

The same day that the Lawrence men were preparing to attack Franklin, David Starr Hoyt (who had lost the rifles on the Missouri River six months before), now a "major" in the free-state army, went on some kind of a mission, the exact nature of which cannot now be determined, into Fort Saunders.* He appears to have depended upon his Masonic affiliation to protect him. After he left the fort he was killed under circumstances that his friends could only guess. This "murder" of Hoyt (a pro-slavery account, if one were available, would probably say he was executed as a spy) made the free-state men more bitter than ever against the garrison of Fort Saunders, and they could scarcely be restrained from attacking the place until preparations were completed.

The very morning after the battle of Franklin, Lane proceeded with all the force he could gather about Lawrence, except Bickerton's artillery company, to a previously arranged rendezvous on Rock Creek, about three miles from Saunders. Here he met Sam Walker with several companies of the "Army of the North," J. A. Harvey with his Chicago company, Dr. Cutter with his Massachusetts men, Henry Shombre with his Indiana party, and possibly others. Bickerton's small company was delayed a day in Lawrence making ammunition for the cannon. While

---

* Early secondary accounts state that Hoyt went to try to negotiate a cessation of hostilities (Holloway, 379; Andreas, I, 142). Captain Sam Walker, who claimed to have known all the circumstances and to have tried to dissuade Hoyt from going, says he went to reconnoiter (*Kansas Historical Collections*, VI, 268-69). O. P. Kennedy, also present at the capture of Fort Saunders, says that Hoyt went as a spy, making a pretext of having a sack of corn ground at a mill Saunders had, but a footnote to the same article, probably by George W. Martin, asserts that he went "on a friendly mission" (*ibid.*, VII, 530). William Crutchfield, a member of the "Stubbs" company, which took part in the capture, says that the Committee of Safety decided to try arbitration and that Hoyt went on this conciliatory mission (*ibid.*, 532).

some made cartridges by preparing paper containers and filling them with powder, Bickerton, with a few helpers, was casting cannon-balls from type of the *Herald of Freedom* that had been salvaged (one account says from the river) after the May raid, and was now commandeered for the purpose. On the night of August 14 all were ready and plans were laid for an attack the following morning. Lane was in command and had between three and four hundred men. Accounts of participants differ as to whether or not shots were exchanged, and also as to whether or not Lane resorted to the ruse of "straw men." The story, as it gained currency later, was that Lane gathered from the neighborhood a large number of farm wagons, set up in each of them a number of stakes bound about with bundles of straw which, at a distance, would look like men, and had the wagons emerge from the woods, thus creating in the blockhouse the impression that a large army was advancing.[45] At all events, as the free-state force approached the fort the garrison fled, and a pursuing party was unable to overtake them. A number of United States muskets, issued to Captain Saunders' militia company, and large stores of ammunition and supplies fell to the victors. After taking possession of these, the free-state men burned the house.[46]

This occurred during the forenoon of August 15. That afternoon Lane turned over his command to Walker and, with a small bodyguard, left for the Nebraska line, presumably to meet the second contingent of the "Army of the North." Walker had just ordered his men to disband and return to Lawrence, when news arrived that some prisoners in Lecompton, the men just arrested for the raid on Franklin, were to be put to death. The men began to clamor to attack the territorial capital. Since Walker, who according to his own story considered that such an attempt would be suicidal, could not resist the men, he started with the whole force toward Lecompton. Near Walker's own cabin on the California road, they met a raiding party under Colonel Titus and a skirmish ensued. Perhaps this gave Walker an idea, though he claimed to have received secret information the next morning that only a few men were at Titus's fort, and that the federal troops would not interfere if he should attack the place. The following morning, on August 16, Walker led his men against Titus's blockhouse. In the midst of heavy musketry from both sides, Bickerton put "Old Sacramento" into position and threw a dozen or more shots into the blockhouse, shouting, "Here's a second edition of the *Herald of Freedom!*" After about half an hour of firing, Titus surrendered his garrison and the house was burned. On each side, several had been wounded and one killed.[47]

Just as the firing ceased, a company of United States troops appeared. Major Sedgwick's command, only a mile distant, had witnessed the whole affair, but had made no effort to intervene. When this company did appear, it was only to prevent an attack on Lecompton. One version has it that Major Sedgwick, who was free-state in sympathy and frequently communicated secretly with Walker, did not even take the precaution of sending a company to the scene until he had gone into Lecompton and there found Governor Shannon, who was too panic-stricken to give any order except for the protection of the town.[48] In his own report of the episode, Major Sedgwick said: "I placed my command between the house and the town, and, the Governor soon after joining us, we moved in the direction of the place attacked. By this time the house had been destroyed, one man killed, Colonel Titus and one other dangerously wounded, the others carried off prisoners . . . . I would also say that I have received no instructions how to act in a conflict with citizens, or when an officer is authorized to fire upon them, except the President's proclamation of February 16, 1856."[49]

All idea of attacking Lecompton was now given up, and Walker returned to Lawrence with his nineteen prisoners. It required all the ingenuity and nerve he possessed (and that was a great deal) to save the life of Colonel Titus, who was most bitterly hated by the free-state men for his many depredations and for his part in the sack of Lawrence the previous May. The next day (Sunday) Governor Shannon went to Lawrence with a detachment of federal troops and negotiated his second treaty with the Committee of Safety. In exchange for Colonel Titus and his men, he agreed to release the fifteen free-state prisoners held by the territorial authorities, including those arrested for participation in the attack upon Franklin, and to return the Abbott howitzer, surrendered by Pomeroy at the sack of Lawrence. He did not demand the surrender of "Old Sacramento" or of other arms taken by the free-state men.[50] Dr. John Doy remarked, "We traded Titus for an old cannon."

This was almost the last official act of Governor Shannon. He carried out the treaty faithfully, refused to call out the territorial militia as demanded by the pro-slavery leaders, and ordered out the whole garrison of Fort Leavenworth to preserve order and prevent reprisals. But this course of action so antagonized the pro-slavery faction that the governor's life was in danger. On August 21, four days after the second Treaty of Lawrence, he resigned and left the territory. That same day, notice of his removal was received from Washington.[51]

With the flight of Governor Shannon, bedlam broke loose again. Immediately following the free-state operations just described, the border press had burst forth with wildly exaggerated accounts of the occurrences, reporting that Titus had been murdered, that Lane's army was driving all pro-slavery men from the territory and burning their houses, that Lecompton had been raided and the "treason" prisoners rescued, and that all pro-slavery towns in Douglas County had been destroyed.[52] The day before Shannon left Kansas, "Major General" W. P. Richardson, of the northern division, territorial militia, had taken the liberty to call out his division; and the first official act of Secretary Daniel Woodson as acting governor, on August 21, was to approve this step and to direct the calling out of the southern division also. On August 25 Acting Governor Woodson issued a proclamation declaring "the said Territory to be in a state of open insurrection and rebellion," and calling upon all law-abiding citizens and all civil and military officers "to aid and assist by all means in their power in putting down the insurrectionists, and in bringing to condign punishment all persons engaged with them."[53]

During these days Atchison collected a "Grand Army" of some five hundred Missourians at New Santa Fe, just across the line in Missouri about fifteen miles south of Westport, intending, apparently, to muster them into "Major General" A. M. Coffey's southern division of the territorial militia. From this base, a raid was made on the Quaker mission on the Shawnee reservation, and supplies were "pressed." On August 25 a free-state force attacked a raiding party from Atchison's command and drove them back across the line.[54] On August 30 a detachment of Atchison's men, estimated to number from two to three hundred, marched upon Osawatomie, piloted by the Reverend Martin White, who had been driven or frightened away from the vicinity by John Brown. They were led by "General" John W. Reid. Approaching the town from the northwest because the crossing of the Marais des Cygnes below the village was guarded by free-state men, Reid's force met Frederick Brown, one of John Brown's sons, and another free-state man, whom they killed on the spot; White claimed that the horse young Brown was riding had been stolen from him. John Brown with seventeen men, Dr. W. W. Updegraff with ten, and Captain Cline with fourteen, took a position along the Marais des Cygnes, protected by the timber and the river bank, and fired upon the Missourians as they advanced. Reid's men returned the fire and brought a cannon into play. When this failed to dislodge the defenders, the Missourians charged through the timber, whereupon the free-state men broke and fled across the river. Two were killed as they were swimming across. Such was the much-discussed "Battle of Osawatomie," which, according to Brown's detractors, was no battle at all. Overwhelmingly outnumbered and short of ammunition, Brown and his associates could only make a faint show of resistance. Having thus dispatched its defenders, Reid's men proceeded to sack the village, burning all but three of four houses. They took seven prisoners, two of whom they killed.[55] Again the Emigrant Aid Company's mill was saved, this time by an old army veteran, Freeman ("Pap") Austin, with his rifle which he called the "Kill Devil."[56] Perhaps no explanation of this blow is necessary, but it has been explained in some quarters as punishment of Osawatomie for harboring John Brown.*

As soon as news of the sack of Osawatomie reached Lawrence, Lane gathered a force of about three hundred men, including a number from Topeka, and marched in pursuit of Reid. He made contact with Reid's men at the pro-slavery rendezvous on Bull Creek on the evening of August 31, but for some unknown reason he delayed the attack until the following morning. During the night Reid escaped.[57]

In the meantime, matters were becoming tense along the Kaw. The militia had gathered at Lecompton, and Woodson ordered a division to place itself between that town and Lawrence to prevent Lane's escape.[58] Despite Woodson's orders to the contrary,[59] houses of free-state people were burned, and settlers were frightened into abandoning their homes and fleeing into Lawrence. At Leavenworth the pro-slavery municipal authorities instituted a reign of terror and drove a large number of free-state sympathizers out of the territory. Supply wagons continued to be seized between Leavenworth and Lawrence until the people of the latter place were in fear of being starved out. Pleas of the Free State Committee of Safety for the opening of the road to Leavenworth and the protection of their property elicited from Acting Governor Woodson only the retort that they could expect no protection or consideration until or unless they would agree to obey the territorial laws,—the "bogus laws."[60] When S. Southerland and G. W. Hutchinson, merchants of Lawrence, went to Lecompton in

---

* Such was the view of Professor F. H. Hodder.

person to protest to the acting governor, they were arrested as spies.[61] General Smith declared that it was absurd to consider as spies men who appeared in their own proper person, but insisted that the case was beyond his control.[62]

On September 1 United States Marshal Donaldson presented to Acting Governor Woodson a formal statement that the ordinary judicial processes were inadequate for the suppression of the insurrection. Thereupon, Woodson issued a requisition to Colonel Cooke, commanding the federal troops in the field, to "invest the town of Topeka, disarm all insurrectionists or aggressive invaders against the organized Government of the Territory to be found at or near that point, leveling to the ground all their breastworks, forts or fortifications, keep the head men or leaders in close confinement, and all persons found in arms against the Government as prisoners, subject to the order of the Marshal of the Territory." This order Colonel Cooke refused to obey.[63]

At this juncture the Committee of Safety decided to make an attack upon Lecompton in an effort to disperse the militia and to free Southerland, Hutchinson, and nine or ten other free-state prisoners who were being held there by the territorial authorities. It was a bold stroke, which could be executed only if it could be done so quickly that the acting governor would not have time to call upon the federal troops, who were encamped in the immediate neighborhood, to intervene. Colonel Harvey was to proceed north of the Kansas River to a point opposite Lecompton to cut off the escape of the garrison, while Lane was to move directly to the attack. Harvey proceeded with his maneuver on schedule, but, as usual, Lane delayed a day. After he had kept his men in hiding the greater part of the day and Lane had failed to appear, Harvey concluded that the project had been abandoned and withdrew his men.[64] The next afternoon Lane appeared with about three hundred men on the hills overlooking Lecompton, and sent Walker with sixty mounted men to place himself between the town and the federal troops. Instead of attacking at once, which offered the

[205]

only chance of success, Lane sent a demand into the town for the surrender of the prisoners. Before his messenger could return with a statement that the prisoners had been released and that the militia were disbanding, Colonel Cooke arrived with six hundred dragoons, lectured the free-state men (all but Lane, who kept out of sight) for their foolhardiness, and announced that he would prevent an attack. Whereupon, Lane, like the fabled king who marched his army up a hill, could only "march back down again." The attacking party returned to Lawrence empty-handed, but they had given the acting governor the scare of his life. The prisoners were released, and the militia, pretending to disband, left Lecompton only to join Atchison's "Grand Army," which was closing in upon Lawrence for what the *Squatter Sovereign* declared was to be the "third and last time."[65]

The next move was to be an attack upon Leavenworth to break up the reign of terror there and to open the road for free-state provisions. Again Lane was to lead the main party, and Harvey a supporting expedition. Harvey carried out his part of the plan by raiding the pro-slavery town of Easton, as a result of which raid his band acquired the appellation, "Colonel Harvey and his forty thieves." Once more Lane failed to appear. Consequently Harvey's men, instead of going on to Leavenworth, started to return to Lawrence by a circuitous route to avoid meeting federal troops. Hearing that a pro-slavery raiding party was encamped on Slough Creek, near the present site of Oskaloosa, Harvey attacked and captured them, and returned safely to Lawrence with his plunder.[66]

Such was the situation in Kansas when Governor John W. Geary arrived on September 7, 1856. Each side had thrown the other into a state of terror. Anarchy reigned. But on the whole, the free-state element faced the darker outlook. To the west of Lawrence a semblance of quiet was returning, but Osawatomie was in ruins, no free-state man dared appear in Leavenworth, and Atchison's "Grand Army" was gathering to wipe out Lawrence. To make matters worse, Lane, stricken with one of his inexplicable moods, suddenly decided to leave Lawrence, accompanied by a strong bodyguard, just when the town was in the greatest danger. Allowing himself to become embroiled in a county-seat fight, Lane was induced by the people of Ozawkie to attack their pro-slavery rival, Hickory Point. Unable to dislodge the defenders of that village, Lane withdrew and sent an order to Lawrence for reinforcements and the two cannons.[67] That evening, receiving Governor Geary's proclamation which ordered *all* armed forces to disband, he dismissed his men and sent a message to Lawrence countermanding his order for reinforcements. Meanwhile, Colonel Harvey left Lawrence with all the men he could muster, thus leaving the town defenseless in the face of Atchison's horde, missed Lane's second messenger, and on the following day engaged in a fruitless foray at Hickory Point, only to see the bulk of his command, including the redoubtable "Stubbs" company, captured by federal troops under Governor Geary's orders.[68]

With Kansas embroiled throughout the summer of 1856 in such a "war to the knife and knife to the hilt," well indeed might the North seethe with excitement over "bleeding Kansas," and well indeed might the administration at Washington shudder for the consequences to the Democratic party.

CHAPTER XI

"Bleeding Kansas"

WHILE CONGRESS WAS DEBATING and the administration was proclaiming, while the Emigrant Aid Company was exerting itself to support the free-state cause in Kansas and the Atchison political organization in Missouri was performing the same function for the pro-slavery cause, while the contestants of both parties in the territory were appealing from the ballot box to the battlefield, both sections of the Union were growing excited over the struggle for Kansas, and were girding their loins for the fray. During the early months of 1856, when the Emigrant Aid Company was still bearing virtually the whole brunt of the Northern efforts, Southerners began to bestir themselves to organize in support of their partisans in Kansas. The most active promoter of the Southern enterprise was Major Jefferson Buford, a lawyer of Eufaula, Alabama.

As early as November 26, 1855, Buford published in his home-town paper, the Eufaula *Spirit of the South,* an appeal for "three hundred industrious, sober, discreet, reliable men, capable of bearing arms," to migrate to Kansas. To each he promised forty acres of land, free passage to Kansas, and support for a year. Although he announced his intention of using twenty thousand dollars of his own money, he appealed for contributions, promising that, for each fifty dollars contributed, he would "place in Kansas one *bona fide* settler, able and willing to vote and fight if need be for our section."[1] On January 7, 1856, Buford sold forty plantation slaves, at an average price of seven hundred dollars, and turned the proceeds into a fund to finance his Kansas venture.[2] He immediately began his recruiting activities in Alabama, while in South Carolina, Georgia and Florida, local "emigrant aid societies" were formed to support his effort.

The South Carolina movement began in December, 1855,

when one E. B. Bell announced his intention of raising a company of one hundred men to go to Kansas to secure homes and to defend Southern institutions.[3] Representative Preston S. Brooks, soon to become famous in the South and infamous in the North for his assault on Senator Charles Sumner, pledged a hundred dollars toward the project, or one dollar for each man who should be enlisted, and thought that other members of the South Carolina delegation in Congress would make similar contributions unless parties should be organized in their own districts.[4]

Apparently nothing came of Bell's effort except to start the agitation, but about the first of March there was formed in Charleston the Kansas Emigration Society of South Carolina. Although this organization was lavish in its denunciation of the New England Emigrant Aid Company, it nevertheless sought to imitate the methods of that Company so far as it understood them. A full corps of officers was elected, an executive committee was created, and a campaign was launched with public meetings and local committees to raise funds and recruit emigrants.[5] Unlike the New England Emigrant Aid Company, this association undertook to purchase full equipment for its emigrants, and to pay their traveling expenses. A party of some sort must have been dispatched early in March, for on March 27, a "second colony" of twenty-eight left Charleston to join Buford.[6] The activity of the society continued on into April, and perhaps longer. On April 1, a meeting in Charleston was addressed by a representative of an association that had been formed in Platte County, Missouri.[7] Other parties of emigrants may have been sent later, but no record of them has come to light.

Apparently similar activities were carried on in Georgia and Florida, for groups from these states were among the Buford party. Indeed, one of the four points of rendezvous designated by Buford was Columbus, Georgia.

About April 1 Buford assembled his host at Montgomery, Alabama. They were estimated to number about four hundred.

Though not armed, they were formed into a military organization as a regiment of four companies, with Buford as colonel.[8] At an expense of approximately $24,000, of which some $14,000 was contributed, Buford fully equipped his men, except for arms, and paid their fare to Kansas. He had an agreement with each member of the expedition by which the man was to enter a claim in Kansas and, as soon as he should acquire title, was to deed one-half of his land as reimbursement for his transportation and support. The expedition left Montgomery on April 7, 1856, in a blaze of glory. Traveling by steamboat up the Mississippi and Missouri rivers, it reached Westport on May 2 in a destitute condition. On the way up the Missouri River, someone, usually assumed to have been a member or members of the party, robbed Colonel Buford of five thousand dollars—all the cash he had with him.[9]

Pomeroy did not appear to take Buford's men very seriously. On May 10 he wrote from St. Louis: "My clerk wrote me here that Col. Buford's party arrived there [Kansas City], slept on the floor, and had to borrow money of Riddlesbarger and Co. to pay their bills. The Colonel and all his party were out of funds. The Southern emigrants are poor and discouraged (Simmons says, who just arrived from Kansas) and will make tracks for home if the aid societies of the border counties do not support them."[10]

The men were enrolled almost at once in the territorial militia and were armed by the territorial authorities. Groups of them participated in most of the conflicts of the spring and summer. Very few of them took claims; and when their friends ceased to support them, most of them either left the territory or engaged in marauding. None, so far as can be learned, ever carried out his contract with Buford.[11]

While these efforts were being made in the far South, proslavery emigrant aid societies were being formed in some of the border counties of Missouri. One of the most active was organized in Platte County, on February 16, 1856, on the ruins of the defunct "Self-Defensive Association."[12] Another was launched about the same time in Lafayette County.[13] There were probably others. These societies undertook not only to promote the migration of pro-slavery settlers to Kansas but to support them in the territory, in the belief, apparently, that they were imitating the Eastern emigrant aid organizations. The Lafayette County society issued an appeal to the people of the South, which was published in *De Bow's Review* of May, 1856. This address announced that "the crisis is at hand," and urged the "absolute necessity of immediate action" on the part of the slaveholding states. The arrival of "the noble Buford" was gratefully acknowledged, but it was asserted that Missouri had borne the brunt of the struggle, and that now the abolitionists were more active than ever and would scruple at nothing. "Missouri has done nobly thus far," ran the appeal, "in overcoming the thousands who have been sent out by the Abolition Aid Societies; but we can not hold out much longer unless the whole South will come to the rescue . . . . Let societies be formed to assist the emigrants. Those who can not emigrate can contribute money to those who can. We have such societies in Missouri, and we can induce more people to emigrate than we are able to support. If the whole South would adopt this system, we should succeed. . . ."[14]

With the publication of this appeal, the powerful *De Bow's Review* entered the fray, and the issues for June and August carried pleas in a similar vein.[15] Many Southern newspapers took up the battle cry. The present study has not revealed the extent to which this campaign resulted in organized effort in the South, but the resultant migration of Southerners to Kansas was sadly disappointing to the friends of the "peculiar institution." However, if this Southern effort resulted in nothing else, it helped to arouse the North. As early as February, 1856, the Northern press began to bristle with appeals to the "friends of freedom" to bestir themselves and put the free-state men in a position to defend their homes against the armed bands that were being raised in the South by Buford, E. B. Bell, and others, "who are going to Kansas, pledged to remain for two years, not as actual settlers, but to reinforce the border ruffians of Missouri."[16]

This discussion, coupled with the general excitement over "bleeding Kansas," aroused the North to a renewal of emigrant aid effort similar to that which had swept the country in the summer of 1854. During February, 1856, there sprang up in various parts of the North, local Kansas Aid Committees, and in several instances these expanded or consolidated during the months following into state committees. One of the first of these of which a record is available was the committee formed in Albany, New York, on February 18, 1856, which, as already noted in chapter IX, expanded into the New York State Kansas Committee.

During February a series of "Kansas aid" meetings were held at various points in Wisconsin, at most of which local committees were created. On March 6, representatives of these local committees held a convention in Milwaukee and organized "an association called the Wisconsin State Kansas Emigrant Aid Society," with objects "similar to [those of] the Massachusetts organization." Officers were James S. Douglas, president; Charles J. Hotchkiss, secretary; and J. A. Lophorn, treasurer. There was a board of twenty-one directors, and an executive committee of five.[17]

It will be recalled that during January and February the Emigrant Aid Company conducted a thorough canvass of New England, calling public meetings in the various towns at which representatives of the Company and members of the Kansas Free State delegation spoke. At these meetings it was common to appoint local Kansas relief committees, which solicited both relief funds and subscriptions to the stock of the Company. As relief supplanted stock subscriptions as the principal motive of this effort, officers of the Company decided that it would be advantageous to organize Boston for relief purposes independently of the Company, since many persons considered the Emigrant Aid Company too much of a business enterprise to handle relief funds properly.* Accordingly, the Company officers, acting in their individual capacities, arranged for a meeting at Faneuil Hall on March 12, which was addressed by members of the Kansas Free State delegation.[18] At this meeting a committee was formed, called officially the Boston Kansas Relief Committee, but commonly referred to as the Faneuil Hall Committee.[19] This committee set to work at once raising funds for Kansas relief, and for a time operated in close co-operation with the Emigrant Aid Company. On June 25 delegates from Kansas Leagues and local Kansas aid committees in the various Massachusetts towns met in convention in Boston and formed the Massachusetts State Kansas Committee, with George L. Stearns as chairman and Patrick T. Jackson as treasurer.[20] This committee almost immediately absorbed the Fanueil Hall Committee. Although officers and directors of the Emigrant Aid Company were purposely omitted from the personnel of the State Committee, many of them were among the most active promoters of the new project, and the two organizations worked in complete harmony.

During the spring the Emigration Aid Society of Northern Ohio,† which had been somnolent for a year, aroused itself and sponsored the formation of an emigrant party by S. N. Wood (leader of the Branson rescue) which started for Kansas on April 8.[21] The raid on Lawrence, on May 21, gave an added impetus to this Kansas aid movement, and soon afterward a number of new organizations sprang up. Mention has already been made of the Chicago committee, formed the very day of the Lawrence

---

* Le Baron Russell stated," . . . the movement in Boston for Kansas relief was actually got up by our Company. Our officers, at the first meeting, appointed the Committee to arrange for the Faneuil Hall meeting. I know this for I nominated them myself. It was then thought better that our officers should not take a very prominent part in the new movement, lest it should prejudice some persons who might have any feelings against the Company. . . . I believe that every member of our Executive Committee and a large number of our Directors and Stockholders have subscribed liberally to this cause as well as to the Company stock" (original letter, Russell to Hale, June 30, 1856, Aid Company Papers).
† See chap. IV.

raid. A few days later there was launched the Iowa State Kansas Committee, with headquarters at Iowa City, then the capital of the state. It had the double purpose of aiding the free-state cause in Kansas with men and supplies, and of promoting the Iowa route for migration. Its officers were W. Penn Clark, chairman; C. W. Hobart, secretary; and H. D. Downey, treasurer.[22] It has not been possible to compile a complete list of the Kansas aid organizations that were operating during the summer of 1856, but in addition to those already mentioned, Dr. Webb, in July, listed the following: the Cleveland Kansas Aid Society, Charles Hickox, president, J. Sterling, secretary; the Detroit Kansas Aid Society, Z. Chandler, president; the Pittsburgh Kansas Aid Association, George W. Jackson, president, E. J. Allen, secretary; the Central Illinois Kansas Committee, C. H. Ray, secretary; the Vermont State Kansas Committee, E. P. Walton, secretary, the Reverend B. B. Newton, general agent.[23]

In June a movement was set on foot to co-ordinate the work of all these assorted agencies by the creation of a National Kansas Committee. Thayer claimed the credit for originating the plan,[24] but such evidence as has come to light indicates that it originated with William Barnes of the New York State Kansas Committee.* At least, Barnes called the first convention and presided at its first session. A "Convention of Delegates of Kansas Aid Associations and Committees"[25] was called to meet at Cleveland, Ohio, on June 20, 1856. The date was changed to June 26, and then moved back to June 20.[26] The Emigrant Aid Company appointed Pomeroy, Waters, and Thayer as delegates,[27] but, because of the shifting of dates, these men were not at the Cleveland meeting. The convention met on June 20 with representatives present from the New York State Kansas Committee, the Emigration Aid Association of Northern Ohio, the Cleveland Kansas Aid Society,

---

* Thayer did correspond with Barnes prior to the first meeting, and made some suggestions that were subsequently followed, but nothing in his letter suggests that he was the author of the plan (original letter, Thayer to Barnes, June 20, 1856, William Barnes Papers).

the State of Indiana, the Kansas Free State Executive Committee, the Pittsburgh Kansas Aid Association, and four Ohio counties.[28] After two days of speech-making, the convention voted an "Address to the Friends of Humanity, Justice and Freedom," and adjourned to meet in Buffalo, New York, on July 9, with a view apparently, to securing a wider representation of Northern organizations.

Between the two meetings, Barnes wrote to Dr. Webb urging that New England be represented at the Buffalo meeting. Webb replied that he would do his best, but that there were no regular organizations in New England outside Massachusetts, and that most of the local committees would act through the Emigrant Aid Company.[29] The Company added Charles J. Higginson to the delegation already appointed.[30] Dr. Webb wrote a letter to Professor A. C. Twining of Yale, urging that Connecticut be represented.[31] The adjourned convention met at Buffalo on July 9 and 10, with delegates present from nearly all the known organizations and relief committees. Thayer represented Massachusetts on the general "Committee on Plan of Action." The convention demanded the immediate admission of Kansas under the Topeka constitution, called upon all states, counties, and towns to organize, endorsed the Iowa route for migration to Kansas, declared in favor of loans to Kansas settlers to pay for their land, and appointed a National Kansas Committee to supervise Kansas relief.[32] After a few changes in personnel, the committee organized with Thaddeus Hyatt as president, A. B. Hurd, secretary, George W. Dole, treasurer, S. G. Howe, financial agent, W. F. M. Arny, general transportation agent.* Headquarters were estab-

---

* The Committee, as finally organized, included, in addition to the officers: William H. Russell, New Haven; Governor W. H. Hoppin, Providence, Rhode Island; Alexander Gordon, Pennsylvania; John W. Wright, Logansport, Indiana; J. H. Tweedy, Milwaukee; W. H. Stanley, Cleveland; F. A. Hunt, St. Louis; Penn Clark, Iowa City; A. H. Reeder, Kansas; J. Y. Scannon, Chicago; S. W. Eldridge, Kansas; Dr. Samuel Cabot, Boston. This roster is taken from the letterhead of the Committee's stationery. Dr. Howe was a director of the Emigrant Aid Company and Dr. Cabot a member of its Executive Committee. Both had been added to the Massachusetts State Kansas Committee. The New York Daily Tribune, August 12, 1856, mentions some changes made from original personnel.

lished in Chicago in charge of an executive committee consisting of Hyatt, Howe, Arny, Dole, Hurd, Scannon, and Webster.[33]

One of the first acts of this subcommittee was to send Howe and Hyatt on the double errand of taking charge of the emigrant train in Iowa and Nebraska, commonly known as "Lane's army of the North," and of investigating conditions in Kansas. Dr. Howe was planning the trip before the Buffalo convention, probably on behalf of the Massachusetts State Kansas Committee.* As previously noted, Howe and Hyatt caught up with the emigrant train at Nebraska City on July 30, got rid of Lane, and arranged for the train to enter Kansas. During July the Committee appointed Eli Thayer as general agent to organize the states and counties.[34] Thayer launched forth with a grandiose plan of creating a county committee in each county, with a corps of solicitors to canvass each school district. On August 1 he announced that he expected to have a state committee functioning in each New England state within ten days.[35] But, although Thayer made much of this in his *Kansas Crusade,* written a quarter of a century later, and gave the impression that he had organized the entire North,[36] all the evidence we have indicates that his practical achievements did not extend beyond his own county. There he organized a county committee of old officers of the Worcester County Kansas League, and enlisted six hundred solicitors to canvass the school districts. He had special subscription books prepared, some of which he sent to Barnes for use in New York.[37] He proposed to use the Frémont Republican Clubs to solicit funds for Kansas,[38] but there is no indication of the extent to which the plan was put into practice. During the early fall, Thayer was busy with his Congressional campaign, but after the election he made an offer to the National Committee to devote all his time to organizing states if the Committee would bear his expenses and pay him for his time. Hurd wrote him a letter offering

---

*Dr. Webb wrote to him on July 1, in regard to the best route to take (Aid Company Letters, Book B, 88-92).

him five dollars a day and expenses,[39] but records are not available to show whether or not he accepted the offer.

The National Kansas Committee, upon its formation, assumed the burden which had been borne by the Emigrant Aid Company alone until the first months of 1856, but which had been shared by the various local and state committees during the spring and early summer, of supporting the free-state party in Kansas. It undertook to stimulate migration, to secure reduced rates for emigrants, to supply arms for the border war, and to afford relief to those who had suffered in body or in purse in the free-state cause. Its methods differed materially from those of the Emigrant Aid Company. It furnished arms openly as an organization. It recruited "emigrants" with the understanding that, although they were expected to remain as permanent settlers, their first work was to be soldiers in the free-state army; and it furnished such direct pecuniary assistance to its "emigrants," that Dr. Webb referred to it as "hiring men to go to Kansas."[40] The National Committee received some large donations from individuals, notably Gerrit Smith, who gave a thousand dollars a month for several months,[41] but it depended chiefly for its financial support upon the state and county committees. Some county and local committees responded, but the state committees showed a disposition to retain for their own use all the money they collected. When the National Committee had been in operation for four months, its secretary stated that only the New York and Massachusetts state committees had sent any money to Chicago.[42]

On the whole, the work of the National Committee was disappointing. At first, money that was badly needed to relieve the distress of actual settlers in Kansas was expanded in recruiting and sending to Kansas "emigrants" who turned out to be only a burden and an embarrassment to the free-state party,* and in

---

* Charles H. Branscomb wrote, November 21, 1856, "It is thought here by many that a great mistake has been made by the National Committee in spending so much money in getting their trains into the Territory" (Aid Company Records, Book II, 201). Philip Schuyler wrote, November 22, "You may send here millions of money to be distributed

the purchase of rifles, most of which never reached Kansas.* When, finally, the Committee did turn its efforts to relief, the work was bungled in a way that caused serious dissatisfaction, and tended to demoralize the recipients.† After six months of activity even the president of the Committee had to admit, "The Central Kansas Committee have utterly failed in their duty in this particular, and for this I blame them."[43] By the end of 1856, most of the responsible leaders in Kansas were writing that the original plan of the Emigrant Aid Company was the best for Kansas. James Redpath wrote to the *New York Tribune*, "Instead of Aid Societies we need Aid Companies; not charitable associations, but moneyed corporations." And in the same issue of the *Tribune,* an editorial by Greeley echoed this sentiment.[44]

While the officers of the Emigrant Aid Company questioned the wisdom of the National Committee's methods, they cooperated with it wholeheartedly, and also with the Massachusetts State Committee.[45] The Company did not relax for a moment its

---

to the settlers, and tens of thousands of men with arms to fight, and it will prove a curse to the cause unless there are facilities and appliances for developing the resources of the country and the making of homes and raising our own food and supplying our own wants" (*ibid.,* 206-07). G. W. Brown wrote, November 26, "The idea of buying up men for Kansas is not a paying investment" (*ibid.,* 211-12). The Rev. E. Nute wrote, December 15, "Kansas will not be aided by the accession of such men as can be picked up in Chicago and other Western cities. A large part of those who were brought here last fall at great expense have been a positive and serious damage to us and to our cause. Many of them have returned, stealing horses to get away on, and selling their rifles in Iowa at one fourth their cost" (*ibid.,* Book III, 11). Amos A. Lawrence wrote to ex-Governor Reeder, December 20, "My opinion is averse to sending men to the Territory at all, unless in an emergency to repel an invasion. Pretty much all those whose expenses were paid by the State Committee and Kansas associations last summer have returned, or only remain in the Territory as hangers on, or something worse. One gang of them have been stealing horses up to this time" (Lawrence Letters, 208).

* Most of the rifles purchased by the Committee, except those placed in the hands of its "emigrants," were stored at Tabor, Iowa, and eventually turned over to John Brown, who used some of them at Harper's Ferry. Iseley, "Sharps Rifle Episode," *American Historical Review,* XII, April, 1907, 546-66.

† In the fall of 1856, A. H. Shurtleff, general agent of the New York State Kansas Committee, sent a questionnaire to the Kansas State Central Committee, to which William Hutchinson, secretary of that committee replied. In answer to the question, "What, if anything, has the Kansas Aid Society done to relieve the settlers?" Hutchinson stated: "Till last week, next to nothing. Not one fifth of the money contributed has reached Kansas in available form. Recently $3,000 in money and $200 worth of clothes have come to hand" (original letter, undated, William Barnes Papers). Many complaints reached Boston that worthy cases were neglected, and most of the letters cited above complained of the demoralizing effect of indiscriminate charity. There were also charges of graft in distribution (Aid Company Letters, Book B, 106, 121, 502-03, 535-36, 559-60).

efforts to raise funds for relief of the needy, and all the money raised for the purpose was sent to Pomeroy, S. N. Simpson, or the Reverend Ephraim Nute in Lawrence to be used where it would do the most good. Dr. Webb suggested to Simpson that in most cases the funds should be furnished as loans, that might or might not be called for later according to circumstances, so as to save the self-respect of the recipients and act as a spur to further exertion.[46] The Company authorized its agent in Lawrence to lend the mill to the Committee of Safety without charge and to lend houses belonging to the Company to persons in need.[47] The Company continued to serve as a transmitting agency for individuals who wished to send money to friends or relatives in Kansas. Such people would deposit their money with Dr. Webb, and he would authorize the beneficiary, or a Company agent for him, to draw for the amount through the Company's forwarding agents. No charge was made for this service.*

One of the biggest relief tasks undertaken by the Emigrant Aid Company was the collection and forwarding of clothing. By arrangement with the Massachusetts State Kansas Committee, the entire responsibility for this work in New England was taken over by the Company, while the Committee undertook to supply provisions. During the summer the relief work was retarded by the blockade of the Missouri River and the lack of overland transportation facilities, but on September 24 Dr. Webb reported that he had already sent twenty-five packages of clothing.[48] Frequent letters during the next two months tell of the number of packages sent from time to time. On December 4 Webb wrote: "From this office alone there have been forwarded over three hundred packages of clothing to the Territory. Our State Kansas Committee have sent already fifteen thousand dollars' worth of provisions."[49] At about the same time the cash book of the Massa-

---

*Several dozen letters, acknowledging receipt of funds for transmission, and a number of others recommending this method of sending funds (there being danger that the actual cash might be stolen on the way), are found in Book B of Aid Company Letters. A package of several dozen receipted drafts are among the Aid Company Papers.

chusetts State Kansas Committee shows that it had expended "in and for Kansas," $35,878.05.[50] Since the distribution in Kansas was in the hands of persons (Pomeroy, Simpson, Nute, and later Robinson) who acted under the joint authority of the Emigrant Aid Company, the Massachusetts Committee, and the National Committee, it was inevitable that confusion should exist in the minds of the people of the territory, and that complaints against the work of the National Committee should reflect upon the Emigrant Aid Company. But in order that there might be no just grounds for complaint so far as the Company was concerned, Dr. Webb directed several relief workers on the ground to seek out worthy cases that had not been reached and to see that they were cared for,[51] while Amos A. Lawrence sought to care for such isolated posts as Osawatomie and the Quaker Mission.[52] Despite complaints that the town of Lawrence was unduly favored, a settler at Wabaunsee wrote to the Company office, on December 1, that clothing was coming in steadily and was doing great good.[53]

But this direct relief work was only incidental to the program of the Emigrant Aid Company. As Amos A. Lawrence put it, the Company acted as almoner only for those who preferred its agency because it had been longer in the field.[54] There were many who did prefer its agency, particularly the Quakers, because they felt that it did not use its money for "Frémont and fighting,"* and as a consequence Webb and Lawrence sent thousands of dollars to Kansas for distribution. But it was the view of most of the officers of the Company that the best way to afford relief was to give employment to those who needed it. The zeal for relief donations completely paralyzed stock subscriptions, and this fact, along with the chaotic state of affairs in Kansas, brought the Company's building program to a standstill. Accordingly, Le Baron Russell suggested late in June that an effort be made

---

* The number of Lawrence's letters to Quakers acknowledging their contributions and indicating how the money would be used suggests that the Aid Company was the principal channel through which the New England Quakers acted.

to divert some of the relief money to the Company for construction work in Kansas; he stated that the Faneuil Hall Committee had expressed a willingness to appropriate two thousand dollars for the purpose, but that, since it was merging its existence into the state committee, he feared the plan might fall through.[55] The idea slumbered while war raged in Kansas; but in the fall, when relative peace had been restored there, Lawrence took it up, and at his suggestion the Executive Committee appropriated some of the relief funds in their hands toward creating employment by building mills.[56] In December the Massachusetts State Committee, largely through the efforts of Lawrence, was persuaded to invest one thousand dollars in Emigrant Aid Company stock to assist in rebuilding the Free State Hotel, which would furnish employment to dozens of men in Lawrence.†

In December Lawrence wrote to Pomeroy, "If we can get clear of politics, we shall get on well."[57] The observation was fitting, for throughout the summer and fall the whole Kansas Aid movement had been enmeshed in the toils of partisan politics. In the face of the undisguised hostility of the administration to the free-state movement and its support of the "bogus" territorial laws, it was inevitable that any movement in support of the Free State party in Kansas should take on an anti-administration political color. Then, when the administration and its spokesmen in Congress sought to place the entire odium of the Kansas troubles on the Emigrant Aid Company, it became doubly inevitable that the whole Kansas Aid movement, which was blurred in the popular mind under the generic concept of "Emigrant Aid Society," should assume a strongly anti-administration tinge. This was meat and drink to the rising Republican party. Had the administration deliberately set about to build up a powerful opposition, it could not have pursued a more fitting course than the one it followed.

---

† November 19, Lawrence explained his plan in a letter to Robinson (Lawrence Letters, 193-95). On January 2, 1857, the Executive Committee accepted the offer of the State Committee and authorized the issuance of fifty shares of stock to the Trustee of the State Committee, P. T. Jackson (Aid Company Records, Book III, 12-13, 20).

As previously noted, the Republican party had been born of the excitement over the Kansas-Nebraska bill and the spectacular fugitive slave cases of 1854; but had there been no excitement in Kansas, it might well have been stillborn. A historian of the early Republican party declares: "Apart from what happened in Kansas . . . the Republican genesis can not be explained. It is scarcely making the case too strong to say that without the constant stimulus offered by events in Kansas, the party would never have crystalized."[58] The excitement died down after the November election of 1854, and the new party was threatened with disintegration; but the "bogus" election in Kansas in March, 1855, followed by the rise of the free-state movement during the summer and fall, gave it a new ground on which to stand. When Kansas affairs reached a crisis in the Wakarusa War and the events which followed it, the Republican party sprang into newness of life. If the party could identify itself with the free-state movement in Kansas, it would have a "cause" which could so arouse Northern voters that even the Presidency itself might not be beyond its grasp. When the Free State delegation went east in February, 1856, its members were much in demand as speakers at Republican rallies. "Bleeding Kansas" became the watchword of the party, while its representatives in Congress espoused the cause of Reeder, demanded a Congressional investigation in Kansas, and rushed to the defense of the Emigrant Aid Company.

Naturally enough, the Republican organizers sought to turn the Kansas Aid movement to political account. Everywhere Republican politicians became enthusiastic promoters of the movement and took the lead in forming local relief committees. Republican rallies were turned into Kansas aid meetings, so that some color was given to the charge, so often reiterated in Congress, that the whole movement was only a partisan political maneuver. In the Emigrant Aid Company, councils were divided. Robinson and Pomeroy, ambitious politicians that they were, very early avowed themselves Republicans, as did most of the younger and more zealous directors. But most of the Company's money had come from older, more conservative men like Lawrence and John Carter Brown. These men were old-line Whigs, —"Hunkers," they called themselves. They were "national men,"* of the Clay-Benton stripe—sincere opponents of slavery extension, but for the Union first. To them the formation of a sectional party would be, of itself, a national calamity, and many of them feared that Republican success would lead to disunion. To their way of thinking, the Republicans should never have been permitted to arrogate to themselves the sponsorship of the free-state movement.[59] Lawrence saw the danger to the Company of permitting it to be dragged into the political melee, and as early as December, 1855, he wrote a warning to Robinson.† Partly because of the efforts of Lawrence and partly because of a speech of Governor Gardiner of Massachusetts, which put the Company in a wrong light, the Executive Committee on March 1 issued a statement in which they expressed sympathy with the Free State party in Kansas but disavowed all connection with party politics at home.[60]

Nevertheless, some of the Republican managers were able to utilize certain Emigrant Aid Company connections. Early in February Robinson wrote a letter to John C. Frémont recalling some of their common experiences in California and suggesting Frémont as a candidate for the Presidency.[61] The writing of this letter was undoubtedly inspired by Frémont promoters in the East, probably by Speaker Nathaniel P. Banks. Under date of March 17, Frémont replied to Robinson in a letter which, while

---

* At the time of the Harper's Ferry raid, Lawrence wrote to Jefferson Davis: "I am the son of Amos Lawrence, now deceased, whom you knew, and who brought me up to be a 'national man,' as we understand that term." After reciting his connection with the Fillmore campaign of 1856, he reaffirmed that he was a Hunker "and even in Missouri should be a law and order man" (Lawrence Letters, 279-80).

† "As a matter of policy," he wrote, "it would have been better for you and Mr. Pomeroy not to be identified with the Republican Party. It is enough to belong to the Free State Party in Kansas. Pretty much all of the Directors of the Emigrant Aid Company have joined it, but by doing so, we are liable to lose the support of the other parties. The largest amount of money has been paid by, and perhaps a majority of the shares belong to 'old Hunkers,' and we want to keep them on our side" (Lawrence Letters, 119).

[223]

guarded in its statements, took a stand in favor of the Free State party. Robinson turned this letter over to G. W. Brown, who, about April 1, published it in the *Herald of Freedom,* and at the same time placed Frémont's name at the *Herald's* masthead as candidate for President.[62] The other two Lawrence papers, the *Free State* and the *Tribune,* at once took up the cry,* as did the *New York Tribune* and the *Cleveland Herald*—and the Frémont campaign was on. This maneuver had the effect of tying the Free State party and, in a measure, the whole Kansas Aid movement to Frémont's chariot wheels, and even created a popular impression that he had the support of the Emigrant Aid Company as an organization.

While the parties were holding their conventions and nominating their candidates, the pot continued to boil in Congress. As the star of the Republicans rose rapidly and steadily, it became increasingly apparent to the administration forces that their little trick of making a political issue of the Emigrant Aid Company had backfired. Instead of having the intended effect of reconciling Northern voters to the administration's policy in Kansas, the outburst enabled the self-appointed political defenders of the Company to hold it up as a martyr and to rally voters to the cause of "Frémont and Free Kansas." There now appeared a marked toning down in the Congressional attacks on the Company,† while the Republicans became more outspoken in its defense.[63] During July the Republicans in the House, with the support of some antislavery "Americans," were able to put through the Grow Bill for the admission of Kansas under the Topeka

---

* Each of the three Lawrence papers claimed the credit of first declaring for Frémont. Brown claimed it for the *Herald of Freedom,* and Crandall and Nevins acknowledge his claim (*False Claims,* II). Colonel Holliday claimed it for the *Tribune* (*Kansas Historical Collections,* V, 50), and R. G. Elliott claimed it for the *Free State* (*ibid.,* X, 192). Unfortunately the question cannot be settled objectively, since no complete files of the three papers are known to exist. It is interesting to note that Robinson, with a bragging propensity second only to that of Thayer, did not in any of his writings claim credit for having originated the Frémont candidacy.

† E.g., the speech of Lewis Cass in the Senate, May 12-13, 1856. He attributed the Kansas trouble to "outside interference," and blamed both the Aid Company and the Missourians (*Congressional Globe Appendix,* 34 Cong., 1 Sess., 512).

constitution,[64] and the Dunn Bill to nullify the "bogus" territorial laws and to restore the Missouri Compromise.[65] Of course no one was so naïve as to suppose that either of these measures could pass the Senate, where the administration forces were in control, but their passage by the House put the opprobrium of defeating them on the Democratic party.

Obviously, if the Democrats hoped to elect Buchanan, they must quiet "bleeding Kansas." The first move in this direction was an enabling act to authorize the formation of a state constitution in Kansas. Douglas had submitted such a bill from the Committee on Territories on March 17,[66] but this apparently was intended only as a reserve weapon, since no effort was made to secure action on it until the Presidential compaign got under way. But when it became clear that Northern voters would not hold the administration guiltless of "the Crime against Kansas" and blame the Emigrant Aid Company, Robert Toombs of Georgia introduced a more elaborate measure, which Douglas accepted as a substitute for his bill.[67] The Toombs bill passed the Senate on July 2. It provided for the registration of the voters in Kansas by a special commission to be appointed by the President, the immediate calling of a constitutional convention, and federal supervision of the territorial election. The bill, if carried out in good faith, might lose Kansas for slavery, but it would quiet the excitement and save the Democratic party.

The maneuver had a real chance of success. In the first place, the Senate could usually coerce the House into accepting anything it proposed. In the second place, if the Republicans wished to avoid an appearance of insincerity in their professions, it would be difficult for them to reject the Toombs bill, at least as a basis for compromise. But for once the House was adamant, and the Republicans wriggled out by asserting that Pierce could not be trusted to execute the act in good faith, and that the registration of voters in Kansas was to take place at a time when most of the free-state settlers had been driven from their homes. Luckily for the Republicans (or was it scheming rather than luck?), the leaders of the Kansas Aid movement took the ground that this peace offer was only a sham. Even the Emigrant Aid Company, despite its proclamation of political neutrality, actively opposed the Toombs bill. Pomeroy was sent to Washington to lobby,[68] several of the directors conferred with influential politicians,[69] and Dr. Webb wrote to William Barnes: "I hope our New York friends are using all their influence among members of Congress to defeat the cunningly devised, but iniquitous Toombs Bill, or at all events to render it harmless by expunging the objectionable portions, and then returning it to the Senate to let it rest with that body to refuse relief to Kansas if willing to incur the odium of such a procedure."[70]

It was no less important to the American party and the Whig remnant that supported them than to the Democrats to quiet the Kansas excitement, since the net effect of that excitement was to strengthen the Republicans. On the other hand, the Americans and Whigs could scarcely be expected to underwrite the administration plan, since to do so would destroy their argument that the problem could not be solved through the Democratic party. Hence, it appeared politically necessary that these groups should offer a plan of their own. On July 10 Senator Crittenden proposed the Whig-American plan in the Senate. It was nothing less audacious than that General Winfield Scott, in whom both sections had confidence, should be sent to Kansas as a dictator.[71] On June 28 L. D. Evans of Texas presented the same proposal in the House.[72] Congress took no action on the proposition, but the suggestion may have influenced the administration in its decision to send Geary to Kansas after the Toombs bill had failed.

Although almost everyone else who was active in Emigrant Aid Company circles went over to the Republicans, Amos A. Lawrence remained a staunch supporter of Fillmore throughout the campaign, much to the embarrassment of his colleagues. This was to be expected in view of his "Hunker" background, his in-

[226]

timate friendship with Fillmore, and his dread of sectional parties; but when he perceived what was obvious to their opponents and is equally obvious to the historian today, "that the straight Republican members of Congress did not act and vote for an equitable settlement of the Kansas question at the last session, but exerted themselves to have it unsettled,"[73] he became convinced that the only hope for an early settlement acceptable to the Free State party lay in Fillmore's election.[74] He labored diligently to secure a "free Kansas" declaration from Fillmore,[75] and to commit S. G. Haven, the Fillmore leader in Congress, to a "free Kansas" program.[76] Fillmore did make private promises to Lawrence,* and Haven introduced a bill, which, by combining the provisions of the Dunn and Toombs bills, sought to find a basis for compromise,[77] but for the American party to have taken a free-soil stand openly would have been suicidal. In the North, where the more pronounced free-soil element of the party had already "bolted" and indorsed Frémont, such a stand could have done little good. In the South, where the American strength consisted chiefly of old Whigs who were as pro-slavery as their Democratic neighbors, the only effect would have been to drive these voters to the support of Buchanan.

In the hope of capitalizing on Lawrence's connections, both with the conservatives and with the Kansas movement, the Americans of Massachusetts nominated him for governor. He hesitated several days, and then declined the nomination. The only reason he gave was that, since he should be elected by factions opposed to each other, he could do no good.[78] But it seems likely that he was influenced in his decision by pressure put on him by his associates in the Emigrant Aid Company. On August 25, while Lawrence's acceptance was hanging fire, one J. M. Bunce of Hartford wrote to Dr. Webb that, in view of Lawrence's nomina-

---

* On September 4, Lawrence wrote to Robinson, "If Mr. Fillmore should come in, he will act promptly with the whole power which the law gives or will give. I have it from him in writing in all shapes, and I believe in him as good for all his promises" (*ibid.*, 174).

[227]

tion by the Know-Nothings and the presumption that the other members of the Aid Company were in sympathy with it, "Earnest friends of freedom in Kansas will hesitate about placing their contributions to promote this where the expenditure will be more or less controlled by Mr. L." Webb replied on August 30: "I was previously fully sensible of the serious injury that would be inflicted upon the cause of freedom, and great obstacles we should encounter in making further appeals for aid to carry forward our Kansas movements in consequence of the false position in which Mr. Lawrence has indirectly allowed the crazy politicians to place him before the public. The moment I learned what was going on, I had an interview with the gentleman and stated in what imminent peril he would place the best interests of Kansas by allowing himself to be placed at the head of the Fillmore ticket in this State . . . . Mr. L. promised me that, whatever decision he might make, he would come out strong for Kansas, and would express himself on that matter in unmistakable language . . . . There is not a single individual of our number associated with Mr. L. in 'this new movement'; on the other hand, everyone who has expressed an opinion deprecates it."[79]

The failure of the Toombs Bill, the refusal of the Republicans to join in any compromise that might deprive them of their sharpest political weapon, "Bleeding Kansas," and the new movement set on foot in the free states to call special sessions of the legislatures to appropriate money for Kansas relief and to demand the opening of the Missouri River, convinced the administration that heroic measures were necessary to save the situation.* About the middle of August it was decided to remove Governor Shannon and to send John W. Geary to Kansas as governor, with instructions to open the Missouri River and to restore peace in the

---

* On July 27, Webb wrote to William Barnes: "My letters from Washington state that the Administration Party begin to be alarmed at the course of events resulting from the recent lawless proceedings and gross outrages committed in the Territory and are busily engaged in contriving counteracting schemes. I should not be surprised to hear of Shannon's recall and LeCompte's condemnation" (original letter, William Barnes Papers).

territory at almost any price. It was decided, too, to release the free-state prisoners held at Lecompton on charges of treason.

All during the summer, Lawrence had been making every possible effort on behalf of these prisoners. First, he wrote to President Pierce and appealed to influential politicians. When this failed, he sent Pomeroy to Washington to appeal directly to the President.* Still getting no satisfaction, he hit upon the idea of playing upon the high esteem in which his stepmother was held by her nephew, President Pierce. But let Bishop Lawrence (son of Amos A.) tell the story:

"He first wrote the draft of such a letter as would have been written by a wife imploring the release of her husband. This letter was then copied by Mrs. Robinson, who took precaution to omit some of the more sentimental passages, and was sent to Mrs. Pierce inclosed with a letter from Mr. Lawrence's stepmother, who was a favorite aunt of the President. Mrs. Pierce, after reading the letter, handed it to her husband, and a few days later Mr. Lawrence was able to write to Mrs. Robinson, 'Not long since the President wrote to my brother that he had given such instructions as would gratify him and his friends here, especially my mother, whose good opinion he valued more than that of all the politicians.' "[80]

Although Lawrence and the Robinsons attributed the release of the prisoners to this intervention, it probably had little if any effect, as they were undoubtedly released for political reasons.

Geary was able to restore a semblance of peace in Kansas and to secure, through Governor Sterling Price of Missouri, the opening of the river, so that by the time of the election the excitement had died down. Pennsylvania was carried by the fact that Buchanan was a "favorite son," reinforced, it was charged in Republican circles, by the outright purchase of votes in Philadel-

---

*Pomeroy went to Washington July 12 on a triple errand. On behalf of Lawrence he was to appeal to President Pierce to release Robinson, and was to sound out S. G. Haven as to the best course for both Haven and Lawrence to pursue to further Fillmore's candidacy (Lawrence Letters, 152-55). On behalf of the Emigrant Aid Company, he was to lobby against the Toombs Bill (Aid Company Letters, Book B, 163, 168, 178).

phia,[81] so that Buchanan was elected. But the "Bleeding Kansas" issue, provided for the Republicans largely through the national Kansas Aid movement and the activities of the Emigrant Aid Company, had changed the course of history none the less. It had carried the Republican party through the most critical campaign of its history, and had cut the ground from under its rival, the American party. Moreover, the inability of the Democrats to avert the issue had forced the administration to abandon the struggle for Kansas, thus enabling the Free State party to consolidate its position so that it could withstand the Lecompton movement of the next year, and take possession of the territorial government. Finally, despite the attacks of the administration upon it, the campaign had left the Emigrant Aid Company unscathed and in a stronger position than it had ever occupied before.

CHAPTER XII

The End of the Crusade

WHEN GOVERNOR JOHN W. GEARY arrived in Kansas on September 9, 1856, the chaos in the territory had reached its zenith. Everywhere "Jayhawking," or plundering enemy settlements, was rife. Lane's raid had thrown Lecompton into panic. The reign of terror at Leavenworth was unchecked. Atchison's "Grand Army" was concentrating against Lawrence, which had been left well-nigh defenseless by the withdrawal of Lane and of the reinforcements he had called to attack Hickory Point. Both sides were committed to a war of extermination, and murder and pillage stalked the land.

Governor Geary went to work with a will. He arrived at Lecompton late at night on September 12, and the next morning delivered his inaugural address in which he announced his intention to "do justice at all hazards," and pleaded with the bona fide settlers to banish outside influence and begin anew. "Let the past be buried in oblivion," he urged: "Let all strife and bitterness cease."[1] The same morning he issued two proclamations, one ordering all armed forces, including the existing territorial militia, to disband, and the other ordering all adult male citizens to enroll themselves for militia duty.[2] These proclamations were followed up the following day by orders to the militia generals to disband the forces under their command.[3] But Geary was not the man to depend on mere orders and proclamations. He had already sent a private agent to Lawrence to investigate rumors. Receiving a message from this agent sometime after midnight, on September 12-13, he called upon Colonel Cooke for an escort and rode the rest of the night to reach Lawrence. Here he assured the people that they would be protected, but seeing no immediate danger to the town, he returned to Lecompton during the afternoon of September 13, to find that village thrown into panic by reports of Lane's and Harvey's activities at Ozawkee and Hickory Point. He at once dispatched a squadron of federal dragoons, which on the night of September 14 captured almost the whole of Colonel Harvey's command, 101 men.[4] Before this expedition had returned, Governor Geary, hearing that Secretary Woodson, whom he had sent to disperse Atchison's army, was unsuccessful, gathered all the troops he could and went to Lawrence on the afternoon of September 15. Placing a battery of artillery on Mount Oread, where their guns could cover the approach from Franklin, Geary went alone in the early morning of September 16 to the pro-slavery camp at Franklin, called the leaders together, and in the name of the President ordered them to disperse.[5] According to a rumor current at the time, he told Atchison that one more raid would ruin the Democratic party. Not daring to do battle with United States troops under the personal command of the governor, the host of 2,700 melted away and Lawrence was saved.

From this moment, peace rapidly returned to Kansas. By enrolling both free-state and pro-slavery men in his new federal militia, Geary was able to break up the guerrilla bands and to restore order. By the middle of December quiet was restored, so that the new militia could be dismissed. Since there was still a scarcity of necessities and an even greater scarcity of employment, it was necessary to continue the relief work on through the fall and winter. But despite this fact, 1857 opened as a boom year in Kansas. Speculation in claims and town lots ran riot. New "paper" towns—and some real ones—sprang up like the proverbial mushrooms. As the spring opened, new settlers swarmed in, and Kansas appeared to have entered upon an era of peace and prosperity.

At first the free-state people did not place much confidence in Governor Geary, but by the time of the Presidential election he had definitely cast his lot with their side. He was particularly intimate with Robinson and Pomeroy. Shortly after the election,

Amos A. Lawrence wrote to both of them to "keep a good influence about" the governor.[6] At nearly the same time, in reply to a letter of congratulations, Geary wrote Lawrence "a large letter, rather flowery, but showing the right spirit,"[7] in which he outlined his program, or such portion of it as he was willing to have known, in a manner highly satisfactory to the officials of the Emigrant Aid Company.[8] But so excessive was the praise showered upon the governor by free-state settlers and newspapers that both Lawrence and Dr. Webb suggested to Pomeroy it might be desirable ostensibly to find some fault, lest Geary be removed as too satisfactory to the Free State party.[9]

As soon as he had a grasp of the situation in Kansas, Geary concocted a scheme by which Kansas was to be admitted under the Topeka constitution and he himself, as an administration Democrat, should be elected state governor. Robinson was taken into the deal and agreed to step aside in favor of Geary. According to the plan, Geary was to secure the backing of the administration, and Robinson was to go to Washington, when Congress should meet, and reconcile the Republicans.[10] To clear the ground for this project (since it would spoil everything for the Emigrant Aid Company to appear to be sponsoring the arrangement), Robinson late in September, 1856, resigned his Company agency.* On October 3 the Executive Committee voted to accept Robinson's resignation, subject to the proviso that his salary as agent should continue for six months and that he should continue to correspond with the Company.[11] About December 1 Robinson explained the plan to Lawrence, who expressed approval of the entire scheme except the sidetracking of Robinson as governor.[12] Both Geary and Lawrence believed that the Democratic party leaders would welcome the arrangement to align Kansas with their party and to save embarrassment to the incoming adminis-

---

* On August 14, Lawrence had written to Robinson, "If your position in regard to the Emigrant Aid Company prejudices you with the people of the Territory, you had better resign it, just making sure that we will make good the deficiency in your income while you devote yourself to the politics of the Territory" (Lawrence Letters, 167).

tration. It was assumed that the Republicans would be content with the glory of having saved Kansas to freedom. But neither the administration nor the Republicans in Congress could be converted to the idea, and the only consequence of the move was to bring about Geary's removal on the very day that Buchanan became president.

During the summer of 1856 the affairs of the Emigrant Aid Company in Kansas had been almost as chaotic as the condition of the territory itself. The regular activities of the Company had come to an almost complete standstill, while all efforts had gone into relief work and politics. No building could take place, and the three mills stored at Kansas City could not be moved. During June the Company had no active agent in Kansas. Robinson was imprisoned at Lecompton. Pomeroy left Kansas immediately after the sack of Lawrence and a few weeks later was sent to Washington, where he remained, except for brief intervals, until Congress adjourned in August. S. N. Simpson, of Lawrence, took charge of the Company's relief work. Late in June it was decided to send Branscomb to Kansas to look after Company business until Pomeroy could return or Robinson should be released.[13] Branscomb left Boston on July 1 and reached Lawrence in about three weeks. As soon as he could make a tour of inspection, he reported to Dr. Webb that the Company's business was in a very bad condition. The mills were earning no rent, while claims against the Company for debts and damages were cropping up on every hand, and creditors were growing impatient.[14] In the face of these circumstances and of the state of war that prevailed in Kansas, the Company sought to set its house in order and to resume normal activities. The officers were eager to move the mills from Kansas City and get them into operation, and to begin the rebuilding of the Free State Hotel.[15] Branscomb was instructed to endeavor to collect rents and other debts owing to the Company, and to check up on the mill machinery stored at Kansas City—to secure descriptions of the packages, the amount of charges, and the like.[16] Although Dr. Webb fretted all summer because Pomeroy was away from Kansas,[17] the Executive Committee would not permit him to leave Washington until the final adjournment of Congress. But on September 1, Pomeroy was sent back to Kansas to take charge of the Company's business in general, while Branscomb was left in charge of the rebuilding of the hotel.[18] About the same time, the Company treasury secured a little money, and Branscomb was directed to pay up to fifty per cent on the most urgent bills, to a total not exceeding a thousand dollars.[19] When Robinson's resignation was received about October 1, Branscomb was designated permanent agent to work in cooperation with Pomeroy, as Robinson had been doing.

In the meantime, an effort was made to tighten the reins on the agents—a reform long overdue. Prior to the summer of 1856 the agents had been allowed a free hand, with only the most general instructions. There had been no adequate system of reporting to the home office, so that the Executive Committee never knew exactly how it stood with debtors, creditors, or even with the agents themselves. Unheard-of creditors were always bobbing up with new demands, and at each accounting with the agents unexpected claims appeared for commissions, expenses, and other miscellaneous items. When the agents' accounts were called in for audit, they were found to have been kept in such haphazard fashion as to be all but meaningless. Indeed, the Executive Committee had only a vague notion as to what property the Company owned in Kansas. When Branscomb was sent out in July, a subcommittee of the Executive Committee, consisting of Le Baron Russell and C. J. Higginson, was appointed to supervise and instruct the agents, and from that time on a more strict accounting was required. On October 1, when Branscomb was appointed a general agent, a new set of instructions was drawn up for both him and Pomeroy. They were to devote themselves exclusively to Company business, and were forbidden to engage in politics or to make private investments. Their first duty was to be the settle-

[235]

ment of accounts, both payable and receivable, and they were to send a detailed statement to the secretary without delay. They were to invoice all property, secure deeds to all real estate held by the Company, and to report the precise items of all existing contracts. They were cautioned especially to be accurate in all their accounts, to send vouchers for all transactions and copies of all future contracts, and to report every two weeks.[20]

At the same time these joint instructions were issued, separate instructions were given to Branscomb relative to work on the hotel. This hotel project had claimed the best efforts of the Company during the first year and a half of its existence, and the destruction of the original building was a staggering blow. However, little time was spent in weeping. On June 3, scarcely a week after news of the destruction had reached Boston, a special meeting of the Executive Committee was called to lay plans for rebuilding.[21] A stock subscription drive was launched for the purpose, but it was soon submerged in relief work. About the middle of June Pomeroy was sent to Washington to lay before Congress a claim for the value of the destroyed building;[22] at the same time he was authorized to hire Colonel Eldridge to remove the rubbish and begin work on the new basement, and an appropriation of two thousand dollars was made for the purpose.[23] Dr. Cabot arranged to have his brother, who was an architect, draw plans for the new building gratis. But Eldridge, who was in the East at the time, did not return to Kansas until fall, so that nothing had been done on the ground when Branscomb was sent to Kansas in July. Branscomb was authorized to proceed with the work, and did so as rapidly as the unsettled state of affairs in Lawrence would permit. By August 11 the Massachusetts State Kansas Committee had turned over to the Emigrant Aid Company one thousand dollars to be used as wages for labor (as a form of relief),[24] and this had been used by Branscomb for work on the hotel. Branscomb's instructions of October 1 were to remain in charge of the hotel, and to continue with the work if conditions seemed to warrant; he was authorized to draw for not more than two thousand dollars for the work.[25]

After the Presidential election the members of the Executive Committee grew discouraged. The treasury was nearly empty, and there seemed to be little prospect of collecting the damage claim against the government. There was much uncertainty as to what Buchanan might do, and as to how the Kansas settlers might react to his policy. At best, it was doubtful whether or not construction work could go on during the winter months, and it appeared much more urgent to get the mills at Kansas City into operation. Accordingly the Committee decided, on November 7, to recommend to Branscomb and Pomeroy that work on the hotel be suspended and that the balance of the letter of credit be used to move the mills.[26] When Branscomb replied urging the continuation of construction, it was definitely decided to suspend the work until funds should be available to complete the building.[27] Branscomb continued in frequent letters to urge the resumption of building operations,[28] but when it was learned that two other hotels were being built in Lawrence by individuals, the Executive Committee was less inclined than ever to push the project, since they did not "care to interfere with individual enterprise."[29] When, early in February, 1857, S. W. Eldridge* offered to purchase the hotel basement, stable, and lots for five thousand dollars, the offer was accepted.[30]

At no time did the Company entirely abandon its efforts to secure stock subscriptions, but as long as the relief work appeared to be paramount, little was accomplished in this direction. After the Presidential election, with quiet restored in Kansas, the Executive Committee decided to renew this activity. On November 14 Dr. Webb wrote to Seth Paddleford, one of the directors: "The reflecting part of the community is becoming more and more convinced that the original plan of the New England Emigrant

---

*Eldridge and his brothers built on this foundation the buiding that was destroyed in the Quantrill Raid of 1863. Today the fourth hotel, still called "Hotel Eldridge," stands on the site.

Aid Company is the true one for saving Kansas; we therefore intend to move again forthwith in the matter of procuring original stock subscriptions."[31] The plan was to call a meeting of persons engaged in a certain trade or business, and make a general appeal; this was to be followed by personal solicitation at the place of business of each prospect. At first these meetings were held in the Company office; later, "parlor meetings" were held.[32] Thayer usually addressed the meetings and helped with the solicitation.[33] It was confidently expected that a hundred thousand dollars could be raised in this manner. For each ten thousand subscribed, the subscribing group should be permitted to select the name of a new town in Kansas to be located by the Company.

The movement started off with a flourish. The first meeting called, that of the shoe and leather dealers, pledged twenty thousand dollars, and selected the names of Claflin and Batcheller (for Lee Claflin and J. and E. Batcheller, shoe and leather dealers of Boston) to be given to two new towns in Kansas.* In his December letters Dr. Webb was jubilant.[34] But success was short-lived. A number of office meetings of various trades were held, and the parlor meetings continued down into March, 1857, but no more large subscriptions were secured. On January 26, 1857, Webb confessed to Branscomb: "Thus far our efforts to increase the stock subscriptions (beyond what was accomplished with the shoe and leather dealers) have not been very successful, and from the lukewarmness which prevails, some of our Board have little faith that much more can or will be accomplished."[35] In this same letter Dr. Webb suggested that it might be necessary to sell some of the mills in Kansas to release funds for additional improvements. During the first six months of 1857 collections on outstanding subscriptions, reinforced by some installment payments from Eldridge on the purchase of the hotel, kept the treasury in a fair condition, but by July the Executive Committee had to face

---

* Report of Assistant Treasurer, April 10, 1854, showed the shoe and the leather subscription as $18,720, of which $17,860 had been paid or was considered good (Aid Company Records, Book III, 97-98).

the fact that no more money could be raised from stock and that for the future the Company must depend upon sales and collections in Kansas.[36] Perhaps it is gratuitous to theorize as to the cause of this stoppage. One reason undoubtedly was that the East was already beginning to feel the pinch of that financial stringency that was to become the following August the "panic of 1857." But the main reason would appear to be that, freedom seeming to be secure in Kansas, men were no longer willing to subscribe money to accomplish that end, whereas, despite the flattering prospects in Kansas during the winter and spring, the stock of the Company did not appeal to Eastern businessmen as either a safe investment or an attractive speculation. So far as Eastern contributors were concerned, the Kansas crusade was ended.

After the unfortunate experience with Dr. Cutter's party, Dr. Webb did not push the emigrant business very energetically, but he did not abandon it entirely. He supplied tickets to the Worcester party under Martin Stowell which left for Kansas on June 27, 1856, and which, as nearly as can now be determined, numbered twenty-seven when it left Worcester.* Small parties left on the 10th and 17th of July. On July 29 there was a party conducted by a "Rev. Mr. Parsons," which numbered "about fifty."[37] Webb, through William Barnes, furnished the tickets for the first party sent by the Vermont Kansas Relief Committee, which left Albany on August 20 and numbered twenty-two.[38] During the latter part of August and all of September Webb reported that no parties were leaving, but that he was ready to send any who might appear each Tuesday. During this time he sent a number of individuals to Chicago to join the emigrant train that Eldridge, Pomeroy, and Robert Morrow were forming under the auspices of the National Kansas Committee.[39]

---

* Dr. Webb mentioned supplying the tickets, but did not state the number (Aid Company Letters, Book B, 50). E. P. Harris, a member of the party, writing from memory about 1900, prepared an account for the *Kansas Historical Collections,* VIII, 313-14. He says the party, as finally organized, numbered thirty-one of whom three joined at New York.

By December Dr. Webb was laying plans for the spring migration, which he expected to be large. He announced that as in former seasons Tuesday would be party day, but that he would sell individual tickets to those who preferred them. He expected to secure reductions in fares of as much as 25 per cent. In letters far too numerous to cite, beginning December 2, 1856, and running well into the spring, he answered inquiries of prospective emigrants stating that parties would start as soon as the Missouri River should be free of ice.[40] The first party of the spring left Boston on March 3; the number is nowhere mentioned, but Webb referred to it as "a small party."[41] For the next few weeks small parties were reported, but most applications were for individual tickets. Since the railroads gave only one conductor's pass with each fifty tickets, conductors were sent only with privately organized parties. On April 23 Webb replied to an applicant who desired to conduct a party: "There has been scarcely a day for a month past that we have not ticketed persons for Kansas. They go in small squads generally, instead of large parties as last year, and consequently there is no necessity for conducting agents."[42] Webb furnished tickets for a party of thirty-five from New Hampshire, which left Boston on March 12, conducted by A. B. Marshall, and settled at Zeandale, near Manhattan.[43] He also furnished tickets for a New Jersey party, organized by A. P. Nixon, which left New York on April 14.[44] By May the party idea was virtually abandoned, although on June 12 Webb informed an applicant, "As Tuesday is still looked upon as party day, it is the one on which you would be most likely to find company."[45] He continued to sell individual tickets until the following spring. The emigrant books indicate that from the beginning of the spring migration in 1857 until the end of July, he sold 370 tickets, and from Aguust, 1857, until April, 1857, 172 more.[46]

But however important the work of the Emigrant Aid Company may have been in stimulating migration to Kansas during the first critical year, its best efforts had become inconsequential

[240]

by 1857. Kansas was filling rapidly, but from the states of the Old
Northwest. Of the many letters from that territory reporting the
volume of the spring migration of 1857, the following from the
Reverend Ephraim Nute of Lawrence, dated April 28, may be
taken as typical: "The immigration continues to increase. Hundreds come to this place [Lawrence] daily, and, at lowest com-
putation, a thousand a day into the Territory, probably three
thousand. They are of the right kind to stay,—families from the
Western states, with their teams, stock, furniture, farming tools,
etc."[47] In this great stream, the few hundred who trickled westward under the auspices of the Emigrant Aid Company were
but as a tiny brook to a mighty river. In this respect, too, as in the
making of investments, the Company's work was done; the Kansas crusade was ended.

"We have in contemplation to establish several towns in different sections of the Territory," wrote Dr. Webb at the close of
1856.[48] The Company had obligated itself to establish two towns
to be called Claflin and Batcheller, and at the beginning of 1857
it set out to comply with the obligation. Early in January, 1857,
Pomeroy made arrangements with some Shawnee Indians to
launch a town at the mouth of the Wakarusa (the present site of
Eudora, then known as Fish's Crossing) as soon as the reservation
should be surveyed and opened to settlement. The Emigrant Aid
Company was to receive a one-sixth interest, and the town was to
be called Batcheller.[49] Pomeroy was authorized to purchase a
Wyandotte float, if necessary, to secure the title.[50] But when, a
few weeks later, John Calhoun's surveyors platted that portion of
the Shawnee Reserve, they left no land in that vicinity open to
pre-emption—"a trick of the pro-slavery officers," Pomeroy declared, "to hurt and prevent the Yankees settling upon the upper
part of the Reserve."[51] About the same time Pomeroy was dickering with several Lawrence men to found a town on Big Sugar
Creek in Linn County,[52] but the project fell through. In March
the Executive Committee authorized Pomeroy to establish a town

[241]

on the Missouri River, as nearly as possible opposite St. Joseph, Missouri, and to locate a sawmill there.[53] As soon as the instructions reached him, Pomeroy made a trip up the river to inspect the proposed townsite, but, as will be explained more fully presently, he was persuaded by the proprietors of Atchison to purchase an interest in that place instead of launching a rival town.

In February, 1857, C. C. Hutchinson and B. B. Newton applied to the Emigrant Aid Company for a mill for a Vermont colony which they proposed to establish in Kansas.[54] In May this group founded the town of Mapleton, north of Fort Scott, and renewed their application for a mill.[55] After several months of dickering, an agreement was reached whereby the Company was to locate one of its mills there, receiving as a bonus one-fourth interest in the town, and the name of the settlement was to be changed to Claflin.[56] One of the smaller mills at Kansas City was assigned to Claflin, but before arrangements could be made to move it, it was levied upon and sold for storage charges.[57] Pomeroy made repeated efforts to recover the mill, resorting to a lawsuit when other means failed, but it was still tied up by litigation when the Company closed out its affairs. Naturally, the proprietors of Mapleton considered themselves absolved from the obligation to change the name of their town or to assign an interest in it to the Emigrant Aid Company; but the Company officials continued to talk of "Claflin," and never quite gave up the idea that the Company owned an interest in the place.

In the fall of 1857, a group of Manhattan men, headed by S. D. Houston, who were projecting a town on the Republican River northwest of Manhattan, proposed to Dr. Webb that they call the place Batcheller, on condition that the Emigrant Aid Company locate a mill there.[58] Negotiations dragged on through the fall and winter, and in the spring of 1858 an agreement was reached.[59] The town was duly christened "Bacheller,"* but this

---

* The man for whom the town was named spelled the name "Batcheller," with the *t*, and this spelling is used in the records and correspondence of the Emigrant Aid Company. In Kansas, however, the name was usually "Bacheller," without the *t*.

became distorted into "Bachelder." After the Civil War the name was changed to "Milford."

Almost from the beginning of its operations, the Emigrant Aid Company had been urged to sponsor German migration to Kansas.[60] Early in 1857, the Executive Committee was persuaded by Dr. Charles F. Kob, a German physician, to do something toward the promotion of such migration, and to assist him in establishing a German language newspaper there.[61] They even toyed with the idea of sending Kob or someone else to Germany to recruit immigrants.[62] The Executive Committee appropriated three hundred dollars to buy type, and appointed Cabot and Hale as a committee to raise such additional funds as might be needed by contributions.[63] In May a pamphlet in German, *Information for German Immigrants,* written by Kob, was published jointly by the Emigrant Aid Company and the Massachusetts State Kansas Committee.[64] About the same time a quadruple contract was formed among the State Kansas Committee, the Emigrant Aid Company, Kob, and Pomeroy (in his capacity of a proprietor of Atchison), according to which Kob was to establish a free-state newspaper in Atchison, to be printed in German and called *Die Kanzas Zeitung.*[65] The Emigrant Aid Company lent the type gratis, and the paper was to be printed on the press of the *Squatter Sovereign,* now free-state in politics. About the first of June Kob left for Kansas, accompanied, according to Pomeroy, by "a large party of fine looking Germans."[66]

While negotiations were in progress with Kob, the Reverend F. M. Serenbetz, a German Congregational minister, applied to the Emigrant Aid Company, through Hale, for assistance in taking his congregation to Kansas.[67] The Executive Committee decided to give Serenbetz a letter of introduction to Pomeroy and to instruct the Company agents to assist him in locating his colony; they also authorized Hale to raise two hundred dollars for the Serenbetz party.[68] The first week in April Serenbetz left for Kansas with thirty of his people, planning for the rest of the congregation to follow later.[69] They arrived in Lawrence destitute, and it cost the various relief agencies there some three hundred and fifty dollars to move them on to their location, one hundred dollars of this being borne by the Emigrant Aid Company.[70] No sooner were the Germans located than Serenbetz wrote to the Company begging for another five hundred dollars.[71] But with all their financial deficiencies, the Serenbetz party did found the town of Humboldt, to which, through them, the Emigrant Aid Company may lay some claim.

During the summer of 1856 a group of Lawrence men, among them C. W. Babcock, B. W. Woodward, and O. E. Learnard, projected the town of Burlington across the Neosho River from the still undeveloped site of Hampden, and a tentative agreement was made with the Emigrant Aid Company to set up their Hampden mill there.[72] Because of the unsettled state of affairs in Kansas, nothing was done to plant the projected settlement until the following spring. At that time a contract was made between the Company and Learnard by which the mill was sold to Learnard for four hundred dollars cash and ten shares in the town of Burlington, he to gather up the machinery "wherever and in whatever condition he may find it."[73] Thus the Company became a part proprietor of the town of Burlington in succession to the interest it was to have had in Hampden.

Soon after his release from the prison camp, Robinson joined with S. N. Simpson and Abelard Guthrie, a Wyandotte Indian, in plans for the town of Quindaro. Robinson straightway wrote to the Emigrant Aid Company offering an interest, to which Dr. Webb replied, on October 7, that while the Company would like to engage in the new settlement, it could not do so because of financial stringency, though it might locate a mill there.[74] A month later the Executive Committee, despairing of being able, for financial reasons, to move the large mill to Lawrence, for which it was intended, authorized Pomeroy to sell it to the Quindaro Association for town shares.[75] Sometime during December

[244]

or January an agreement was reached whereby, in payment for the mill, the town company paid the $1,688.28 freight and storage charges, Dr. Robinson cancelled his account of $1,962.53 against the Emigrant Aid Company, and the Company received ten shares or one hundred lots in the town of Quindaro.[76] About the same time negotiations were opened with the proprietors of the rival town of Wyandotte to locate one of the small mills there, but no agreement was reached.

By far the most important interest acquired by the Emigrant Aid Company in 1857 was in Atchison. When, early in April, Pomeroy went up the Missouri River to spy out a location for Claflin or Batcheller, he fell in with Robert McBratney, representing an emigrant aid organization in Cincinnati, who had an offer from the Atchison town company to sell a controlling interest in the town, and who proposed to let Pomeroy in on the deal for the Company. Pomeroy agreed tentatively. While McBratney stopped at Atchison to see what could be done, Pomeroy went on to St. Joseph, but decided that no site in that locality was comparable to Atchison.[77] Accordingly, he returned to Atchison, and he and McBratney closed the deal. Between them they agreed to buy fifty-one of the one hundred shares into which the town stock was divided, arranging for an immediate apportionment of the lots represented. In addition, Pomeroy bargained for the purchase of a three-story frame hotel and of the *Squatter Sovereign,* and agreed to build a flour mill. Since he had no authority from the Emigrant Aid Company to enter into such a transaction, he bought in his own name, offering to relinquish to the Company all or any part of the purchase.[78] C. J. Higginson and Martin Brimmer, members of the Executive Committee, had left for Kansas on a tour of inspection a few days before Pomeroy's first letter about the Atchison proposal was received. A letter was dispatched immediately urging them to hurry to Atchison, decide what part of Pomeroy's purchase the Company could assume, and draw on the treasury to complete such part of the transaction.[79]

When Higginson and Brimmer reached Atchison they found that Pomeroy's purchases would involve $11,000 cash, as much more in six months, and the obligation to spend $50,000 on improvements. In view of the complete stoppage of stock subscriptions, this was obviously beyond the capacity of the Company to handle. Accordingly, they agreed, on behalf of the Company, to take one hundred lots at five dollars each, and the hotel and its site at three thousand dollars. They agreed, further, to put up a flour mill.[80] Pomeroy purchased the *Squatter Sovereign* in conjunction with McBratney and F. G. Adams. These two partners published the paper for a time; then Pomeroy bought them out, and sold the business to O. F. Short. The next year, it passed into the possession of John A. Martin, who changed the name to *Freedom's Champion* and published the paper until his death in 1889. Despite some assertions to the contrary, the Emigrant Aid Company never owned an interest in the paper.

Closely interwoven with the matter of town interests was the question of mills. All during the summer and fall of 1856, the Executive Committee wrestled with the problem of the three mills stored at Kansas City. They were especially desirous of setting up the large mill at Lawrence to replace the old one that was partially disabled, and even considered diverting relief funds to that purpose.[81] Efforts were made to sell the smaller mills or to find parties who would pay the freight and storage charges, move the mills at their own expense, and get them into operation, taking their pay in the earnings of the mills—but without success.[82] A fruitless effort was made to sell the old mill at Lawrence for enough to move and set up the new one there.[83] In the meantime Branscomb reported that the storage charges on the mills at Kansas City were eating up their value.[84] In November, 1856, despairing of being able to set up the large mill at Lawrence, the Executive Committee decided to let it go to the proprietors of Quindaro on the best terms they could get.[85] The resulting arrangement has already been discussed. When, a month later, the shoe and leather subscription was obtained, it was decided to hold the two smaller mills to be located in Claflin and Batcheller when those towns should be established.[86] However, before instructions to this effect reached Pomeroy in Kansas, he had accepted an offer from the proprietors of Wabaunsee and, as had been originally intended, had assigned one of the smaller mills to that settlement. The arrangement was that some one, on behalf of the town company, should move the mill and set it up, taking pay in sawing at four dollars per hundred, and that the mill site and four shares in the town should be assigned to the Emigrant Aid Company as a bonus.[87] The mill was moved during the spring,[88] but did not get into operation until the following December or January.[89]

During the spring stock drive of 1856, a Mr. Morris sold the Company a grist mill for stock.[90] During the summer this mill could not be shipped because of border conditions, and in the fall funds were not available for the purpose until the season was so far advanced that the Missouri River was ice-blocked. Consequently the Morris mill lay in storage in Boston until March, 1857. During February, 1857, J. N. Buffum of Lynn, Masachusetts, and Isaac Adams of Boston each offered the Company an engine, for which they would take part pay in stock.[91] After several weeks' delay, during which time special committees inspected the engines and dickered on terms, both offers were accepted.[92] The Buffum engine, a planing mill purchased with it, and the Morris grist mill were shipped by water via New Orleans during the last week in March, 1857.[93] The Adams engine was shipped by rail on May 2.[94] Before the Buffum engine reached Kansas, the Atchison agreement had been made, according to which the Company was to build a flour mill there; therefore, this engine was forwarded immediately to Atchison.[95] The Adams engine, with the planing mill and the Morris grist mill, appears to have been stored at Quindaro, and several months later it was assigned to

[247]

Batcheller.* In June Pomeroy bought flour mill machinery for Atchison from W. W. Hamer & Co., of Cincinnati.[96]

During the early months of 1857, requests poured in upon the Emigrant Aid Company for aid in all sorts of local development projects. Practically every settlement with which the Company had connections wanted a hotel, one or more churches, a schoolhouse, and some dwelling houses for rental.† Obviously, in its embarrassed financial condition, the Company could not comply with all these requests, even in the hope that such developments would enhance the value of its property in the various localities. But when Higginson and Brimmer were in Kansas in April, 1857, they did obligate the Company on several of these proposals. They promised, conditionally, subscriptions of one thousand dollars each toward the building of hotels in Manhattan and Osawatomie.[97] They arranged for the building of a schoolhouse in Topeka (the Executive Committee had already voted to build it if the office building in Lawrence could be sold)[98] and pledged a hundred dollars toward a schoolhouse for Manhattan.[99] Bishop Kemper, happening to be in Lawrence at the time, persuaded them to promise to donate a lot there for an Episcopal church (the only such donation ever made by the Emigrant Aid Company).[100] When Higginson reported back to the Executive Committee, they objected to becoming partners in the two hotel projects for fear of subsequent liabilities. Instead, they proposed that at Manhattan the Emigrant Aid Company advance the thousand dollars as the purchase price of additional town shares, the town proprietors, who were also the projectors of the hotel, to invest

---

* There is some confusion as to whether the Batcheller mill was the one purchased from Adams or the one previously sold to Quindaro, but a careful analysis of the correspondence indicates that it was the Adams mill. Earlier writers were probably confused by references to the Batcheller mill as "the mill at Quindaro."

† Some of the letters making requests, most of them dated in January or February, 1857: from O. C. Brown, Osawatomie, wanting a hotel (Aid Company Records, Book C, 26); from C. B. Lines, Wabaunsee, wanting a church and a schoolhouse (*ibid.*, 25); from M. C. Dickey, Topeka, wanting a church and a schoolhouse (*ibid.*, 39-41); from N. S. Storrs, lessee of the mill at Osawatomie, wanting a hotel and some rental houses (*ibid.*, 44-45); from Branscomb urging the building of a hotel in Topeka (*ibid.*, 105); from the Rev. C. E. Blood, Manhattan, wanting a schoolhouse (*ibid.*, 112-16).

this in the hotel project.[101] It is impossible to tell from either the correspondence or the account books whether or not this plan was carried out. The agreement finally reached at Osawatomie was that the Company should release to the hotel company six of its town shares to be sold at not less than $250 each, the hotel company agreeing to repay in two years the amount raised by the sale of the shares.[102] The hotel was built; but when the loan fell due, the proprietors pleaded inability to pay,[103] and so far as the records show, it was never collected.

The lot promised to the Episcopalians was eventually deeded.[104] It was not the policy of the Company to give direct aid to churches, although it appears that Pomeroy, on behalf of the Company, made a pledge to the Methodist church at Manhattan which was paid by remitting the charges for sawing at the Company's mill and crediting the amount to the miller on his rent.[105] Dr. Webb's information pamphlet for May, 1857, carried an appeal for building funds for the various denominations in Lawrence;[106] and Webb, Hale, Williams, and Lawrence exerted themselves personally to raise such funds. A part of the contributions for the building of the Plymouth Congregational Church in Lawrence were handled through the Company office in Boston,[107] and Amos A. Lawrence, although himself an Episcopalian, gave a thousand dollars toward it.[108]

During the summer and fall of 1857, the company built on two of its own lots in Topeka a two-story brick schoolhouse,[109] at a cost of two thousand dollars.[110] By the end of the year, it was occupied by a school "free to the pupils and supported by subscription," and on Sundays by the Methodists and Congregationalists as a place of worship.[111] The hundred-dollar subscription to the Manhattan schoolhouse was paid by sawing at the mill.[112] During the first two winters, the Emigrant Aid Company gave the use of a room in its office building in Lawrence for a subscription school.[113] In the fall of 1856, with the help of Edward Everett Hale, E. B. Whitman and the Reverend Ephraim

[249]

Nute raised money to build a Unitarian church in Lawrence, the basement of which was fitted up as a schoolroom.[114] During the winter of 1856-57 a free school, giving some high school work as well as elementary instruction, was operated in this room, supported by Whitman, Nute, and Amos A. Lawrence. Lawrence was always much interested in education in Kansas, and as early as 1855 began talking about endowing a "Memorial College" for the town of Lawrence. In February, 1857, he placed in the hands of Robinson and Pomeroy as trustees, two $5,000 notes of Lawrence University, Appleton, Wisconsin (which he had previously founded), an assignment of $1,000 accrued interest, and one hundred shares of stock in the Emigrant Aid Company,[115] to serve as the nucleus of an endowment for such a college. Until the money should be used for that purpose, he directed that the income, six hundred dollars a year, be used for the support of Sunday schools and day schools in Kansas.[116] Eventually, this fund was devoted to the establishment of the University of Kansas at Lawrence.[117] In July of 1857, the Emigrant Aid Company was solicited for a contribution to a proposed college in Manhattan.[118] The question was deferred from time to time, but about a year later the Executive Committee voted to assign twenty of its lots in Manhattan to the Bluemont Central College Association to be sold, one-half of the proceeds to be devoted to the college, the other half paid to the Company.[119] The agreement was carried out, and in the fall of 1859 the lots were deeded to the college, the Company receiving $785 as one-half their value.[120] A few years later Bluemont Central College became the Kansas State Agricultural College.[121]

The Emigrant Aid Company had been urged repeatedly to build rental houses in several of the settlements to encourage the development of the towns and enhance the value of the property, including its own, but only in Lawrence was anything of the sort done. In April, 1857, the Executive Committee authorized its agents to expend two thousand dollars for buildings in Lawrence, suggesting four simple cottages on as many lots.[122] While Higginson and Brimmer were in Kansas, they, together with Branscomb, selected two lots and arranged for the building of a stone house on each.[123] These were built during the summer at costs of $1,440.00 and $1,382.84 respectively.[124]

The annual meeting of stockholders of the Emigrant Aid Company occurred on May 26, 1857.[125] Amos A. Lawrence, who was in Wisconsin at the time, sent in his resignation as treasurer. With the substitution of Charles J. Higginson for Lawrence as treasurer, the same officers were re-elected. Lawrence was placed on the Board of Directors. Several of the old crusaders were dropped as directors and replaced by some of the new stockholders.* The Executive Committee chosen by the Board of Directors for the ensuing year consisted of J. M. S. Williams, chairman, Eli Thayer, Samuel Cabot, Jr., R. P. Waters, Le Baron Russell, Charles J. Higginson, Edward Everett Hale, and Martin Brimmer.[126]

In many respects, this annual meeting may be taken as marking, for the Emigrant Aid Company, the end of the Kansas crusade. In his letter of resignation as treasurer, Lawrence said: "The main object for which the association was formed, viz. the incitement of free emigration to Kansas, has been successfully accomplished. The corporation must hereafter be considered a land company and be managed as such."[127] A few weeks later he wrote to the Reverend Mr. Nute: "We look upon the great question as now settled, and all political movements in Kansas as having chiefly a local interest."[128] By the end of the year, Dr. Webb was ready to agree with John Carter Brown, president of the Company, that the work was done. "I consider with you," he wrote to Brown, "that our great mission is nearly accomplished; and I

---

* Those dropped were: H. C. Bowen, William Cullen Bryant, John Lowell, E. D. Morgan, Samuel Tobey, George B. Upton, and Francis Weyland. Those added, besides Lawrence were: Oliver Ames, Jr., Easton; Tyler Batcheller, Boston; Richard Bigelow, St. Louis; William P. Bullock, Providence; Abner Curtis, Abbington; Jacob A. Dresser, Boston; James H. Duncan, Haverhill; and George L. Stearns, Medford.

think that after fulfilling the stipulations already made, we should proceed to wind up the affairs of the Company as speedily as can be done consistently with the best interests of the stockholders."[129] Opponents of the Company also recognized that the battle was over. While negotiating the purchase of an interest in Atchison, Pomeroy wrote that both B. F. Stringfellow and his partner P. T. Abell had done their utmost to facilitate the bargain. "They both declare," he stated, "that they have done all they could to make Kansas a slave State; now they want to make some money, which, to quote from B. F. Stringfellow, 'can only be done by falling in with manifest destiny and letting it become a free State.' "[130]

From the spring of 1857 there was a shift of emphasis in Company affairs. The crusading spirit gave way to an attitude of business. To be sure, some of the Company's greatest works of benevolence were done after that time, as already noted, but the stress was laid on so managing the property as to return something to the stockholders. After his retirement from the treasurership, Amos A. Lawrence, the greatest crusader of all, took only a passing interest in Company affairs. Eli Thayer, although he retained his vice-presidency and his membership in the Executive Committee, lost interest in the concern and rarely attended committee meetings. He had been elected to Congress in the fall of 1856, and, after the spring of 1857, divided his attention between politics and a private colonization venture in western Virginia (now West Virginia), where his colonists founded the town of Ceredo.[131] John Carter Brown retained the presidency of the Company, but like Lawrence and Thayer, he took only a passing interest in its affairs after he regarded the Kansas question as settled. When the "Lecompton swindle," as the Lecompton constitution move was called in Emigrant Aid Company circles, came to a head, the Company officers took considerable interest in the outcome; but it had little, if any, effect on their actions or policies. It will be necessary in another chapter to sketch briefly the heroic

[252]

efforts of the Executive Committee to save something from the financial wreckage, but at best this part of the story is an anticlimax. It is utterly devoid of historical significance, and might be omitted entirely except that the average reader may be presumed to have a mild curiosity to learn what became of an organization about which such violent controversy had raged. The real work of the Company was done. The Kansas crusade was ended.

CHAPTER XIII

The Loaves and Fishes

THE DIRECTORS and the Executive Committee of the Emigrant Aid Company at no time lost sight of their goal of making the enterprise at least repay to the stockholders their original investment, and if possible, some margin of profit. During the days of the Kansas Conflict, this objective was crowded into the background, but when, in the spring of 1857, they became convinced that Kansas was safe, the directors turned their major attention to the pecuniary object. Already, during the preceding autumn, they had set about to restore some order in the Company's business affairs; and this effort had revealed the fact that the treasurer's books were hopelessly out of balance, and that the accounts were in a chaotic condition. In February, the Executive Committee undertook to work out a budget for the year. At the second weekly meeting of the month, Higginson and Thayer were made a committee to estimate the income in sight, to figure the current expenses, and to recommend appropriations.[1] A week later, February 20, this committee reported that the probable income for the next six months would be $26,736, of which $3,130 would be required for running expenses, and $3,000 was already appropriated for setting up a mill. Appropriations of the rest were recommended, chiefly for the purchase of more mills.[2] But in working out their figures, they had found discrepancies between the treasurer's books and Pomeroy's accounts. Accordingly, the Executive Committee directed Pomeroy to come East at once, bringing all his books and accounts for a check-up, and instructed the treasurer "to open a new set of books for the Company, to be kept by double entry here; and to arrange a system of accounts that shall insure exactness on the part of all agents and officers of the Company, conformity of books here with those in the Territory, and a frequent comparison of them through accounts current, trial balances, etc." This new set of books was opened by C. J. Higginson when he became treasurer three months later,[4] but they made little improvement in the condition of the Company's accounts.* During this same period the Committee on Agencies was attempting to compile a "Property Book" that would show a complete invoice of the Kansas property.[5] The old set of treasurer's books had contained no invoice of property, but had merely charged against each settlement in which the Company had property, a fixed proportion of general expenses; as a consequence, no one in Boston knew exactly what the Company owned, or what the various items had cost.† One of the purposes of sending Higginson and Brimmer to Kansas in the spring of 1857, was to have them invoice and evaluate the various items of Company property there.

But despite the confused state of the Company's business, the outlook during the spring and summer of 1857 was bright. It was a boom season in Kansas, and speculation was rife. Despite the Company's financial stringency, the agents and Executive Committee was dubious as to the advisability of selling property, believing that values must go higher; and several opportunities to make cash sales at substantial profits were passed up. So flattering were the prospects, that in May the Executive Committee took under consideration the proposal of Colonel Daniel Ruggles, of the United States Army, to operate in western Texas,[6] where they had already given some aid and encouragement to a colony of German settlers.[7] In June, a special Texas Committee was created, which prepared an elaborate report recommending that

---

* Only these later account books are preserved. Containing only summary entries of the first two years' transactions, they tell almost nothing about the operations of that period, and even for later transactions they were kept in such a manner that even expert accountants who have examined them have been able to learn little from them.

† Undated note of Le Baron Russell to A. A. Lawrence asking that Mr. Stone (the assistant treasurer) "ascertain from his books and such documents as Dr. Webb has or can find" the cost of certain items. The note concludes, "I do not wish to have the proportion of *general expense* charged on the Treasurer's books to any of these items, appear at all on the property book." Attached is a penciled sheet in Stone's handwriting giving the cost of some of the items and leaving others blank, thus indicating that there was no means of ascertaining them (original documents, Aid Company Papers).

the Company undertake operations in Texas as soon as funds should be available and the requisite information could be obtained. Ruggles and Frederick Law Olmsted* were engaged to work on the project[8] and an effort was made to interest English cotton manufacturers.[9] But before anything tangible had been achieved, the "Panic of 1857" had broken upon the country, and the project was put aside for the time.

But even this economic depression, which seriously retarded the operations of the Company, did not at once dampen the ardor of the Executive Committee. The condition was regarded as only transitory, and it was even suggested that the hard times in the East would stimulate migration to Kansas, and so revive boom conditions there by the summer of 1858. At the annual stockholders' meeting, May 25, 1858, Le Baron Russell, for the directors, gave a long report in a most optimistic tone, reciting the achievements of the Company during the preceding year and hinting at brilliant prospects for the immediate future.[10] At this meeting the same officers were re-elected. The roster of directors was changed only by the addition of Dr. Webb and Judge Thomas Russell, and by the dropping of several who had ceased to be active.[11] The only change in the Executive Committee was the addition of Judge Thomas Russell.[12]

However, despite the note of cheerfulness, the Company was having its troubles. It was finding its Kansas property unprofitable and well-nigh impossible to manage. People in Kansas appeared to assume that ordinary standards of honesty did not apply in dealings with the Emigrant Aid Company; all seemed to consider it fair plunder. This may be explained, on the one hand, by the reputation the Company had acquired as a benevolent institution, and on the other, by the Westerner's ingrained distrust of all corporations—especially absentee corporations. The mills

---

*Frederick Law Olmsted, previously mentioned in these pages in connection with the Abbott Howitzer, is known to students of American history as the author of *Journey in the Seaboard Slave States* and *Journey through Texas*. He was also a noted landscape architect who laid out Central Park in New York and had many other achievements to his credit.

offered an especially perplexing problem. Inevitably, they deteriorated from ordinary wear and tear, but even more from neglect and abuse. They were operated by lessees, who with rare exceptions, failed to take even ordinary care of machinery·and buildings, and, more often than not, defaulted on their rent. In every case the lease required the tenant to keep the mill in repair at his own expense, but the millers either did not make the needed repairs at all or tried to hold the Company for them, usually at outlandish figures, and to deduct the charges from their rent.* It was a part of Branscomb's job as agent to keep a check on the mills. At best this would have been difficult, with their wide distribution and the difficulties of travel and communication, but it is obvious that Branscomb did not make any great effort to perform this duty.

Similar difficulties were experienced with other properties. Tenants of the Lawrence houses and the Topeka schoolhouse were seeking to have additions or repairs made and to take the cost out of rents. Odd claims were always bobbing up. O. E. Learnard, purchaser of the Hampden-Burlington mill, claimed that the Company was obligated to buy him a circular saw, and a board of arbitration awarded $120 after he had offered to settle for $85.[13] Then the mills were damaged by the elements. At Manhattan, high water in the Blue River washed away the bank until there was danger that the mill would fall into the river.[14] In February, 1857, the Osage River overflowed at Osawatomie, completely submerging the mill.[15] The damage was soon repaired, and the mill was again put in operation, but sometime during the summer or fall it was burned.†

---

* The Manhattan mill is a good illustration. In May, 1857, Branscomb removed C. S. Stevens from the tenancy of the mill because he failed to make repairs and had fallen several months behind on his rent. The mill was then leased to D. A. Butterfield (later prominent as an operator of stage coach lines), and the Company agreed to buy him a lath mill provided he would set it up at his own expense .No sooner was the lath mill installed than Butterfield sent a bill for $453 charges for setting it up and refused to pay any more rent until his bill should be allowed. Meanwhile, Butterfield let the mill fall into disrepair until it was in danger of fire.

† Hale stated in the *Directors' History* that the mill was burned during the attack on Osawatomie. This was an error. The date of the fire is not mentioned in the letters or records, but it was in the late summer or early fall of 1857.

With a view to remedying these conditions, insofar at least as they were due to laxity on the part of agents, it was determined in February, 1858, to reorganize the agencies.[16] Branscomb having offered his resignation (by request), Martin F. Conway was employed as general agent at a salary of $1,000 a year and traveling expenses, to begin March 1. He was to recommend to the Executive Committee for appointment a local agent for each of the outlying settlements—Topeka, Manhattan, and Osawatomie. These local agents were to be paid a commission of 5 per cent on all cash collected for sales and rents, and were to be held strictly accountable to the general agent. Conway was to look after local matters in Lawrence. Pomeroy was continued at this old salary, and was to act as local agent at Atchison and to have charge of pending litigation in Kansas City relative to the American Hotel.[17]

When Conway took over the general agency from Branscomb, he found the accounts in a deplorable state. There was no adequate invoice of property, and no memoranda of existing contracts. It was impossible to tell what the Company owed or what was owed to it, and Branscomb, pleading inability to remember, was suspected of deliberately withholding information.[18] The Company had already had trouble with Branscomb for ignoring or violating his instructions in disposing of Company property. When his final accounts were presented, it was found that he had padded both his salary account and his expense account.[19] By his own figures he owed the Company $692.88 (it claimed several hundred dollars more) which he was unable to pay.[20] The matter dragged on until August when, being threatened with suit, Branscomb settled with the Company by giving his notes for $1,000 secured by mortgages on property owned by him.[21] During the summer of 1859, Pomeroy let the affairs of the Company in Atchison get into such a muddle that it was necessary to send Conway to straighten them out. The Executive Committee, however, did not suspect Pomeroy of actual dishonesty, but considered that

[258]

his preoccupation with politics and private business ventures had led him to neglect Company affairs.[22]

One purpose in retaining Pomeroy as an agent in 1858 was to have his services in the effort then under way to clear up the status of the hotel in Kansas City; in 1855, the Company had sold the hotel to S. W. Eldridge for $10,000 (the price they had originally paid for it). Eldridge, in turn, sold the hotel to H. W. Childs, who defaulted on his contract, and Eldridge failed to keep up his payments to the Company.[23] Pomeroy tried several schemes to protect the Company's equity, but when the Company closed out its property a year later, the hotel was still tied up in litigation.

Another problem with which the Company was constantly wrestling during these years was that of securing titles to its real estate. Of course, the various communities that had pledged town lots to the Company could convey no better title than a bond for a deed, until the town itself should secure title from the federal government. Even these bonds could not be given until the towns became incorporated, which they steadfastly refused to do until the Free State party gained control of the Territorial Legislature at the end of 1857. Therefore, until 1858, the Company's title to town lots in the various settlements rested on nothing more substantial than memoranda of town associations. Some difficulty over titles arose in almost every settlement in which the Company had an interest, and the agents were constantly being sent from this town to that to check up on the matter. In Lawrence, a question arose as to the validity of title under the Wyandotte float located there early in 1855. For months the Emigrant Aid Company was in doubt as to its ability to maintain its holdings in Lawrence.[24] Disputes of one kind or another arose over the Company's holdings in Manhattan,[25] Topeka,[26] and Burlingame,[27] but these were finally settled in a manner satisfactory to the Company. In Osawatomie an involved legal tangle developed over the respective rights of the three proprietors (the Emigrant

Aid Company, O. C. Brown, and William Ward).[28] When the last entry on the subject was made in the minute books of the Company, the matter had still not been cleared up.

Yet, despite all the difficulties, the Company received, during 1860, deeds to practically all the real estate to which it laid claim.[29] Although some titles were still disputed and several lawsuits were pending when the Company closed its affairs, it owned, clear of incumbrance, property which, could it have been sold at any reasonable estimate of its value, would have been ample to pay all debts and to have returned to the stockholders several cents on the dollar.

But although these problems of property titles were of major significance in determining the possibility of ultimate returns on the stock, the most pressing problem of the years 1857-1861 was that of making ends meet. As noted in the last chapter, the Company, by July, 1857, had despaired of raising any more money by the sale of stock and was entirely dependent on rents and sales in Kansas to meet all expenses. At that time Amos A. Lawrence wrote to John Carter Brown: "As to the Emigrant Aid Company, I have very much the same view as yourself: as to the stock, its value will probably become steadily less, as no sales of land can be made to keep down expenses. The property is all there, which we ever had (except what has been burned) and it must require constant expenditures to protect it and to pay our agents. The rents, including that of the hotel, would have paid all our running expenses, but cannot now."[30] The Company had fixed annual expenses of about six thousand dollars in salaries, office expense, and agent's expense accounts.* In 1858, the towns in Kansas began to levy taxes. These totaled $534.00 for the Company's fiscal year of 1858-59, $1,446.17 for the year 1859-60, and $516.38 for 1860-61.[31] Then there were variable irregular ex-

---

* Salaries were: Dr. Webb, $1,500; A. J. Stone, $850; Pomeroy, $1,000; Branscomb (later Conway), $1,000. The rent on the Boston office was $400 a year until March 1, 1858, when one room was given up and rent was reduced to $250. Agents' expense accounts and miscellaneous expenses in Boston exceeded $1,000 a year.

penses: upkeep and repairs on the property, the cost of sending Company officers to Kansas on several occasions to check up affairs, costs of lawsuits, and no end of claims that were always turning up. Some of these claims were preposterous, as for example, the claim of a Mrs. Wilder for the value of a carpet lent to Robinson in 1856 to fit up a room for the Howard Congressional Committee and burned in the Free State Hotel,[32] and the twin claim of G. W. Deitzler for $534.55 for articles furnished to the Congressional Committee and also burned in the hotel.[33] A. D. Searl wanted the Company to pay him for surveying and mapping Lawrence.[34] Of course, the Executive Committee rejected many of these claims, but in some cases the agents had so involved the Company that there was no way of escape left open. The Company was again and again victimized by padded accounts and exorbitant charges for services. One such bill Dr. Webb said reminded him of "the French Company's charge during the American Revolu-ion,—so much for the broom, and so much for the various materials and time used in making the broom."[35] It seemed that everyone in Kansas was trying to exploit the Emigrant Aid Company.

Then, too, the Company was subjected to some severe losses. The most severe, of course, was the burning of the Free State Hotel in the spring of 1856. The claim against the federal government for reimbursement for the loss was pushed diligently, and at one time the Committee on Claims of the House of Representatives was ready to recommend that the claim be allowed, but was unable to get the floor to report.[36] Another heavy loss was sustained in the burning of the Osawatomie mill. The mill, with its building, had cost about $7,000. The machinery was apparently little damaged by the fire, but a man engaged to clean and box it had done his work so indifferently that much of it was ruined by weather. Then Branscomb, in his irresponsible manner, told Cyrus Tator, who was building a mill privately, to use what he could of the old machinery and pay whatever he thought it was worth.

[261]

Eventually, Conway collected from Tator $650 for such of the machinery as he used.[37]

Another source of heavy loss was bad debts. The agents always found it difficult to collect debts owed the Company. Considerable amounts were lost on delinquent rents. Often when agents could not get cash, they would take the notes of renters or purchasers, only to find, when the notes fell due, that they could not be collected; and the best they could do was to take back the property after standing the expense of the lawsuit. Sometimes property was sold for town shares, which soon depreciated or became entirely valueless. The two most flagrant cases of bad debts were those of S. W. Eldridge and G. W. Brown. It is not clear just how much the Company lost on Eldridge. He finally paid the entire purchase price of the Lawrence hotel, after delaying nearly a year and trying to get the Company to credit him with amounts he had had to pay on existing construction contracts.[38] But he never did complete his delinquent payments on the Kansas City hotel. The only indication of the amount his delinquency cost the Emigrant Aid Company is a letter of instructions to Pomeroy in June, 1858, that Eldridge should be sued unless he would undertake to pay within four months the $2,500 overdue on the purchase price with interest, and that Pomeroy should try to hold him for the expense to which the Company had been put by reason of his nonperformance of his contract.[39]

While G. W. Brown was held as a "treason" prisoner during the summer of 1856, his wife toured the East raising funds to revive the *Herald of Freedom*. It reappeared about November 1, 1856. Since Brown's business seemed to be prospering, and the Emigrant Aid Company was hard pressed for funds, Dr. Webb, on the last day of February, 1857, wrote a very friendly letter to Brown asking him to make arrangements to repay the $2,000 which the Company had advanced to him in 1854.[40] Brown replied that he thought the services he had rendered to the cause and to the Emigrant Aid Company entitled him to continued favors at its

[262]

hands.[41] When the agents pushed him for a settlement, he demanded proof of the debt.[42] When such proof was furnished, he offered to pay in Emporia town shares, the value of which was then entirely speculative and exceedingly doubtful.[43] For a year and a half, the Company, through its agents and by direct correspondence, pushed him for a settlement. Finally, in July, 1858, he had the audacity to deny that he owed the Company anything, saying that the bill of sale which he had delivered as security constituted an actual sale, so that when his press was destroyed in the Lawrence raid the loss was the Company's.[44] The Company ledger shows the debt paid February 6, 1860, in territorial scrip, none of which was ever redeemed, so that the $2,000 was a total loss.[45]

A contributory cause of the difficulty in collecting debts owed to the Company was the general economic depression in the fall of 1857. Money was "tight" throughout the country, but especially in Kansas. Conway wrote in May, 1858, that little money had come into the Territory during the spring, and what little there was had gone out again through the land office.[46] Credit was so stringent in Kansas that loans commanded from 6 to 10 per cent a *month*.[47] As early as January, 1858, Branscomb had written that owing to the stringency of money, tenants and other debtors were unable to pay even when willing.[48] Moreover, conditions in Kansas failed to improve during the next three years; many who could have paid made the depression an excuse for refusing to do so.

But although this inability to make collections was a serious matter to the Company, it was not the most disastrous result of the depression. With the tightening of credit, the Kansas boom collapsed. The first of December, 1857, F. A. Hunt wrote to Webb that city lots and shares had dropped 50 per cent. Of course, cash sales became virtually impossible; Pomeroy wrote that his offer to sell the Atchison mill for cash was taken as a joke.[51] Even credit sales to responsible parties became almost impossible except at ruinously low prices. At first, the members of the Executive Committee believed that the condition would be of short duration and refused to sell lots except for cash. Mills and rental properties which would deteriorate rapidly or involve expensive upkeep, they were willing to sell for part cash and part credit, but they refused offers at sacrifice prices. However, as time passed and the Company became desperate for money, they began urging the agents to sell anything they could on almost any terms they could get so long as they got part cash. The Executive Committee even considered resorting to auction sales.[52] During 1858, 1859, and 1860 almost every letter to the agents urged greater efforts to make sales. During these years a few lots were sold in Lawrence and Atchison, but the proceeds of these sales aggregated only about $6,000.[53]

In this desperate state of affairs, the Executive Committee found it necessary, at the beginning of 1858, to resort to a loan, pledging Company property as security. Since the Boston banks would not make the loan on this basis, Amos A. Lawrence, John Carter Brown, and Martin Brimmer signed the note for $6,000, taking a mortgage on Company property as security.[54] At the beginning of 1859, this indebtedness was increased to $10,000; at the beginning of 1860, to $12,000; and at the beginning of 1861, to $15,000. When the first note was given, it was expected that within the year the depression would lift and that sales in Kansas would permit the loan to be paid at maturity. At the first renewal it was still believed that matters would soon right themselves. But by the spring of 1861, it was apparent to all that the Company faced bankruptcy, and the endorsers renewed their signatures only with the understanding that the property should be sacrificed to liquidate the debt.

By the spring of 1861, the Company was facing other discouragements. Officers were losing interest, and it was becoming almost impossible to secure quorums at meetings of the Executive Committee and the Board of Directors. In 1859, the discovery of gold in western Kansas (present Colorado) caused an exodus of settlers from the settlements in the eastern part of the Territory, and this tended to depress still further the already sadly deflated value of town lots. At the same time, mills and houses were deteriorating, and it was becoming increasingly difficult to find renters, and impossible to find buyers.

The most severe blow of all was the great drought of 1859-60. There were no accurate weather records in those days, and accounts of old settlers differ as to details, but the stories agree that for a period varying with the locality from twelve to sixteen months, the only rain was a few scattered showers, too light to relieve vegetation. In the growing season of 1860, almost nothing was raised in Kansas. Coming on the heels of two years of economic depression, the drought rendered fully a third of the settlers destitute and dependent upon outside aid for the necessities of life.[55] Sales and collections in Kansas, difficult for the preceding two years, became absolutely impossible, and real estate values dropped to almost nothing. Pomeroy reported that the Emigrant Aid Company's flour mill at Atchison was useless because there was nothing to grind.[56] This was the death knell of the Company's hope of realizing on its Kansas property.

Early in 1860, Thaddeus Hyatt organized a Kansas relief movement and undertook to supply the destitute settlers with food, clothing, and, later, seed. An organization was formed in Kansas to co-operate with S. C. Pomeroy and W. F. M. Arny as distributing agents. A depot was established at Atchison, where Pomeroy doled out provisions to applicants from all parts of the Territory. A report of the Kansas Committee, under whose auspices Pomeroy and Arny worked, shows that they received and distributed 8,090,951 pounds of provisions and seed grain, $83,-869.52 in money, besides great quantities of clothing, medicines, and garden seeds.[57] Although there was much criticism of the manner in which Pomeroy and Arny conducted the relief work, some even charging them with outright dishonesty, those in the best position to know insisted that Pomeroy, at least, was absolutely faithful to his trust, that he worked hard and diligently, and did as well as anyone could have done.[58] Despite the common belief in Kansas to the contrary (due probably to the fact that Pomeroy had charge of the relief and that Conway assisted him more or less), the Emigrant Aid Company as such did not participate in the relief work of 1860. However, a Kansas Relief Committee was formed in Boston with George L. Stearns (at the time a member of the Executive Committee of the Emigrant Aid Company) as chairman, and Dr. Webb as secretary-treasurer. Headquarters were maintained at the Emigrant Aid Company office at No. 3 Winter Street. Of the twelve members of the committee, seven were directors of the Emigrant Aid Company, four of these being members of the Executive Committee.[59] Apparently, this Boston committee was formed originally to co-operate with Hyatt, but in the hope of avoiding some of the complaints raised against his organization (chiefly, its involvement in politics and the unnecessary hardship of requiring all applicants to go to Atchison for relief), they sent an agent of their own, George W. Collamore, to Kansas and operated independently. They raised and spent $27,100.32, mainly for seed grain, and sent considerable quantities of contributed clothing.[60]

As early as 1857, Lawrence and John Carter Brown had favored liquidating the holdings of the Emigrant Aid Company, feeling that its mission was accomplished. At the first quarterly directors' meeting after the floating of the six-thousand-dollar loan, the board went on record as favoring the conversion of the property into cash as rapidly as possible.[61] At the annual stockholders' meetings of 1858, 1859, and 1860, proposals were made to sell the property at auction for what it would bring in order to pay the debts and close the Company's operations, but in each case a majority felt that business conditions must improve within a year and that it would be foolish to sacrifice the property. By the fall of 1860, when it became necessary to authorize an increase of the indebtedness to $14,000, the Executive Committee had become sufficiently discouraged to appoint a committee "to take into consideration the propriety of disposing of the Company's property."[62] Although this committee did not devise a workable plan, a new committee was appointed early in May to propose a plan to the directors and stockholders at the time of the annual meeting.[63] When May 28, 1861, the day of the annual meeting, arrived, the directors, as was customary, held a special meeting before the stockholders assembled, and Dr. Le Baron Russell, for the special committee, recommended the sale of the Company's entire property for $20,000 to a group of stockholders to be formed for the purpose. With only Dr. Webb dissenting, the directors voted to approve the course and to recommend it in turn to the stockholders.[64]

At the annual meeting of the stockholders the same day, the treasurer's report showed that during the year collections from all sources, sales, rents, and old accounts, had aggregated only $1,454.98, while interest on the standing debt had been $1,117.73, and the debt had had to be increased by $2,680.00. The Executive Committee offered a report stating that the "special purpose" of the Company had been completed with the recent admission of Kansas to the Union as a free state and that, while they did not absolutely despair of making the investment profitable, the long series of discouragements, culminating in the drought, constituted a condition "most difficult to struggle against," and that means must be found to release from their responsibility "those gentlemen who have lent the credit of their names to the Company."[65] In the face of these representations, and the added fact (which, though not mentioned in the minutes, must have been in the mind of everyone present) that the country was plunging into civil war, the stockholders voted to authorize the sale of all the property of the Company in Kansas and Missouri for any amount sufficient to pay the debts, and also voted to recommend that such of the stockholders as might care to participate form an association with a capital of $20,000 to make the purchase.[66] Amos A. Lawrence was again elected treasurer for the express purpose of carrying out the liquidation.* At this meeting three estimates of the value of the property were presented: one of $136,700, made by Conway in 1858; one of $52,540, made just before the meeting by Dr. Webb; and one of $34,070, just made by Dr. Russell. It was still hoped that the claim against the federal government might be collected and so some small return be made to the stockholders.[67]

Lawrence, Webb, and Russell at once tried to carry out the edict of the stockholders. Early in the summer an association of stockholders was formed to purchase the property for $20,000, which would have paid the debt and left $5,000 as contingent fund to push the Lawrence hotel claim; but when the subscribers of this association heard the new complications in regard to the title of the Kansas City hotel, they withdrew their offer.[68] At this juncture, Henry H. Elliott, one of the New York directors, entered a protest against a forced sale, urging that the directors renew the loan for another year, reduce the expenses to the minimum, and redouble their efforts to collect the claim for the destruction of the Free State Hotel. Accordingly, in a special meeting on June 18, the directors voted that the sale should be postponed if enough directors could be found to guarantee the debt, and instructed the treasurer and the Executive Committee to see what could be done.[69] The Executive Committee voted on July 22† to dismiss the secretary, close the Boston office, and reduce the salary of the agent in Kansas to $750 a year.[70] Lawrence then sent a circular letter to all the directors asking each to guarantee a portion of the debt;[71] but of the forty addressed only three responded, and the project was dropped.[72] The effort was then resumed to make up

---

* All other officers were re-elected. John Carter Brown presented his resignation as president, but was persuaded to reconsider. Except for a few shifts in the Board of Directors, no changes were made in the roster by the annual meetings of 1859 and 1860.

† After this meeting, there are no minutes of the Executive Committee until March 20, 1862, when a special meeting was called to ratify the sale of the property. Apparently meetings were held at irregular intervals during this period, but whoever kept the minutes did not enter them in the record books. Dr. Webb continued to be secretary of the Directors and of the Company after his salary ceased, but he no longer attended meetings of the Executive Committee.

a group of stockholders to purchase the holdings. A circular letter was sent to the stockholders inviting them to subscribe in $500 units.[73] By January 10, the date set for closing the list, $22,000 was subscribed; but it was decided to make an initial bid of $15,000, the amount of the debt, and not to go above $16,000. The sale was set for February 12, 1862, at the Parker House, and other stockholders were invited to bid individually or in groups.

On the appointed day, interested stockholders met at the Parker House, but some of them objected that, in view of developments since the preceding May, it would be improper to proceed with the sale without further authorization from the body of stockholders. Therefore, the sale was postponed until the twenty-seventh. At that time, Lawrence, who was bidding for the regular group, made an initial bid of $16,000. Three other parties each raised the bid fifty dollars, whereupon the property was knocked down to Henry A. Ayling and Isaac Adams, representing six stockholders, for $16,150.[74] Thus, a body of property, carried at a book valuation of $143,322.98,[75] was sacrificed for just enough to pay the debts, saving the Company from public bankruptcy, and to leave a small margin for the winding up of affairs.

It is impossible to say just what had been the initial cost of this property; the officers of the Company were never able to figure it out to their own satisfaction. But it is probable that, charging to each item all expenses properly belonging to it, the total represented an investment of around a hundred thousand dollars. There has been a great deal of speculation among Kansas writers as to how so large an investment could shrink to a paltry $16,000, the late William E. Connelley going as far as to hint rather broadly that someone cleared around $80,000 on the deal.[76] The present study, like the smaller one made by William Herbert Carruth half a century ago,[77] has revealed nothing to substantiate such a suspicion. The reasons for the Company's financial failure are entirely obvious. Listed in the approximate order of their importance, they may be briefly summarized as follows:

[269]

By far the most important cause of failure was the economic depression of 1857-60, followed and prolonged in Kansas by the great drought. This condition rendered it impossible for the Company to make collections or sales. Whatever might have been the value of the property had times been normal, in such times as these it had no market value at all. Had the Company been able, or had its principal stockholders been willing, to hold on until after the Civil War, considerable sums might have been realized from its real estate, although the buildings and machinery would inevitably have deteriorated.

The reason that probably deserves to be ranked second was poor management. For this, in turn, there were several reasons, first among which was the distance of the field of operations from the home office and the inadequacy of communications. This meant that too much discretion had to be left to agents, and that no system of checking or accounting the managers could devise was adequate to keep the officers in Boston in sufficiently close touch with what was going on in Kansas. Closely related to this last difficulty was the inexperience of those in control of the Company affairs with the corporate form of business organization. The corporation, as a business form, was still in the experimental stage, and the techniques by which the modern business enterprise checks and controls its branches and agencies had not yet been devised. A third reason for the poor management was the attempt to mix the philanthropic (one might add, the political) with the business motive. Too much was done "for the cause," and too much latitude and liberality were allowed for political purposes to permit the affairs to be kept on a workaday business basis.

A third cause of financial failure was direct losses during the border war and later from the elements. The Free State Hotel and the Osawatomie mill were cases in point. A great deal of freight, not all of it rifles, was lost or destroyed on the Missouri

[270]

River or in warehouses in Kansas City, the value of which the Company was never able to recover.

Closely akin to this was the indeterminate loss due to the attitude of people in Kansas toward the Company, discussed at some length in this chapter. Carruth told of an old settler who said to him, "We understood the Aid Company to be a benevolent institution, and we regarded anything of the Company's that came in our way as a gift."[78]

Finally, and perhaps this reason should be placed higher on the list, the financial failure of the Company was due to the character of the agents who represented it in Kansas. No one of the four was a business genius. All were too lenient in Company affairs. All four neglected Company business for political activity or private gain. Dr. Webb once wrote to Pomeroy, "Many of our losses, I fear, are justly chargeable to the laxity of our agents,"[79] and again and again he lectured each of them for their carelessness or indifference. Branscomb, at least, was not entirely honest, and Robinson and Pomeroy were each called to account, on occasion, for apparent irregularities. It would be going beyond what the evidence justifies to suggest that either Pomeroy or Robinson ever transgressed the legal bounds of honesty in his dealings with the Company, but certainly each of them, on more than one occasion, construed his rights or obligations in a manner favorable to himself. It would certainly not be true to consider the agents as the primary cause of the Company's failure, but it it equally certain that their handling of affairs tended to make a bad matter worse.

CHAPTER XIV

Dotage

WHEN THE EMIGRANT AID COMPANY closed out its Kansas affairs in the early spring of 1862, it was decided to keep the organization alive, at least for the time being, in order to push the claim against the federal government for the destruction of the Free State Hotel, as well as because of the hope that the Company might be able to operate in the South either during or after the Civil War. In the spring and summer of 1862, the Executive Committee held occasional meetings for special purposes,—to authorize the deeds to Adams and Ayling, to audit the treasurer's books, to arrange for the annual stockholders' meeting, to press the hotel claim—but when, on August 5, 1862, they failed to muster even the three members required for a quorum, they adjourned to meet at the call of the secretary.* Although an Executive Committee was named each spring, no meetings are recorded after the one just mentioned, until December 5, 1864, when a new and smaller committee was created by the directors to deal with the proposals to operate in Florida.[1]

The annual meeting, May 27, 1862, re-elected John Carter Brown president, against his expressed wishes. Other officers chosen at the time were the following: R. P. Waters, vice president (the directors a week later added Amos A. Lawrence as second vice president); Martin Brimmer, treasurer; C. J. Higginson, secretary.[2] It was voted to reduce the number of directors to fifteen, three to constitute a quorum.† The directors continued

* Recorded meetings of the Executive Committee: March 20, 1862, to authorize deeds; April 10, to audit the treasurer's books; and May 20, to call the annual meeting (Aid Company Records, Book V, 251-53). After the annual meeting the Executive Committee met June 5, June 14, June 24, June 27, July 8, and August 5; these meetings dealt chiefly with plans to operate in the South and with efforts to push the hotel claim (ibid., 254-57).

† The directors for the year 1862-63 were: Oakes Ames, Easton; Martin Brimmer, Boston; William Cullen Bryant, New York; Horace Bushnell, Hartford; S. Cabot, Jr., Boston; E. D. Morgan, New York; Seth Paddleford, Providence; Le Baron Russell, Boston; Nathan

to hold quarterly meetings during the Civil War years, but the usual minute is, "No quorum present. No business transacted."

At their first quarterly meeting of 1862, the directors "determined to print some extracts from former reports made to the stockholders and directors, arranged in such form and with such connection as should give a short history of the Company's operations from its beginning."[3] The subject was referred to the Executive Committee,[4] who designated Edward Everett Hale for the work.[5] Hale labored several weeks on the project, reading sections of his pamphlet to each meeting of the Executive Committee for approval or corrections. It was completed in July and printed under the title *History of the New England Emigrant Aid Company, with a Report on Its Future Operations, Published by Order of the Board of Directors.*[6] Five hundred copies were made, one of which was sent to each stockholder as a sort of final accounting.

During 1862 and 1863, Dr. Webb devoted much of his time to pushing the claim against the federal government for the destruction of the Free State Hotel in Lawrence. After his dismissal as full-time secretary of the Emigrant Aid Company in the summer of 1861, he became secretary of the Massachusetts Institute of Technology (a position he occupied until his death in the fall of 1866), but he found time to make several trips to Washington to work on this claim.[7] Dr. Webb succeeded in getting the matter before the committee on Claims of the United States Senate in February, 1863, but as usual, the claim died in committee. After the spring of 1863, there is no further record of efforts to push the claim until 1866.

After the Quantrill raid on Lawrence, Kansas, the directors raised some money by subscription for relief work there.[8] The records of the fund have not come to light; hence it is impossible

---

Durfee, Fall River; T. M. Edwards, Keene, New Hampshire; Caleb Foote, Salem; E. E. Hale, Boston; C. J. Higginson, Boston; E. P. Waters, Beverly; and J. P. Williston, Easthampton. Morgan and Williston resigned and the vacancies were not filled (Aid Company Records, Book "Company," 120-21). These same officers and directors were continued through the year 1863-1864 (*ibid.*, 125-26).

to say how much was raised or how it was expended, but the amount must have been ample since Brimmer, who as treasurer of the Company administered the fund, considered that there would probably be a residue which could be used for relief elsewhere.

As the time approached for the annual meeting of 1864, a new group came forward, headed by Edward Atkinson, who proposed to reorganize the Company with a view to aiding immigration from Europe. All of the old officers agreed to step aside to clear the way for the project (Brown had been seeking to resign as president for three years).[9] At the annual stockholders' meeting, May 24, the new group took charge. The by-laws were amended to eliminate one vice president and to reduce the number of directors to nine. The stock of George Atkinson was transferred to Edward Atkinson, M. D. Ross, and C. L. Flint to render them eligible to the directorate.* The following roster was elected: R. P. Waters, president; E. E. Hale, vice president; Edward Atkinson, treasurer; T. H. Webb, secretary.[10]

Nothing came of the proposal to aid immigrants from Europe. At their first two quarterly meetings, August 30 and November 9, 1864, the new directors failed to muster a quorum.[11] An attempt to revive the Executive Committee was also unsuccessful.

During the last three years of its Kansas activity, the Emigrant Aid Company had under consideration several proposals to operate elsewhere. In November, 1858, the directors had discussed at some length the question as to whether, when Kansas affairs should be closed up, it would be better to disband the Company or to seek another field of operations. Missouri and the Cherokee Country (later Oklahoma) were mentioned as possibilities, but the prevailing sentiment favored reviving the project of 1857 to operate in Texas, where the German colony provided a nucleus for free-soil settlement. In the spring of 1860, a Texas committee,

---

*The directors elected were: M. D. Ross, C. L. Flint, E. E. Hale, George S. Winslow, Edward Winslow, Edward Atkinson, T. H. Webb, R. P. Waters, and Thomas D. Morris.

that had been appointed some months before,[12] recommended operation in Texas and proposed the raising of $50,000 for the purpose.[13] The Executive Committee voted to launch a stock-subscription drive for the purpose,[14] but the matter forthwith disappears from the minutes; since there is no record of stock issued at this time, evidently nothing came of the effort.

In their annual report for 1861, the Executive Committee suggested that a proposal be made to the federal government, recently turned over to the Republicans, that the government finance operations of the Company to the south of Kansas.[15] It is not recorded that the directors took any action on this recommendation, but from that time until the close of the Civil War the Company was constantly flirting with the idea of co-operation with the federal government in the colonization of the South with people from the North. In March, 1862, Higginson launched a campaign to have the Company undertake colonization independently. He recognized that money would be the great problem, but he thought a patriotic appeal to the old stockholders might bring in some.[16]

Early in June, the directors took up the question. Fearing that money could not be raised for land purchases, they decided to try to persuade Congress to confiscate the estates of Confederates and open the confiscated land to pre-emption by Northern colonists.[17] Efforts were made to interest members of the Cabinet and members of Congress in the proposal, the Company disclaiming any expectation of profit, but nothing came of them.[18] The Executive Committee also toyed with the idea of operating in Virginia and Maryland without government help. They even sent a special agent to look into the possibilities,[19] but as usual the idea had to be dropped for lack of funds.

The one project of the Civil War years that showed any signs of getting off the ground was a plan of Edward Everett Hale to assist the migration of unmarried women to Oregon, first proposed in August of 1854.[20] Hale undertook to raise $2,000 by popular subscription for the venture, and actually secured $850.[21] In December he sent what he called a "pioneer party" of about half a dozen young women.[22] No profit motive was involved. He made elaborate plans to charter a ship which would carry a party of a hundred or more and advertised the plan in the newspapers. He continued to work on this project into the summer of 1865, when he prepared a report for the directors, but apparently the ship never sailed.[23]

In July of 1865, a Colonel Stevens of Washington, D. C., presented to the Executive Committee the plans of "The United States Mutual Protection Company" for the colonization of the South, and sought the co-operation of the Emigrant Aid Company.[24] This concern appears to have been formed by politicians and government officials in Washington, and may have been inspired by the earlier activities of the Emigrant Aid Company.* S. C. Pomeroy, then a senator from Kansas, was its vice president. It is not clear whether the directors of the Emigrant Aid Company ever did any more than discuss the idea of co-operating with the Mutual Protection Company (which, so far as this study has revealed, never really did anything), but at all events, Colonel Stevens succeeded in reviving among them an interest in Southern colonization, and they set about to interest such influential men as George L. Stearns, Governor Andrews of Massachusetts, and J. M. Forbes, builder of the Burlington Railway, in the "plantation movement."[25]

The eleventh annual meeting of the stockholders, called for May 30, 1865, failed to muster a quorum, though an adjourned meeting a week later re-elected the same officers and directors with a few minor changes.[26] At the twelfth annual meeting, on May 29, 1866, the only thing worth noting was that J. M. Forbes was placed on the Board of Directors.[27] Dr. Webb died about the

---

* Later this organization was metamorphosed into the American Emigrant Aid and Homestead Company, and in 1867 its president corresponded with the New England Emigrant Aid Company proposing co-operation in Florida.

first of November, 1866, and the directors appointed T. B. Forbush to succeed him as secretary, and General J. F. B. Marshall to replace him on the Board.[28]

As early as the Company's annual meeting of 1863 the proposal to operate in Florida had been discussed, and a committee, headed by Hale, had been appointed to take up the matter with the federal government.[29] At two directors' meetings during the ensuing year, Hale reported in favor of such action;[30] but with an empty treasury nothing could be done, and interest in the matter lapsed until it was revived by Colonel Stevens in the late summer of 1865. One can only guess at developments during the next year; but on November 5, 1866, in a special meeting called to consider Florida emigration, the directors were so impressed by the representations of a "Colonel Scott of Florida" that they authorized a newspaper advertisement urging emigration to that state and adjourned for a week.[31] Directors' meetings now came thick and fast; there were five during November, all devoted to Florida. By November 21, the directors were ready to vote an application for permission to issue preferred stock, to launch an emergency drive for $3,000, and to establish regular weekly meetings.[32] The half-dead Emigrant Aid Company had suddenly sprung into newness of life.

Steps were taken immediately to reopen the Boston office. Temporary desk space was obtained in the rooms of the Soldiers Memorial Society at 23 Chauncy Street.* Here, for about three months, the directors held their weekly meetings, and here the Reverend T. B. Forbush maintained office hours, dispensed information about Florida, and answered correspondence. In January, the Company took a part of Edward Winslow's office at 80 State Street.[33] When Winslow's lease expired, March 31, 1867, a room was rented at 40 Tremont Street for fifty dollars a month,[34] and the office was maintained there through September.

---

*Apparently, this arrangement was made before the directors' meeting of November 5, 1866 (the first recorded in a year), since the minutes of that meeting are dated "at the Office of the Company, 23 Chauncy St."

The same directors' meeting that chose General J. F. B. Marshall to fill the vacancy on the board created by the death of Dr. Webb appointed a committee to confer with him about going to Florida as agent of the Company.[35] Arrangements were completed in a few weeks, and, about the middle of December, 1866, Marshall started on his mission.[36] He was to receive a salary of $200 a month and expenses.[37] He spent three months traveling about Florida, looking over the country and investigating offers for the sale of land. On March 16, he was back in Boston and reported to a special meeting of the directors.[38]

In the meantime, the directors were wrestling with the old problem of finance. The renewal of activities inevitably meant the renewal of expenses. No steps could be taken toward selling the new preferred stock until the Legislature should meet and amend the charter to authorize its issue. As already noted, the directors voted in November to raise an emergency subscription of $3,000 for immediate expenses, but voting such a subcription was one thing, and raising it was quite another. A subscription list shows a total of $2,290 subscribed during 1866 and 1867,[39] but the money came in slowly. At each weekly meeting of the directors, the treasurer reported the amount on hand, and it was usually small. In March, a loan of $1,000 was voted to pay General Marshall,[40] but apparently the sum could not be borrowed. At the time of the annual meeting, May 28, only $580.00 had been received, of which $534.40 had been expended.[41]

As soon as the Massachusetts Legislature met, a petition was presented asking permission to issue preferred stock.[42] In due course an act was passed, and signed by Governor Bullock, February 23, 1867, amending the charter. It authorized the Company to issue preferred stock to an amount of $150,000, to be divided into hundred-dollar shares; this stock was to receive a dividend of 8 per cent before anything should be paid on the common stock. Holders of the old stock who wished to participate in the new activities and to receive any dividends that might be earned

[278]

were required to register their stock with the treasurer of the Company within thirty days of the giving of public notice. The charter was to expire thirty years from the passage of the act.[43]

A special meeting of the stockholders was called for March 6, 1867, to approve the revision of the charter. Lacking a quorum of the old stock, the meeting appointed a committee to collect proxies and adjourned for a week.[44] The meeting reconvened March 13. The act to amend the act of incorporation was approved and referred to the directors for execution. The by-laws were amended so that each share of preferred stock should have five votes, each share of registered common, one; one-sixth of the preferred and registered common should constitute a quorum. A resolution was adopted calling upon the directors to issue an address to the stockholders inviting subscriptions to the new stock, and a committee of twenty was appointed to solicit subscriptions.[45] At the annual meeting, May 28, the by-laws were further amended to provide for twelve directors, all of whom must be holders of preferred stock. The following officers were elected: president, John M. Forbes; vice president, E. E. Hale; secretary, T. B. Forbush; treasurer, Martin Brimmer.[46]

As early as January, 1867, the directors decided that a necessary adjunct to their operations would be a "loyal" newspaper, and appointed Hale and one of the new directors a committee to see what could be done.[47] This committee found that the publishers of the *Florida Times* at Jacksonville would sell a controlling interest in their paper for $2,500. Hale was authorized to close the deal and secure an editor whenever subscriptions to the new stock should provide the funds.[48] In about a month, arrangements were completed with Edward M. Cheney, an employee of the *Christian Register,* by which, the Emigrant Aid Company providing the necessary $2,500, Cheney was to purchase the *Times* and hold it in the name of the Company. In lieu of salary, he was to have all profits above 8 per cent, as well as the right to purchase the paper at any time by repaying the amount advanced to him together with interest. He was to have complete charge as editor and publisher, agreeing to keep the paper thoroughly loyal in character, and to manage it in close co-operation with the Emigrant Aid Company.[49] At about the same time, the Executive Committee commissioned him to act as agent of the Company in Florida without pay.[50]

When Cheney reached Jacksonville, he violated his agreement to the extent of purchasing the *Florida Union* outright for $3,000 instead of the contemplated interest in the *Times*.[51] At first, the directors objected and threatened to repudiate the deal; but when Cheney assumed the $500 difference himself, and parties in whom the directors had confidence wrote from Florida justifying his course, they became reconciled to the arrangement.[52] On July 1, 1867, Cheney issued a four-page pamphlet advertising the *Union*. The pamphlet carried a quarter-page advertisement of the "Florida Agency of the New England Emigrant Aid Company," signed "Edward M. Cheney, Agent."[53] Cheney operated his paper for several years as a staunch supporter of the "Carpet-bag" Republican regime. He appears to have kept up his interest payments to the Emigrant Aid Company faithfully, and ultimately to have repaid the principal.

As soon as the reorganization was effected under the amended charter, a drive was begun for subscriptions to the preferred stock. Hale prepared an "Address to the Stockholders" suggesting prospects of "a handsome profit."[54] By the first week in June, $5,300 had been subscribed.[55] At that time a plan was launched to sell shares in blocks of five or more to prospective emigrants, agreeing to redeem the stock at par in land to be provided by the Company at five to ten dollars per acre.[56] A circular was issued describing the plan;[57] during June and July, seven persons subscribed for forty shares ($4,000) under this plan,[58] and, according to the secretary, $3,000 more was promised.[59] Prospective emigrants besieged the Company office, eager to go to Florida under

Company auspices, or to buy land there when the Company should have it to sell.[60]

But things did not go smoothly, and by July a crisis was reached. Forbush had warned Hale in March that the stock could not be marketed in single shares, but that it must be taken by a comparatively few men who believed that money could be made and who would take it in large enough blocks to be personally interested in the management of the Company.[61] But men of affairs would risk only a few hundred dollars each. By the middle of June, subscriptions (except under the land-stock plan) had reached a standstill, while all the money that came in was needed for current expenses, leaving nothing for land purchases. When a meeting of the directors was called to consider the situation and the prospects of the Company, all agreed that unless $25,000 could be raised, it was futile to attempt to go on. A committee set up to see what could be done[62] decided "that the project of the Emigrant Aid Company was perfectly feasible and very promising, so far as they could see, but if capitalists like Messrs. Forbes and Brimmer who understand the whole matter won't get into it and use their influence, it is not worth the while of younger men, who are very busy and have very little money, to attempt it."[63] At an adjourned meeting of the directors, July 11, the committee reported less bluntly but to the same effect. The discussion that ensued brought out general agreement that unless the Company could find "a president who should be well known on the street among business men, and who should be able to give time and attention to the affairs of the Company sufficient to make him the managing and responsible head thereof," and also a competent agent in Florida, the enterprise must be abandoned. Forbes, who was present, stated that he could not give the necessary attention to meet the requirement, and offered his resignation. On his motion, the meeting resolved: (1) that unless $25,000 should be pledged by August 31, arrangements should be made to close affairs on October 1; (2) that the Company go

[281]

ahead and print the Florida pamphlet which Forbush had prepared; (3) that a committee be appointed to raise $1,600 to pay
existing debts; (4) that pending the raising of $25,000, no more
subscriptions be taken on the basis of the land-stock circular.[64]

During the next two months, Hale and Forbush, and possibly
one or two others, worked frantically to find a new president
who would take hold in earnest and induce his business associates to put money into the venture, but without success. Prospective emigrants continued to apply until Forbush, at his wits' end
to know what to tell them, finally shut up the office to avoid answering their questions.[65] Forbes became convinced that failure
was inevitable, and so hastened it by refusing to advance another
cent. "I have paid already a good deal more than my share," he
wrote to Hale, "and I don't propose to pay any more."[66]

When the directors met for their quarterly meeting, September 5, 1867, it was apparent that matters had reached a dead end.
Still the directors present were loath to admit defeat, and determined to make one more effort. They adjourned for only a week,
to give Marshall an opportunity to interview some men from
Florida whom, it was hoped, they might induce to take hold and
save the Company.[67] During this week Forbush proposed a plan
to extinguish the old stock and get five or six men to put in $500
each and reorganize the Company; but the men he had in mind
could not be reached, or were unwilling to take the plunge.[68]
Marshall was unable to find his Florida men, and a final appeal
to Forbes proved fruitless. Consequently, when the directors convened in their adjourned meeting, September 11, and none of
their well-to-do members appeared, there was nothing to do but
vote to close up affairs by October 1, and endeavor to keep the
charter alive. Hale was made chairman of a committee to close
up business. At this meeting the treasurer reported that he had
received during the year $5,194.78, and had paid out $5,050.73,
and had on hand $144.05; liabilities to October 1 were $1,411.00,
assets $944.05 (raised by Hale toward the $1,600 he was author-

ized to secure), leaving a deficit of $466.95.[69] This did not include $1,400 claimed by Forbush as back salary. Enough was raised by Hale from wealthy directors to pay the deficit (except Forbush's salary, which never was paid in full) and to leave a small amount for incidental expenses.

The next day after this meeting Forbush wrote to Hale, "We shall want either a box in the Post Office, or better still, a place where we can set up our desk, nail up a mail box, and where I can run in occasionally and see if there are any matters to be attended to. There will be letters coming in all this autumn which must in some way be responded to, and I suppose, as I am in the matter, I had better look after them. Cheney will have to pay us a little money the first of September and some more the first of May, and that will pay postage and leave something for my trouble . . . . I am sorry the thing breaks up in this way. I feel a little rebellious about it, but if everybody else lets go of it, it is no use for you and me to hold on."[70]

Again desk space was secured at 23 Chauncy Street, and there, for the next six months, Forbush maintained a sort of Florida information bureau, answering questions, and referring those who intended to migrate to Cheney in Jacksonville for assistance in locating. Hale and Forbush issued a little circular announcing that the Company had decided not to go on with the proposed colony.[71] Early in the year the directors had instructed the secretary to prepare a pamphlet of Florida information.[72] The first edition of one thousand was printed in July, and by the time active operations were suspended, between six and seven hundred copies had been given out.[73] It was a twenty-page booklet, similar in character to Webb's *Information for Kansas Emigrants.* Forbush continued to furnish these free to prospective emigrants, and when the first edition was exhausted, brought out a second edition dated February, 1868. A prefatory note to this second edition declares: "In response to many letters received from all sections of the country since the first issue of this pamphlet, the

[283]

Secretary desires to say very emphatically that the New England Emigrant Aid Company *furnishes no pecuniary assistance* to parties wishing to go to Florida; *neither has it any colonies located, organized, or in the process of organization,* nor any interest in the purchase or sale of any lands. It proposes to scatter information concerning Florida—the advantages and inducements which its soil, climate and productions offer to those seeking new homes —through the North; and to leave each individual to emigrate when and locate where he sees fit. At the same time, it will cheerfully give any further information which it may possess, and such advice as its experience prompts, to all who shall apply."[74]

Three attempts were made during the fall of 1867 to hold a directors' meeting, but in no case was a quorum obtained. A regular meeting was held March 3, 1868, at which Forbush resigned as secretary and assistant treasurer to take a pastorate in Cleveland. General Marshall was elected to both positions, and was instructed to move the Company headquarters to his own offices.[75] For the next two years, Marshall devoted some small fragment of his time to Aid Company correspondence, and was allowed fifty dollars a year for his services, paid out of interest received from Cheney.[76] On April 20, 1868, a meeting of the directors was called (the last ever recorded) in response to the request of the president, J. M. Forbes, and Cheney, then secretary-treasurer of the Florida Republican Executive Committee, that the Company assist in marketing bonds of the state of Florida (Carpet-bag) for the Republican campaign fund in that state.[77] Some little effort was made by Marshall and Hale, and a few of the bonds were disposed of.[78]

The Company kept up a shadow of an organization until 1870, but the only minutes are those of annual stockholders' meetings. The only excuse for existence during these years was the collection and disposition of small payments from Cheney and the hope of collecting the old hotel claim. The fourteenth annual meeting was held at Marshall's office, May 26, 1868. After receiving a few routine reports, the meeting voted to reduce the number of directors to nine, and elected the following roster: president, J. M. Forbes; vice president, E. E. Hale; secretary-treasurer, J. F. B. Marshal.[79] The same officers and directors were re-elected at the fifteenth annual meeting, May 28, 1869.[80] This last meeting, after electing officers for "the ensuing year," voted that when the balance should be collected from the *Florida Union,* it should be distributed among those who had contributed to make up the deficit in 1867-1868, and that the president, the vice president, and the treasurer be a committee to prosecute the hotel claim.[82]

This was the last annual meeting. A letter of Marshall to Hale two months after this meeting indicates that the officers were working on the hotel claim;[83] but with the failure of this final effort, the Company ceased to function. Since the charter still had twenty-seven years to run, the Company may be said to have lived on as a sort of disembodied spirit. By implication, the officers elected in 1870 continued to hold office indefinitely, and at least one of them, Hale, took his position rather seriously.

The epilogue of the story came in 1897. The charter would expire by limitation on the nineteenth of February of that year. J. M. Forbes, president of the Company, lay on his deathbed. J. F. B. Marshall, the secretary, had died in 1888. Edward Everett Hale, as vice president, called a meeting of stockholders for February 15, and by diligent effort, gathered up enough proxies to constitute a quorum. Most of the original stockholders were dead, and their heirs were not aware that they held stock in the Company; some had never even heard of it.[84] Only Hale and John A. Higginson attended the meeting but they represented 256 shares. They voted to petition for an extension of the charter and to transfer to the University of Kansas* the Company's claim against the federal government.[85]

---

*The transfer of the hotel claim was made at the suggestion of William Herbert Carruth (original letter, Carruth to Hale, February 9, 1897, Aid Company Papers). The University of Kansas has made several unsuccessful attempts to collect the claim.

On February 18, 1897, the day before the old charter would expire, the governor of Massachusetts approved an act of the Legislature extending the charter of the Emigrant Aid Company for ten years.[86] It is not clear what Hale wanted with the extension; it may have been just a matter of sentiment with him. Certainly, no use was ever made of it, but it served to fulfill for another ten years the old ambition of the directors to "keep the charter alive." The extension expired February 19, 1907. Thus passed away, unmourned and unnoticed (except perhaps by the aging Edward Everett Hale, the last survivor of the Kansas Crusade), the "powerful moneyed corporation" whose name had once convulsed the nation.

CHAPTER XV

Dividends

SPEAKING TO A REUNION of Kansas old settlers in 1879, Edward Everett Hale, after telling of the work of the Emigrant Aid Company in Kansas and mentioning the amount of money raised and spent concluded his speech thus: "No subscriber to that fund ever received back one cent from the investment. But all the same we had our dividends long ago. They came in Kansas free, a nation free, in the emancipation of four million black men, and in the virtual abolition of slavery over the world."[1]

The financial failure of the Company has been discussed at some length. There is little or nothing more to be said on that score. The hope of actually making money on the investment was probably futile after the destruction of the Free State Hotel, but, except for the depression and the drought, some return could probably have been made to the stockholders. Again, something might have been saved from the wreck had the Company been managed consistently as a purely business venture—but it never was. Eli Thayer declared to Hale in 1867 when the effort was being made to reorganize the Company for operations in Florida: "The great error of the directors of the old Company in Kansas times was a total disregard of money making. Had the capabilities of the Company been steadily developed to that object, it would have accomplished a hundred times more in colonizing at that time, and would have been before this the most powerful moneyed organization on this continent. But allowing its agents in Kansas to become rich at its own expense, and to monopolize all the best bargains on their own private accounts, while the Company paid them for the time used in their own interest, it soon dwindled into insignificance."[2] It is highly doubtful that Thayer could have done any better, but he

[287]

certainly stated the truth as to the laxity of the Company's business methods.

The primary reason for this laxity was the fact that, almost entirely until the summer of 1857, and to a considerable extent even after that, the stress in Company affairs was laid upon "saving Kansas," rather than upon making money. Early in 1858, Dr. Webb wrote to a new director: "The prime object of instituting the organization, as you are undoubtedly aware, was to advance the cause of justice and humanity by extending and securing the blessings of freedom to our territorial possessions. . . . As regards pecuniary gain by means of our operations, that was a subordinate affair, a minor consideration with most of those who were induced to become stockholders; still, I think in this particular, we shall be successful if prosperous times soon bless the country again. But even should funds all 'evaporate and come to nought,' so far as filthy lucre is concerned, we shall have the proud satisfaction of knowing that by our humble efforts the blighting curse of slavery has been arrested in its course, and the area of freedom materially enlarged."[3] That is the tone which permeates most of the minutes and correspondence. Again and again one comes upon allusions to "this great object."

This fact suggests an affirmative answer to the question that naturally presents itself, whether or not the stockholders were reconciled to their financial loss. There were some, of course, who were not—particularly among those who subscribed in New York and Brooklyn in 1856 through the efforts of Thayer.* But in the main it seems that the stockholders were ready, with Hale, to take their dividends in the satisfaction of having helped to save Kansas to freedom. Lawrence's views are too well known to require restatement. He had never expected the stock to pay; and when it became necessary to sacrifice the Kansas holdings,

---

* These were represented by Henry H. Elliott of New York, who protested in a directors' meeting in 1861 against the sacrifice of the property (Aid Company Records, Book V, 227-28).

he took it as a matter of course. John Carter Brown, one of the heaviest stockholders and most liberal contributors, wrote to Lawrence on the occasion of the closing out of the property: "I shall feel fully satisfied in sinking the stock I originally had in the Company and the other expenses incurred, in the reflection that in so doing I assisted in making Kansas a free state and saving her from the clutches of the slave drivers."[4] In resigning the treasurership in 1857, Lawrence stated that there was not one of the directors "who would not at any time, and who would not *now*, sacrifice his own share in this [the Company's property] and much more, to open the Territory to the labor and enterprise of our citizens, and to perpetuate there our free American institutions."[5] In his report in 1861, recommending the closing out of the property, Dr. Le Baron Russell stated: "It is considered by the Directors that the chief object of the Company, which was to aid in the settlement of Kansas by a free population, is successfully accomplished." He added that, although it had once been anticipated that the stockholders should receive back their investment with interest, and possibly a profit, "It is probable that few, if any, subscribed to the stock with that expectation."[6]

Since, then, most of the stockholders appeared willing to sacrifice their investment in order to keep slavery out of Kansas, one cannot help wondering what was behind such an intense interest in the checking of its extension. Many of them, of course, were actuated, so far as they were consciously aware, only by sentimental considerations—abstract notions of right and justice. This was particularly true of young idealists like Edward Everett Hale, and was probably true of most of the ministers and college professors, who were numerous among the smaller shareholders. Undoubtedly, too, many of the business and professional men acted on a similar impulse. These people were simply caught in the rising tide of antislavery sentiment and were carried on with the current.

[289]

But it seems likely that the businessmen as a class—those from whose ranks came all the larger shareholders—were influenced directly or indirectly by social and economic considerations which might be expected to be reflected ultimately in their ledger sheets. One aim that is frequently mentioned is that of relieving an excess population. From the days when its representatives in Congress had opposed the ratification of the Louisiana Purchase Treaty down through the time of the nullification controversy, when the resolution of Foote of Massachusetts to restrict Western land sales had precipitated the Webster-Hayne debate, the business interests of the Northeast had opposed migration to the West, fearing, apparently, not only an overturn of the political balance, which would diminish the influence of that section in the counsels of the nation, but also the draining off of its labor supply, which must inevitably mean a higher wage scale. But by the 1850's, immigration and mechanical improvements had created a surplus of laboring population, a fact which tended to breed discontent and to increase the cost of public charity. One easily suspects, without being able to prove its existence, a connection between the anti-foreign feeling that gave rise to Know-Nothingism and the desire to thin out the population.

Then there was the feeling that the rapid filling of the West would create new markets for Eastern goods, and it was believed that a free state would be a better customer than a slave state. Thayer stressed this in his appeals for stock subscriptions in New York in 1856. Later he told how he had argued ". . . that New York merchants were more interested pecuniarily in this result than were any other people in the Union; that if they would compare their sales to Kentucky with those of Ohio, they would need no further argument to show that their money interest was all on the side of making Kansas free."[7] Thayer related also that Horace B. Claflin told him a dozen years after the Kansas conflict "that the six thousand dollars* which he paid to the

---

* In fact, Claflin paid only $3,000, but at that he was the largest stockholder of the Company, with 150 shares (Aid Company Account Books, Stock Ledger).

Emigrant Aid Company in 1856 had been several times repaid by the excess of profit on goods sold to merchants in Kansas and Kansas City over what it would have been if slavery had prevailed in that State."[8] There is no reason to believe, however, that this consideration directly influenced the men who, through 1854 and 1855, advanced the funds that first got the Company into operation. There is no hint of it in any of Lawrence's letters, or in any of the correspondence of John Carter Brown, J. M. S. Williams, or others of this original group, that has come to light in this study.

Another interest that may have influenced some of the stockholders was concern for Kansas as a route for the proposed Pacific Railway. As Professor F. H. Hodder has shown, this matter loomed much larger in the organization of Kansas Territory than is generally realized.[9] Pomeroy was certainly interested in it,* and it would seem to be a safe assumption that some of the railway promoters among the stockholders must have been. One of the best-known of these was John M. Forbes, who, in 1854, took fifty shares ($1,000) of Emigrant Aid Company stock, and who, in 1867, became the president of the Company. In the 1850's he was actively engaged in the building of the Hannibal and St. Joseph Railway (now a part of the Burlington system), which must inevitably seek an outlet through Kansas Territory.

But while these economic considerations were influencing various classes of individuals, there was another and more subtle force, of which individuals may have been only dimly conscious, that must have influenced the businessmen as a class and the Northeast as a section. This was the growing conviction that the domination of the federal government by the slaveholding interest was deleterious to the business prosperity of the Northeast.

---

* In a letter dated July 27, 1854, probably to J.M.S. Williams, Pomeroy mentioned the route for the Pacific Railway as one of his interests in Kansas. In a signed but undated article on the Emigrant Aid Company, apparently written in 1854 and intended for newspaper publication, he lists "the position of the Territory as including the belief that it is upon the great highway of the nation to the Pacific" as one of the attractions for migration (originals of both in Pomeroy's handwriting, Aid Company Papers).

It was clear to everyone who gave it serious thought in the 1850's that the plantation agrarianism of the South and the rapidly developing industrial capitalism of the Northeast represented not only divergent, but actually hostile, social and economic systems. The industrial section needed an expanding market, and a home market protected by tariff. In the early 1840's, politicians of the Liberty Party had preached that the federal government, controlled by the "Slaveocracy," discriminated against Northern businessmen in tariff legislation.[10] It is clear that Southerners resented the growing industrial supremacy of the North, and the tariff tinkering of 1857 suggests that they were willing to sacrifice the welfare of Northern capitalists in the interest of cheaper consumer's goods.[11] It is probably not without significance that the Republican party early espoused protection (though with reference to Pennsylvania rather than to New England), and that the Confederate constitution prohibited a protective tariff;[12] and Professors Beale and Miller have shown that sectional differences on tariff were, in a large measure, behind the Radical reconstruction program.[13]

It is true that there is not a single reference to tariff in the minutes or correspondence of the Emigrant Aid Company or in the letters, so far as they have been examined in this study, of those who took part in its activities. However, frequent allusion to the merits of "free labor," and disparaging remarks about the "slave power," suggest that the Emigrant Aid Company men were conscious of the fundamental antagonism between the two economies. This is not to say that men like Amos A. Lawrence, John Carter Brown, and J. M. S. Williams were consciously acting with a view to changing the national tariff policy; there is not one word in any of their letters or recorded remarks to suggest that they were prompted by anything but a philanthropic motive in their opposition to the extension of slavery.* But it

---

* Lawrence expressed his feelings in a letter he wrote on July 18, 1857, to the Reverend Ephraim Nute of Lawrence, Kansas: "Some of us stood ready to have made a much

seems likely that the business class, of which they were a part, was groping toward the control of the federal government in the interest of business; and the way to achieve the goal was to stop the making of slave states.

But, whatever may be the final analysis of the interest these men had in checking the advance of slavery, they rested content in the belief that the Emigrant Aid Company had saved Kansas to freedom. Of course, there were then, and there have been since, many to dispute this claim; and it is not a part of the purpose of the present discussion to enter into the controversy. Indeed, it would be little short of childish to revive the old dispute as to who saved Kansas and to attempt to prove that the major credit belongs to the Emigrant Aid Company.* At all events, the leaders of the Company believed that their efforts had been the determining factor. In 1855, J. M. S. Williams stated: "We were too quick for them. The first blow struck by the Emigrant Aid Company kept the slave immigration in suspense; that encouraged emigrants from the free States."[14]

In their annual report for 1857, the Directors declared:

In view of the present conditions in Kansas, but three years ago a wilderness, now teeming with a busy and intelligent population, your Committee may be pardoned for dwelling with pride and satisfaction upon the reflection that this grand result has been chiefly owing to the operations of the New England Emigrant Aid Company. Other associations of later date (first organized by the suggestions and personal efforts of members of this Board) have materially aided the cause .... But this Company took the

---

greater sacrifice had it been necessary, somewhat commensurate with that made by yourself and others. For months I felt as though I held my property and even my life by an uncertain tenure; but with a numerous family of children and a loving wife, I did not intend to part with either until it was necessary to bring up the 'forlorn hope' .... Please do not show this to anyone, for I never wrote it before, and never reflect upon it without devout gratitude to God for having spared me so great a sacrifice" (Lawrence Letters, 263-64).

*For years writers on early Kansas wrangled over the question of who deserved the principal credit for "saving" Kansas. Robinson and Thayer argued for the Emigrant Aid Company, Connelley for Jim Lane, F. B. Sanborn for John Brown, and R. G. Elliott for the "unsung pioneers" from the Old Northwest. For a scientific historian's analysis of the claims made for John Brown, see Malin, *John Brown and the Legend of Fifty-Six.*

initiative at a time when its course was looked upon with distrust and suspicion . . . . Your Directors would not be understood to claim that the present population of Kansas, or even any considerable portion of it, has been sent to the Territory directly through the agency of the Company; but they do believe that, but for the encouragement given to emigration in the early days of its settlement by the operations of the Company in planting capital there, in diffusing information for emigrants, in combining them into parties and aiding them to establish the first towns on its soil, the Territory would still be a wilderness.[15]

At the beginning of 1858, John Carter Brown, president of the Company, wrote: "The Emigrant Aid Company, so far as Kansas is concerned, has done its work; and if Kansas is ever a free State, it will be owing to the movements of this Association. We have made all or nearly all the substantial improvements thus far,—and locations made by us Yankees were so many centers around which all free elements from the West and elsewhere collected."[16] When, in 1861, the Executive Committee made their report recommending the closing out of the Kansas property, they stated with pride that, at the recent admission of Kansas to statehood, "Of the four agents that the Company have had in Kansas during the six years of our work there, one occupied the Congressional Chair, one the Governor's, and a third has since been elected to the United States Senate. These facts, occurring entirely without management on the part of the Company, among a population of fully 100,000, indicate unmistakably that the effect of this Company's operations in helping to place the State of Kansas in the position now occupied, has nowhere and at no time been exaggerated, although the nature of the operations themselves have been much misrepresented."[17]

Since the members of the Company were so firmly convinced that the State of Kansas was largely their handiwork, it may be appropriate to summarize briefly just what the Company contributed toward the building of the free commonwealth. In the first place, it raised and spent in its Kansas enterprise about $190,000.

Because of the confusion of the account books, it is impossible to construct an exact financial statement, but the following, pieced together from the account books, the treasurer's reports, scattered items in the minute books, and a few wild guesses, furnishes a rough approximation:

RECEIPTS

Stock (not counting the preferred of 1867)	$130,340.00
Donations	8,405.16
Sales and rents (partly original estimates)	38,000.00
Borrowed	15,000.00
	$191,745.16

EXPENDITURES

Estimated original cost of Kansas property	$ 91,324.75
Boston office (all Boston expenses)	30,465.00
Agents' salaries, fees, and expense accounts	27,000.00
Miscellaneous	42,955.41
	$191,745.16

The sales and rents do not include the $16,150 received at the final auction, nor is the expenditure of this sum in payment of debts included under expenditures, since the two items would balance each other, and their inclusion would create a false impression as to the amount of money spent by the Company. The miscellaneous item under expenditures included taxes, upkeep, and repairs on the property, payment of various claims against the Company, freight and storage costs not charged to individual properties, fees of special agents, litigation costs, money advanced for various local development projects (such as the Osawatomie and Manhattan hotels), territorial scrip and town shares accepted for sales which turned out to be worthless, losses due to bad debts, and various other odds and ends. It is impossible to say whether or not, if all items could be tabulated, there would be an unaccounted loss.

In the second place, the Company sent to Kansas a number of "emigrants" which probably approached three thousand. The five emigrant books that are preserved show 1,774 tickets sold to April 2, 1858. But the books covering the period from April 17, 1855, to May 6, 1856, are lost and this gap must account for several hundred. During this interval, Dr. Webb reported to the Executive Committee parties totaling over two hundred,[18] and judging by the records in the emigrant books, he must have furnished at least an equal number of tickets to Barnes in Albany, to branch societies, and to individuals. When allowance is made for persons who joined the Aid Company parties en route and for individual tickets sold after April 2, 1858, it is evident that the number who traveled to Kansas under Company auspices must have been between twenty-five hundred and three thousand. In addition, the propaganda carried on by the Emigrant Aid Company must have influenced many others to migrate, particularly those sent out by organizations formed in imitation of the original Company.

Of course, even with the most liberal allowances, this showing is not very impressive, and small as it is, it is subject to deductions. There were many duplications among the ticket sales; some individuals traveled to Kansas on Emigrant Aid Company tickets four or five times. Furthermore, certainly not more than two-thirds, and probably not many more than half, of the Aid Company "emigrants" remained as permanent settlers. And there are those who insist that the bluster frightened away more settlers than it attracted.[19] Indeed, the federal census of 1860 showed but 4,208 Kansas inhabitants of New England birth in a population of 107,206,[20] and many of these probably migrated to Kansas from the states west of the Appalachians. Still, the Emigrant Aid Company settlers were a real force in the making of Kansas. They were clustered in centers of free-state activity, they took a more active interest in the "cause" than did the pioneers from the West, and they furnished a disproportionate share of the leadership. Moreover, they brought an element of culture which the Westerners lacked, and they took the lead in the founding of schools, churches, libraries, and colleges. Finally, it was they, more than any other coherent group, who fixed the traditions of the state.

In the third place, it was the agents and settlers of the Emigrant Aid Company who established all the towns that were centers of free-state activity: Lawrence, Topeka, Osawatomie, and Manhattan. This has been adequately discussed elsewhere, and need only be mentioned here. If the necessity for the Kansas conflict be conceded, it is difficult to overestimate the importance of these towns as "cities of refuge" and centers of defense.*

In the fourth place, the Company made improvements for the benefit of the settlers which, though sometimes inadequate and disappointing, were nevertheless substantial. These have all been mentioned, and need only to be summarized. Machinery was sent for ten mills in all, located at Lawrence, Topeka, Manhattan, Osawatomie, Burlington, Wabaunsee, Quindaro, Atchison, Batcheller (Milford), and Claflin (Mapleton). All of these except for the one intended for Mapleton were actually put into operation during the territorial period. All but the one at Atchison were primarily sawmills, although grist mills were set up in connection with these at Osawatomie, Manhattan, Wabaunsee, and Milford. Nine or ten small mills do not appear to be a very great contribution to the building of a state until one compares it with the total milling facilities available to the Kansas settlers. Professor H. A. Richardson, who years ago made an extensive study of early milling in Kansas, was able to discover only twenty-four mills of all kinds established in Kansas prior to 1860 in addition to those sent by the Emigrant Aid Company. Of these,

---

* Hale laid heavy stress on this importance of towns in the speech cited at the opening of this chapter (Gleed, *Kansas Memorial*, 140-48).

five belonged to the federal government (located at military points) and two to Indian missions. Of the seventeen remaining, several were small affairs that operated only for a short time.[21] Hence, it would probably not be far wrong to assert that about half of the mills actually available to the settlers of territorial Kansas were sent out by the Emigrant Aid Company.*

The Company endeavored to provide hotel accommodations in the settlements. Besides temporary huts in Lawrence, it bought a hotel in Kansas City, built the Free State Hotel in Lawrence, bought and remodeled a hotel in Atchison, and aided, to the extent of a thousand dollars each, the building of hotels in Osawatomie and Manhattan. It gave room for a school in Lawrence, built a schoolhouse in Topeka, and contributed toward the building of one in Manhattan. It made possible the launching of the *Herald of Freedom* and the *Kanzas Zeitung*. Books collected and sent by Dr. Webb laid the foundation of libraries in Lawrence and Topeka. Agents and officers of the Company, and in one instance the Company itself, took an active part in the organization of churches and in the erection and equipment of places of worship. The University of Kansas grew out of the benevolence of Amos A. Lawrence, and Kansas State College is the outgrowth of an institution founded by Emigrant Aid Company settlers and aided by a donation of town lots by the Company itself. The Company engaged extensively in relief work in 1856, and its officers and agents carried on similar work in 1860 and 1863. Finally, it was the officers of the Emigrant Aid Company who furnished the first arms for the free-state militia.

Of course, the entries in the ledger of history are not all on the credit side of the Emigrant Aid Company's account. Some of its spokesmen made too lavish promises that could not be fulfilled, talking in terms of millions of dollars when they had only thousands to spend. The settlers held exaggerated expectations,

---

* William Phillips declared in 1856, "Near one-half of the saw mills in the Territory were brought there by its capital" (Phillips, *Conquest of Kansas*, 24).

which were inevitably doomed to disappointment. Many were embittered by the inadequacy of the Company's efforts, and free-state settlers from the West were sure that the Company was only making matters worse. The Missourians and their allies in Washington were not the only ones who blamed the Emigrant Aid Company for all the troubles in Kansas. Such statements were made repeatedly by the *Kansas Free State* as spokesman for the Western settlers.[22]

To say that there would have been no Kansas conflict but for the agitation of the Emigrant Aid Company is either to ignore other factors in the situation—the determination of the pro-slavery politicians to redress the Senate balance upset by the admission of California (which they soon despaired of redressing by the annexation of Cuba), and the explosive elements in Missouri state politics—or to assume that the free-soil settlers, who would of necessity have drifted into Kansas with or without the existence of the Emigrant Aid Company, would have submitted tamely to the establishment of slavery in an area free by the terms of the Missouri Compromise; certainly, Atchison and his backers in Washington would not have stood by with folded hands and have permitted slavery to be voted out of Kansas without a struggle. Still, the activity of the Emigrant Aid Company, particularly its propaganda, was undoubtedly *one* of the factors in bringing the Kansas conflict to a head. It antagonized the South, it gave Atchison the talking point he needed to arouse the border, and it gave the Administration at Washington the necessary pretext to support the party of "law and order." Whether responsible for the conflict or not, once it had started, the Emigrant Aid Company helped to carry it on. It not only armed the free-state settlers, but it supported the Free State party almost unaided until the country became aroused in the summer of 1856.

There is, of course, ample room for differences of opinion as to just what place the Emigrant Aid Company should hold in the history of Kansas, but there can be no doubt that it deserves a place. Kansas would have been settled, certainly, if the Company had never existed; it might have been settled just as rapidly —possibly more rapidly.* In all probability it would have become a free state ultimately, but that it would have done so without a struggle seems most unlikely. At any rate, in the events that actually occurred, the Emigrant Aid Company had a part, and that part, if not decisive, was by no means trivial.

The Company deserves also a place in the history of New England. First of all, it was largely the early activity and propaganda of the Emigrant Aid Company that aroused New England on the Kansas question, performing much the same function as did the Republican uprising in the Middle West. While the western states were holding mass meetings to protest the repeal of the Missouri Compromise, and were looking to political action to redress the grievance, New England was listening to the appeals of the Emigrant Aid Company for direct action. Politically, outside of Maine and Vermont, where something like pioneer conditions still prevailed, New England turned first to the Know-Nothing movement after the collapse of the Whigs; in 1854, the Know-Nothings won every state office and control of the legislature in Massachusetts. Two years later all New England was ready to turn to the Republicans. One cannot scan the New England newspapers of that day and find the name of the Emigrant Aid Company linked with every article and editorial on Kansas, without sensing that the activity of the Company was a major factor in bringing about this change.

The result was effected not only by pouring into the ears of New Englanders an uninterrupted stream of propaganda, but by providing a method of action which gave the people of the section an actual part in the movement and made them feel a sort of proprietary interest in the free-state cause. The Company, at

* At least the *Kansas Free State* asserted repeatedly that the activities of the Emigrant Aid Company were driving settlers away (see Connelley, *Appeal to the Record,* for quotations).

the height of its activity, had almost a thousand stockholders, located all over New England, and drawn chiefly from the most
influential classes: wealthy business men, ministers, college professors, physicians, lawyers, and public officials; here was a leaven
which must inevitably leaven the whole lump of public opinion.
Amos A. Lawrence wrote to Robinson in 1857, when Robinson
was inclined to grumble over real or imagined grievances: "You
are not strong enough to stand against it [the Emigrant Aid
Company] in this part of the country a single day. Its financial
power is trifling, but its moral power here, if exerted against any
individual, would destroy his influence and standing. This arises
from the character of most of the men who compose its Board
of Directors. Any opinion that they might deliberately form and
promulgate on almost any subject, but especially on any subject
relating to Kansas, would be final, and would have more weight
than a ruling of the United States Court."[23] With such a power
throwing its weight into the scales, it is small wonder that in
1856 the Republicans, who stood, or pretended to stand, for the
same cause for which the Emigrant Aid Company was working,
swept all New England.

Moreover, the Emigrant Aid Company offered a common
medium through which divergent, and hitherto discordant, elements could work. Capitalist and laborer, Hunker Whig and
Free Soiler, the religious zealot and the unbeliever, each of whom
felt an interest in retarding the spread of slavery, could all join
forces in support of the Aid Company. Says Professor Henry
Greenleaf Pearson, ". . . the movement to save Kansas was important in Massachusetts because it provided a common ground
for action by men who had hitherto stood apart."[24]

To sum up the influence of the Emigrant Aid Company on
New England history, it may be said that first of all, the Company popularized the Kansas issue in the region. Then, by furnishing a job in which all groups of the population could unite, it
prepared the way for the success of the Republican party in New

[301]

England in 1856. It is, of course, futile to attempt to say what might have happened had things been otherwise, but it seems unlikely that, without the support of New England, the Republicans could so easily have swept on to that victory of 1860 which precipitated the Civil War.

Finally, one must inquire what place should be accorded to the Emigrant Aid Company in the history of the nation. On the national stage it did to a lesser degree what it had done in New England. By its agitation, it helped to nationalize the Kansas conflict. Its advertising and propaganda were a factor in creating Northern sentiment in support of the free-state cause. It set the pattern for the wider Kansas Aid movement of 1856 which went further than the New England organization alone could have ever done in consolidating Northern opinion in behalf of "bleeding Kansas." This furnished the new Republican party with a highly emotionalized popular issue that enabled them to consolidate their position and win a moral victory in 1856. When, soon after the opening of the thirty-fourth Congress, the Administration made the Emigrant Aid Company an issue in an effort to shunt responsibility for its own unpopular course in Kansas, it played directly into the hands of the Republicans. Defense of the Emigrant Aid Company became the rallying ground for all forces in Congress opposed to the administration, and so provided a bridge over which many a representative and senator, elected as Know-Nothing, crossed over to the Republican lines. This development forced the administration to abandon the Kansas struggle in order to save the Democratic party in the approaching election, and enabled the free-state settlers of Kansas to take possession of the territorial government. With the loss of Kansas, Southern leaders despaired of redressing the senatorial balance; and they turned more and more to the belief that, if they should lose control of the federal government to the "Black Republicans," they must leave the Union in order to save their social and economic system.

It is impossible to say just how far the course of national events was changed by the existence or the activities of the Emigrant Aid Company. No human wisdom can say to what extent things would have been different if the Company had never been formed. The Kansas struggle would probably have come anyway, though it might have run a much different course. The Republican party would have been launched in any case, but it might or might not have made the rapid headway it did. The administration certainly would have had to look elsewhere for a scapegoat in 1856; and without the defense of the Emigrant Aid Company as a rallying point, the opposition groups might or might not have been able to force the abandonment of the Kansas struggle. But without attempting to fix too definitely the exact place of the Company in American history, one may safely conclude that, for better or for worse, the thread of the Emigrant Aid Company history is woven inextricably into the fabric of events that led up to the Civil War, and that it deserves at the hands of the historians a clearer understanding and a more adequate treatment than it has had heretofore.

But whatever importance the judgment of history may finally assign to the Emigrant Aid Company, its story is a moving real-life drama. The consecration of its leaders to a great cause, their struggles, frustrations, and heartaches in carrying on their crusade, and even their futile efforts to save something from the financial wreckage for their stockholders, all make up a human-interest story that sounds more like imaginative fiction than drab historic facts. The poetic line that Eugene Ware ("Ironquill") wrote about John Brown would seem to be even more appropriate if applied to the crusaders of the Emigrant Aid Company: they "dared begin." They "lost, but losing won."

Notes

I

1. Mary J. Klem, "Missouri in the Kansas Struggle," Mississippi Valley Historical Association, *Proceedings for the Year 1917-1918*, IX, 393-413.
2. James G. Blaine, *Twenty Years of Congress* (Norwich, Conn., 1884), I, 119-22.
3. E. L. Craik, "Southern Interest in Territorial Kansas," *Kansas Historical Collections*, XV, 348 ff.; Klem, *loc. cit.*
4. *De Bow's Review*, XX, 741.
5. *New York Daily Times,* May 27, 1854.
6. Eli Thayer, *A History of the Kansas Crusade* (New York, 1889), 250-51.
7. G. O. Ward, *The Worcester Academy* (Worcester, Mass., 1918), 33-42.
8. A. A. Lawrence to Moses Grinnell, June 21, 1854. Letters of Amos A. Lawrence about Kansas Affairs and to Correspondents in Kansas from June 10, 1854, to August 10, 1861 (bound typewritten copies, hand-indexed, prepared under the direction of Mrs. A. A. Lawrence from letterpress copies. Kansas State Historical Society, Topeka, Kansas), hereinafter cited as Lawrence Letters, 3.
9. W. E. Connelley, *A Standard History of Kansas and Kansans* (Chicago and New York, 1918), I, 341.
10. W. W. Rice (Secretary of the Worcester County Kansas League during the period of the Kansas conflict), remarks at a meeting of the Worcester Society of Antiquity, 1887. Worcester Society of Antiquity, *Collections*, VII, 26.
11. Ward, *Worcester Academy,* 40. There are numerous allusions to Ceredo in the minutes and correspondence of the Emigrant Aid Company.
12. Account books of the New England Emigrant Aid Company, Kansas State Historical Society, Topeka, Kansas, hereinafter cited as Aid Company Account Books, Journal, 13.
13. Edward Everett Hale, *Memories of a Hundred Years* (New York, 1897), II, 151-53. A copy of this pamphlet is preserved among the papers and effects of the New England Emigrant Aid Company in the Archives of the Kansas State Historical Society, Topeka, Kansas; hereinafter cited as Aid Company Papers.
14. Hale, *Memories,* II, 155.
15. Eli Thayer, *The New England Emigrant Aid Company* (Worcester, 1887), 13.
16. Pamphlet, *Organization, Objects and Plan of Operations of the Emigrant Aid Company* (Boston, 1854), preserved among Emigrant Aid Company Collected Pamphlets, Kansas State Historical Society, Topeka, Kansas. This pamphlet states that it is a part of the plan of the Emigrant Aid Company "to return a handsome profit to the stockholders upon their investment."
17. "Report of the Special Committee Appointed to Investigate the Troubles in Kansas," No. 200, *House Reports*, 34 Cong., 1 Sess., commonly known and hereinafter cited as *Howard Report*, 885.
18. Thayer, *New England Emigrant Aid Company*, 13.
19. *National Cyclopedia of American Biography*, VIII, 372-73.
20. Hale, *Memories*, II, 155.
21. *Ibid.*, 165.
22. Thayer, *Kansas Crusade*, 33, 225.
23. Lawrence Letters, 66.
24. Letterpress copies of letters written by Thomas H. Webb and others on behalf of the New England Emigrant Aid Company, preserved in the Archives of the Kansas State Historical Society, Topeka, Kansas, hereinafter cited as Aid Company Letters; Book A, 34.
25. *Ibid.*, Book B, 512.
26. J. B. Quincy, "Memoir of Thomas H. Webb, M. D.," Massachusetts Historical Society, *Proceedings*, XIX, 336-38.
27. Lawrence Letters, 140.
28. *Ibid.*, 167.

29. B. P. Redmond (president of Lawrence College, Appleton, Wisconsin), *Hon. Amos A. Lawrence* (Appleton, 1886).

30. These impressions of Amos A. Lawrence have been gleaned almost entirely from his letters and from the minutes and correspondence of the Emigrant Aid Company.

II

1. Notes on this petition are among certain notes taken by Professor Robert F. Moody (Boston University) and generously lent to the writer. These notes are chiefly on letters written to Amos A. Lawrence and preserved among the original Lawrence papers. Hereinafter these will be cited as Moody Notes.

2. Edward Everett Hale, "The Colonization of Kansas," in W. T. Davis (ed.), *The New England States* (Boston, 1897), I, 82.

3. *Ibid.*, 81-82.

4. Engrossed copy of Act of Incorporation among Aid Company Papers; also, official printed copy of "House Bill No. 164, Commonwealth of Massachusetts," in New England Emigrant Aid Company Collected Pamphlets.

5. Original letter among Aid Company Papers.

6. Except as otherwise indicated, all information about these preliminary meetings is gleaned from scattered newspaper clippings in the Webb Scrap Books, Book I. These scrapbooks are seventeen volumes of newspaper clippings on the Emigrant Aid Company and Kansas matters generally, collected and prepared by Thomas H. Webb, Secretary of the Emigrant Aid Company, and preserved in the Library of the Kansas State Historical Society, Topeka, Kansas.

7. Thayer, *New England Emigrant Aid Company*, 25.

8. *Howard Report*, 883.

9. A. A. Lawrence to Professor A. S. Packard, October 30, 1854. Lawrence Letters, 37.

10. Lawrence Correspondence (letters written to Amos A. Lawrence and preserved among the Lawrence papers), Book XI, 149. Moody Notes.

11. Lawrence Letters, 1.

12. A copy of the unamended Articles of Association is not accessible. This summary is based upon P. T. Jackson's letter cited in note 10.

13. Jackson's letters to Lawrence cited in note 10.

14. Thayer, *New England Emigrant Aid Company*, 25-27.

15. Lawrence Letters, 3.

16. Lawrence Correspondence, Book XI, 157. Moody Notes.

17. *Ibid.*, 160.

18. Undated printed copy of Act of Incorporation among Aid Company Papers.

19. Thayer to Lawrence, June 29, 1854. Lawrence Correspondence, Book XI, 161. Moody Notes.

20. No specific record of this fact has come to light, but incidental allusions in the correspondence would indicate that such was the case.

21. Jackson to Lawrence, June 30, 1854. Lawrence Correspondence, Book XI, 161. Moody Notes.

22. Lawrence Letters, 7.

23. *Ibid.*, 8.

24. Lawrence Correspondence, Book XI, 175. Moody Notes.

25. In all preserved correspondence July 18 is the date mentioned. The newspaper account of the meeting gives July 19 as the date. *New York Daily Tribune*, July 20, 1854, Webb Scrap Books, Book I, 66.

26. Lawrence Letters, 15.

27. Edward Channing, *A History of the United States* (New York, 1905), VI, 161.

28. Robert F. Moody, "The First Year of the Emigrant Aid Company," *New England Quarterly*, IV, Jan., 1931, 148-55.

29. Lawrence Letters, 10.

30. See note 28.

31. Lawrence Correspondence, Book XI, 176. Moody Notes.

32. Lawrence Letters, 10.

33. Copies of both in Lawrence Letters, 11-15.

34. Printed copy, "Articles of Agreement and Association of the Emigrant Aid Company," in New England Emigrant Aid Company Collected Pamphlets.

35. Original minute books of the Emigrant Aid Company containing the minutes of the Trustees, the Stockholders, the Directors and the Executive Committee, in the Archives of the Kansas State Historical Society, Topeka, Kansas, hereinafter cited as Aid Company Records; Book I, 5-6.

36. *Ibid.*, 17.

37. Certified copy of the act among the Aid Company Papers.

38. Webb Scrap Books, Book I, 170.

39. Aid Company Records, Book I, 68-69. Also printed copy of circular letter to the stockholders, dated Feb. 26, 1855, in New England Emigrant Aid Company Collected Pamphlets.

40. Lawrence Letters, 52.

41. *Ibid.*, 56.

42. *Ibid.*, 58.

43. Hale, in Davis, *The New England States,* I, 89. Also pamphlet, *The John Carter Brown Library* (published by Brown University, Providence, 1905).

44. Aid Company Records, Book "Company," 43-48.

45. Complete minutes of the meeting, *ibid.*, 39-49.

46. *Ibid.*, Book I, 73-75.

47. *Ibid.*, Book "Company," 52.

48. *Ibid.*, Book I, 139.

III

1. Edward Everett Hale, *Kanzas and Nebraska* (Boston, 1854), 216-19.

2. E. E. Hale, Jr., *The Life and Letters of Edward Everett Hale* (Boston, 1917), I, 252.

3. Lawrence Letters, 18.

4. *Howard Report,* 886.

5. *Ibid.*, 874.

6. Gleaned chiefly from the Emigrant Books, which listed purchases and sales of tickets, and from correspondence in Aid Company Letters. These Emigrant Books are Dr. Webb's accounts of all transactions relative to tickets. Besides dealings with the railway passenger agents, they list the name of each person who bought tickets from the Company. Five are preserved; at least two are missing.

7. Hale, *Memories of a Hundred Years,* II, 157.

8. Copies of several editions of this pamphlet are among the New England Emigrant Aid Company Collected Pamphlets.

9. *Howard Report,* 886.

10. So stated in various Aid Company publications, verified by the correspondence, and testified to by J. Riddlesbarger, Kansas City forwarding agent of the Emigrant Aid Company, before the Howard Commitee. *Ibid.*, 884.

11. Hale, *Memories,* II, 157.

12. Thomas H. Webb, *Information for Kansas Emigrants* (Boston, 1855-1857, several editions), 5th and all later editions, 4.

13. *Howard Report,* 874-75 (Lawrence), 884 (Thayer), 886-87 (Stone).

14. Original among Aid Company Papers.

15. Webb, *Information,* 5th and later eds., 7.

16. *Howard Report,* 874.

17. Webb, *Information,* 13th and later eds., 10.

18. Lawrence Letters, 53-55. There are other letters in a similar vein.

19. Webb, *Information,* all eds., 3-4; 13th and later eds., 41-42.

20. New England Emigrant Aid Company Collected Pamphlets.

21. Records of these requests are scattered through the Aid Company Records and Aid Company Letters.

22. Russell K. Hickman, "Speculative Activities of the Emigrant Aid Company," *Kansas Historical Quarterly,* IV, Aug., 1935, 235-67. Connelley asserted repeatedly that this was the primary purpose of the Emigrant Aid Company.

23. *Howard Report,* 885.

24. Lawrence Letters, 20.

25. *Ibid.*, 22-23; Thayer, *Kansas Crusade*, 58-59.
26. Lawrence Letters, 75; Paul Wallace Gates, "A Fragment of Kansas Land History," *Kansas Historical Quarterly*, VI, Aug., 1937, 227-40.
27. *History of the New England Emigrant Aid Company with a Report on Its Future Operations* (published by Order of the Board of Directors, Boston, 1862), hereinafter cited as *Directors' History*, 23.
28. See Gates, cited in note 26, above.
29. Part of the papers of the Kansas Land Trust, filed under "Miscellaneous Papers," are in the Archives of the Kansas State Historical Society, Topeka, Kansas. Lawrence wrote Robinson several letters about it; Lawrence Letters, 205, 247, 259, 277.
30. Thayer, *Kansas Crusade*, 59.
31. Charles Robinson, *The Kansas Conflict* (Lawrence, Kansas, 1898), 182.
32. W. E. Connelley, *An Appeal to the Record* (Topeka, 1903), 109.
33. Stock Ledger, Aid Company Account Books.
34. Webb to William Tyler, Pawtucket, R.I., Oct. 4, 1854, Aid Company Letters, Book A, 7. Numerous other letters say essentially the same thing.
35. Connelley, *Appeal to the Record*, 7.
36. W. H. Carruth to E. E. Hale, February 9, 1897. Original letter among Aid Company Papers.
37. Quoted by W. H. Carruth, "The New England Emigrant Aid Company as an Investment Society," *Kansas Historical Collections*, VI, 90-96.

IV

1. Exact dates are not available. Robinson states (*Kansas Conflict*, 69) that they passed Jefferson City on July 4.
2. Robinson, *Kansas Conflict*, 69-70.
3. Lawrence Letters, 8-9.
4. John Doy, *The Narrative of John Doy* (New York, 1860), chap. I. Account of Newell Philbrick, one of the party, in *Worcester Daily Spy*, August 31, 1854. Original letter (undated, but written about 1880) of C. W. Smith, Secretary of the Kansas Old Settlers Association, to F. G. Adams, Secretary of the Kansas State Historical Society, Aid Company Papers.
5. Aid Company Records, Book I, 7-8.
6. Lawrence Correspondence, Book XI, 190. Moody Notes.
7. F. W. Blackmar, *The Life of Charles Robinson* (Topeka, Kansas, 1902).
8. Josiah Royce, *California* (Boston, 1886), 476-78; H. H. Bancroft, *California inter Pocula* (San Francisco, 1888), 410.
9. Lawrence Letters, 261-62.
10. *Ibid.*, 18-20.
11. Aid Company Records, Book I, 13-15.
12. *National Cyclopedia of American Biography*, XII, 69-70.
13. Original letter of Pomeroy, unaddressed, but probably to J. M. S. Williams, dated July 27, 1854. Aid Company Papers.
14. W. H. Carruth, "The New England Emigrant Aid Company as an Investment Society," *Kansas Historical Collections*, VI, 90-96.
15. Aid Company Records, Book I, 13-15.
16. F. W. Blackmar, *Kansas: A Cyclopedia of State History* (Chicago, 1912) I, 230.
17. Gleaned from Aid Company Letters and Aid Company Records.
18. This information about Thayer's work is taken from newspaper clippings in the Webb Scrap Books and from scattered allusions in the correspondence and minutes of the trustees.
19. Constitution of the Worcester County Kansas League in New England Emigrant Aid Company Collected Pamphlets.
20. Hale in Davis, *New England States*, I, 83-84. Hale reproduces Thayer's outline from which he worked. The original, in Thayer's handwriting, is among the Aid Company Papers.
21. Copies in Collected Pamphlets. An abridgment of the report is given in Thayer, *Kansas Crusade*, 27-29. The "Plan" is summarized here in some detail because of the extensive allusions to it that must be made in later chapters.

NOTES (pp. 62-71)

22. Copies of 2nd, 3d, and 4th editions in Collected Pamphlets.
23. Aid Company Records, Book I, 25.
24. *Ibid.*, 19.
25. Webb Scrap Books, Book I, 59.
26. Lucy Larcom to John G. Whittier, Feb. 27, 1858. Quoted by Grace L. Shepherd, "Letters of Lucy Larcom to the Whittiers," *New England Quarterly*, July, 1930.
27. Copies among Aid Company Papers.
28. Aid Company Records, Book I, 5-6.
29. William Lawrence, *Life of Amos A. Lawrence* (Boston and New York, 1888), 84.
30. Lawrence Letters, 20.
31. *Ibid.*, 24-25.
32. Aid Company Records, Book I, 16.
33. Professor Moody found a printed copy of this circular among the Lawrence papers. Moody Notes.
34. Lawrence Letters, 36-37.
35. *Ibid.*, 39-40.
36. Lawrence, *Amos A. Lawrence*, 85.
37. *Howard Report*, 829-30.
38. Copy in Collected Pamphlets.
39. Lawrence Letters, 16-18.
40. Aid Company Letters, Book A, 31.
41. Several original letters among Aid Company Papers.
42. *New York Daily Times*, Aug. 31, 1854.
43. Aid Company Records, Book I, 51-53; Aid Company Letters, Book A, 79.
44. Several circulars of the New York Kansas League are among the Aid Company Papers. One, entitled *The Great Kansas Enterprise*, issued in conjunction with the American Settlement Company, is in Collected Pamphlets. Frequent mention of its activities and several of its advertisements appear in the *New York Daily Times*.
45. Copy of constitution, prospectus, and other materials in Max Greene, *The Kansas Region* (New York, 1856), 188-91. Greene was a member of the exploring party sent out by the Settlement Company.
46. George Walter, *History of Kansas. Also Information Regarding Routes, Laws, etc.* (New York, 1855). More pretentious but less complete and reliable than Webb's *Information*.
47. *New York Daily Times*, March 31, 1855, and June 4, 1855.
48. *Ibid.*, Aug. 31, 1854.
49. Galley sheet, "Ohio Kansas Movement," dated Oberlin, Aug. 21, 1854. Webb Scrap Books, Book I, 96.
50. *Oberlin Evangelist*, Sept. 27, 1854.
51. Several copies of Howe's statement, clipped from different newspapers, in Webb Scrap Books, Book II.
52. Clayton S. Ellsworth, "Oberlin and the Anti-Slavery Movement" (unpublished thesis, Cornell University, 1930), chap. V.
53. Webb Scrap Books, Book I, 158.
54. C. B. Boynton and T. B. Mason, *Journey through Kansas* (Cincinnati, 1855), Preface.
55. William H. Mackey, "Looking Backward," *Kansas Historical Collections*, X, 642-51. Mackey went to Kansas as a member of this colony.
56. An excellent sketch of the enterprise, based on original research, is Russell Hickman, "The Vegetarian and Octagon Settlement Companies," *Kansas Historical Quarterly*, II, Nov., 1933, 377-85. Diary of one of the settlers, describing the plan and reproducing various circulars issued by the Vegetarian Company, Mrs. Miriam D. Colt, *Went to Kansas* (Watertown, Mass., 1862); circulars describing octagon plan, 280-82.
57. Items about and advertisements of the Octagon Company, *New York Daily Tribune*, Aug. 10, 1855; Feb. 23, 26, 28, 1856.
58. Circular of the Vegetarian Company reproduced in Colt, *op cit.*, 13-21.
59. Hickman, cited in note 56.

V

1. W. H. T. Wakefield, "Squatter Courts in Kansas," *Kansas Historical Collections,* V, 71-74.

2. Annie Abel (Henderson), "Indian Reservations in Kansas and the Extinction of Their Title," *Kansas Historical Collections,* VIII, 72-109.

3. Wakefield, cited in note 1.

4. Quoted in full in A. T. Andreas, *History of Kansas* (Chicago, 1883), I, 83.

5. George W. Martin, "The First Two Years in Kansas," *Kansas Historical Collections,* X, 120-48.

6. Wakefield, cited in note 1.

7. S. N. Wood, "The Pioneers of Kansas," *Kansas Historical Collections,* III, 426-31.

8. In 1856 Thaddeus Hyatt, president of the National Kansas Committee, visited Kansas to investigate the need for relief. He took depositions from a large number of settlers from all parts of the country. Nearly all testified that they had migrated to Kansas for the purpose of bettering their economic condition. Ninety-five of these depositions, called the "Hyatt Manuscripts," are preserved in the Archives of the Kansas State Historical Society, Topeka, Kansas. Excerpts, *Kansas Historical Collections,* I-II, 203-21. Evidence of the same kind is offered by E. L. Craik, "Southern Interest in Territorial Kansas," *Kansas Historical Collections,* XV, 338 ff., and by Wallace E. Miller, *The Peopling of Kansas* (Columbus, Ohio, 1906), 45-46.

9. Wood, cited in note 7.

10. P. P. Wilcox, letter to the Kansas State Historical Society, Jan. 24, 1886, *Kansas Historical Collections,* III, 467.

11. Wood, cited in note 7.

12. Reported by Dr. Webb to the Trustees. Aid Company Records, Book I, 25, 27, 34, 37, 41, 42, 43.

13. Emigrant Books. This counts half-fare tickets sold for children.

14. Indicated by letters of Dr. Webb to B. Slater, St. Louis forwarding agent of the Emigrant Aid Company, Aid Company Letters, Book A, 19-20.

15. Thayer, *Kansas Crusade,* 54.

16. Aid Company Records, Book I, *passim.*

17. Thayer, *Kansas Crusade,* 56.

18. Aid Company Letters, Book A, 30-31.

19. Richard Cordley, *A History of Lawrence, Kansas, from the Earliest Settlement to the Close of the Rebellion* (Lawrence, 1895), 15.

20. *Howard Report,* 125, 153, 336, 830, 832, 835, 836, 845, 852, 857, 862, 899, 1160, 1172.

21. "Address to the People of the United States," quoted in *Howard Report,* 879. Also issued as a tract, Aid Company Papers.

22. Webb to Pomeroy, Nov. 6, 1854, Aid Company Letters, Book A, 47-48. Webb to Robinson, Nov. 27, 1854, *ibid.,* 67-68. Webb to Pomeroy, April 23, 1855, *ibid.,* 138. There are several others.

23. *New York Daily Times,* April 9, 1855.

24. Original letter, undated, C. W. Smith to F. G. Adams, based on records of Kansas Old Settlers Association, Aid Company Papers.

25. Robinson, *Kansas Conflict,* 89.

26. Smith letter, cited in note 24.

27. For rival versions of the controversy see Robinson, *Kansas Conflict,* 78-89, and R. G. Elliott, *Foot Notes on Kansas History* (Lawrence, 1906), 14-21. Contemporary newspaper account of early phase of the affair, *New York Daily Times,* Oct. 30, 1854.

28. Webb to Pomeroy, March 26, 1855, Aid Company Letters, Book A, 103-04. Webb to Robinson, May 8, 1855, *ibid.,* 147-49.

29. E.g., William Phillips, *The Conquest of Kansas by Missouri and Her Allies* (Boston, 1856), 26-33.

30. *Springfield Republican,* Feb. 21, 1855, Webb Scrap Books, Book III, 7.

31. *New York Daily Times,* Oct. 21, 1854; *ibid.,* April 4, 1855. *Telegraph and Pioneer,* Dec. 16, 1854, *ibid.,* Book II, 61. These are only a few samples.

32. Aid Company Letters, Book A, 39-41.

33. *Ibid.*, 56-67.

34. Webb, *Information* (13th ed.), 56. Charles Robinson, "Topeka and Her Constitution," *Kansas Historical Collections,* VI, 291-305.

35. F. W. Giles, *Thirty Years in Topeka* (Topeka, 1886), 20-22. Giles was one of the nine founders and was secretary of the association. Wallace S. Baldinger, "The Amateur Plans a City," *Kansas Historical Quarterly,* XII, Feb., 1943, 3-13. On the naming of Topeka see Giles, *op. cit.,* and *Kansas Historical Collections,* X, 404.

36. Letter of William Chestnut, one of the party, dated Dec. 12, 1854, in *New York Tribune,* Jan. 23, 1855. Ely Moore, Jr., told a conflicting story, attributing the founding to Missourians and asserting that he was present on the occasion. The essential agreement of his story with newspaper accounts of the founding of Paola (only ten miles away) suggests that, either deliberately or inadvertently, he must have confused the two. Ely Moore, Jr., "The Naming of Osawatomie," *Kansas Historical Collections,* XII, 338-46.

37. Minutes of the Executive Committee for June 20, 1855, Aid Company Records, Book I, 151-52. Isaac T. Goodnow, "Personal Reminiscences," *Kansas Historical Collections,* IV, 244-53.

38. Testimony of Isaac S. Haskell, *Howard Report,* 1035-37.

39. Goodnow, cited in note 37. A. R. Greene, "Kansas River Navigation," *Kansas Historical Collections,* IX, 317-58.

40. Aid Company Letters, Book B, 142-43, 487-89.

41. Webb, *Information* (13th ed.), 69. Andreas, *History of Kansas,* I, 647. Minutes of Executive Committee, Aid Company Records, Book I, 121, 126, 132.

42. *Hampshire Gazette,* May 29, 1855, Webb Scrap Books, Book IV, 111.

43. J. M. Bisbey, "Early Day Transportation," *Kansas Historical Collections,* XI, 594-97. Bisbee was one of the original settlers of Wabaunsee.

44. Aid Company Letters, Book A, 331-38.

45. Original deed of William Gillis to Robinson and Pomeroy, "agents, in trust for the Emigrant Aid Company of Boston, Massachusetts," dated Sept. 14, 1854, Aid Company Papers. Apparently Gaius Jenkins, nominal owner of the hotel, had never received a deed to it.

46. Letter of Pomeroy, *The Puritan Recorder* (Boston), Nov. 16, 1854, Webb Scrap Books, Book II, 13.

47. Lawrence Letters, 9-11, 27. Aid Company Letters, Book A, 46-47.

48. Lawrence Letters, 34. Aid Company Letters, Book A, 46-47.

49. Cordley, *History of Lawrence,* 13, 17.

50. Aid Company Records, Book V, 24-25, 27-28. Duplicate copy of deed (consideration one dollar) is among Aid Company Papers.

51. Aid Company Letters, Book A, 30, 54, 59, 104, 137.

52. Webb, *Information* (13th ed.), 46.

53. Lawrence Letters, 28.

54. Aid Company Letters, Book A, 28.

55. *Ibid.,* 44-45.

56. *Ibid.,* 138.

57. Reported by Brown in letter to Hale, July 25, 1855. Original letter, Aid Company Papers.

58. Aid Company Letters, Book A, 21, 24, 32-33. Aid Company Records, Book I, 14, 24-25, 28, 30, 37, 39.

59. Lawrence Letters, 53-55. See above, chap. III, note 18.

60. Aid Company Records, Book A, 82-83. Lawrence Letters, 64-65, 69-70.

61. Lawrence Letters, 72.

VI

1. Jonas Viles, "Sections and Sectionalism in a Border State," *Mississippi Valley Historical Review,* XXI, June, 1934, 3-22.

2. Lucien Carr, *Missouri, a Bone of Contention* (Boston and New York, 1888), 221-26.

3. Theodore Roosevelt, *Thomas Hart Benton* (Boston and New York, 1887), 342-43; chap. XIV.

4. *New York Daily Tribune,* July 26, 1854, Webb Scrap Books, Book I, 67.

5. *Boston Daily Advertiser,* June 21, 1854, *ibid.,* 20.

6. *New York Daily Times*, Aug. 18, 1854.
7. Testimony of J. H. Day, a Missouri farmer. *Howard Report*, 526.
8. This view of the situation, expounded at the time by the Bentonite newspapers, is supported by E. L. Craik in his doctoral dissertation, "Southern Interest in Territorial Kansas," *Kansas Historical Collections*, XV, 348.
9. W. M. Paxton, *Annals of Platte County, Missouri* (Kansas City, 1897), 184. Andreas, *History of Kansas*, I, 90. Some newspaper accounts of this meeting give the date as July 20 (Webb Scrap Books, Book I, 104).
10. Webb Scrap Books, Book I, 112.
11. Andreas, I, 90.
12. George W. Martin, "Early Days in Kansas," *Kansas Historical Collections*, IX, 126-43.
13. *Boston Atlas*, Dec. 4, 1854, copied from *Platte* (Missouri) *Argus*, Webb Scrap Books, II, 28. *National Era* (Washington, D. C.), Dec. 12, 1854, copied independently from the *Argus*, *ibid.*, 32.
14. Copied from the *Intelligencer* (date not given) in *New York Daily Times*, Nov. 23, 1854.
15. "Address to the People of the United States," in *Howard Report*, 887. Also published as a broadside, Aid Company Papers.
16. *Howard Report*, 356, 838, 856, 896-97, 902, 903.
17. Robinson, *Kansas Conflict*, 92-100; Leverett W. Spring, *Kansas, The Prelude to the Civil War* (Boston and New York, 1907), 38-42.
18. W. F. Switzler in C. R. Barnes (ed.), *Switzler's History of Missouri* (St. Louis, 1879), 277-78; *New York Daily Times*, Jan. 13, 1855; Jan. 16, 1855; Feb. 6, 1855.
19. *New York Daily Times*, Feb. 6, 1855.
20. Copy of item from *St. Louis Democrat* (date not given) in *New York Daily Times*, Sept. 17, 1855.
21. *St. Louis Evening News*, May 16, 1855, quoted in Craik, "Southern Interest in Territorial Kansas," *Kansas Historical Collections*, XV, 341.
22. Spring, *Kansas*, 43. Many stories were told of efforts of pro-slavery men to pad the registration. See Holloway, 138-39, and James R. McClure (one of the census takers), "Taking the Census and Other Incidents of 1855," *Kansas Historical Collections*, VIII, 227-50.
23. Holloway, 139. William Barbee, one of the census takers and a pro-slavery man, testified that Governor Reeder issued the call for the election the same day that he (Barbee) turned in the census returns for his district (*Howard Report*, 244).
24. So many persons testified to the prevalence of these rumors that it is impossible to cite them all. For a few samples, see *Howard Report*, 356, 361, 384, 385, 410, 412, 859, 860, 897, 899, 1145.
25. Newspaper accounts of some of these meetings are preserved in the Webb Scrap Books, Book II (Ray County) 187, (Glasgow) 187, (Fayette) 188, (Lexington) 266. "Kansas Meetings" are known to have been held in all the border counties.
26. Lawrence Letters, 62-64.
27. Aid Company Letters, Book A, 395.
28. *Ibid.*, 83-84.
29. *Ibid.*, 98-99.
30. *Howard Report* 30. There is, of course, no way of telling exactly how many fraudulent votes were cast.
31. I. T. Goodnow, "Personal Reminiscences," *Kansas Historical Collections*, IV, 244-53.
32. *Howard Report*, 887-93.
33. So stated J. N. O. P. Wood, a settler from Illinois, who was a free-state man until the fall of 1855, when he changed sides (*ibid.*, 653-60). There is ample corroborative evidence in miscellaneous newspaper allusions and reminiscences of old settlers.
34. Robinson to Thayer, April 2, 1855, quoted in W. H. Iseley, "The Sharps Rifle Episode in Kansas History," *American Historical Review*, XII, 546-66; quoted also in Blackmar, *Life of Charles Robinson*, 131-33.
35. Robinson, *Kansas Conflict*, 169.
36. *Ibid.*, 176-77, 179-80.

37. This summary is based on Holloway, 178-81, and Andreas, *History of Kansas,* I, 106-08.
38. Quoted in *Kansas Conflict,* 145-52.
39. W. H. Stephenson, *The Political Career of General James H. Lane* (Topeka, 1930), 42-44.
40. Robinson, *Kansas Conflict,* 170, 217.
41. Holloway, 182-89; Andreas, 108-10.
42. Andreas, 110-13; Robinson, *Kansas Conflict,* 175-79.
43. Hodder Lectures; also Robinson, *Kansas Conflict,* 179-80.
44. Andreas, 113-16.

VII

1. Lawrence Correspondence, Moody Notes.
2. Minutes of the Trustees, 32nd meeting, Feb. 23, 1855, Aid Company Records, Book I, 128.
3. Lawrence to Robinson, Lawrence Letters, 49.
4. Lawrence to Williams, Feb. 20, 1854, *ibid.,* 52. Lawrence to Pomeroy, same date, *ibid.,* 52-53.
5. *Ibid.,* 57.
6. Aid Company Records, Book "Company," 48-49.
7. Lawrence to Pomeroy, March 14, 1855, Lawrence Letters, 58-59. Lawrence to Wm. J. Rotch, New Bedford, *ibid.,* 60.
8. Aid Company Records, Book I, 25.
9. Lawrence Letters, 66, 68.
10. *Ibid.,* 66.
11. *Ibid.,* 75-76.
12. Several copies of this tract among Aid Company Papers. Copied in full in Thayer, *Kansas Crusade,* 130-33; also in *Kansas Historical Collections,* I-II, 194-96.
13. Printed copies of form letters sent out by these committees in Collected Pamphlets.
14. An article in the *Kansas Historical Collections,* I-II, 193-202, reports that the Kansas State Historical Society had at that time (1880) 232 of these letters, and prints the list. In the present study, 160 of them were found among the Aid Company Papers and examined. The others are either lost or filed elsewhere.
15. These figures are taken from a newspaper clipping pasted in the small account book in which Hale kept a record of ministerial subscriptions and contributions. The notebook itself shows $917.25 collected, $840 in twenty-dollar blocks for which shares were issued. This was probably the amount that Hale collected himself.
16. Aid Company Records, I, 170, 173-74, 181, 185.
17. Lawrence to Williams, Sept. 26, 1855, Lawrence Letters, 100-01. To J. C. Brown, same date, *ibid.,* 101-02. To Williams, Sept. 27, *ibid.,* 102-03.
18. Lawrence to J. C. Brown, Oct. 3, 1855, *ibid.,* 104.
19. Aid Company Letters, Book A, 165-66.
20. Aid Company Records, Book I, 178-81. Also original correspondence between Russell and Hale among Aid Company Papers. Hale received $20 a week and expenses.
21. Minutes of the Executive Committee, Aid Company Records, Book I, 190-92, 193-95, 203-06, 207-10, 218-22.
22. Minutes of the Trustees, *ibid.,* 5-6.
23. Lawrence to Webb, March 17, 1855, Lawrence Letters, 66-67.
24. Lawrence to Williams, same date, *ibid.,* 67-68.
25. Original letter, Russell to Hale, Dec. 14, 1855, Aid Company Papers.
26. Minutes of the Executive Committee, Aid Company Records, Book I, 181. Also letters of Williams, Sept. 29 and Oct. 1, 1855, Moody Notes.
27. Aid Company Records, Book I, 193-94; Book II, 10.
28. Minutes of the Executive Committee, *ibid.,* 81, 85-86, 90, 91, 94, 100, 107-08, 114-15, 118-19, 125, 128-29, 150, 177. Louise Barry, "The New England Emigrant Aid Company Parties of 1855," *Kansas Historical Quarterly,* XII, Aug., 1943, 227-68.
29. *New York Daily Times,* May 29, 1855.
30. Holloway, *History of Kansas,* 156.

31. *Ibid.,* 156-57.
32. Webb to Pomeroy, May 8, 1855, Aid Company Letters, Book A, 160.
33. *Ibid.,* 124.
34. *Ibid.,* 105-10.
35. *Ibid.,* 80-82, 96-99.
36. Original letter, W. D. Haley (Alton, Illinois) to Hale March 9, 1855, Aid Company Papers.
37. Aid Company Letters, Book A, 113-14, 123.
38. Each statement in this paragraph is based on one or more newspaper items taken from either the files of the *New York Times* or the Webb Scrap Books.
39. Mrs. Robinson recorded Nov. 29, 1855, "The large hotel is complete externally . . ." (Sara T. D. Robinson, *Kansas, Its Interior and Exterior Life* [Boston, 1856], 119 [later editions, 140]).
40. Aid Company Records, Book I, 13-15.
41. Aid Company Letters, Book A, 10-12, 40.
42. Giles, *Thirty Years in Topeka,* 30-35.
43. The *Kansas Free State* (Lawrence), March 3 and July 9, 1855, quoted in Connelley, *Appeal to the Record,* 125-26.
44. Aid Company Records, Book I, 127-28.
45. *Ibid.,* 145-46, 148, 155, 161. Also original letter, Pomeroy to Branscomb (Acting Secretary), Aug. 6, 1855, Aid Company Papers.
46. Original letter, Pomeroy to Branscomb, Aug. 11, 1855, Aid Company Papers. Same, Sept. 1, 1855.
47. Original letter, Pomeroy to Branscomb, Sept. 15, 1855.
48. Aid Company Records, Book II, 25-26, 97-98.
49. *Ibid.,* Book I, 154.
50. *Ibid.,* 207-10.
51. *New York Daily Times,* May 24, 1855.
52. The late W. H. Iseley worked out this story more than fifty years ago and published it under the title, "The Sharps Rifle Episode in Kansas History," in the *American Historical Review* of April, 1907. The present study has gone over the ground thoroughly, but has brought to light almost nothing that would modify Iseley's findings.
53. Letter to Thayer quoted in Blackmar, *Robinson,* 131-33. Original letter to Hale preserved among Aid Company Papers.
54. Letter of George W. Deitzler to J. S. Emery of Old Settlers' Committee, dated San Francisco, Sept. 8, 1879, describes the episode from memory. Quoted in full in Charles S. Gleed (ed.), *The Kansas Memorial* (Kansas City, 1880), 184; quoted in abridged form in Robinson, *Kansas Conflict,* 123-24.
55. Aid Company Letters, Book A, 146-47. Quoted in abridged form on pp. 226-27 of F. B. Sanborn's "Early History of Kansas," *Massachusetts Historical Society Proceedings,* XLI. Evasiveness prompted by fear letter might be intercepted.
56. Letter to Webb, acknowledging the order and inclosing invoice, signed by J. C. Palmer, president of Sharps Rifle Manufacturing Company, printed in Hale, *Memories of a Hundred Years,* II, 165-66.
57. Lawrence Letters, 87.
58. An incomplete list is given in Lawrence, *Amos A. Lawrence,* 97. The full list, taken from a memorandum in handwriting of Dr. Cabot among Lawrence papers, is given by F. B. Sanborn (cited in note 55), 227. There is some question whether it was the first or second hundred rifles that this group paid for, but for the present purpose, it is immaterial.
59. Lawrence Letters, 82.
60. *Ibid.,* 85.
61. *Ibid.,* 86.
62. Quoted in unsigned article (probably by F. G. Adams), "The Abbott Howitzer," *Kansas Historical Collections,* I-II, 222. Quoted also in Robinson, *Kansas Conflict,* 124-25.
63. *Ibid.*
64. Lawrence Letters, 90-91.
65. *Ibid.,* 89-90.
66. Letter of Abbott, written in 1881 on occasion of presenting the howitzer to the Kansas State Historical Society, quoted in "The Abbott Howitzer," cited in note 62. The same article reproduces several letters of Olmsted relative to the howitzer.

67. F. B. Sanborn (cited in note 55; see p. 349 in his discussion) was convinced that the cost of sending arms was charged as "freights" in the "Kansas Expense" account. Professor F. H. Hodder suspected that some of the entries of "Sundries" in the account books of the Emigrant Aid Company may cover expenditures for rifles (remark made orally to the writer).

68. Iseley found in the Massachusetts Historical Society the small notebook in which Dr. Cabot kept his rifle account. It shows $12,443.63 raised and spent (Iseley, cited in note 52).

69. James C. Malin, "The Pro-Slavery Background of the Kansas Struggle," *Mississippi Valley Historical Review*, X, Dec., 1923, 285-305.

70. Lawrence Letters, 121.

71. Lawrence to Robinson, Oct. 17, 1854, *ibid.*, 35.

72. Nov. 21, 1854, *ibid.*, 44.

73. To Pomeroy, Oct. 7, 1854, and Nov. 7, 1854, Aid Company Letters, 13, 50. To Robinson, Oct. 9, 1854, *ibid.*, 16.

74. Webb to Robinson, Dec. 21, 1854, *ibid.*, 76-78.

75. *Ibid.*, 101-02.

76. Lawrence Letters, 73.

77. Lawrence to Professor Packard, July 14, 1854, *ibid.*, 81-82. Lawrence to Robinson, Aug. 18, *ibid.*, 94.

78. July 14, 1855, *ibid.*, 82.

79. July 15, 1855, *ibid.*, 84.

80. *Ibid.*, 84-85.

81. *Ibid.*, 85.

82. *Ibid.*, 86.

83. Aug. 10, 1855, *ibid.*, 88-89.

84. Aug. 16, 1855, *ibid.*, 91-92.

85. Lawrence to Brown, Sept. 1, 1855, and Sept. 11, 1855, *ibid.*, 96-98. The quotation is from letter of September 11.

86. Original letters to Branscomb and Williams are among Aid Company Papers. Lawrence's reply, dated Sept. 22, indicates that he received a letter similar to the others (Lawrence Letters, 98-99).

87. Original letter, Robinson to Lawrence, Sept. 28, 1855, Aid Company Papers.

VIII

1. Newspaper accounts of some of these county meetings, Webb Scrap Books, Book IV, 103, 109, 117.

2. *New York Herald*, July 20, 1855, reprinted from *Lexington* (Missouri) *Weekly Express*, July 14, 1855. Loose clipping in Webb Scrap Books, Book IV.

3. Aid Company Records, Book I, 172-73, 175-76, 179, 182.

4. Printed circular in New England Emigrant Aid Company Collected Pamphlets. Printed in full in *Congressional Globe Appendix*, 34 Cong., 1 Sess., 151.

5. April 8, 1856, *ibid.*, 464.

6. Holloway, *History of Kansas*, 205; Robinson, *Kansas Conflict*, 129.

7. *Howard Report*, 416, 905-10, 912-13, 922, 922-24, 947. Constitution and ritual printed in full in *Congressional Globe Appendix*, 34 Cong., 1 Sess., 99-100.

8. S. N. Wood's own account of the rescue, Robinson, *op. cit.*, 184-86. Much confusion exists as to details of the affair, owing to diverse accounts of participants.

9. Document in full, Holloway, *op cit.*, 220-21.

10. *Ibid.*, 221-22; *Kansas Historical Collections*, III, 291-92.

11. Holloway, 223-25; *Kansas Historical Collection*, III, 294-95.

12. Governor Shannon's letter to President Pierce justifying his handling of the matter, *Kansas Historical Collections*, III, 299-301.

13. Holloway, 228.

14. Shannon's telegram and Pierce's reply, *Kansas Historical Collections*, V, 243. Free State appeals to President, signed by Robinson and Lane, *ibid.*, 245-46, 247.

15. Above, note 12.

16. *Kansas Historical Collections*, III, 296-97.

17. *Ibid.*, V, 246-47.

18. Letter of Senator Sumner to E. E. Hale, quoted in letter of Dr. Webb to R. A. Chapman, March 17, 1856, Aid Company Letters, Book A, 328.

19. Holloway, 294.

20. A. A. Lawrence to N. Gamwell, Nov. 17, 1855, Lawrence Letters, 121.

21. Dr. Webb wrote several letters to arrange speaking dates for members of the delegation (Aid Company Letters, Book A). Each week their activities were reported to the Executive Committee of the Emigrant Aid Company (Aid Company Records, Book II).

22. Quoted from letter of H. H. Morrill, Gardiner, Maine, *ibid.*, 68.

23. Such letters were written Dec. 10, 1855, Dec. 20, 1855, Jan. 31, 1856, and Feb. 12, 1856; Lawrence Letters, 116-17, 119-20, 128-29, 133.

24. *Congressional Globe Appendix*, 34 Cong., 1 Sess., 4.

25. *Congressional Globe*, 34 Cong., 1 Sess., 296-98.

26. Letter reproduced, *Kansas Historical Collections*, V, 245-46. Quoted, Holloway, 285, and Robinson, 223.

27. *Kansas Historical Collections*, V, 247; Robinson, 223-24.

28. J. D. Richardson, *Messages and Papers of the Presidents* (Bureau of National Literature and Art, 1909), V, 390-91; *Kansas Historical Collections*, V, 259-60.

29. Dispatches of Jefferson Davis, Secretary of War, to Colonel Sumner, and of W. L. Marcy, Secretary of State, to Governor Shannon, communicating authorization for use of troops, 34 Cong., 1 Sess., *Senate Executive Documents*, No. 23.

30. *Congressional Globe Appendix*, 34 Cong., 1 Sess., 168-69.

31. *Ibid.*, 154.

32. *Ibid.*, 149-51.

33. *Ibid.*, 193-95.

34. *Ibid.*, 306-10.

35. *Ibid.*, 551-52.

36. *Congressional Globe*, 34 Cong., 1 Sess., Part I, 415.

37. *Congressional Globe Appendix*, 34 Cong., 1 Sess., 89-90.

38. *Ibid.*, 96-100.

39. *Ibid.*, 106-07.

40. "Report of the Committee on Territories on Affairs in Kansas," *Senate Reports*, 34 Cong., 1 Sess., No. 34.

41. *Congressional Globe Appendix*, 34 Cong., 1 Sess., 287-88.

42. *Ibid.*, 202-03.

43. *Ibid.*, 370.

44. *Ibid.*, 361.

45. *Ibid.*, 464-65.

46. *Ibid.*, 401.

47. Aid Company Letters, Book A, 327-28.

48. *Congressional Globe Appendix*, 34 Cong., 1 Sess., 537-38.

49. Patrick Laughlin (Pro-slavery) and G. P. Lowrey (Free State) both testified that pro-slavery people believed that the hotel was built as a fort and equipped with portholes (*Howard Report*, 907, 1078). Similar testimony from contemporary newspaper items is quoted in Phillips, *Conquest of Kansas*, 309, and Malin, "Pro-Slavery Background of the Kansas Struggle," *Mississippi Valley Historical Review*, X, 303.

50. The indictment is given in full in Holloway, 314-16.

51. Robinson, *Kansas Conflict*, 235.

52. Proclamation in full, Holloway, 318. *Kansas Historical Collections*, IV, 392 (in Free State memorial to President, dated May 22, 1856).

53. Holloway, 317.

54. Letter of the Committee and Governor Shannon's reply, *ibid.*, 318-19. Committee's letter, *Kansas Historical Collections*, V, 393. Governor's reply, *ibid.*, 394.

55. Holloway, 323-28. Appeal to Donaldson, *Kansas Historical Collections*, V, 395. Reply, *ibid.*, 395-96.

56. Holloway, 331. Account in memorial to the President, *Kansas Historical Collections*, V, 392-403.

IX

1. Aid Company Records, Book I, 206, 215-16.
2. Contract in full, Aid Company Letters, Book A, 178-79.
3. Thayer, *Kansas Crusade,* 203-05, 209.
4. Aid Company Account Books, Journal, 13.
5. Aid Company Letters, Book A, 195 ff.
6. The plan is outlined in a letter of Webb to J. S. Emery of the Kansas delegation, April 4, 1856. In the same letter Webb asks Emery to address several meetings in the interest of the Company and of Kansas relief. *Ibid.,* 386.
7. *Ibid., passim.*
8. Report of J. M. S. Williams for the Finance Committee to the quarterly meeting of the Directors, Nov. 27, 1855. Aid Company Records, Book I, 200-01.
9. Treasurer's report to annual meeting. *Ibid.,* Book "Company," 46.
10. *Kansas Crusade,* 46 note. This amount should probably be discounted somewhat in view of Thayer's known proclivity for exaggeration.
11. *Worcester Daily Spy,* Feb. 11, 1856. Webb Scrap Books, Book IX, 85-86 (Dr. Webb omitted the part of the clipping telling about Thayer's offer to pay for ten rifles, but other clippings on pages 94, 110, 116, 117, and 119, indicate the substance of the missing portion). Senator H. S. Geyer of Missouri read the account from the *Spy* in the Senate, April 8, 1856, as proof of the seditious character of the Emigrant Aid Company (*Congressional Globe Appendix,* 34 Cong., 1 Sess., 486). Robinson also told of the incident in his *Kansas Conflict,* 224.
12. Aid Company Letters, Book A, 188-91.
13. *Ibid.,* 212.
14. Original letter, Hoyt to Pomeroy, Aid Company Papers.
15. Original bill of lading; also original letter of F. A. Hunt, the St. Louis forwarding agent, to Webb, March 14, 1856, reporting the shipment and seizure of the rifles. Aid Company Papers.
16. F. B. Sanborn, "Early Kansas History," Massachusetts Historical Society, *Proceedings,* XLI, 227-28.
17. For examples of such replies, see Aid Company Letters, Book A, 283, 315, 319.
18. *Ibid.,* 382. Other similar letters, *ibid.,* 364, 372, 378.
19. *Ibid.,* 367, 378, 382.
20. Webb to Robinson, sending receipt for a rifle on which $14 was due. Apparently, Robinson was expected to collect this in Kansas (*ibid.,* 398).
21. April 2, Webb sent Robinson three receipts, subject to his order, for rifles "loaned" by Dr. Cabot to emigrants (*ibid.,* 380).
22. Such offers are found in letters to S. W. Cone, Haverhill, New Hampshire, L. D. Bailey, Bradford, Maine, and Martin Stowell, Worcester (*ibid.,* 364, 366, 372).
23. Original letter, William Barnes Papers, Kansas State Historical Society, Topeka, Kansas.
24. Lawrence Letters, 143.
25. Aid Company Letters, Book A, 220.
26. *Ibid.,* 249.
27. *Ibid.,* 262-63.
28. *Ibid.,* 265, 273.
29. Webb Scrap Books, Books IX-X, *passim.*
30. Aid Company Letters, Book A, 301-03.
31. *Ibid.,* 415-17.
32. Original letter, Stone to Pomeroy, May 26, 1856. Aid Company Papers.
33. *Boston Daily Evening Traveller,* Feb. 13, 1856. The letter, dated "Free State Hotel, Headquarters, January 25, 1856," is signed "W." It was probably written by J. M. Winchell. Webb Scrap Books, Book IX, 115. See also James C. Malin, *John Brown and the Legend of Fifty-Six* (Philadelphia, 1942), 69.
34. Aid Company Records, Book I, 221.
35. *Ibid.,* 203, 219, 221.
36. *Ibid.,* Book II, 21, 31, 35.
37. Aid Company Letters, Book A, 225, 256-57, 362.

38. Aid Company Records, Book II, 97-98.
39. *Ibid.,* 65-66; Aid Company Letters, Book A, 369, 373-74.
40. Aid Company Records, Book II, 65-66.
41. Original letter, A. J. Stone to Pomeroy, April 23, 1856, reports the shipping of the mills. Aid Company Papers.
42. Aid Company Records, Book I, 93-94.
43. *Ibid.,* 96-97.
44. *Ibid.,* 176; Book II, 56.
45. *Ibid.,* 68-69.
46. *Ibid.,* 84-85.
47. Aid Company Letters, Book A, 377.
48. *Ibid.,* Book B, 172.
49. *Ibid.,* Book A, 199.
50. Lawrence Letters, 72; Aid Company Letters, Book A, 306.
51. Aid Company Records, Book II, 105-06; Aid Company Letters, Book A, 432-33.
52. Aid Company Records, Book II, 141; Aid Company Letters, Book B, 108.
53. Aid Company Letters, Book A, 172, 179½, 263, 292-93, 345. In one instance, however, J.M.S. Williams offered to pay a certain individual one dollar each for all recruits he could get over the first fifty (*ibid.,* 179½).
54. Aid Company Letters, Book A, 284 (C. B. Lines, New Haven), 324 (Mr. Cole, Exeter, New Hampshire), 343 (David Ryerson, Newton, New Jersey), 360 (Mr. Perry, Providence, Rhode Island). At the meeting of the Executive Committee, April 5, 1856, Dr. Webb stated that many of the fifty-eight letters received during the preceding week had announced the formation of parties. Aid Company Records, Book II, 95.
55. Aid Company Letters, Book A, 360. On April 4, 1856, Dr. Webb wrote to J. S. Emery of the Free State delegation, asking him to speak at some of Cone's meetings in New Hampshire: "Cone's principal object is to raise recruits, ours to raise money for the relief fund; of course the two objects can be promoted at the same time" (*ibid.,* 386).
56. *Kansas Historical Collections,* VII, 530 note, 576.
57. Dr. Webb reported to the Executive Committee that he supplied them 38 tickets (Aid Company Records, Book II, 96).
58. Aid Company Letters, Book A, 370-71, 375.
59. *Ibid.,* 401, 428.
60. Speech of C. B. Lines at Old Settlers' Reunion, Bismarck Grove, September 16, 1879; reproduced in Gleed, *The Kansas Memorial,* 121-29.
61. *Ibid.;* Thayer, *Kansas Crusade,* 187-88.
62. Aid Company Letters, Book A, 284, 342.
63. *Ibid.,* 306, 364, 385, 405, 411, 412.
64. Above, note 55.
65. Aid Company Records, Book II, 103.
66. Aid Company Letters, Book A, 423.
67. *Kansas Historical Collections,* VII, 377. On June 26, Dr. Webb wrote an endorsement of Messrs. Cone, urging "whom it may concern" to render them assistance in establishing their paper. The Executive Committee had declined to aid them directly (Aid Company Letters, Book B, 65).
68. *Ibid.,* 93-94, 113.
69. *Ibid.,* 50; *Kansas Historical Collections,* VIII, 313.
70. Aid Company Letters, Book A, 420.
71. Aid Company Records, Book II, 88.
72. Aid Company Letters, Book A, 344.
73. Above, note 58.
74. Aid Company Records, Book II, 96, 99.
75. *Ibid.,* 99, 101.
76. *Ibid.,* 103.
77. Aid Company Emigrant Books, Book "April, 1856, to April, 1857."
78. Aid Company Letters, Book A, 442.
79. Webb Scrap Books, Books IX-X.
80. Aid Company Letters, Book A, 186-87, 325; Aid Company Records, Book II, 79-81. In April, 1856, Pomeroy made some sort of agreement with F. A. Hunt & Company, but its provisions are not known.

81. Aid Company Letters, Book A, 406-07, 425-26.
82. *Ibid.*, 406-07, 409-10.
83. *Ibid.*, 307-09, 350.
84. *Ibid.*, 406-07.
85. *Ibid.*, 342.
86. Letter to F. A. Sumner, general agent of one of the railroads (no indication of which one), Feb. 22, 1856; *ibid.*, 292-93.
87. Webb to William Barnes, April 4, 1856; *ibid.*, 384.
88. Print of a circular letter inviting the recipient to attend the meeting of March 13, among the papers and effects of the New York State Kansas Committee in the Kansas Historical Society, Topeka, herein cited as William Barnes Papers.
89. Printed circular, "Freedom for Kansas," signed by these officers, *loc. cit.*
90. Printed circular dated April 18, 1856, *loc. cit;* also announcement in *New York Tribune,* April 28, 1856.
91. Webb to Barnes, March 20, 1856. Original in William Barnes Papers; copy, Aid Company Letters, Book A, 349. Generally, the contents of Barnes's letters can only be inferred from Webb's answers. Barnes's letter books, if he kept any, are not preserved, and in only a few instances are the originals of his letters found among the Aid Company Papers.
92. Aid Company Letters, Book A, 384.
93. A large number of these receipts, signed by officers of the Committee and countersigned by various local agents are among the William Barnes Papers.
94. Aid Company Records, Book "Company," 46.
95. For roster of directors, 1855-1856, see chap. II, p. 30 note.
96. Aid Company Records, Book "Company," 50.
97. *Ibid.*, 48-51.
98. *Ibid.*, Book II, 117.
99. Aid Company Records, Book II, 39, 45-46.
100. Letter reproduced in Hale, *Memories of a Hundred Years,* II, 162-63.
101. Aid Company Records, Book II, 84-88; Aid Company Letters, Book A, 332.
102. One of these is preserved among the New England Emigrant Aid Company Collected Pamphlets. The history of the memorial can be traced in detail from Aid Company Letters and Aid Company Records.
103. Aid Company Letters, Book B, 57.
104. *Congressional Globe Appendix,* 34 Cong., 1 Sess., 853. The memorial is there reproduced in full.
105. Aid Company Records, Book II, 121-22. The entire Executive Committee signed the "Address to the People of the United States."
106. Several copies are still extant. One is in the William Barnes Papers. Several are among the Aid Company Papers.
107. *Howard Report,* 875.

X

1. Andreas, *History of Kansas,* I, 131; Holloway, *History of Kansas,* 340.
2. Statement of James Townsley, one of Brown's party, made in 1879, quoted in Robinson, *Kansas Conflict,* 265-67. Slightly different statement by Townsley, made on another occasion, quoted in Andreas, I, 603-05. Pro-Brown account, S. J. Shively, "The Pottawatomie Massacre," *Kansas Historical Collections,* VIII, 177-87. Account by August Bondi, one of Brown's men, but not present on the occasion, *ibid.*, 280-81. Bondi claimed to have had his account from Theodore Weiner, who was with Brown when the men were killed.
3. Andreas offers other evidence to corroborate Townsley's testimony. For one thing, descriptions given by widows of the slain men tallied perfectly with the appearance of Brown. For a historian's analysis of the evidence, see Malin, *John Brown and the Legend of Fifty-Six,* chap. XXVII.
4. Hale, "Colonization of Kansas," in Davis, *The New England States,* I, 87.
5. Thayer, *Kansas Crusade,* 190-91.
6. Remarks of Amos A. Lawrence at meeting of the Massachusetts Historical Society, May, 1884. *Proceedings 1884-1885,* Series II, Vol. I, 183.

7. Lawrence Letters, 245, 246, 247, 250. Lawrence, *Amos A. Lawrence*, chap. VIII.
8. Emigrant Aid Company Stock Register.
9. F. B. Sanborn, *Life and Letters of John Brown* (Boston, 1885), 380-84.
10. *Ibid.*, 111-12.
11. Observation of Professor F. H. Hodder, who said in a lecture that Brown did irreparable harm to the cause which "he intended or pretended to serve."
12. Andreas, I, 232; Holloway, 352-56; August Bondi, "With John Brown in Kansas," *Kansas Historical Collections*, VIII, 275-89.
13. Andreas, I, 232-33; Holloway, 356-58.
14. Andreas, I, 134.
15. *Ibid.*, 133-34; Holloway, 358-60; G. W. E. Griffith (one of Shore's men), "The Battle of Black Jack," *Kansas Historical Collections*, XVI, 524-28; Captain Sam Walker's account, *ibid.*, VI, 259-60.
16. Andreas, I, 134; Holloway, 361-62. Holloway was of the opinion that six or seven prisoners were killed.
17. Andreas, I, 134, 886; Holloway, 361-62; contemporary account by an eyewitness in letter of Charles Cranston to his family, read in the United States Senate June 25, 1856, by L. F. S. Foster, *Congressional Globe Appendix*, 34 Cong., 1 Sess., 680; Colonel Sumner's account in his report to the Adjutant General, *Kansas Historical Collections*, IV, 439-40 (also quoted in Robinson, *Kansas Conflict*, 295).
18. Andreas, I, 140-41; Holloway, 369-76; Spring, *Kansas*, 129-35; James Redpath's contemporary account from the *Chicago Tribune*, *Kansas Historical Collections*, IX, 540-45.
19. Andreas, I, 141.
20. Dispatches of S. Cooper, Adjutant General, U. S. A., containing memoranda of Jefferson Davis, Secretary of War, reprimanding Colonel Sumner, and Colonel Sumner's replies, *Kansas Historical Collections*, IV, 450-53.
21. So stated by Elliot, *Foot Notes on Kansas History* (Lawrence, 1906), 10, and frequently asserted by free-state emigrants.
22. C. B. Lines, Bismark Grove speech, Sept. 16, 1879, quoted in Gleed, *Kansas Memorial*, 121-29.
23. W. M. Paxton, *Annals of Platte County, Missouri* (Kansas City, 1897), 214. Andreas (I, 138) quotes an excerpt from the *Squatter Sovereign* of July 1, 1856, reporting an overland party of twenty-five from Illinois and Indiana turned back in Platte County. No date is given. This may have been the same party.
24. Webb to William Barnes, June 14, 1856; Aid Company Letters, Book B, 19. Original of letter in William Barnes Papers.
25. June 21, Aid Company Letters, Book B, 92.
26. Andreas, I, 138.
27. *Ibid.* Aid Company Letters, Book B, 92.
28. *Ibid.*, 93-94.
29. Andreas, I, 139-40 (quoted pro-slavery press as authority); O. G. Richards, "Kansas Experiences," *Kansas Historical Collections*, IX, 545-46. Richards started in Strawn's party, but with five others took the land route.
30. Aid Company Letters, Book B, 127.
31. *Ibid.*, 221.
32. *Ibid.*, 204-06.
33. Original letter, begun Aug. 26, finished Sept. 6, 1856; William Barnes Papers.
34. Letter of Peter Page of the Chicago Committee, to William Barnes, June 30, 1856; *ibid.*
35. E. G. Ross, *A Reminiscence of the Kansas Conflict* (Albuquerque, New Mexico, 1898).
36. Robert Morrow, "Emigration to Kansas in 1856," *Kansas Historical Collections*, VIII, 302-15.
37. Charles S. Gleed, "Samuel Walker," *Kansas Historical Collections*, VI, 249-76. Gleed quotes Walker's own story of the affair (*ibid.*, 266-68).
38. Account by E. P. Harris, one of the Stowell party, in footnote to the Morrow article cited in note 36; *ibid.*, VIII, 312-14.
39. Above, note 36. See also W. E. Connelley, "The Lane Trail," *Kansas Historical Collections*, XIII, 268-79. Here as elsewhere, allowance must be made for Connelley's

violent pro-Lane partisanship. There is no evidence that Lane marked this trail. The markers, piles of stones called "Lane's chimneys," may have been erected by John Brown, but this is uncertain.

40. Correspondence of the War Department with military officers stationed in Kansas, from Annual Report of the Secretary of War for 1856, *House Executive Documents*, No. 1, 34 Cong., 3 Sess., I, Part II, reproduced in *Kansas Historical Collections*, IV, 424-519. This letter of General Smith, *ibid.*, 457.

41. Correspondence between free-state men and Acting Governor Daniel Woodson, *ibid.*, III, 329-34.

42. General Percifer F. Smith to the Adjutant General, War Department correspondence, *Kansas Historical Collections*, IV, 459.

43. Andreas, I, 141; *Kansas Historical Collections*, VII, 532.

44. Two accounts by Captain Bickerton, one contemporary and one written in 1881, *Kansas Historical Collections*, I-II, 218-21. Contemporary account by R. B. Foster, a participant, *ibid.*, 226-28. Secretary Woodson's report of the affair to President Pierce, asserting that the post office was robbed, *ibid.*, III, 333-35.

45. The story is told by John Speer in the *Lawrence Tribune* of July 20, 1876, and repeated by Robinson in his *Kansas Conflict*, 306. Sam Walker, writing years after the event, told the story. Other participants, in their accounts, either ignore the story or deny it.

46. Walker's account, *Kansas Historical Collections*, VI, 268-70. Other statements by participants: R. B. Foster, *ibid.*, I-II, 227; N. W. Spicer, *ibid.*, 230-31; O. P. Kennedy, *ibid.*, VII, 530-31; William Crutchfield, *ibid.*, 532. Secretary Stanton's report to President Pierce, *ibid.*, III, 335.

47. Bickerton's account, *ibid.*, I-II, 220-21; R. B. Foster's account, 227-28; Sam Tappan's account, 228-29; N. W. Spicer's account, 231; Walker's account, VI, 270-72; William Crutchfield's account, VII, 533-34.

48. Holloway, 381.

49. *Kansas Historical Collections*, IV, 463.

50. Foster's statement, *ibid.*, I-II, 228; Tappan's statement, 229-30. Governor Shannon's statement, IV, 461; Major Sedgwick's statement, 463; Walker's statement, VI, 273.

51. Andreas, I, 143.

52. Such an account from the Weston, Missouri, *Platte County Argus* of August 18, 1856, was incorporated into General Smith's report to the Adjutant General, Aug. 29, 1856, with the comment that, although such reports were exaggerated, there was an element of truth in them (*Kansas Historical Collections*, IV, 466-70).

53. Dispatches and documents, taken from the executive minutes of the governor's office during the administrations of Reeder, Shannon, and Woodson (*ibid.*, III, 197-337). This proclamation on pp. 234-35.

54. Andreas, I, 145; account by Captain Samuel Anderson, who commanded one of the companies, *Kansas Historical Collections* (I-II, 210-11). Other companies were commanded by Captains Cline and Shore. The free-state force consisted of 78 men.

55. Holloway, 386-88; Andreas, I, 145, 871, 876-77.

56. There are two versions of this story, one told by Andreas (I, 877), the other by August Bondi, who claimed to have got his account from Austin himself (*Kansas Historical Collections*, VIII, 279-80 note).

57. Holloway, 388-89; Andreas, I, 145-46.

58. Woodson's order, *Kansas Historical Collections*, III, 326.

59. *Ibid.*, 327.

60. Correspondence reproduced in full, *ibid.*, 329-34.

61. Letter of Daniel Woodson, *ibid.*, 332-33.

62. Letter of Major George Deas, Adjutant General (on behalf of General Smith) to Colonel Cooke, *ibid.*, 482-83.

63. All the documents reproduced, *ibid.*, 327-29.

64. Holloway, 391; J. C. Malin, "Colonel Harvey and His Forty Thieves," *Mississippi Valley Historical Review*, XIX, June, 1932, 57-76.

65. Colonel Cooke's account (report to General Smith written the same evening), *Kansas Historical Collections*, IV, 485-87. Walker's account (written several years after), *ibid.*, VI, 273-74.

66. Malin (cited in note 64); account of Slough Creek raid by Charles W. Smith, an "old settler," *Kansas Historical Collections,* VII, 535.
67. Account by S. J. Reeder, a participant, George A. Root (ed.), "The First Day's Battle at Hickory Point," *Kansas Historical Quarterly,* I, Nov., 1931, 32-49.
68. Charles W. Smith, "The Battle of Hickory Point," *Kansas Historical Collections,* VII, 534-36; Malin, cited in note 64. One hundred and one of Harvey's men were taken; he himself escaped with a small bodyguard.

XI

1. W. L. Fleming, "The Buford Expedition to Kansas," *American Historical Review,* VI, Oct., 1900, 38-48.
2. *Ibid.*
3. *New York Evening Post,* Feb. 8, 1856, copied from *Edgefield* (S.C.) *Advertiser* (undated). Webb Scrap Books, Book IX, 72.
4. *Ibid.*
5. *Charleston Daily Courier,* March 13-24, 1856, carried daily advertisements of the Kansas Emigration Society of South Carolina, with several news stories of its activities.
6. *Ibid.,* March 28, 1856.
7. Advertisement of the meeting, *ibid.,* April 1, 1856; news account of it, *ibid.,* April 2, 1856.
8. Fleming, "Buford Expedition," cited in note 1. See also footnote, probably by G. W. Martin, *Kansas Historical Collections,* VII, 37.
9. Fleming, cited in note 1.
10. Quoted by Dr. Webb in a letter to J. M. S. Williams, Aid Company Letters, Book A, 452.
11. Fleming, cited in note 1.
12. Report from (St. Louis) *Missouri Democrat,* March 12, 1856, copied from *Weston Reporter* (undated), read in U. S. House of Representatives, March 17, 1856, by S. Galloway of Ohio. *Congressional Globe Appendix,* 34 Cong., 1 Sess., 212.
13. *De Bow's Review,* XX, May, 1856, 635-37.
14. *Ibid.*
15. *Ibid.,* June, 1856, 741-44; XXI, Aug., 1856, 187-94.
16. Many such clippings are scattered through the Webb Scrap Books, Books IX-XI. This quotation is from the *Boston Evening Transcript,* Feb. 9, 1856, *ibid.,* Book IX, 76.
17. Original letter, Charles J. Hotchkiss to E. E. Hale, March 10, 1856. Aid Company Papers.
18. Aid Company Letters, Book A, 318, 324, 328.
19. *Ibid.,* Book B, 17, 20, 76.
20. Circular dated July 2, 1856, signed by George L. Stearns. William Barnes Papers.
21. C. S. Ellsworth, "Oberlin and the Anti-Slavery Movement" (unpublished thesis, Cornell, 1930), chap. V.
22. Circular of the Committee, dated July 4, 1856, addressed "To the Friends of Free Kansas," New England Emigrant Aid Company Collected Pamphlets; copy, *Kansas Historical Collections,* XIII, 268-69.
23. Webb, *Information for Kansas Emigrants* (11th ed., July 26, 1856), 58-59.
24. Thayer, *Kansas Crusade,* 212.
25. Aid Company Records, Book II, 126.
26. Aid Company Letters, Book B, 46.
27. Aid Company Records, Book II, 126.
28. Pamphlet, *Kansas Aid Societies,* issued by National Kansas Committee. William Barnes Papers.
29. Webb to Barnes, June 27, 1856; Aid Company Letters, Book B, 95. Original in William Barnes Papers.
30. Aid Company Records, Book II, 137.
31. Aid Company Letters, Book B, 96.
32. Pamphlet, *Kansas Aid Societies.*
33. *Ibid.* Also printed form letter, dated in blank, signed by "W. F. M. Arny, General Transportation Agent," William Barnes Papers.

34. Original letters, A. B. Hurd to William Barnes, Aug. 1, 1856, and Thayer to Barnes, same date. William Barnes Papers.

35. Original letters, Thayer to Barnes, July 26 and Aug. 1, 1856, *ibid.* The plan is elaborated in Thayer, *Kansas Crusade,* 172-75.

36. *Ibid.,* 44.

37. Original letter, Thayer to Barnes, July 26, 1856, William Barnes Papers. In 1887, Thayer sent to the Secretary of the Kansas State Historical Society a specimen of these subscription booklets, on the flyleaf of which he had written a brief summary of the plan and a statement that six hundred of the booklets were used in Worcester County. He wrote in also the names of the six members of the Worcester County Committee, three of whom had been active in the Worcester Kansas League in 1854. Collected Pamphlets.

38. Original letters, Thayer to Barnes, Aug. 1 and Aug. 8, 1856. William Barnes Papers.

39. Original letter, Hurd to Thayer, Nov. 14, 1856. Aid Company Papers.

40. Webb to G. L. Stearns, Aug. 20, 1856. Aid Company Letters, Book B, 244. Webb to Henry Ward Beecher, Dec. 10, 1856, *ibid.,* 506-08.

41. F. B. Sanborn, "Early Kansas History," Massachusetts Historical Society *Proceedings,* XLI, 347-49.

42. Original letter, Hurd to Thayer, Nov. 14, 1856. Aid Company Papers.

43. Original letter, Thaddeus Hyatt to Horace Greeley, Jan. 10, 1857. William Barnes Papers.

44. *New York Daily Tribune,* Dec. 23, 1856. All the letters from Kansas cited above said essentially the same thing.

45. Letters too numerous to cite in Aid Company Letters, Book B, and Lawrence Letters, show the close co-operation that existed between the Emigrant Aid Company and these two committees during the summer and fall of 1856.

46. Webb to S. N. Simpson, June 27, 1856. Aid Company Letters, Book B, 71-72.

47. C. J. Higginson to Branscomb, June 27, 1856. *Ibid.,* 79.

48. Webb to Thaddeus Hyatt, Aid Company Letters, Book B, 329. To Thayer, *ibid.,* 330.

49. *Ibid.,* 496-98.

50. Aid Company Papers.

51. Webb to Nute, Nov. 21, 1856, Aid Company Letters, Book B, 473. To Colonel Dickey, Topeka, Dec. 31, *ibid.,* 552-53. To Branscomb, same date, *ibid.,* 559-60.

52. Lawrence to Pomeroy, Dec. 5, 1856, Lawrence Letters, 198-99. To "Mr. Mendenhall, Osawatomie," April 23, 1857, *ibid.,* 255.

53. Aid Company Records, Book II, 216.

54. Lawrence Letters, 212-14.

55. Original Letter, Russell to Hale, June 30, 1856. Aid Company Papers.

56. Aid Company Records, Book II, 182-83.

57. Lawrence Letters, 200.

58. A. W. Crandall, *The Early History of the Republican Party* (Boston, 1930), 107.

59. Lawrence to Robinson, April 7, 1856. Lawrence Letters, 138-39.

60. Aid Company Records, Book II, 73-75.

61. Crandall, *Republican Party,* 164. C. K. Holliday, "The Presidential Election of 1856," *Kansas Historical Collections,* V, 48-60, especially 50. Blackmar, *The Life of Charles Robinson,* 161.

62. Crandall, 164. Allan Nevins, *Frémont, the West's Greatest Adventurer* (New York and London, 1928), II, 479-80. G. W. Brown, *False Claims of the Historians Truthfully Corrected* (Rockford, Illinois, 1902), 11. The letter is reproduced in Blackmar, *Charles Robinson,* 161-62.

63. Remarks in defense of the Emigrant Aid Company were made in the House of Representatives by Anson Burlingame, June 21, and in the Senate by L. F. S. Foster (Connecticut), June 25, Benjamin F. Wade (Ohio), July 2, and Henry Wilson (Massachusetts), July 9. *Congressional Globe Appendix,* 34 Cong., 1 Sess., 653-56, 683-90, 749-57, 852-57.

64. July 3, 1856, *Congressional Globe,* 34 Cong., 1 Sess., 1541.

65. July 29, *ibid.,* 1814-18.

66. *Ibid.,* 663.

67. *Ibid.*, 1439.
68. Aid Company Letters, Book B, 178-80. Lawrence Letters, 152-55, 156-57.
69. So Webb wrote to Pomeroy. Aid Company Letters, Book B, 178-80.
70. Original letter, July 25. William Barnes Papers. Webb did not enter this letter in the Aid Company Letter book.
71. *Congressional Globe,* 34 Cong., 1 Sess., 1381.
72. *Congressional Globe Appendix,* 34 Cong., 1 Sess., 693-97.
73. Lawrence to S. G. Haven, Oct. 10, 1856. Lawrence Letters, 185. Lawrence had written to Robinson July 24: "If your particular friends in Congress, or those who make the greatest professions, were less anxious about their party politics, something would have been accomplished before this" (*ibid.*, 159). He wrote, on Aug. 7, to S. N. Simpson that he was losing hope of a settlement of the Kansas trouble because "our Republican friends in Congress are too eager to insist on the adoption of grand principles, rather than meet on business terms and adopt practical measures, which there would be no difficulty in doing." *Ibid.*, 165. On Aug. 14, he wrote again to Robinson: "Our Kansas friends in Congress are not at all reliable when practical results are to be reached. . . and though they have the cause sincerely at heart, they are biased by the prospect of the presidential election" (*ibid.*, 166).
74. He so wrote Robinson July 24, and again Aug. 14 (*ibid.*, 158-59, 166-67).
75. Lawrence's letters to Fillmore, July 18, *ibid.*, 157-58; Aug. 15, *ibid.*, 169; Aug. 30, *ibid.*, 171-72.
76. Lawrence to Haven, July 12, *ibid.*, 152; July 15, *ibid.*, 155-56; July 28, *ibid.*, 161-63; July 29, *ibid.*, 163-64.
77. *Congressional Globe,* 34 Cong., 1 Sess., 1556. Content of bill from two letters of Lawrence to Haven, July 28 and 29, 1856, commenting on details. Lawrence Letters, 161-64.
78. Lawrence to Fillmore, Aug. 30. Lawrence Letters, 171-72. To Robinson, Sept. 16, *ibid.*, 179.
79. Aid Company Letters, Book B, 269-71.
80. Lawrence, *Amos A. Lawrence,* 110-11. The letter is reproduced in Blackmar, *Charles Robinson,* 432-35.
81. C. K. Holliday, "The Presidential Campaign of 1856," *Kansas Historical Collections,* V, 48-60. Colonel Holliday gave what he represented to be the inside story of the transaction.

XII

1. John H. Gihon, *Geary and Kansas* (Philadelphia, 1857), 123-26, reproduces the message in full. Gihon was secretary to Governor Geary.
2. Gihon reproduces both in full, *ibid.*, 126-27.
3. Copies of the correspondence, *ibid.*, 134-37.
4. *Ibid.*, 138-43.
5. *Ibid.*, 148-53. Governor Geary's letter to Secretary Marcy giving report of his activities, *ibid.*, 153-57.
6. Lawrence to Robinson, Nov. 19, 1856, Lawrence Letters, 195. To Pomeroy, Dec. 5, 1856, *ibid.*, 199.
7. Lawrence to Robinson, Dec. 15, 1856, *ibid.*, 204-05.
8. Webb to Pomeroy, Dec. 16, 1856, Aid Company Letters, Book B, 518-19.
9. *Ibid.* On Dec. 30, Lawrence wrote the same to Pomeroy, and suggested that to get Governor Geary soundly abused by some of the newspapers would do more good than ten times as much praise. Lawrence Letters, 216-17. On Feb. 5, 1857, Lawrence suggested the same to Governor Geary himself (*ibid.*, 229-30).
10. Robinson summarized the plan in his *Kansas Conflict,* 339-40. The outlines of it can be gleaned from Lawrence's correspondence.
11. Attested copy of the minutes signed by Dr. Webb, Aid Company Letters, Book B, 372-73.
12. Lawrence to Robinson, Dec. 16, 1856, Lawrence Letters, 204-05. To A. H. Reeder, Dec. 20, *ibid.*, 209. To S. G. Howe, Dec. 22, *ibid.*, 210.
13. Aid Company Records, Book II, 130, 134; Aid Company Letters, Book B, 72, 77-81.

14. Webb to Pomeroy (in Washington), Aug. 11, reporting two letters from Branscomb, *ibid.,* 217-18.

15. Webb to Thayer, July 30, *ibid.,* 171.

16. C. J. Higginson to Branscomb, July 31, *ibid.,* 176.

17. Webb to Pomeroy, July 29, Aug. 2, and Aug. 11, *ibid.,* 169, 188, 217-18. In all of these letters Dr. Webb bewailed the condition of the Company's affairs in Kansas, and insisted that matters would go to ruin if Pomeroy did not soon return.

18. Higginson to Pomeroy, Sept. 1, letter of instructions, *ibid.,* 276-80.

19. Minute of the Executive Committee, Sept. 5, 1856, Aid Company Records, Book II, 163-64.

20. Letter of instructions signed by Russell and Higginson, Aid Company Letters, Book B, 356-64.

21. Aid Company Records, Book II, 120.

22. Letters of instruction to Pomeroy, Aid Company Letters, Book B, 57, 67. This time Pomeroy remained in Washington only a few weeks. Before his return to the Capital in July, he spent several weeks soliciting stock subscriptions in New England and Philadelphia.

23. Aid Company Records, Book II, 128, 131. Aid Company Letters, Book B, 57.

24. Aid Company Records, Book III, 12-13.

25. Aid Company Letters, Book B, 356-57.

26. Aid Company Records, Book II, 187. Aid Company Letters, Book B, 443.

27. Aid Company Records, Book II, 192, 194.

28. Letters from Branscomb dated Dec. 1, Dec. 5, Dec. 10, and Dec. 15, 1856, and Jan. 1, 1857, Aid Company Records, Book II, 209-10, 212, 218; Book III, 10, 22.

29. Webb to Branscomb, Jan. 26, 1857, Aid Company Letters, Book B, 605.

30. Minutes of special meeting of the Executive Committee, Feb. 7, 1857, Aid Company Records, Book III, 34-37. Martha B. Caldwell, "The Eldridge House," *Kansas Historical Quarterly,* IX, Nov., 1940, 347-70.

31. Aid Company Letters, Book B, 452.

32. The plan was explained in the letter to Paddleford just cited (note 31) and in a letter to P. C. Schuyler, Dec. 24, 1856, *ibid.,* 539-40. The "parlor meetings" are discussed in a letter to W. J. Rotch, a New Bedford Director, Jan. 13, 1857, *ibid.,* 578.

33. Thayer's part in the work is mentioned in all three of these letters (note 32) and also *ibid.,* 450, 489, 491, 495, 497, 504, 515, 517½.

34. Webb to Pomeroy and Branscomb, Dec. 13, 1856, Aid Company Letters, Book B, 518½. To G. W. Brown, Dec. 22, *ibid.,* 531. To P. C. Schuyler, Dec. 24, *ibid.,* 539-40.

35. Aid Company Letters, Book B, 625.

36. *Ibid.,* Book C, 73, 79.

37. Aid Company Letters, Book B, 184. In another letter Webb said there were "about sixty" in the party, *ibid.,* 167.

38. *Ibid.,* 186-87, 221, 226-27, 249.

39. *Ibid.,* 249, 295, 308, 317. Account of this emigrant train by Robert Morrow, one of the conductors, *Kansas Historical Collections,* VIII, 302-06. The train entered Kansas Oct. 10, 1856, and contained between 200 and 300 persons.

40. Aid Company Letters, Book B, 490 ff.

41. *Ibid.,* 699, 671, 673, 690, 692.

42. *Ibid.,* Book C, 30.

43. *Ibid.,* Book B, 672, 673, 707. Letter from Marshall reporting arrival, Aid Company Records, Book, III, 103-04.

44. Webb to Pomeroy, April 6, stating that Nixon's party "will go out under our auspices" (*ibid.,* Book C, 8). Advertisements of the party in *New York Daily Tribune,* March 17, March 31, and April 6, 1857. One of these advertisements says, ". . . as we go out under the auspices of the New England Emigrant Aid Company, we shall have important and serviceable aid from its agents in the Territory."

45. Aid Company Letters, Book C, 55.

46. Emigrant Books, among Aid Company Papers.

47. Original letter, Nute to Hale, Aid Company Papers.

48. Dec. 22, 1856, Aid Company Letters, Book B, 530.

49. Letters of Pomeroy, Jan. 6 and Jan. 27, 1857, Aid Company Records, Book III, 24, 42-44.

50. *Ibid.,* 49.
51. Letter of Pomeroy, Feb. 2, 1857, *ibid.,* 51.
52. Letter of Pomeroy, Jan. 21, 1857, *ibid.,* 41. Letter of John B. Wood of Lawrence, *ibid.,* 45-46.
53. *Ibid.,* 69-70, 73-74.
54. Letter of C. C. Hutchinson, Feb. 13, 1857, *ibid.,* 47-48.
55. Letter of William Hutchinson, Lawrence, May 11, 1857, *ibid.,* 187-88.
56. *Ibid.,* 208-10, 221-22, 241-42.
57. *Ibid.,* 255-56; Book IV, 12-14.
58. *Ibid.,* Book III, 203-04, 205-06, 208-10.
59. *Ibid.,* Book IV, 175-76.
60. Editorial, "The German Immigration," *New York Daily Times,* Jan. 6, 1855. Several original letters, Aid Company Papers.
61. Aid Company Records, Book III, 13-14, 19-20, 59-60.
62. *Ibid.,* 80; Aid Company Letters, Book B, 701.
63. Aid Company Records, Book III, 67.
64. *Ibid.,* 139-40, 157. Hale bought the font of type for $228.86 ($254.29 less 10 per cent discount for cash) and had it shipped to Branscomb; receipted bill among Aid Company Papers.
65. Aid Company Records, Book III, 156-57.
66. *Ibid.,* 168-69.
67. Original letters, Serenbetz to Hale, March 2 and March 14, 1857. Aid Company Papers.
68. Aid Company Records, Book III, 87-88.
69. Aid Company Letters, Book C, 7.
70. Original letters, Branscomb to Hale, April 25, 1857, and Nute to Hale, April 28, 1857, Aid Company Papers.
71. Aid Company Records, Book III, 165-66.
72. Original contract between Learnard and Pomeroy (for Emigrant Aid Company), dated Aug. 11, 1856, Aid Company Papers.
73. Aid Company Records, Book III, 84, 127. Original papers involved in transaction, Aid Company Papers.
74. Aid Company Letters, Book B, 377.
75. *Ibid.,* 438-39.
76. Original memorandum of transaction, Aid Company Papers.
77. Letter from Pomeroy, dated St. Joseph, April 10, 1857, Aid Company Records, Book III, 109-12.
78. Letter from Pomeroy, dated Atchison, April 18, 1857, *ibid.,* 119-20.
79. *Ibid.,* 121; Aid Company Letters, Book C, 33-34.
80. Letter of Higginson, dated Atchison, April 26, 1857, Aid Company Records, Book III, 127.
81. Lawrence to Pomeroy, Dec. 6, 1856, Lawrence Letters, 198.
82. Aid Company Letters, Book B, 360, 362-63, 605-06.
83. *Ibid.,* 189-90, 204-05, 278.
84. *Ibid.,* 171.
85. *Ibid.,* 438-40.
86. *Ibid.,* 518-21.
87. Letters from Pomeroy, Dec. 3, 1856, and Jan. 22, 1857, Aid Company Records, Book II, 214; Book III, 43.
88. Account of the moving of the mill by a man who worked on the job, J. M. Bisbee, "Early Day Transportation," *Kansas Historical Collections,* XI, 594-97.
89. Branscomb wrote from Lawrence, Jan. 14, 1858, that the Wabaunsee sawmill was finished and in operation. Aid Company Records, Book IV, 44.
90. Aid Company Letters, Book B, 440.
91. Buffum made his offer to Thayer, who reported it to the Executive Committee Feb. 13, 1857, Aid Company Records, Book III, 48; Aid Company Letters, Book B, 648. Adams made his offer in writing, Feb. 24, 1857, Aid Company Records, Book III, 71-72.
92. *Ibid.,* 66-67, 71-72.
93. Aid Company Letters, Book B, 721-22; Book C, 35.

94. *Ibid.,* 32-35.

95. Aid Company Records, Book III, 154-55.

96. *Ibid.,* 168.

97. Higginson's report to the Executive Committee, *ibid.,* 141-42.

98. *Ibid.* Also letter from Branscomb, *ibid.,* 175. Minutes of the Executive Committee, April 3, 1857, *ibid.,* 87.

99. Higginson's report, *ibid.,* 131-42.

100. Letter of the Rev. Charles Reynolds, Lawrence, quoting letters of Bishop Kemper, *ibid.,* Book V, 24-25.

101. *Ibid.,* Book III, 154, 188; Aid Company Letters, Book C, 45, 98, 110-12, 118-19, 133-34.

102. *Ibid.,* 183-84, 440-41; Aid Company Records, Book IV, 31-34, 231.

103. *Ibid.,* Book V, 70. Original letter, Webb to M. F. Conway, June 4, 1859, Aid Company Papers.

104. Minute of the Executive Committee, Jan. 28, 1859, authorizing transfer of the lot. Copy of the deed among Aid Company Quit Claims (book, labeled "Quit Claims," containing exact copies on printed forms of all quitclaim deeds executed by the Emigrant Aid Company, among the papers and effects of the Company in Topeka; herein cited as "Aid Company Quit Claims").

105. Original note to Pomeroy, May 1, 1857, signed by John Pipher and Charles Barnes, to credit C. S. Stevens (the miller) with $46.30 for sawing "on your subscription to the M. E. Church of this place." Notation on the back, "Copy sent to Boston, May 18, '57," indicates that the subscription was on behalf of the Emigrant Aid Company rather than by Pomeroy personally. Aid Company Papers.

106. Webb, *Information for Kansas Emigrants* (13th ed., May 14, 1857), 55-56.

107. Aid Company Records, Book I, 116, 150; Aid Company Letters, Book A, 104, 142, 163-64.

108. Original letter, the Rev. James F. Clark (Pastor, Church of the Disciples, Boston) to Pomeroy, April 24, 1856, Aid Company Papers. Clark raised $2,000 for Plymouth Church, and reported $3,000 raised elsewhere, including Lawrence's $1,000. Amos A. Lawrence in letters to S. N. Simpson, Aug. 9 and Aug. 30, 1856, authorized drafts for his $1,000 contribution, Lawrence Letters, 164-65, 170-71.

109. Aid Company Letters, Book C, 98, 127-28.

110. Receipts of the contractor, Abner Doane, for payments on the contract, totaling $2,000, Aid Company Papers.

111. Letter from Branscomb, Jan. 14, 1858, Aid Company Records, Book IV, 43.

112. Accepted order on the miller for $100 in full of the Emigrant Aid Company's subscription for building schoolhouse in Manhattan, dated July 24, 1857, and signed by C. E. Blood, Aid Company Papers.

113. George F. Moorehouse, "Probably the First School in Kansas for White Children," *Kansas Historical Collections,* IX, 231-35.

114. Webb, *Information* (13th ed.), 56. Original letter, Nute to Hale, Aug. 3, 1857, Aid Company Papers.

115. Lawrence Letters, 205-06, 231-33. Certificate of 100 shares of stock in the Emigrant Aid Company to Robinson and Pomeroy, Trustees, Aid Company Papers.

116. Lawrence Letters, 227-28, 232-33, 236.

117. F. H. Snow, "The Beginnings of the University of Kansas," *Kansas Historical Collections,* VI, 70-75.

118. Aid Company Records, Book III, 186.

119. *Ibid.,* Book IV, 203-04.

120. *Ibid.,* Book V, 84-85. Copy of the deed, Aid Company Quit Claims.

121. J. T. Willard, "Bluemont Central College, the Forerunner of Kansas State College," *Kansas Historical Quarterly,* XIII, May, 1945, 323-57.

122. Aid Company Records, Book III, 95; Aid Company Letters, Book C, 23-24.

123. Aid Company Records, Book III, 136.

124. Original contracts for the houses and receipts for payments, Aid Company Papers.

125. Aid Company Records, Book "Company," 55-60.

126. *Ibid.,* Book III, 149-50.

127. *Ibid.,* Book "Company," 56.

128. Lawrence Letters, 263.
129. Aid Company Letters, Book C, 177-78.
130. Aid Company Records, Book III, 121.
131. Thayer, *Kansas Crusade*, 219-23. On the Ceredo venture see F. B. Sanborn, *Life and Letters of John Brown* (Boston, 1885), 381, 383. There are numerous allusions to Ceredo in the Aid Company correspondence.

XIII

1. Aid Company Records, Book III, 50.
2. *Ibid.,* 51-52.
3. *Ibid.,* 53-57; letter of Webb to Lawrence requesting the opening of a new set of books, Aid Company Letters, Book B, 668.
4. Aid Company Records, Book III, 157, 164.
5. *Ibid.,* Book II, 181-82; Book III, 204. This "Property Book" cannot be found among the Aid Company Papers, but several invoices from it are preserved.
6. Aid Company Records, Book III, 131, 139.
7. Aid Company Letters, Book A, 184-85, 229; Book B, 319. Original letters, Frederick Law Olmsted to Hale, July 23, 1855, Dec. 23, 1855, and Jan. 17, 1856, Aid Company Papers. Hale raised some money and Dr. Webb sent more to help D. A. Douai maintain a Free Soil newspaper in San Antonio. Early in 1857, Hale and Webb joined with Olmsted in circulating propaganda for antislavery colonization in Texas, but for strategic reasons the name of the Emigrant Aid Company was not connected with the movement. Original letters, Olmsted to Hale, Jan. 10, Jan. 23, Jan. 27, and Jan. 30, 1857, Aid Company Papers.
8. Aid Company Records, Book III, 166, 169-72.
9. *Ibid.,* Book III, 179-80, 183; Aid Company Letters, Book C, 66; Percy W. Bidwell, "The New England Emigrant Aid Company and English Cotton Supply Associations," *American Historical Review,* XXIII, Oct., 1917, 114-19, quotes letter of Olmsted to Dr. Cabot, dated July 26, 1857.
10. Aid Company Records, Book "Company," 60-65.
11. *Ibid.,* 66-67. Professor Silliman was put back on the Board a year later.
12. *Ibid.,* Book IV, 147-48.
13. Aid Company Letters, Book C, 234-35, 376-85, 432-33, 488.
14. *Ibid.,* 112-13; Aid Company Records, Book IV, 194.
15. *Ibid.,* 78, 92.
16. Aid Company Records, Book IV, 50.
17. Report of Committee on Agencies recommending the plan, presented to and adopted by the Executive Committee, Feb. 5, 1858, Aid Company Records, Book IV, 51-59. Plan explained in a letter to Conway, Feb. 6, 1858, Aid Company Letters, Book C, 217-22.
18. Aid Company Records, Book IV, 93-98.
19. Aid Company Letters, Book C, 326-29, 356-57, 391-94.
20. *Ibid.,* 326-29, 456-59.
21. Aid Company Records, Book IV, 199-201.
22. *Ibid.,* Book V, 78-81; original letters or certified copies, Higginson to Pomeroy, Aug. 31, 1859, and Sept. 3, 1859; Higginson to Conway, Sept. 4, 1859; Aid Company Papers.
23. Aid Company Records, Book II, 211; Book III, 15, 95, 153-54, 177, 212; Book IV, 34-36, 42, 97-98, 119-20; Aid Company Letters, Book C, 23, 145.
24. Letters of Branscomb about Lawrence titles, Dec. 10, 1856, Jan. 1, 1857, and April 27, 1857, Aid Company Records, Book II, 216-18; Book III, 20-22, 125.
25. Aid Company Records, Book IV, 156-57; Aid Company Letters, Book C, 435-36.
26. Aid Company Records, Book V, 140, 142-45.
27. *Ibid.,* 148-52, 174-77, 180-81.
28. *Ibid.,* 201-02.
29. *Ibid.,* 128-30, 161, 171.
30. Lawrence Letters, 151.
31. Annual reports of the treasurer, Aid Company Records, Book "Company," 74, 86, 96.

32. *Ibid.,* Book IV, 183-84; Aid Company Letters, Book C, 474-75.
33. Deitzler's statement, original paper, Aid Company Papers.
34. Original letter, Webb to Conway, April 12, 1859, *ibid.*
35. Aid Company Letters, Book C, 26.
36. Aid Company Records, Book V, 204.
37. *Ibid.,* Book IV, 125-26; Aid Company Letters, Book C, 414, 416-17.
38. Aid Company Records, Book III, 126, 162, 216.
39. Aid Company Letters, Book C, 435-36.
40. *Ibid.,* Book B, 684.
41. Aid Company Records, Book III, 106-07.
42. Aid Company Letters, Book C, 48, 98.
43. *Ibid.,* 347-48.
44. Aid Company Letters, Book IV, 195.
45. Aid Company Account Books, General Ledger, 70.
46. Aid Company Records, Book IV, 129.
47. Letter of Conway, July 12, 1858, *ibid.,* 181-82.
48. *Ibid.,* 24-25.
49. Letter of Conway cited in note 47.
50. Aid Company Records, Book III, 265.
51. *Ibid.,* Book IV, 14.
52. *Ibid.,* 93, 180-82, 221, 239.
53. Copies of deeds, Aid Company Quit Claims.
54. Aid Company Records, Book IV, 11-20, 48-49; Aid Company Letters, Book C, 168-70.
55. E. C. Manning, "In at the Birth and—," *Kansas Historical Collections,* VII, 202-05; William H. Coffin, "Settlement of the Friends in Kansas," *ibid.,* 322-61 (especially 354); George W. Martin, "The Territorial and Military Combine at Fort Riley," *ibid.,* 361-90 (especially 384-85).
56. Letter from Pomeroy, Oct. 24, 1860, Aid Company Records, Book V, 181.
57. Report, dated March 15, 1861, signed by W. W. Guthrie, F. P. Baker, and C. B. Lines as Committee, *Kansas Historical Collections,* IX, 483-84.
58. George W. Glick (governor of Kansas 1883-1885), "The Drought of 1860," *ibid.,* 480-85. Governor Glick, who lived in Atchison and knew Pomeroy intimately, defended him against all allegations in regard to this relief work. In a footnote (*ibid.,* 482) he quoted a statement of Hyatt, made in 1872, praising the fidelity of both Arny and Pomeroy.
59. Circular of Boston Kansas Relief Committee, dated March 13, 1861, Aid Company Papers.
60. *Ibid.* Also papers of the Boston Kansas Relief Committee, including bills for supplies purchased and hundreds of receipts for either goods or money received from "George W. Collomore, Agent for the New England Kansas Relief Committee," Aid Company Papers.
61. Feb. 23, 1858, Aid Company Records, Book IV, 73-75.
62. *Ibid.,* Book V, 171.
63. Ibid., 198-200.
64. *Ibid.,* 206.
65. Report signed for the Executive Committee by C. J. Higginson, *ibid.,* 201-05.
66. *Ibid.,* 212-13.
67. *Ibid.,* Book "Company," 104-08.
68. Printed circular letter to the stockholders, dated Jan. 16, 1862, signed by Dr. Webb, reciting the history of all negotiations to date. Copy, Aid Company Papers.
69. Minutes of Directors, Aid Company Records, Book V, 227-28.
70. *Ibid.,* 236-40.
71. Copy of printed circular letter, Lawrence to the stockholders, dated Aug. 28, 1861, Aid Company Papers.
72. Webb's circular letter cited in note 68.
73. Copy of printed circular letter, Lawrence to the stockholders, dated Dec. 14, 1861, Aid Company Papers.
74. Aid Company Records, Book "Company," 113-18.
75. "Kansas Expense" account, General Ledger, Aid Company Account Books.

76. Connelley, *Appeal to the Record*, 7.
77. W. H. Carruth, "The New England Emigrant Aid Company as an Investment Society," *Kansas Historical Collections*, VI, 90-96.
78. *Ibid.*
79. Aid Company Letters, Book C, 423.

XIV

1. Aid Company Records, Book V, 275-77.
2. *Ibid.*, 254.
3. Report of the secretary to the annual meeting, May 27, 1863, *ibid.*, Book, "Company," 122.
4. *Ibid.*, Book V, 254.
5. *Ibid.*, 255.
6. Cited extensively in these pages as the *Directors' History*, so called because Hale's authorship is not indicated in the publication. Copies are to be found today in most well-stocked libraries. See Hale, *Life and Letters of Edward Everett Hale*, 343.
7. Aid Company Records, Book "Company," 120; Book V, 262. Also "Memorial of the New England Emigrant Aid Company Praying Indemnification for the Destruction of Property at Lawrence, Kansas, May 21, 1856," 37 Cong., 3 Sess., *Senate Miscellaneous Documents* No. 29.
8. Original letter, Brimmer to Hale. Aid Company Papers.
9. Original letter, Higginson to Hale, May 19, 1864, *ibid.*; minutes of Directors, May 24, 1864, Aid Company Records, Book V, 268-69.
10. *Ibid.*, Book "Company," 128-30.
11. *Ibid.*, Book V, 273, 274.
12. *Ibid.*, Book IV, 265-70.
13. *Ibid.*, Book V, 101-07.
14. *Ibid.*, 108.
15. *Ibid.*, 205.
16. Original letter, Higginson to Hale, March 28, 1862, Aid Company Papers.
17. Original letter, Higginson to Hale, June 4, 1862, *ibid.*
18. Printed copy of circular letter sent to Cabinet members and members of Congress, New England Emigrant Aid Company Collected Pamphlets.
19. Aid Company Records, Book V, 254.
20. *Ibid.*, 273.
21. Original subscription paper, Aid Company Papers.
22. Aid Company Records, Book V, 280.
23. Undated, unsigned draft of a report in writing that looks like Hale's, Aid Company Papers. There are also a number of letters and other documents relating to Oregon, among them about thirty letters from young women, dates running from Jan. 9 to Aug. 8, 1865. Some wanted to go; others only inquired.
24. Aid Company Records, Book V, 288. Pamphlet of the United States Mutual Protection Company, Aid Company Papers.
25. Original letter, Webb to Hale, Nov. 27, 1865, urging Hale to get some of these men out for a meeting with Stevens, Aid Company Papers.
26. Aid Company Records, Book "Company," 131.
27. *Ibid.*, 133.
28. *Ibid.*, Book V, 291-96.
29. Aid Company Records, Book "Company," 125-27.
30. *Ibid.*, Book V, 266, 267.
31. *Ibid.*, 292-93.
32. *Ibid.*, 297.
33. Aid Company Records, Book V, 302, 305. The first minutes dated at the new office were Jan. 23, 1867, *ibid.*, 307.
34. *Ibid.*, 319, 320.
35. *Ibid.*, 296.
36. *Ibid.*, 298, 299, 301.
37. Original bill presented by General Marshall, March 15, 1867: salary for three months, $600.00; expenses (itemized), $425.80; total $1,025.80. Aid Company Papers.

38. Aid Company Records, Book V, 316.
39. Aid Company Papers.
40. Aid Company Records, Book V, 324.
41. *Ibid.*, Book "Company," 141.
42. *Ibid.*, Book V, 302, 304, 305. The petition was drafted by Governor Andrew.
43. Officially attested copy of the Act, Aid Company Papers; copy in minutes of the stockholders, Aid Company Records, Book "Company," 137-38.
44. *Ibid.*, 135.
45. *Ibid.*, 136-40.
46. *Ibid.*, 141-42.
47. *Ibid.*, Book V, 307.
48. *Ibid.*, 314-15.
49. *Ibid.*, 322-24.
50. *Ibid.*, 325.
51. *Ibid.*, 326.
52. *Ibid.*, 327, 330, 332.
53. Copy of the pamphlet, Aid Company Papers.
54. Aid Company Records, Book V, 317-18; printed copy, Collected Pamphlets.
55. Aid Company Records, Book V, 330.
56. This plan was first proposed by Hale, March 29, *ibid.*, 325; it was presented in detail by Marshall June 5, *ibid.*, 330-31.
57. Copy, Aid Company Papers.
58. Original subscription paper, *ibid.*
59. Aid Company Records, Book V, 338.
60. Original letters, Forbush to Hale, March 18 and April 3, 1867, Aid Company Papers.
61. Original letter, Forbush to Hale, March 18, 1867, *ibid.*
62. Aid Company Records, Book V, 324; original letter, Forbush to Hale, July 6, 1867, Aid Company Papers.
63. Original letter, Forbush to Hale, July 8, 1867, reporting meeting of the committee, *ibid.*
64. Aid Company Records, Book V, 335-37.
65. Original letter, Forbush to Hale, Aug. 26, 1867, Aid Company Papers.
66. Original letter, Forbes to Hale, Aug. 18, 1867, *ibid.*
67. Aid Company Records, Book V, 338-39.
68. Original letter, Forbush to Hale, Sept. 6, 1867, Aid Company Papers.
69. Aid Company Records. Book V, 339-40.
70. Original letter, Forbush to Hale, Sept. 12, 1867, Aid Company Papers.
71. Copy, *ibid.*
72. Aid Company Records, Book V, 302.
73. *Ibid.*, 338.
74. Several copies of second edition among Aid Company Papers and in Collected Pamphlets. Copies are to be found in many libraries.
75. Aid Company Records, Book V, 343.
76. *Ibid.*, Book "Company," 145, 147.
77. *Ibid.*, Book V, 343-44.
78. Original correspondence between Marshall and Hale, Aid Company Papers.
79. Aid Company Records, Book "Company," 143.
80. *Ibid.*, 145.
81. *Ibid.*, 146.
82. *Ibid.*, 146-47.
83. Original letter, July 26, 1870, Aid Company Papers.
84. Original letters, Aid Company Papers.
85. Aid Company Records, Book "Company," 148-51.
86. Officially attested copy of the Act, Aid Company Papers.

XV

1. Speech at Bismark Grove, Lawrence, Kansas, Sept. 16, 1879, reported in Gleed, *Kansas Memorial*, 140-48.

2.. Original letter, Thayer to Hale, April 16, 1867, Aid Company Papers.
3. Webb to Richard Bigelow, Feb. 3, 1858, Aid Company Letters, Book C, 269-70.
4. Brown to Lawrence, Jan. 28, 1862. Original in Lawrence Papers, Moody notes.
5. Aid Company Records, Book "Company," 58.
6. *Ibid.*, Book V, 219, 221.
7. *Kansas Crusade,* 203. This is verified by a letter from C. H. Branscomb, dated New York, Jan. 26, 1856, describing one of Thayer's meetings, Aid Company Records, Book II, 27-28.
8. Thayer, *Kansas Crusade,* 209.
9. F. H. Hodder, "The Railroad Background of the Kansas-Nebraska Act," *Mississippi Valley Historical Review,* XII, June, 1925, 3-22.
10. Julian P. Bretz, "The Economic Background of the Liberty Party," *American Historical Review,* XXXIV, Jan., 1929, 250-64.
11. A. M. Schlesinger, *Political and Social Growth of the United States 1852-1933* (revised ed., New York, 1933), 8-9.
12. Howard K. Beale, "The Tariff and Reconstruction," *American Historical Review,* XXXV, Jan., 1930, 276-94.
13. *Ibid.*; C. L. Miller, *The States of the Old Northwest and the Tariff 1865-1888.* (Emporia, Kansas, 1929), 32-34.
14. Quoted by Amos A. Lawrence in letter to John Carter Brown, Nov. 9, 1855, Lawrence Letters, 111-12.
15. *Directors' History,* 18.
16. Aid Company Records, Book IV, 27.
17. *Ibid.*, Book V, 201-05.
18. *Ibid.*, Books I and II, *passim.* The nine parties for which Dr. Webb recorded the numbers totaled 199, but he mentioned two other parties without stating their numbers.
19. William O. Lynch, "Popular Sovereignty and the Colonization of Kansas 1854 to 1860," Mississippi Valley Historical Association, *Proceedings,* 1917-1918, IX, Part III, 380-92.
20. *Ibid.*
21. H. A. Richardson, "A History of Milling in Kansas" (unpublished monograph, written 1928), chap. I.
22. See Connelley, *Appeal to the Record,* for excerpts from the *Free State* criticizing the Emigrant Aid Company.
23. April 29, 1857, Lawrence Letters, 256-57.
24. Henry Greenleaf Pearson (Professor of English, Massachusetts Institute of Technology), "Preliminaries of the Civil War (1850-1860)," chap. XVI of Vol. IV of A. B. Hart (ed.), *Commonwealth History of Massachusetts* (New York, 1930), 473-78.

Bibliography

I. SOURCES

A. Manuscripts

1. Papers and effects of the New England Emigrant Aid Company in Archives of the Kansas State Historical Society, Topeka, Kansas.

   Account Books, consisting of Cash Book, Journal, General Ledger, Kansas Ledger, three Stock Registers, Stock Ledger.

   Emigrant Books. Five small memorandum books containing records of purchases and sales of railway tickets with names of purchasers, from September, 1854, to April, 1858, with a gap from April, 1855, to April, 1856.

   Letters, three bound volumes of letterpress copies, from September 29, 1854, to August 28, 1858. A fourth volume is known to be missing.

   Papers. Files of original correspondence, memoranda, and miscellaneous papers.

   Quit Claims. Two books of copies of quitclaim deeds on printed forms.

   Records. Six bound volumes of Minutes of the Trustees, the Executive Committee, the Directors and the Stockholders.

2. Other manuscript material in the Archives of the Kansas State Historical Society.

   Barnes, William, Papers. Papers and effects of William Barnes as Secretary of the New York State Kansas Committee, 1856-1857.

   Lawrence Letters. Bound volume of typewritten copies of letters of Amos A. Lawrence about Kansas affairs and to correspondents in Kansas, prepared in 1888 under the direction of Mrs. Sarah E. Lawrence.

   Miscellaneous Papers. File under that title. Consulted for some original letters of Amos A. Lawrence to relatives and for papers of the Kansas Land Trust.

3. Lawrence Correspondence, Moody Notes. Letters written to Amos A. Lawrence, preserved among the Lawrence Papers in Boston, Massachusetts. Notes on some of the letters in Folio XI taken by Professor Robert F. Moody.

B. Published Documents

1. United States Government Documents.

   "Annual Report of the Secretary of War, December 1, 1856," 34 Congress, 3 Session, *House Executive Documents*, I, Part II, No. 1.

   Davis, Jefferson, Secretary of War. Despatches to Colonel E. V. Sumner, and Marcy, W. L., Secretary of State, to Governor Wilson Shannon, 34 Congress, 1 Session, *Senate Executive Documents*, No. 23.

   "Memorial of the New England Emigrant Aid Company Praying Indemnification for the Destruction of Property at Lawrence, Kan-

[332]

sas, May 21, 1856," 37 Congress, 1 Session, *Senate Miscellaneous Documents,* No. 29.

"Report of the Committee on Territories on Affairs of Kansas, January 24, 1856," 34 Congress, 1 Session, *Senate Report,* No. 34.

"Report of the Special Committee appointed to Investigate the Troubles in Kansas," 34 Congress, 1 Session, *House Report,* No. 200. Cited and commonly known as *Howard Report.*

2. Documents published by the Kansas State Historical Society.

Barnes, Lela, ed., "Letters of Cyrus Kurtz Holliday, 1854-1859," *Kansas Historical Quarterly,* VI, August, 1937, 241-94.

"Correspondence of Governor Geary," quoted from 35 Congress, 1 Session, *House Executive Documents,* VI, No. 17, *Kansas Historical Collections,* IV, 385-402.

"Corespondence of Governor Shannon" [and Acting Governor Woodson], quoted from 34 Congress, 3 Session, *House Executive Documents,* I, Part I, No. 1, *Kansas Historical Collections,* IV, 385-403.

"Documentary History of Kansas. Governor Geary's Administration," *Kansas Historical Collections,* V, 264-89.

"Documentary History of Kansas. Governor Reeder's Administration," *Kansas Historical Collections,* V, 163-234.

"Documentary History of Kansas. Governor Shannon's Administration," *Kansas Historical Collections,* V, 234-64.

"Excerpts from the Report of the Secretary of War," Military Despatches, Kansas Territory and Department of the West, 1856, quoted from 34 Congress, 3 Session, *House Executive Documents,* I, Part II, No. 1, *Kansas Historical Collections,* IV, 424-519.

"Executive Minutes of the Governor's Office during the Administration of Governor John W. Geary," quoted from 34 Congress, 3 Session, *House Executive Documents,* I, Part I, No. 1, 85-173; 34 Congress, 3 Session, *House Executive Documents,* III, No. 10, 1-36; 35 Congress, 1 Session, *Senate Executive Documents,* VI, No. 17, 27-208; *Kansas Historical Collections,* IV, 520-742.

"Executive Minutes of the Governor's Office during the Administration of Governor Andrew H. Reeder," abstract of manuscript volume in office of the Secretary of State, *Kansas Historical Collections,* III, 226-78.

"Executive Minutes of the Governor's Office during the Administration of Governor Wilson Shannon" [and Acting Governor Daniel Woodson], abstract of manuscript volume in office of Secretary of State, *Kansas Historical Collections,* III, 283-337.

"Letters of New England Clergymen," eight samples of letters received in response to Hale's appeal to the clergy in 1855, with list of all letters received and amount of money sent in each case [original letters in Archives of Kansas State Historical Society], *Kansas Historical Collections,* I-II, 193-202.

Lovejoy, Julia Louise, "Letters from Kanzas," *Kansas Historical Quarterly,* XI, 29-44.

"Selections from the Hyatt Manuscripts," seven selected depositions from among fifty-two in Archives of the Kansas State Historical Society (out of several hundred taken by Thaddeus Hyatt in Kansas during the winter of 1856-1857), *Kansas Historical Collections,* I-II, 203-33.

3. Documents published privately.

Bidwell, Percy W., "The New England Emigrant Aid Company and English Cotton Supply Associations," a letter of Frederick Law Olmsted to Dr. Samuel Cabot, Jr., relative to the proposal to interest British cotton manufacturers in a scheme for the colonization of Texas, *American Historical Review,* XXIII, October, 1917, 116-19.

Hyatt, Thaddeus, *Kansas,* "The Prayer of Thaddeus Hyatt to James Buchanan, President of the United States, in behalf of Kansas, asking for a Postponement of all the Land Sales in that Territory, and for Other Relief, together with Correspondence and Other Documents Setting Forth its Deplorable Destitution from Drought and Famine." Washington, 1860.

Kansas, University of, *Memorial in Support of Senate Bill No. 2677.* Lawrence, Kansas, 1897. Contains important documents as supporting exhibits.

Ray, P. O., "Some Papers of Franklin Pierce, 1852-1862," *American Historical Review,* X, October, 1904, 110-27.

Richardson, James D., *A Compilation of the Messages and Papers of the Presidents.* 10 vols. Published by the Authority of Congress, 1899. Also edition published by Bureau of National Literature and Art, 1909.

Shepherd, Grace L., "Letters of Lucy Larcom to the Whittiers," *New England Quarterly,* III, July, 1930, 501-18.

C. Contemporary Publications

1. Publications of the New England Emigrant Aid Company.

Articles of Agreement and Association of the Emigrant Aid Company. Boston, 1854.

[Forbush, T. B.], *Florida: The Advantages and Inducements Which It Offers to Immigrants.* 2nd ed. Boston, 1868.

[Hale, Edward Everett], *History of the New England Emigrant Aid Company with a Report on Its Future Operations.* Published by Order of the Board of Directors. Boston, 1862.

[Hale, Edward Everett, and Thayer, Eli], *Organization, Objects, and Plan of Operations of the Emigrant Aid Company.* 2nd and 3rd eds. Boston, 1854.

Pamphlets and Tracts. Miscellaneous assortment, most of them without names.

Report of the Committee of the Massachusetts Emigrant Aid Company with the Act of Incorporation and Other Documents. Boston, 1854.

Two Tracts for the Times. Boston, 1855. Contains: Stringfellow, B. F., "Negro Slavery No Evil," and Goodloe, D. R., "Is It Expedient to Introduce Slavery into Kansas?"

Webb, Thomas H., *Information for Kansas Emigrants.* 17 eds. Boston, 1855-1857.

2. Propaganda publications.

Hale, Edward Everett, *Kanzas and Nebraska.* Boston and New York, 1854.

Phillips, William, *The Conquest of Kansas by Missouri and Her Allies.* Boston, 1856.

Robinson, Sara T. L. [Sara D. T. in later editions], *Kansas, Its Interior and Exterior Life.* 1st ed., Boston, 1856. 10th ed., Lawrence, Kansas, 1899.

3. Emigrant guide books and descriptive books.

Boynton, the Reverend C. B., and Mason, T. B., *A Journey through Kansas.* Cincinnati, 1855.

Greene, Max, *The Kanzas Region.* New York, 1856.

[McNamara, J. M.], *Three Years on the Kansas Border,* by a Clergyman. New York and Auburn, New York, 1856.

Parker, Nathan H., *The Kansas and Nebraska Handbook for 1857-1858.* Boston, 1857.

Walter, George, *History of Kansas, Also Information Regarding Routes, Laws, etc.* New York, 1855.

4. New England Emigrant Aid Company Collected Pamphlets. A file of pamphlets, circulars and miscellaneous printed material published by or relating to the New England Emigrant Aid Company or similar organizations. Library of the Kansas State Historical Society, Topeka, Kansas.

5. Contemporary histories.

Brewerton, G. Douglas, *The War in Kansas.* New York, 1856.

Gihon, John H., *Geary and Kansas.* Philadelphia, 1857.

Tomlinson, William P., *Kansas in Eighteen Fifty-eight.* New York, 1859.

6. Personal narratives.

Colt, Mrs. Miriam D., *Went to Kansas.* Watertown, Massachusetts, 1862.

Doy, John, *The Narrative of John Doy of Lawrence, Kansas.* New York, 1860.

[Ropes, Mrs. Hanna], *Six Months in Kansas,* by a Lady. Boston, 1856.

D. Accounts by Participants

Hale, Edward Everett, "New England in the Colonization of Kansas," in Davis, William T., ed., *The New England States.* 4 vols. Boston, 1897. I, 79-90.

Robinson, Charles, *The Kansas Conflict.* Lawrence, Kansas, 1898.

Thayer, Eli, *A History of the Kansas Crusade, Its Friends and Its Foes.* Introduction by Edward Everett Hale. New York, 1889.

The New England Emigrant Aid Company and Its Influence, through the Kansas Conflict, upon National History. Worcester, Massachusetts, 1887.

E. Reminiscences and Memoirs

Bisbey, J. M., "Early Day Transportation," *Kansas Historical Collections,* XI, 594-97.

Blaine, James G., *Twenty Years of Congress.* 2 vols. Norwich, Connecticut, 1884.

Bondi, August, "With John Brown in Kansas," *Kansas Historical Collections,* VIII, 275-89.

Coffin, William H., "Settlement of the Friends in Kansas," *Kansas Historical Collections,* VII, 323-61.

Crutchfield, William, "The Capture of Fort Titus, August 16, 1856," *Kansas Historical Collections,* VII, 532-34.

Elliott, R. G., "Autobiography of Robert G. Elliott," *Kansas Historical Collections,* X, 190-96.

"The Twenty-first of May," *Kansas Historical Collections,* VII, 521-30.

Gable, Frank H., "Memoirs of a Pioneer Kansan," *Kansas Historical Collections,* XVI, 576-81.

Gleed, Charles S., ed., *The Kansas Memorial.* Kansas City, Missouri, 1880. Contains addresses delivered and letters read at Old Settlers' Meeting, Bismarck Grove, Lawrence, Kansas, September 15-16, 1879.

Goodnow, Isaac T., "Personal Reminiscences and Kansas Emigration, 1855," *Kansas Historical Collections,* IV, 244-53.

Green, Charles R., *Early Kansas History.* Olathe, Kansas, 1914.

Griffith, G. W. E., "The Battle of Black Jack," *Kansas Historical Collections,* XVI, 524-28.

Hale, Edward Everett, *Memories of a Hundred Years.* 2 vols. New York, 1902.

Holliday, Cyrus K., "The Presidential Election of 1856," *Kansas Historical Collections,* V, 48-60.

Kennedy, O. P., "The Capture of Fort Saunders, August 15, 1856," *Kansas Historical Collections,* VIII, 530-31.

Mackey, William H., "Looking Backward," *Kansas Historical Collections,* X, 642-51.

McClure, James R., "Taking the Census and Other Incidents of 1855," *Kansas Historical Collections,* VIII, 227-50.

Majors, Alexander, *Seventy Years on the Frontier.* Denver, 1893.

Manning, E. C., "In at the Birth and ———," *Kansas Historical Collections,* VII, 202-05.

Moore, Eli, Jr., "The Naming of Osawatomie and Some Experiences with John Brown," *Kansas Historical Collections,* XII, 338-46.

Morrow, Robert, "Emigration to Kansas in 1856," *Kansas Historical Collections,* VIII, 302-15.

[336]

Richards, O. G., "Kansas Experiences of O. G. Richards in 1856," *Kansas Historical Collections*, IX, 545-48.
Robinson, Charles, "Topeka and Her Constitution," *Kansas Historical Collections*, VI, 291-305.
Root, George A., ed., "The First Day's Battle of Hickory Point" [Diary and Reminiscence of S. J. Reeder], *Kansas Historical Quarterly*, I, November, 1931, 32-49.
Ross, Edmund G., *A Reminiscence of the Kansas Conflict*. Albuquerque, N. M., 1898.
Shaw, the Reverend James, *Early Reminiscences of Pioneer Life in Kansas*. Atchison, Kansas, 1886.
Smith, Charles W., "The Battle of Hickory Point, September 13, 1856," *Kansas Historical Collections*, VII, 534-36.
Wakefield, W. H. T., "Squatter Courts in Kansas," *Kansas Historical Collections*, V, 71-74.
Wilcox, P. P., Letter to the Kansas State Historical Society, January 24, 1886, *Kansas Historical Collections*, III, 467.
Wood, Samuel N., "The Pioneers of Kansas," *Kansas Historical Collections*, III, 426-31.

F. Periodicals

1. Historical collections.
Kansas Historical Collections, known also as *Transactions of the Kansas State Historical Society*. 17 vols. Published biennially with some irregularities and omissions from 1881 to 1928. Important articles are listed separately.
Massachusetts Historical Society, *Proceedings*. Published annually.
Worcester Society of Antiquity, *Collections*. Published annually.
2. Newspapers and magazines.
Besides particular issues (mentioned in the Notes) of such publications as the *Charleston Daily Courier*, the *Congressional Globe*, *De Bow's Review*, the *New York Daily Times*, the *New York Tribune*, and the *Oberlin Evangelist*, the author has made extensive use of the following:
Webb Scrap Books. Seventeen volumes of newspaper clippings relating to the Emigrant Aid Company and Kansas affairs, 1854-1860, prepared by Dr. Thomas H. Webb. Library of the Kansas State Historical Society, Topeka, Kansas.

II. SECONDARY MATERIAL

A. Biography

Blackmar, Frank W., *The Life of Charles Robinson*. Topeka, 1902.
Brown University, *The John Carter Brown Library*. Providence, Rhode Island, 1905. Memorial pamphlet commemorating the dedication of the Library Building, issued by the University. Contains biographical material about John Carter Brown.

Connelley, William E., *John Brown*. Topeka, 1900.
"Personal Reminiscences of F. B. Sanborn," *Kansas Historical Collections,* XIV, 63-70.
Gleed, Charles S., "Samuel Walker," *Kansas Historical Collections,* VI, 249-74.
Hale, Edward Everett, Jr., *The Life and Letters of Edward Everett Hale.* 2 vols. Boston, 1917.
Hinton, Richard J., *John Brown and His Men.* New York, 1894.
Lawrence, William, *Life of Amos A. Lawrence.* Boston and New York, 1888.
Nason, Reverend Elias, *The Life and Public Services of Henry Wilson.* Boston, 1881.
Nevins, Allan, *Frémont, The West's Greatest Adventurer.* 2 vols. New York and London, 1928.
Raymond, B. P., *Discourse in Memory of Hon. Amos A. Lawrence.* Appleton, Wisconsin, 1886.
Rice, W. W., Remarks on Eli Thayer at meeting of the Worcester Society of Antiquity, 1887, Worcester Society of Antiquity, *Collections,* VII, 26.
Roosevelt, Theodore, *Thomas Hart Benton.* Boston and New York, 1887.
Sanborn, F. B., *Life and Letters of John Brown.* Boston, 1885.
Thayer, Eli, *Six Speeches with a Sketch of the Life of Hon. Eli Thayer.* Boston, 1860. Reprint of six of Thayer's speeches in Congress with an anonymous campaign biography.
Ward, George O., "Eli Thayer, the Fourth Principal," *The Worcester Academy.* Worcester, Massachusetts, 1918.
Williams, H. Clay, ed., *Biographical Encyclopedia of Massachusetts of the Nineteenth Century.* 2 vols. New York, 1879, 1883.
Wilson, Hill Peebles, *John Brown, Soldier of Fortune, a Critique.* Boston, 1913.

B. Articles and Monographs

"The Abbott Howitzer—Its History" [probably by Franklin G. Adams], *Kansas Historical Collections,* I-II, especially 221-24.
Baldinger, Wallace S., "The Amateur Plans a City," *Kansas Historical Quarterly,* XII, February, 1943, 3-13.
Barry, Louise, "The Emigrant Aid Company Parties of 1854," *Kansas Historical Quarterly,* XII, May, 1943, 115-55.
"The New England Emigrant Aid Company Parties of 1855," *ibid.,* August, 1943, 227-68.
Beale, Howard K., "The Tariff and Reconstruction," *American Historical Review,* XXXV, January, 1930, 276-94.
Bretz, Julian P., "The Economic Background of the Liberty Party," *American Historical Review,* XXXIV, January, 1929, 250-64.
Caldwell, Martha B., "The Eldridge House," *Kansas Historical Quarterly,* IX, November, 1940, 347-70.

Carruth, William H., "The New England Emigrant Aid Company as an Investment Society," *Kansas Historical Collections*, VI, 90-96.

Cole, Arthur C., *The Whig Party in the South*. Washington, 1913.

Connelley, William E., "The Lane-Jenkins Claim Contest," *Kansas Historical Collections*, XVI, 21-176.

"The Lane Trail," *Kansas Historical Collections*, XIII, 268-79.

Cordley, Richard, "The Schools of Kansas," *Kansas Historical Collections*, III, 419-22.

Craik, Elmer L., "Southern Interest in Territorial Kansas," *Kansas Historical Collections*, XV, 348-450. Ph.D. thesis, University of Kansas.

Crandall, Andrew W., *The Early History of the Republican Party 1854-1856*. Boston, 1930. Ph. D. thesis, University of Pennsylvania.

Ewing, C. A. M., "Early Kansas Impeachments," *Kansas Historical Quarterly*, I, August, 1932, 307-25.

Fitz, L. A., "The Development of the Milling Industry in Kansas," *Kansas Historical Collections*, XII, 53-59.

Fleming, Walter L., "The Buford Expedition to Kansas," *American Historical Review*, VI, October, 1900, 38-48.

Glick, George W., "The Drought of 1860," *Kansas Historical Collections*, IX, 480-85.

Godsey, Flora R., "The Early Settlement and Raid on the Upper Neosho," *Kansas Historical Collections*, XVI, 451-63.

Greene, Albert R., "The Kansas River—Its Navigation," *Kansas Historical Collections*, IX, 317-58.

Haskell, John G., "The Passing of Slavery in Western Missouri," *Kansas Historical Collections*, VII, 28-39.

Hickman, Russell, "The Vegetarian and Octagon Settlement Companies," *Kansas Historical Quarterly*, II, November, 1933, 377-85.

"Speculative Activities of the Emigrant Aid Company," *Kansas Historical Quarterly*, IV, August, 1935, 235-67.

Hodder, Frank Heywood, "The Railroad Background of the Kansas-Nebraska Bill," *Mississippi Valley Historical Review*, XII, June, 1925, 3-22.

Iseley, W. H., "The Sharps Rifle Episode in Kansas History," *American Historical Review*, XII, April, 1907, 546-66.

Klem, Mary J., "Missouri in the Kansas Struggle," Mississippi Valley Historical Society, *Proceedings, IX*, Part III (1917-1918), 393-413.

Langsdorf, Edgar, "S. C. Pomeroy and the New England Emigrant Aid Company, 1854-1858," *Kansas Historical Quarterly*, VII, August, 1938, November, 1938, 227-45; 379-98.

Lynch, William O., "Popular Sovereignty and the Colonization of Kansas from 1854 to 1860," Mississippi Valley Historical Society, *Proceedings, IX*, Part III (1917-1918), 380-92.

Malin, James C., "Colonel Harvey and His Forty Thieves," *Mississippi Valley Historical Review*, XIX, June, 1932, 57-76.

John Brown and the Legend of Fifty-Six. Memoirs of the American Philosophical Society, XVII, Philadelphia, 1942.

"The Pro-Slavery Background of the Kansas Struggle," *Mississippi Valley Historical Review*, X, December, 1923, 385-405.

Martin, George W., "A Chapter from the Archives," *Kansas Historical Collections*, XII, 359-75.

"Early Days in Kansas," *Kansas Historical Collections*, IX, 126-43.

"The First Two Years of Kansas," *Kansas Historical Collections*, X, 120-48.

"The Territorial and Military Combine at Fort Riley," *Kansas Historical Collections*, VII, 361-90.

Miller, Clarence L., *The States of the Old Northwest and the Tariff 1865-1888*. Emporia, Kansas, 1929. Ph. D. thesis at Columbia University.

Miller, Wallace E., *The Peopling of Kansas*. Columbus, Ohio, 1905. Ph. D. thesis at Columbia University.

Moody, Robert F., "The First Year of the Emigrant Aid Company," *New England Quarterly*, IV, January, 1931, 148-55.

Morehouse, George P., "Probably the First School in Kansas for White Children," *Kansas Historical Collections*, IX, 231-33.

Shively, S. J., "The Pottawatomie Massacre," *Kansas Historical Collections*, VIII, 177-87.

Snow, Francis H., "The Beginnings of the University of Kansas," *Kansas Historical Collections*, VI, 70-76.

Viles, Jonas, "Sections and Sectionalism in a Border State," *Mississippi Valley Historical Review*, XXI, June, 1934, 3-22.

Walters, J. D., "The Kansas State Agricultural College," *Kansas Historical Collections*, VII, 167-88.

Ware, Abby Huntington, "Dispersion of the Territorial Legislature of 1856," *Kansas Historical Collections*, IX, 540-45.

Willard, J. T., "Bluemont Central College, the Forerunner of Kansas State College," *Kansas Historical Quarterly*, XIII, May, 1945, 323-57.

C. State and Local Histories

Andreas, Alfred T., ed., *History of the State of Kansas*. 2 vols, Chicago, 1883.

Bancroft, Hubert H., *California inter Pocula*, Vol. VI of *History of California*. 7 vols. San Francisco, 1888.

Barnes, C. R., ed., *Switzler's History of Missouri*. St. Louis, 1879.

Blackmar, Frank W., "Annals of a Historic Town" [Lawrence, Kansas], American Historical Association, *Annual Report for 1893*, 481-99.

"Kansas," in Goodspeed, W. A., ed., *The Province and the States*. 6 vols. Madison, Wisconsin, 1905. IV, 223-366.

Ed., *Kansas: A Cyclopedia of State History*. 4 vols. Chicago, 1912.

Carr, Lucian, *Missouri, a Bone of Contention*. Boston and New York, 1888.

Case, Theo. S., ed., *History of Kansas City, Missouri*. Syracuse, New York, 1888.

Connelley, William E., *A Standard History of Kansas and Kansans*. 5 vols. Chicago and New York, 1918.
Cordley, Richard, *A History of Lawrence, Kansas, from the First Settlement to the Close of the Rebellion*. Lawrence, Kansas, 1895.
Giles, F. W., *Thirty Years in Topeka*. Topeka, 1886.
Hart, Albert Bushnell, ed., *Commonwealth History of Massachusetts*. 5 vols. 1927-1930.
Holloway, J. N., *History of Kansas*. Lafayette, Indiana, 1868.
Paxton, W. M., *Annals of Platte County, Missouri*. Kansas City, Missouri, 1897.
Royce, Josiah, *California*. Boston and New York, 1886.
Sanborn, F. B., "Early Kansas History," Massachusetts Historical Society, *Proceedings*, XLI, 219-29, 331-59, 452-98.
Spring, Leverett W., *Kansas, The Prelude to the Civil War*. Revised ed. Boston and New York, 1907.
Tuttle, Charles R., *A New Centennial History of the State of Kansas*. Madison, Wisconsin, and Lawrence, Kansas, 1876.
Wilder, Daniel W., *The Annals of Kansas*. Topeka, 1875.

D. Controversial Writings

Brown, George W., *False Claims of the Historians Truthfully Corrected*. Rockport, Illinois, 1902.
Connelley, William E., *An Appeal to the Record*. Topeka, 1903.
Elliott, R. G., *Foot Notes on Kansas History*. Lawrence, Kansas, 1906.
Lecompte, Samuel D., "A Defense by Samuel D. Lecompte," *Kansas Historical Collections*, VIII, 389-405.

E. Unpublished Material

Ellsworth, Clayton S., "Oberlin and the Anti-Slavery Movement up to the Civil War." Ph. D. thesis at Cornell University, 1930.
Flint, Herbert, "Journalism in Territorial Kansas." Master's thesis, University of Kansas, 1916.
Hodder, Frank H., Lectures delivered in class in Presidential Administrations, University of Kansas. Cited as Hodder Lectures.
Richardson, Hayes A., "History of Milling in Kansas." Manuscript article intended for magazine publication.

Index

Abbott, James B.: sent east to procure arms, 126, 136; in Branson rescue, 138; in attack on Franklin, 186

Abbott Howitzer, the: Frederick Law Olmsted purchases, 127; arrives in Kansas, 140; surrendered by Pomeroy, 159; mention, 186; recovered by free-state men, 202

"Abolitionist," Southern use of, 5, 5n

Actual Settlers Association, 73

Adams, Franklin G.: president, Cincinnati Kansas League, 69; buys interest in *Squatter Sovereign,* 246

Adams, Isaac: sells steam engine to Emigrant Aid Company, 247; bids in Kansas property, 269

"Address to the People of Missouri," 135-36

"Address to the People of the United States," 180

"Address to the Stockholders," 280

Agencies, committee on, to compile property book, 255

Agents, Kansas: appointment of, 53; Charles Robinson, 53-55; Samuel C. Pomeroy, 55-58; Charles H. Branscomb, 55, 58-59; Martin F. Conway, 59; new instructions, 235-36

Agreement and Association, Articles of. *See* Articles of Agreement and Association

Albany Kansas League, 68

American Hotel (Kansas City): bought by Emigrant Aid Company, 42; operation of, 86-87; threatened with destruction, 155n; Eldridge defaults on payments, 259. *See also* Gillis House; Kansas City Hotel; Hotels

American ("Know-Nothing") party: A. A. Lawrence and, 14, 226-27; proposes Gen. Scott as Kansas dictator, 226. *See also* "Doniphan Know-Nothings"

American Settlement Company: founds Council City (Burlingame), 67; joint office with New York Kansas League, 67-68; sketch, 67-68; proprietor of Council City, 85-86

Anthony, Daniel R., joins "Pioneer Party," 52, 52n

"Anti-Abolition" ticket, nominated under Topeka Constitution, 145

"Anti-Bentonite" Democrats (Missouri), 93

Apeal to the Clergy, amount raised, 115. *See also* Clergy, appeal for funds

Arming of settlers. *See* Barnes, William; Emigrant Aid Company, arms; Sharps rifles

"Army of the North, Lane's": mention, 166; reports of, 191; Chicago, Cutter and Stowell parties take land route, 193; real

nature of, 193-94; pro-slavery preparation to resist, 194; led into Kansas by M. C. Dickey, 195; second contingent enters Kansas, 196

Arny, W. F. M.: agent, National Kansas Committee, 215; distributes drought relief, 265-66

Articles of Agreement and Association: first formed, 18; tentative organization under, 19; provisions, 19, 20; liability under, 20; revised form adopted, 25; final provisions, 25-26; organization under, 53. *See also* Emigrant Aid Company, trusteeship; "Voluntary association"

Assistant treasurer, employed, 116, 117. *See also* Blanchard; Stone, Anson J.

Atchison, David R.: in Missouri politics, 93, 95; purpose of intervention in Kansas, 95; speech at Liberty, Missouri, 95-96; strategy in Kansas, 95-96; agitation against Emigrant Aid Company, 134; in Wakarusa War, 142; collects "Grand Army," 203

Atchison (Kansas): Emigrant Aid Company interest in, 85; pro-slavery center, 86; Emigrant Aid Company buys share in, 245-46

Atrocities, pro-slavery, alleged, 137. *See also* "Border Ruffians"

Austin, Freeman ("Pap"), saves Osawatomie mill, 204

Ayling, Henry A., bids in Kansas property, 269

Babcock, Carmi W.: in Lawrence claim dispute, 79, 80; mission to Gov. Shannon, 141; projector of Burlington (Kansas), 244

Bacheller, Kansas spelling of Batcheller, 242

Baldwin, John, in Lawrence claim dispute, 79, 80

Baldwin, William, in Lawrence claim dispute, 79, 80

Banks, Nathaniel P., promotes nomination of Frémont, 223-24

Barber, Thomas W., killed in Wakarusa War, 143-44

Barnes, William: co-operation with Emigrant Aid Company, 35; arming of free-state settlers, 166; secretary, New York State Kansas Committee, 176; plans National Kansas Committee, 214

Batcheller, J. and E., town to be named for, 238

Batcheller (Milford, Kansas): mention, 85; efforts to establish, 241-42; established by Manhattan (Kansas) men, 242

Batcheller mill. *See* Mills, Batcheller mill

Beecher, Henry Ward, arms C. B. Lines colony, 173

"Beecher's Bible," origin of term, 173

"Beecher's Bible Rifle Church," Wabaunsee, 85

"Beecher's Bible Rifle" colony: mention, 61; settles at Wabaunsee, 84-85; details, 173. *See also* Lines, C. B.

Bell, E. B., raises recruits in South Carolina, 209, 212

Benton, Thomas Hart: Senator and party leader, 92; interest in Pacific Railway, 92; candidate for Senator, 1855, 98-99

Benton fight, the (Missouri), 92-93

Bentonite Democrats (Missouri), 93

Bickerton, Thomas, captain of artillery company, 198, 200

Bigelow, John (ed., *New York Evening Post*), supports financial drive, 162

Big Springs Convention: called to organize Free State party, 106; organizes Free State party, 107-08; importance of, 108

Black Jack, battle of, 185-86

Blanchard, part-time assistant treasurer, 117

"Bleeding Kansas": effect on stock subscriptions, 49; gives Republicans an issue, 143

Blood, James: meets "Pioneer Party," 53; picks site of Wabaunsee, 84; sketch, 84n

"Blue Lodges," in border conflict, 97, 98

Bluemont Central College (Manhattan, Kansas), Emigrant Aid Company contribution to, 250. *See also* Kansas State Agricultural College

"Bogus election": mention, 74, 123; territorial election called, 102. *See also* Fraudulent voting

"Bogus Laws": enacted, 103; free-state leaders refuse to recognize, 137

"Bogus Legislature": territorial legislature called, 103; adjourns to Shawnee Mission, 103; expels Free State members, 103; enacts "Bogus Laws," 103; antagonizes western settlers, 106

Books: Dr. Webb solicits for Kansas libraries, 88; boxes of rifles marked, 88

Boone, Col. A. G., appeal to rally borderers, 139

"Border Ruffians": Lawrence claimants called, 80; all Missourians called, 102; atrocities alleged, 111

Border War: breaks out in Kansas, 181; resumed in August, 196-97

Boston (Kansas), early name of Manhattan, 83

Boston office (Emigrant Aid Company): No. 3 Winter Street, 29; negotiation of railroad and steamboat rates, 35. *See also* Emigrant Aid Company office

Boynton, the Rev. Charles, visits Kansas for Cincinnati Kansas League, 69

Branscomb, Charles H.: sent to Kansas, 51; appointed general agent, 55-56; sketch, 58-59; assists in fund raising, 162; acting secretary, 166; and steamboat owners, 175; in charge of rebuilding Free State Hotel, 235, 236-37; neglects Kansas property, 257, 257n; removed as agent, 258-59

Branson, Jacob, rescued from Sheriff Jones, 138

Brimmer, Martin: concludes arrangement for interest in Atchison, 245-46; mission to Kansas, 248, 251; member, Executive Committee, 251; signs note for Emigrant Aid Company, 264; treasurer, Emigrant Aid Company, 272, 279

Brown, George W.: editor, *Herald of Freedom*, 89-90; loan from Emigrant Aid Company, 89-90; indicted for treason, 157; debt on *Herald of Freedom*, 262-63

Brown, John: associated with Osawatomie, 82; in Wakarusa War, 144; in Pottawatomie Massacre, 183; relation to Emigrant Aid Company, 184-85; in battle of Black Jack, 185-86; goes to Nebraska City, 195; in battle of Osawatomie, 203

Brown, John, Jr., captain, Pottawatomie Rifle Company, 182

Brown, John Carter: president, New England Emigrant Aid Company, 28-29; sketch, 28-29; remits $1,500, 113; threatens to resign, 115; considers sending political agent to Kansas, 131-32; signs note for Emigrant Aid Company, 264; favors liquidation of Kansas property, 266; resigns as president, 274

Brown, Orville C., founder and part proprietor of Osawatomie, 82

Brown, R. P., murder of, 145

Bryant, William Cullen (ed., *New York Times*): supports financial drive, 162; elected director, 178

Buchanan, James: elected President of the United States, 229-30; Emigrant Aid Company distrust of, 237

Budget Committee, Thayer and Higginson appointed, 254

Buffalo (New York), and "Pioneer Party," 51

Buffalo (New York) Kansas Aid Convention: Emigrant Aid Company representatives, 215; forms National Kansas Committee, 215. *See also* National Kansas Committee

Buffum, J. N., sells steam engine to Emigrant Aid Company, 247

Buford, Jefferson, plan to promote emigration, 208

Buford Expedition, 208, 209-10

Burlington (Kansas): settled by Hampton

County colony, 61; founded, 84; projected by Lawrence (Kansas) men, 244
"Bushwhacking," guerrilla tactics, 182, 182n. *See also* "Jayhawkers"
Butler, the Rev. Pardee, set adrift on raft, 137

Cabot, Dr. Samuel: member, Executive Committee, 31, 251; work on finance, 113; finance committee, 116; orders Sharps rifles, 124-25; raises rifle fund, 125-26; treasurer, rifle fund, 127; work for rifle fund, 161, 162-63. *See also* Sharps rifles; Rifle fund
Calhoun, John, Surveyor General for Kansas and Nebraska, 73n
California, Robinson's experience in, 54
"California Road," highway in Kansas, 198n
Cato, Judge Sterling G., in killing of Barber, 144
Cemetery, Lawrence (Kansas), Pomeroy to lay out, 88
Ceredo (West Virginia), founded by Eli Thayer, 11, 252
Chapman, R. A. (director, Emigrant Aid Company): solicits funds in Springfield, 116; prepares reply to Douglas's charges, 178-79
Charters, Emigrant Aid Company. *See* Emigrant Aid Company charters
Cheney, Edward M.: buys Florida newspaper, 279-80; Florida agent, Emigrant Aid Company, 280
Chicago party, turned back on Missouri River, 191
Childs, H. F. (or Chiles, H. W.): American Hotel leased to, 155n; defaults on hotel contract, 259
Churches: Emigrant Aid Company aid to, 41; Plymouth Congregational (Lawrence, Kansas), 87-88; Episcopal (Lawrence, Kansas), 88, 248; Unitarian (Lawrence, Kansas), 88, 249-50; Methodist (Manhattan, Kansas), 249; Emigrant Aid Company raises funds for, 249. *See also* Emigrant Aid Company, aid to churches
Cincinnati Kansas League: formed, 69; helps found Ashland, 69; settlers at Manhattan (Kansas), 83
Claflin, Horace B.: supports financial drive, 162; elected director, 168
Claflin, Lee, town to be named for, 238
Claflin (Mapleton, Kansas): mention, 85; efforts to establish, 241-42; name of Mapleton to be changed to, 242
Claim disputes, common in Kansas, 138
"Claim jumping," in Kansas, 73
Claims (land), staked by settlers, 72
Clark, G. W. (Indian agent), in killing of Barber, 144

Clergy, appeal to for funds; first effort, 64; conducted by E. E. Hale, 114-15
Cleveland (Ohio) Kansas Aid Convention, 214-15. *See also* National Kansas Committee
Cline, Captain, in battle of Osawatomie, 203
Clubb, Henry S., temperance leader, 69-70. *See also* Octagon Settlement Company; Vegetarian Settlement Company
Coleman, Franklin W., killing of C. W. Dow, 138. *See also* Wakarusa War
Collamore, George W., in drought relief, 1860, 266
Committee of Safety (Lawrence, Kansas). *See* Safety, Committee of
Compromise of 1850, 4, 5
Conductors (Emigrant Aid Company parties): plan, 37; inadequacy of (1855), 119-20; practice discontinued, 174; forwarding agent expected to pay steamboat passage, 175. *See also* Kansas settlers, Emigrant parties
Cone, S. W. and D. D., settlers armed by Dr. Cabot, 166. *See also* Millard City
Congressional debates: House of Representatives, 149-50; Senate, 150-54; Administration strategy, 154-55; effect of, 154-55; helps consolidate Republican party, 224
Connelley, William E.; critic of Eli Thayer, 9, 9n; claims Emigrant Aid Company was speculative project, 46; claims profit made on Kansas property, 269
Conspiracy, Pro-slavery, alleged, 72
Conway, Martin F., appointed general Kansas agent, 258. *See also* Kansas agents
Cook, Captain Joe, alias of James H. Lane, 198
Cooke, Col. Philip St. George: refuses troops to Woodson, 205; intercepts attack on Lecompton, 206; supplies troops to Gov. Geary, 231-32
Council City (Burlingame, Kansas), founded by American Settlement Company, 85
Cracklin, Joseph, captain, Lawrence "Stubbs" Company, 197, 198
Crane, Samuel, owner, Franklin blockhouse, 198-99
Cranston, Charles, saves Osawatomie mill, 188
Cutter, Dr. Calvin: leader of Emigrant party, 166; joins fighting forces, 196; in attack on Ft. Saunders, 199
Cutter party: armed by Dr. Webb, 166; turned back on Missouri River, 173-74, 192

Davis, Jefferson (Secretary of War): dominates Pierce Administration, 154; reprimands Col. Sumner, 189

Debates in Congress. *See* Congressional debates

DeBow's Review: mention, 5; campaign in support of Pro-slavery party, 211

Debts, bad, examples, 262-63

Defense fund, contributions, early 1856, 163-64. *See also* Rifle fund

Delahay, Mark W., publisher, (Leavenworth) *Territorial Register,* 144-45

Democratic party: need to quiet "bleeding Kansas," 225; raid on Lawrence (Kansas) would ruin, 232

Depression of 1857. *See* Panic of 1857

Development projects, local: Emigrant Aid Company attitude toward, 41-42; Emigrant Aid Company asked to aid, 171-72; Higginson and Brimmer promise help for, 248-49. *See also* Emigrant Aid Company, local development projects

Dickey, M. C.: Topeka settler, 81; leads Lane's "Army" into Kansas, 195

Dietzler, George W.: sent East to procure arms, 124; indicted for treason, 157

Directors, Emigrant Aid Company. *See* Emigrant Aid Company directors

Directors' History, issued 1862, 273

Donaldson, J. B. (U. S. marshal), summons posse, 157-58

Doniphan, A. W., candidate for Senator, 98

"Doniphan Know-Nothings": in Missouri senatorial politics, 99; mention, 135

Douglas, Stephen A.: mention, 7; report and speech in Senate, 151-52

Dow, Charles W., killed by F. N. Coleman, 138. *See also* Wakarusa War

Doy, Dr. John, joins "Pioneer Party," 52

Drafts: Pomeroy reckless with, 57; early 1855, 112

Drought of 1859-60: effects in Kansas, 265; factor in financial failure of Emigrant Aid Company, 270. *See also* Kansas relief

Dwight, Theodore: and Emigrant Aid Company of New York and Connecticut, 66; secretary, New York Kansas League, 67; president, American Settlement Company, 67

Easton, Lucian J., urged to call out Platte County Rifles, 139

"Education, Temperance, Freedom, Religion in Kansas," pamphlet directed to clergy, 114

Eldridge, Shailer D.: proprietor, American Hotel, 86; leads second "Army of the North," 196; hired to clear hotel rubble, 236; buys Free State Hotel, 237; payments on Free State Hotel, 238; defaults on American Hotel payments, 259; debts to Emigrant Aid Company, 262

Election, territorial. *See* "Bogus election"

Election, territorial delegate: Free State election called, 107-08; A. H. Reeder elected in Free State election, 108; J. A. Whitfield elected in Pro-slavery election, 108

Elliott, Henry H., objects to sale of Kansas property, 268

Elliott, R. G., editor, *Kansas Free State,* 80

Emigrant Aid Company: projected by Eli Thayer, 7; aid to schools and churches, 41; local development projects, 41-42, 171-72; investment policies, 41-42; question of speculation, 42-44; exaggerated reports on border, 94; Kansas territorial election, 99, 100-01; relation to Free State Movement, 129-33; blamed for Kansas troubles, 143; profits from Kansas excitement, 161; participates in Buffalo convention, 215; co-operates in National Kansas Movement, 218; relief activity, 1856, 218-21; collects clothing for Kansas relief (1856), 219; involvement in politics, 221, 222-23; and Republican party, 222-23; reason for continuing organization after 1862, 272; deficiencies of, 298-99; national importance, 302-03. *See also* New England Emigrant Aid Company

—arms: refuses to arm individuals, 165-66; begins arming individuals, 166. *See also* Rifle fund; Sharps rifles

—Building (Lawrence, Kansas), uses of, 87

—charges against, 8, 94, 143

—charter, Connecticut (The Emigrant Aid Company): Thayer seeks, 20; granted, 21; provisions, 21; reaction of Boston men, 21; A. A. Lawrence and, 21, 22, 23; organization under, 22, 23; New England Emigrant Aid Company and, 23

—charter, first Massachusetts (Massachusetts Emigrant Aid Company): mention, 7; petitioners, 11, 16; accepted, 17; petition for, 16-17; incorporators, 17; act passed, 17; provisions, 17; failure to organize under, 18, 19

—charter, second Massachusetts (New England Emigrant Aid Company): applied for, 26; act passed, 27; provisions, 27; organization under, 27; amended 1867, 278; last extension, 285; final expiration, 286

—claims against, 261. *See also* Emigrant Aid Company finance, claims against Company

—claims for, 8, 293-94

—directors: elected, 1855, 30n; changes, 1856, 178; changes, 1857, 251, 251n; changes, 1858, 256; meetings during Civil War, 272-74; number reduced, 272; changes, 1865, 274n; decide to operate in Florida, 277

—emigrants. *See* Emigrants, Kansas; Kansas Settlers

—finance: needs, 1855, 111-12; report of 1856, 177; condition, spring of 1857, 254; bright outlook, early 1857, 255; stringency after July, 1857, 260; annual expenses, 260-61; claims against Company, 261; losses suffered, 261-63; losses on bad debts, 262-63; loan for operating expenses, 264; reasons for financial failure, 270-71, 287-88; problems of 1866, 278; financial summary, 294-95. *See also* Financial drives

—imitators: similar organizations, 8; organizations in imitation, 65-70

—management: condition of Company affairs, 1856, 234-35; factor in financial failure of Company, 270; discussion of, 287-88

—motives: philanthropy or money making, 45-46; views of leaders, 46-47; crusading motive, 50; profit motive, 50, 254

—office: temporary, Massachusetts Historical Society, 36, 52, 111; No. 3 Winter Street, 29; closed, 268; reopened, 277; 23 Chauncy Street, 283; General Marshall's office, 284

—officers: elected, 1855, 27-30; and rifle fund, 127-28; and Free State Movement, 129-33; sell Kansas territorial scrip, 146; contributions to relief funds, 168; re-elected 1856, 177; set up Massachusetts State Kansas Committee, 212-13; and party politics, 222-23; changes, 1862, 272; changes, 1865, 274; changes, 1866, 279; market Florida bonds, 284

—organization: A. A. Lawrence's ideas, 15; early difficulties, 16; first charter accepted, 17; first charter abandoned, 18, 19; "voluntary association," 25-26; reorganization under second Massachusetts charter, 27, 111; New Haven meeting, 52; new persons take over, 1864, 274; reorganization under revised charter, 1867, 279; maintained until 1870, 284-85

—trusteeship: first provision for, 18; difficulties of organizing, 24-25; Articles of Agreement and Association, 25-26. *See also* "Voluntary association"

—of Massachusetts, 26

—of New York and Connecticut: name adopted, 26; sketch, 66

Emigrant Aid Movement, Southern: Buford expedition, 208, 209-10; Georgia and Florida, 209; South Carolina, 209

Emigrant Aid Societies, Missouri, 210-11

Emigrant Aid Society: use of term, 8; A. A. Lawrence prepares constitution for, 25; confusion of terms, 38, 39, 70, 221; name applied to Emigrant Aid Company, 49-50

—Wisconsin State Kansas, 212

Emigrant handbooks: Webb, *Information for Kansas Emigrants*, 36; Walter, *History of Kansas*, 68; [Serenbetz] *Information for German Emigrants*, 243

Emigrant parties (Emigrant Aid Company): plan, 33; conductors, 37; organization and arrangements, 37; "Party Day," 37; accessions en route, 75-76; private parties, 75, 173-74, 239; size, 1854, 75-76; size, 1855, 117-18. *See also* Kansas settlers, Emigrant parties

Emigrants, Kansas: question of recruiting, 36; complaints against Emigrant Aid Company, 37-38, 40-41; relation to Company, 37-38, 39; monetary aid, 38-39; loans to, 39; no pledge required, 39-40; not stockholders, 39-40; promises to, 40-41; efforts to safeguard, 119-21

Emigration to Kansas: plan to promote, 33; propaganda to stimulate, 36; problems of, 117-18; work on, 1856, 172-75

Emigration Aid Association of Northern Ohio: sketch, 68-69; S. N. Wood leads party to Kansas, 156; revived in 1856, 213

Emporia (Kansas), 85

Episcopal Church (Lawrence, Kansas), Emigrant Aid Company donates lot for, 248, 249. *See also* Churches

Executive Committee (Emigrant Aid Company): authorized, 30; members, 1855-56, 31; employs assistant treasurer, 116, 117; sends Dr. Webb to Kansas, 123; considers request for rifles, 125; considers Kansas politics "unofficially," 133; changes, 1856, 178; members, 1857-58, 251; decision to dismiss secretary and close office, 268; occasional meetings during Civil War, 272; after Civil War, 273, 275, 276; proposes federal aid for Company, 275

Evarts, William M.: supports financial drive, 162; elected director, 178

Fabian policy, A. A. Lawrence recommends, 147

Fain, W. P. (deputy U. S. marshal): Reeder defies, 157; makes arrests in Lawrence, 159

Faneuil Hall Committee, promoted by Emigrant Aid Company, 212-13

Federal authority, free-state men warned against resistance to, 137-38

Finance, Emigrant Aid Company. *See* Emigrant Aid Company finance

Financial drives (Emigrant Aid Company): fall, 1854, 59; drive launched, 1855, 116; success, early 1856, 161-63; volunteer workers, 162-63; amount raised, 163. *See also* Emigrant Aid Company finance.

Flenniken, R. P., candidate for territorial delegate, 98

Florida project: promoted by E. E. Hale, 277; interest in *Florida Union* purchased, 280; effort to interest business leaders, 281-282; abandoned, 282-83; Florida pamphlet issued, 283-84; T. B. Forbush on abandonment of, 283. *See also* Forbush, T. B.; Marshall, J. M. S.

Florida bonds marketed, 284

Forbes, J. M.: contributor to rifle fund, 126; elected director, 276; president, Emigrant Aid Company, 279; forces abandonment of Florida project, 281-82; railroad interests, 291

Forbush, T. B.: secretary, Emigrant Aid Company, 277, 279; author of Florida pamphlet, 283; on abandonment of Florida project, 283

Foreign immigrants, plans to aid, 34

Fort Leavenworth, visited by Robinson, 51

Forts, pro-slavery: principal, 197; Georgia Fort, 197; Ft. Saunders, 197; attack on Ft. Saunders, 199-200; Ft. Titus, 197; battle of Ft. Titus, 200-01

Forwarding agencies: St. Louis, 35, 59, 175; Kansas City, 51, 59. *See also* Hunt, F. A.; Riddlesbarger, J.; Slater, B.

Franklin (Kansas): pro-slavery center, 86; mention, 139, 140; first attack on, 186; second attack on, 198-99

Fraudulent voting (Missourians in Kansas), 98, 101, 103. *See also* Voting, fraudulent

"Freedom, a Plan of," editorial series by Horace Greeley, 19

Frémont, John C., Robinson and nomination of, 223-24. *See also Herald of Freedom*

Free State Hotel: work begun, 87; preliminary work on, 112; progress on, 1855, 121; serves as barracks, 140; claimed to have been built as fort, 155, 169-70; "presented" as nuisance by grand jury, 158; destroyed in sack of Lawrence, 159; destruction not mentioned by stockholders, 177; rebuilding commenced, 236; sold to S. W. Eldridge, 237

—claim against government for loss. *See* Hotel claim

Free State Movement: role of Emigrant Aid Company officers, 129-33; relation of Emigrant Aid Company to, 129-33

Free State party: beginning of, 103-05; permanent organization plan, 106; steps in organization, 107-08; executive committee established, 109

Free State propaganda delegation: sent east by territorial executive committee, 146; headquarters at Emigrant Aid Company office, 146; Emigrant Aid Company

makes use of, 161; aids Republican party, 222

Fugitive Slave Law (1850), unpopularity in North, 4, 5

Geary, John W. (Governor): decision to send to Kansas, 189; arrives in Kansas, 206; orders all armed forces disbanded, 207, 231; purpose of appointment, 228-29; prevents attack on Lawrence (Kansas), 232; forms new militia, 232; friendly with free-state leaders, 233; scheme to secure admission of Kansas, 233-34; removal of, 234

Georgia Fort, attacked and burned, 197. *See also* Forts, pro-slavery

German migration: Emigrant Aid Company interest in, 243-44; settlement in Texas, 255

Geyer, Henry S.: elected Senator from Missouri, 93; quotes "Address to the People of Missouri' 'in Senate, 136; attacks Emigrant Aid Company in Senate, 150, 153

Gillis House: option to purchase, 51; purchase, 86, 112. *See also* American Hotel; Kansas City Hotel

Goodnow, Isaac T., founder of Manhattan, 83

Goodrich, John Z., president, Union Emigration Society, 65, 66

Grasshopper Falls (Valley Falls, Kansas), 86

Greeley, Horace: editorial series, "A Plan of Freedom," 19; helps raise funds for arms, 127

Grinnell, Moses H.: proposed as director, 19; selected as trustee, 20; treasurer, Emigrant Aid Company of New York and Connecticut, 66; supports financial drive, 162

Grow Bill (for admission fo Kansas), passes House of Representatives, 224-25

Guerrillas, free-state, 181-82

—pro-slavery, 182

Guthrie, Abelard, proprietor of Quindaro, 244

Hale, Edward Everett: Texas pamphlet, 1845, 10; sketch, 11-12; on foreign immigrants, 34; speaking tours for Emigrant Aid Company, 36; in charge of appeal to clergy, 114; full-time subscription agent, 116, 162; writes "Address to the People of Missouri," 135; director and member of Executive Committee, 178; raises money for Serenbetz, 243-44; author, *Director's History,* 273; handles Oregon project, 274-76; promotes Florida project, 277; vice president, 279; secures final extension of charter, 285; Bismark Grove speech, 287

Hale, John P., defends Emigrant Aid Company in Senate, 151
Hampden (Kansas), founded, 84
Hampden mill. *See* Mills, Hampden mill
Hampton colony: mention, 61; tickets from Emigrant Aid Company, 75n
Hartford, steamboat: Manhattan settlers, 83; boiler bought for Lawrence mill, 83; burned, 83, 171
Harvey, Col. James A.: in planned attack on Lecompton, 205; raids Easton and Slough Creek, 206; in battle of Hickory Point, 207
Haskins, Nathan: agrees to provide mills, 122; additional mills bought from, 170-71
Haven, S. G., proposes compromise on Kansas, 227
Havens, R. N.: in formation of New York and Connecticut Company, 23; vice president, Emigrant Aid Company of New York and Connecticut, 66
"Hay tent": St. Nicholas Hotel, 81; used as church in Lawrence, 87
Herald of Freedom (newspaper): Emigrant Aid Company organ, 89; establishment of, 89-90; relation to Emigrant Aid Company, 90; nationwide importance, 90-91; "presented" as nuisance by grand jury, 158; office wrecked, 159; type used for cannon balls, 200; "second edition of," 201; declares for Frémont, 224; publication resumed, 262. *See also* Brown, George W.
Hickory Point (1), beginning of Wakarusa War, 138
Hickory Point (2), battle of, 207
Higginson, Charles J.: members, Executive Committee, 31, 251; committee on agencies, 235; mission to Kansas, 245-46, 248, 261; buys interest in Atchison for Emigrant Aid Company, 245-46; elected treasurer, 251; budget committee, 254; secretary, Emigrant Aid Company, 272
Higginson, J. A., attends last stockholders' meeting, 285
"Hirelings, army of," Emigrant Aid Company accused, 8, 37
Hoar, E. Rockwood, contributor to rifle fund, 126
Hoar, Samuel, contributor to rifle fund, 126
Holliday, Cyrus K., founder of Topeka, 81
Holton (Kansas), founded, 196
Hotel claim: Pomeroy presents to Congress, 236; prospect of collecting, 237; pushed in Congress, 261; decision to press, 268; company kept alive to prosecute, 272; transferred to University of Kansas, 285
Hotels: Manhattan, Emigrant Aid Company subscription, 248; Osawatomie, Emigrant Aid Company subscription, 248. *See also* American Hotel; Free State Hotel; Gillis House; Kansas City Hotel
Houses, rental: built by Emigrant Aid Company in Lawrence, 250-51; demands of tenants, 257
Howard Committee: appointed, 108, 149; tries to aid Robinson's escape, 157
Howe, Dr. Samuel G.: sketch, 11; elected director, 178; proposes shortening memorial to Congress, 179; inspects emigrants at Nebraska City, 194; financial agent, National Kansas Committee, 215; sent to Nebraska and Kansas, 216
Hoyt, David S.: sent to Kansas with rifles, 164-65; rifles seized at Lexington (Missouri), 165; killing of, 199
Humboldt (Kansas): founding of, 85; settled by F. M. Serenbetz, 244
Hunt, F. A.: St. Louis forwarding agent, 175; reports decline of Kansas values, 263. *See also* Forwarding agents
Hutchinson, G. W., seized as spy, 204-05
Hyatt, Thaddeus: director, New York Kansas League, 67; supports financial drive, 162; inspects emigrants at Nebraska City, 194; president, National Kansas Committee, 215; sent to Nebraska and Kansas, 216; organizes drought relief, 265

Indian land titles. *See* Land titles, Indian
Independent Democrats, Appeal of the, 3
Information for Kansas Emigrants (Webb): first issue, 36; copies supplied to William Barnes, 177. *See also* Webb, Thomas H.
Information for German Emigrants, published by Emigrant Aid Company and Massachusetts State Kansas Committee, 243
Information Service, Dr. Webb, 36
Iowa emigrant route, 191
Iowa State Kansas Committee, organization and officers, 214

Jackson, Claiborne F., author of Jackson Resolutions, 92-93
Jackson, Patrick T.: enlists A. A. Lawrence, 18-19; early organization activity, 21; withdraws from project, 22; elected director, 178; treasurer, Massachusetts State Kansas Committee, 213
"Jayhawkers": Montgomery uses Hoyt rifles, 165; free-state guerrillas, 182n
Jenkins, Gaius: proprietor, Gillis House, 51; indicted for treason, 157
Jones, Samuel J. (sheriff): arrests Jacob Branson, 138; shot in Lawrence, 156; sack of Lawrence, 160
Junction City. *See* Millard City

Kansas, credit for saving claimed, 293-94

Kansas agencies (Emigrant Aid Company); reorganization of, 258; factor in financial failure of Company, 271. *See also* Agents, Kansas

Kansas Aid Committees (1856). *See* National Kansas Committee

Kansas Aid organizations, listed by Dr. Webb, 214

Kansas and Nebraska, division into two territories, 6

Kanzas and Nebraska (Hale): written, 12; mention, 34; Emigrant Aid Company propaganda, 36; prepared for Emigrant Aid Company, 62

Kansas Anseidlungsverein, Cincinnati, Ohio, 69

Kansas City (Missouri): Robinson and Branscomb visit, 51; mills stored at, 122, 171, 246

Kansas City forwarding agency. *See* Forwarding agencies

Kansas City hotel: involved in litigation, 259; litigation delays sale of Company property, 268. *See also* American Hotel; Gillis House

Kansas Committee, National. *See* National Kansas Committee

Kansas conflict: abandoned by Pierce administration, 230; influence of Emigrant Aid Company on, 299-300

Kansas Emigration Aid Society of South Carolina, 209

Kansas emigrants. *See* Emigrants, Kansas

Kansas emigration retarded: factors, 1855, 118; spring, 1856, 174-75

Kansas Free State (newspaper): hostile to New Englanders, 77; established in Lawrence, 89; objects to Aid Company mills, 122; "presented" as nuisance by grand jury, 158; office wrecked, 159. *See also* Elliott, R. G.

Kansas improvements (Emigrant Aid Company), summary, 297-98

Kansas Land Trust, 44-45

Kansas Leagues: Worcester County constitution, model for others, 60n; organized in New England, 60-61; New York, 66-68; Albany, 68; Cincinnati, 69

Kansas Legion, 136-37

Kansas meetings: called to support Emigrant Aid Company, 60; in Missouri, 99, 134; held throughout North, 191

Kansas Movement, National. *See* National Kansas Committee

Kansas-Nebraska Bill: mention, 3, 4, 7, 16, 72; Southern support of, 5; proposals for counteracting, 6-7; purpose of dividing territory, 94

Kansas property (Emigrant Aid Company): problems of, 256-58; titles to real estate, 259-60; inability to sell,

263-64; A. A. Lawrence and J. C. Brown favor liquidation, 1857, 266; liquidation considered by stockholders, 266-68; estimates of value, 268; sold at auction, 269; probable cost of, 269

Kansas relief, drought of 1860: organization and operation, 265-66; Boston committee formed, 266. *See also* National Kansas Committee

Kansas settlers: from Ohio valley, 72; motives of, 72-74; sources of, 73-74; views on slavery, 74; Western, characteristics, 76-77; provision for medical care, 88; attitude toward Emigrant Aid Company, 256; gold rush to Colorado (1859), 264-65

—Emigrant Aid Company: "Pioneer Party," 23, 24, 51-53, 74-75; second party reaches site of Lawrence, 75; voting in territorial election, 101-02; complaints of, 119-21; disappointed, 120-21; private parties, 1856, 173-74; parties, 1856, 173-74, 239; sent, 1857, 240; declining importance of, 240-41; number sent, 296; influence on Kansas, 296-97. *See also* Emigrant parties

—free-state: molested on Missouri River, 190-91; Chicago party turned back, 191; turned back in Platte County (Missouri), 191; Cutter party turned back, 173-74, 192

—New England: peculiarities, 76-77; difficulties, 77-78; return of, 77-79

Kansas State Agricultural College, 250. *See also* Bluemont Central College

Kansas Tribune (newspaper), established in Lawrence, 89

Kansas, University of, A. A. Lawrence's contributions toward, 15, 250

Kanzas Zeitung, Die, established in Atchison, 243

Kemper, Bishop Jackson, secures donation of lot for church, 248

Kentucky Kansas Association, helps found Ashland, 69

"Kickapoo Rangers," pro-slavery militia company, 145

"Know-Nothing" party. *See* American party; "Doniphan Know-Nothings"

Kob, Charles F., Emigrant Aid Company assists, 243

Land claims, *See* Claims, land

Land titles, Indian: Robinson and Branscomb investigate, 51; Pomeroy to observe, 58; extinction of, 72

Lane, James H.: motives, 74; joins Free State party, 106-07; sketch, 107; chairman, Free State Executive Committee, 109; second in command, Free State militia; 140; signs Treaty of Lawrence, 142; elected Senator by Topeka Legislature, 145; indicted for treason, 157; in charge at Nebraska City, 194; returns to Kansas with Walker, 195; in battle of Franklin, 198; attack on Ft. Saunders, 199-200; "straw men" story, 200; leaves Walker in command, 200; in planned attack on Lecompton, 205-06; in projected attack on Leavenworth, 206; in battle of Hickory Point, 207

—"Army of the North." *See* "Army of the North, Lane's"

Larcom, Lucy, song, "Call to Kansas," 63

"Law and Order party." *See* Pro-slavery party

Lawrence, Amos A.: critical of Thayer, 9, 52, 90; sketch, 14-15; "Hunker Whig," 14; "Know-Nothing" nomination for Governor (Massachusetts), 14, 227; motives, 14-15; opposes Republican party, 14, 223, 223n, 226-27; supports Fillmore for President, 14, 226-27; treasurer, Emigrant Aid Company, 15; trustee, Emigrant Aid Company, 15, 18, 26; advances to Company, 15, 51, 65, 112-13; donations for Kansas projects, 15; ideas of Emigrant Aid organization, 15, 25; and Connecticut charter, 21, 22, 23; treasurer, New England Emigrant Aid Company, 30; views on speculation by Company, 43-44; Lawrence, Kansas, named for, 79; contributions to Lawrence (Kansas) churches, 88, 249; loan to *Herald of Freedom*, 90; threatens to resign, 115; part-time help as treasurer, 116-17; gives note for rifles, 125; contributions to rifle fund, 127; letters to President Pierce, 130; correspondence with Robinson about politics, 130-31; considers sending political agent to Kansas, 131-32; contributions to John Brown, 184; Company officers embarrassed by nomination for Governor, 227-28; effort to secure release of treason prisoners, 229; approves Geary's plan for admission of Kansas, 233; contribution for "Memorial College," 250; resigns as treasurer, 251; signs note for Emigrant Aid Company, 264; favors liquidation of Kansas property, 266; reelected treasurer to liquidate property, 267-68; vice president, 1862, 272

Lawrence, Sara D. T., marries Charles Robinson, 54. *See also* Robinson, Sara D. T.

Lawrence, Bishop William (son of Amos A. L.), describes effort to secure release of treason prisoners, 229

Lawrence, Dr. William R. (brother of

Amos A. L.), contributor to rifle fund, 126

Lawrence Association, organized, 79

Lawrence (Kansas): founded, 75, 79; named for Amos A. Lawrence, 79; claim dispute, 79-80; temporary accommodations for settlers, 87; beginning of library, 88, meetings to launch Free State party, 105-06; Fourth of July celebration (1855), 106; town meeting on Branson rescue, 139-40; Treaty of, 142-43; nominating convention under Topeka Constitution, 145; destruction desired by Pro-slavery party, 155; appeals to Governor Shannon, 158; marshal's posse gathers, 158-59; sack by Sheriff Jones, 160; sack of, begins Civil War in Kansas, 181; Atchison's "Grand Army" prepares to attack, 206

Learnard, O. E.: projector of Burlington (Kansas), 244; dispute with Emigrant Aid Company, 257

Leavenworth (Kansas): convention to organize Pro-slavery party, 110; William Philips attacked, 118; free-state men seized as spies, 204-05; free-state plan to attack, 206

Leavenworth, Fort. *See* Fort Leavenworth

Lecompte, Samuel D., presides at treason indictments, 157

Lecompton (Kansas): pro-slavery center, 86; militia to gather at, 139; plan to attack, 205

Lecompton Constitution, concern of Emigrant Aid Company, 252

Legislature, Bogus. *See* "Bogus Legislature"

Legislature, territorial. *See* "Bogus Legislature"

Legislature, Topeka. *See* Topeka Legislature

Lenhart, Charles, guerrilla leader, 182

Lexington (Missouri), convention, 134-35

Liberty (Missouri): Atchison's speech at, 95-96; arsenal raided, 141-42

Lines, C. B., leader, "Beecher's Bible Rifle" colony, 171, 173

Local development projects. *See* Development projects, local

Lowell, John: director, 31, 32; dropped from Executive Committee, 178

Lowrey, G. P., mission to Governor Shannon, 141

Lum, the Rev. S. Y.: suggests name for Topeka, 81; Congregational minister, Lawrence (Kansas), 87

Lykins, the Rev. Johnston, suggests name for Wabaunsee, 84

Lykins, William (son of the Rev. Johnston L.), in Lawrence claim dispute, 79, 80

INDEX

McBratney, Robert, buys interest in Atchison (Kansas), 245-46
Mace, Daniel, director, Union Emigration Society, 65
Management, Emigrant Aid Company. *See* Emigrant Aid Company, management
Manhattan (Kansas): founding of, 83; Emigrant Aid Company interest in, 83; Dr. Webb's interest in, 83, 123; beginning of library, 88; carried by Free State party, 102. *See also* Bluemont Central College
—mill. *See* Mills, Manhattan mill
—schoolhouse, Emigrant Aid Company subscription for, 248
Manypenny, George W. (Commissioner of Indian Affairs), visits Kansas, 72
Mapleton (Kansas), name to be changed to Claflin, 242
Marshall, J. F. B.: placed on Board of Directors, 277; mission to Florida, 278; secretary and assistant treasurer, 284; secretary-treasurer, 285
Martin, John A., changes *Squatter Sovereign* to *Freedom's Champion,* 246
Mason, T. B., visits Kansas for Cincinnati Kansas League, 69
Massachusetts Historical Society, temporary office of Emigrant Aid Company, 36, 52, 111
Massachusetts State Kansas Committee: Emigrant Aid Company officers in formation of, 212-13; absorbs Faneuil Hall Committee, 213; buys Emigrant Aid Company stock for work relief, 221, 236
Memorial to Congress (Emigrant Aid Company), prepared and presented, 179
Meetings, community (New England), to raise funds for Kansas, 162-63
Migration, early plans for directing, 34
Milford (Kansas), name of Batcheller changed to, 243
Military companies (free-state), formed, 1855, 136
Millard City (Junction City): mention, 86; settled by S. W. and D. D. Cone, 166
Miller, Josiah, editor, *Kansas Free State,* 80
Mills, Emigrant Aid Company: need for in Kansas, 89; sent in 1855, 89; three sawmills installed, 111-12; purchased by Robinson and Pomeroy, 121; Rochester mill reaches Kansas City, 121; purchased from Nathan Haskins, 122; Emigrant Aid Company blamed for inadequacy, 122; stored at Kansas City, 122, 171, 246; freight and storage charges, 122; first grist mills sent by Emigrant Aid Company, 123; supplies purchased, 170
—Atchison mill: flour mill promised for Atchison, 246; Buffum engine sent, 247;

machinery purchased, 248; unable to sell, 263; nothing to grind, 265
—Batcheller mill: sawmill sent from Quindaro, 247; grist mill purchased and sent, 247-48
—Hampden mill: moved to Burlington, 170; sold to O. E. Learnard, 244
—Lawrence mill: steamboat boiler purchased for, 83; too small, 89; inadequate, 122
—Manhattan mill: hauled to Manhattan, 122; in operation, 170; problems of, 257, 257n
—Osawatomie mill: hauled to Osawatomie, 122; in operation, 170; saved by miller, 188; again saved by miller, 204; damaged by flood and burned, 257; loss of, 261-62
—Quindaro mill, sold for town shares, 244-45, 246-47
—Topeka mill: too small, 89; in operation, 121-22; inadequate, 122
—Wabaunsee mill, in operation, 247
Missouri: county meetings, 134; reaction to Robinson's Fourth of July speech, 135
—Legislature, fails to elect Senator, 98-99
—politics, and Kansas Conflict, 135
—western: attitudes, 4; secret societies, 97-98
"Missouri, Address to the People of," effects, 135-36
Missouri Compromise, 3, 5, 16
Missouri River, blockade of: extent of, 189-91; interference with freight, 193; Governor Geary procures opening, 229. *See also* Kansas settlers, free-state
Missourians: reaction to propaganda, 94-95; first illegal voting in Kansas, 98; voting in Kansas territorial election, 101; voting in Kansas blamed on Emigrant Aid Company, 101-02; called "Border Ruffians," 102
Money problems: expenses (1854), 63; efforts to sell stock (1854), 64-65. *See also* Emigrant Aid Company, finance
Montgomery, James ("Jayhawker"), uses Hoyt rifles, 165
Morrow, Robert, leads second "Army of the North," 196
Mount Oread. *See* Oread, Mount

National Kansas Committee: relief committees, 1856, 167; sends Howe and Hyatt west, 194; Kansas Aid meetings and committees, 212; planned by William Barnes, 214; Cleveland convention, 214-15; steps to organize, 214-16; Buffalo convention, 215; officers, 215; members, 215n; headquarters in Chicago, 215-16; Thayer appointed organization agent, 216-17; methods and results com-

[351]

pared with Emigrant Aid Company's, 217-19; undertakes support of Free State Movement, 217-19

National Kansas Movement. *See* National Kansas Committee

Nebraska City (Nebraska): rendezvous on emigrant land route, 193-94; council of war, 195. *See also* "Army of the North, Lane's"

Negroes, exclusion of: in Free State party platform, 107; submitted to free-state voters, 108-09

New England: interest in slavery question, 290-91; influence of Emigrant Aid Company on, 300-02

New England Emigrant Aid Company: and Connecticut charter, 23; named in second Massachusetts charter, 27; name under new charter, 111. *See also* Emigrant Aid Company

Newspapers, Lawrence (Kansas), question which first declared for Frémont, 224n

New York Kansas League: origin, 66-67; additions to Emigrant Aid Company parties, 67; joint office with American Settlement Company, 67-68; settlers found Osawatomie, 82

New York State Kansas Committee: railway tickets, 35; sketch, 176; co-operation with Emigrant Aid Company, 176-77. *See also* Barnes, William

New York Times, editorial on Sharps rifles, 123

New York Tribune: editorial series "A Plan of Freedom," 19; western influence, 95. *See also* Greeley, Horace

Northeast (section), attitudes in, 4

Nute, the Rev. Ephraim (Unitarian Minister, Lawrence, Kansas): distributes relief funds, 167; distributes Emigrant Aid Company relief, 219

Octagon Settlement Company, sends colony to Kansas, 69-70

Ohio Valley: attitude of farmers, 1854, 4; Kansas settlers from, 72

"Old Sacramento" (cannon): attempt to capture, 186; captured, 198; at Fort Titus, 201

Oliver, Mordecai (Representative from Missouri): member, Howard Committee, 148n; attacks Emigrant Aid Company in Congress, 149, 150

Olmsted, Frederick Law: purchases brass howitzer, 127; work on Texas project, 256; personal note, 256n

Oread, Mount: named for Oread Collegiate Institute, 53; posse camps on, 159; Robinson's house on, burned, 159; federal artillery posted on, 282

Oread Collegiate Institute, Mt. Oread named for, 53

Oregon project, party of women sent, 275-76

Organization, Objects, and Plan of Operation of the Emigrant Aid Company: pamphlet, 36; proposals in, 61; history of, 61-62; propaganda use on border, 95; quoted in Senate by Stephen A. Douglas, 152

Osawatomie (Kansas): associated with John Brown, 82; Emigrant Aid Company interest in, 82; founded by New York Kansas League settlers, 82; naming of, 82; raid on, 187-88; battle of, 203-04

Osawatomie mill. *See* Mills, Osawatomie mill

Overcharge of emigrants, explanation of, 119-21

Pacific railroad: Pomeroy's interest in, 56; Benton's interest in, 92; factor in Kansas conflict, 291

Packard, Prof. A. S., 64

Paddleford, Seth (director), solicits funds in Providence, 116

Palmer, J. C., president, Sharps Rifle Company, 126

Palmyra (Baldwin, Kansas): mention, 86; battle expected, 186

Pamphlets, Emigrant Aid Company: *Information for Kansas Emigrants,* 36, 62; *Nebraska and Kansas: Report of the Committee of the Massachusetts Emigrant Aid Company with the act of incorporation and other documents,* 61; *Organization, Objects and Plan of Operation of the Emigrant Aid Company,* 61; *Information for German Emigrants,* 243

Panic of 1857: Emigrant Aid Company reaction, 256; conditions in Kansas, 263; factor in financial failure of Company, 270

Paola (Kansas), 86

"Parallels, law of," 6

Park, George S.: writes description of Kansas for Emigrant Aid Company pamphlet, 61; editor, *Parkville Luminary,* 118

Parkville Luminary, destruction of office, 118

Parrott, Marcus J., sent to Washington as lobbyist, 146

Pate, Henry Clay, in battle of Black Jack, 185-86

Paupers, Company accused of shipping to Kansas, 37

Pawnee (Kansas): designated territorial capital, 86; settlers vote in territorial election, 102; legislature meets at, 103

Philips, William, attacked in Leavenworth, 118

Phillips, Wendell, contributor to rifle fund, 126

Pierce, Franklin (President of U. S.): A. A. Lawrence related to by marriage, 130; Free State Memorial sent to, 140; Gov. Shannon asks him to call out troops, 140-41; annual message, December, 1855, 147; special message on Kansas, 147; free-state leaders appeal to, 147-48; authorizes use of federal troops, 148; proclamation on Kansas, 148

Plan of operations (Emigrant Aid Company), sketch, 33-34

Platte County (Missouri), free-state settlers turned back in, 191

—Regulators, border secret society, 98

—Rifles, in Wakarusa War, 142

—Self-Defensive Association: declaration against emigrant aid societies, 96; referred to in Senate debate, 150

Platte Purchase (Missouri): settlers from, 72; farmers of, 94-95

"Pioneer Party" (Emigrant Aid Company). See Kansas settlers, "Pioneer Party"

Plumb, Preston B., and Emigrant Aid Association of Northern Ohio, 69

Plumb, Samuel, agent, Emigrant Aid Association of Northern Ohio, 68-69

Plymouth Congregational Church (Lawrence, Kansas), Emigrant Aid Company handles contributions for, 249. See also Churches

Politics, Emigrant Aid Company involvement: Kansas territorial election, 99, 100-01; Kansas, 133; national, 221, 222-23

Pomeroy, Samuel C.: appointed general agent, 55-56; sketch, 55-57; U. S. Senator, 57, 276; powers as agent, 57-58; compromises Lawrence claim dispute, 80; part proprietor of Osawatomie, 82; helps organize Plymouth Church, 87; recalled from Kansas to raise money, 113; speaking tour, early 1855, 114n; memorial of, presented in Senate, 150; chairman, Lawrence (Kansas) Committee of Safety, 158; opinion of Buford's men, 210; kept in Washington by Company, 235; presents hotel claim to Congress, 236; bargains for interest in Atchison (Kansas), 245; discrepancies in accounts, 254; duties under reorganized agencies, 258, 259; distributes drought relief, 265-66; U. S. Mutual Protection Company, 276

Pottawatomie Massacre: account of, 183; theories of, 183; effects of, 185. See also Brown, John

Pottawatomie Rifle Company, starts for relief of Lawrence, 182-83. See also Brown, John, Jr.

Pre-emption act, extended to Kansas, 72

Preferred stock: authorized by Massachusetts Legislature, 278; offered to old stockholders, 280; land-stock plan, 280-81; sale inadequate, 281

Press, Northern, reaction to Kansas-Nebraska Bill, 6

—Pro-slavery, attacks on free-state men, 136

Price, Sterling: proposed for Senator, 98; opens Missouri River, 229

Propaganda, Emigrant Aid Company: early, 36; campaign launched, 59

Propaganda delegation, Free State. See Free State propaganda delegation

Property (Emigrant Aid Company), Kansas. See Kansas property

Property losses, factor in financial failure of Company, 270-71

Pro-slavery party: Gov. Shannon supports, 109; organized at Leavenworth, 110

Pro-slavery press, attacks on free-state men, 136

Quakers, New England, send relief through Emigrant Aid Company, 220

Quantrill raid (on Lawrence, Kansas), Emigrant Aid Company directors raise relief funds, 273-74

Quindaro (Kansas): Emigrant Aid Company interest, 85; founded by Robinson and others, 244

Railway companies, negotiations with, 176-77

Railway tickets: sale of, 35; handling of money, 35-36; sale continued through 1859, 36; passes furnished to conductors, 37

Reeder, Andrew H.: interest in Pawnee, 86; calls election for territorial delegate, 98; census of Kansas, 99; calls election for legislature, 99; sketch, 99n; removed as Governor, 103; joins Free State party, 106-07; nominated for territorial delegate, 107; elected Senator by Topeka Legislature, 145; claims Whitfield's seat as territorial delegate, 148; indicted for treason, 157; flees Kansas, 157

Reid, John W., attacks Osawatomie, 203

Relief: committees of 1856, 167; drive for funds, 1856, 167-69; unearmarked funds applied to, 169; New England committees promoted by Emigrant Aid Company, 212-13; Company collects clothing, 219; Company transmits private aid, 220; work of Company, 1856, 218-21; Quantrill raid, 273-74. See also Kansas relief; National Kansas Committee

Republican party: outgrowth of Kansas excitement, 8; helped by Wakarusa War, 142; gains by Congressional debate on Emigrant Aid Company, 154-55, 224; in National Kansas Movement, 221-22; dependence on Kansas issue, 222; achievement in election of 1856, 230. *See also* "Bleeding Kansas"

Republicans in Congress: pass Grow and Dunn Bills in House, 224-25; defeat Toombs Bill, 226; unwilling to settle Kansas issue, 227

Rice, W. W., loan to *Herald of Freedom*, 90

Richardson, W. P.: major general, Pro-slavery militia, 139; killing of Barber, 144; calls out militia division, 202

Riddlesbarger, J. (Kansas City forwarding agent): offers to serve, 51; appointed, 59; Buford borrows money from, 210

Rifles: boxes marked "Books," 88; Executive Committee considers request for, 125. *See also* Cabot, Dr. Samuel; Emigrant Aid Company, arms; Rifle fund; Sharps rifles
—Sharps. *See* Sharps rifles

Rifle fund: Dr. Cabot handles, 125-26, 127, 161, 162-63; contributors to, 126; Emigrant Aid Company officers and, 127-28; amount raised, 127-28. *See also* Cabot, Dr. Samuel; Sharps rifles

Riley, Fort, visited by Branscomb, 51

Robinson, Charles: instructions as agent, 34-35; sent to Kansas, 51; writes description of Kansas for pamphlet, 51; appointed general agent, 53; sketch, 53-55; instructions to, 55; conductor of second party, 55; founding of Topeka, 81; helps organize Unitarian Church (Lawrence, Kansas), 88; plans Free State party, 103-05; on aims of Free State party, 104; motives in free-state movement, 104-05; Fourth of July oration (1855), 106; asks Thayer for Sharps rifles, 124; asks for additional rifles, 126; correspondence with Lawrence about politics, 130-31; and Branson rescue, 139-40; commander, Free State militia, 140; signs Treaty of Lawrence, 142; elected Governor under Topeka Constitution, 145; indicted for treason, 157; attempts to flee, 157; house on Mt. Oread burned, 159; informed of preparations to resist Lane, 194; sends Samuel Walker to Nebraska City, 195; promotes nomination of Frémont, 223-24; resigns Emigrant Aid Company agency, 233; proprietor of Quindaro, 244

Robinson, Sara D. T., copies Lawrence's

letter to Mrs. Pierce, 229. *See also* Lawrence, Sara D. T.

Rochester (New York), settlers join Emigrant Aid Company party, 52

Ross, Edmund G., leads party of Wisconsin settlers, 194

Russell, Le Baron: member, Executive Committee, 31-32; finance committee, 116; helps draft reply to S. A. Douglas, 179; committee on agencies, 235

Russell, Judge Thomas: director, Company, 256; member, Executive Committee, 256

Safety, Committee of (Lawrence, Kansas): formed, 140; appeals to Gov. Shannon, 141; second committee, 158

St. Louis Evening News (newspaper), criticism of D. R. Atchison, 99

St. Louis forwarding agents. *See* Forwarding agents; Slater, B.; Hunt, F. A.

St. Louis Intelligencer (newspaper), predicts Atchison's strategy, 97

Saunders, Fort, preparations to attack, 197, 198. *See also* Ft. Saunders

Schoolhouse, Emigrant Aid Company Building in Lawrence used as, 87
—Manhattan, Emigrant Aid Company subscription for, 248
—Topeka: Emigrant Aid Company promises, 81; Company agrees to build, 248. *See also* Topeka Schoolhouse

Scrip, territorial: issued by Territorial Executive Committee, 146; Emigrant Aid Company officials sell, 146

Schuyler, Philip, Council City and Burlingame, 85-86

Searle, A. D.: surveys Lawrence townsite, 79; surveys Osawatomie townsite, 82

Sedgwick, Major John: expected to protect Osawatomie, 187; report on Ft. Titus, 201

Seeds, garden, sent to Kansas settlers, 88, 265

Senate balance, southern interest in, 5

Serenbetz, F. M., Emigrant Aid Company assistance to, 243-44

Seward, William H.: Senate speech, May 25, 1854, 7, 9; defends Emigrant Aid Company in Senate, 153

Shannon, Wilson: appointed Governor of Kansas, 109; supports Pro-slavery party, 109; proclamation to support Sheriff Jones, 139; calls out militia, 139; intervenes in Wakarusa War, 141-42; signs Treaty of Lawrence, 142; orders militia to disband, 143; visits Washington, 148; second treaty with Lawrence Committee of Safety, 201-02; flees and is removed as Governor, 202

Sharps Rifle Company, 125

Sharps rifles: mention, 33; first appeal for,

INDEX

104-05; Emigrant Aid Company accused of sending, 124; inside story, 124-28; spelling of name, 123n; Robinson asks additional rifles, 126; question, did Company furnish, 128; second shipment arrives, 140; relied on to offset opponents' numbers, 141; surrendered by Pomeroy, 159; Thayer offers to pay for, 164; Hoyt rifles seized, 165. *See also* Rifle fund

Shawnee Mission: Legislature meets at, 106; appeal to Gov. Shannon at, 141

Shombre, Henry J.: killed at Ft. Titus, 196; in attack on Ft. Saunders, 199

Shore, Samuel T., in battle of Black Jack, 185-86

Simpson, S. N.: distributes Emigrant Aid Company relief, 219; part proprietor of Quindaro, 244

Slater, B. (St. Louis forwarding agent): appointed, 59; Dr. Webb's trouble with, 118-19; joins F. A. Hunt and Company, 175

"Slave Power," 4

Smith, George W., indicted for treason, 157

Smith, General Percifer F., reports on conditions in Kansas, 196

Smith, Gerrit: contributor to rifle fund, 126; contribution to National Kansas Committee, 217

Snodgrass, Dr. J. E., vice president, American Settlement Company, 67, 68

Song, prize offered for, 63

"Song of the Kansas Emigrant" (Whittier), sung by Emigrant Aid Company parties, 62-63

Songs, *Lays of the Emigrants,* 63

"Sooners," in Kansas, 72

South (section): attitudes in, 4, 6; Emigrant Aid Company considers operating in, 274-75; federal aid sought for operation in, 275. *See also* Florida project

Southerland, S., seized as spy, 204-05

Southern Emigrant Aid project. *See* Emigrant Aid Movement, Southern

Southern reaction to Kansas conflict, 208

Speaking tours: early, 36; E. E. Hale, 36; Thayer, 59-60; Pomeroy, 114n; Free State delegation, 146-47, 161

Speculation (Emigrant Aid Company): question of, 42-44; Thayer's attitude, 43; Lawrence's attitude, 43-44; charged by W. E. Connelley, 46

Speer, John, editor, *Kansas Tribune* (newspaper), 89

Spirit of the South (Eufaula, Alabama), Buford advertises for emigrants, 208

Spooner, William B.: director, 31; benefactor, University of Kansas, 31; member, Executive Committee, 178

"Squatters": enter Kansas, 72; antagonized by Territorial Legislature, 106

Squatters' associations, formed in Kansas, 73

Squatters Claim Association, declaration of, 73

"Squatters' rights," protection of, 73

Squatter Sovereign, The (Atchison, Kansas): proclaims war in Kansas, 158; Pomeroy agrees to purchase, 245; name changed to *Freedom's Champion,* 246

"Squatter sovereignty": in Compromise of 1850, 5; Thayer accepts challenge, 7

State election (Topeka Constitution), 145

Steamboat line, Emigrant Aid Company considers establishing, 172

Steamboats, Missouri River, negotiation of fares, 175

Stearns, Clark, squatter on Lawrence townsite, 79

Stearns, George L.: chairman, Massachusetts State Kansas Committee, 213; in drought relief, 1860, 266

Stock, Emigrant Aid Company: distribution of, 48; assessments on, 64

—preferred. *See* Preferred stock

Stockholders, Emigrant Aid Company, annual meetings: 1855, 29-30; 1856, 177-78; 1857, 251; 1858, 256; 1861, 267-68, last, 285

—attitude toward financial loss, 288-89

—motives of, 48-49, 289-93

Stock subscriptions: appeals for, 36, 48-49; basis of, 48-49; effect of "bleeding Kansas," 49; guaranteed by trustees, 64; amount subscribed to February, 1855, 112; outside Boston, 113; plan to secure from business groups, 237-39; shoe and leather subscription, 238; stoppage of, 238-39, 260

Stock subscription agents: William A. White, 63-64; E. B. Whitman, 113, 161; two employed, 1855, 115; Bartholomew Wood, 115, 161; E. E. Hale, 116, 162; H. A. Wilcox, 161; Thayer, 162; use of, 161-62; discontinuance, 162-63

Stock transfers: meaning of, 49; A. A. Lawrence, 49; Thayer, 49

Stone, Anson J.: mention, 35, 36; appointed assistant treasurer, 117

Stone, William, partner of A. A. Lawrence, 127

Stowe, Calvin E.: declines to serve as director, 29; signs appeal to clergy, 114

Stowell, Martin: settlers armed by Dr. Webb, 166; party enters Kansas through Nebraska, 174. *See also* Kansas settlers, emigrant parties

"Straw men" story, Lane at Ft. Saunders, 200

[355]

Strawn, William, party turned back on Missouri River, 192

Strickler, Hiram J., major general, Pro-slavery militia, 139

Stringfellow, B. F.: candidate for Senator, 93; acknowledges defeat of pro-slavery cause, 252

Stringfellow, J. H., editor, *Squatter Sovereign*, 158

"Stubbs" Military Company (Lawrence): attacks Franklin, 186; attacks Georgia Fort, 197

Sumner, Charles (Senator from Massachusetts): mention, 101; defends Emigrant Aid Company, 143; speech, "Crime against Kansas," 153-54; suggests reply to S. A. Douglas, 179; assaulted by Preston Brooks, 185

Sumner, Col. E. V.: urged to protect Lawrence (Kansas), 140; Gov. Shannon asks for troops, 140; disperses opposing forces at Palmyra, 187; disperses Topeka Legislature, 188-89; reprimanded and removed, 189

Supplies, free-state, intercepted and captured, 204

Tappan, S. F., resists arrest, 156

Tariff, relation to Kansas Conflict, 291-92

Taxes, levied in Kansas, 260

Tension, growth of in Kansas, 137-38

Tents for settlers, furnished by Emigrant Aid Company, 81

Territorial election. *See* "Bogus election" —supplementary, 103

Territorial Executive Committee, 146

Territorial Register (newspaper, Leavenworth, Kansas), plant destroyed, 144-45

Texas, How to Conquer, before Texas Conquer us, pamphlet by E. E. Hale, 10

Texas, German colony in, 255 —proposal of Emigrant Aid Company to operate in: suggestion of Col. Daniel Ruggles, 255; work of Frederick Law Olmsted, 256; Texas committee appointed, 274-75

Thayer, Eli: accepts challenge, 7; sketch, 8-9; source of ideas, 9-10; motives, 10-11; trustee, Emigrant Aid Company, 18, 20, 26; launches project in New York, 19; seeks new charter, 20; New York and Connecticut Company, 22-23; vice president, New England Aid Company, 30; speaking tours, 36; attitude toward speculation by Company, 43; conducts "Pioneer Party," 52; handling of loan to *Herald of Freedom,* 89-90; solicits stock subscriptions, 113; recruits emigrants, 117; full-time subscription agent, 162; and defense funds, 164; corre-

spondence with John Brown, 184; organization agent, National Kansas Committee, 216-17; elected to Congress, 252; budget committee, 254

Titus, Col. Henry J., captured and exchanged, 201-02

Titus, Fort. *See* Pro-slavery forts, Ft. Titus

Toombs Bill: passes Senate, 225; Emigrant Aid Company opposition, 226

Topeka (Kansas): founded, 81-82; naming of, 81-82; beginning of library, 88

Topeka Constitution: mention, 82; drafted, 108; ratified, 109; and Free State strategy, 141; election to ratify, 144-45

Topeka Constitutional Convention, 108-09

Topeka Convention, first: called, 106; calls Constitutional Convention, 108

Topeka Legislature: meeting of, 145-46; dispersal of, 188-89

Topeka mill. *See* Mills, Topeka mill

Topeka movement: purpose of, 109; name applied to free-state group, 109. *See also* Free State Movement

Topeka schoolhouse: Emigrant Aid Company agrees to build, 248; used by churches, 249; tenants demand repairs, 257. *See also* Schoolhouse, Topeka

Town lots: expected profits from, 33; given to Company, 42 —assigned to Emigrant Aid Company: Lawrence, 79; Manhattan, 83; Topeka, 81

Towns, founding of: Lawrence, 75, 79; Topeka, 81-82; Osawatomie, 82; Manhattan, 83; Hampden (Burlington), 84; Wabaunsee, 84-85; Batcheller (Milford), 85; Claflin (Mapleton), 85; Humboldt, 85; Zeandale, 85 —Emigrant Aid Company, free-state centers, 79 —free-state, importance of, 296-97 —non-political, mention, 86 —pro-slavery, listed, 86

Townsley, James, and Pottawatomie Massacre, 183

Transportation rates: reduced, 35; fares to Kansas, 35

Treason, Free State leaders indicted for, 157

Treason prisoners: rescue feared, 202; release of, 229. *See also* Lawrence, A. A., effort to secure release of treason prisoners

Treasurer's books: out of balance, 254; new set opened, 254-55

Treaty of Lawrence. *See* Lawrence (Kansas), Treaty of

Twining, Prof. A. C. (director), solicits funds in New Haven, 116

Union Emigration Society, 65

United States Mutual Protection Company, 276

Upton, George B.: proposed as president of Emigrant Aid Company, 28; supports financial drive, 162; elected director, 178

Vegetarian Settlement Company, 69-70
"Voluntary association," 26, 53, 111. See also Emigrant Aid Company trusteeship

Voting, fraudulent (Missourians): first occasion, 98; in "Bogus election," 98, 101-02. See also "Bogus election"

Wabaunsee (Kansas): mention, 61; beginning of, 84-85; Emigrant Aid Company interest, 84-85. See also "Beecher's Bible Rifle" colony

Wabaunsee mill. See Mills, Wabaunsee mill

Wakarusa, early name of Lawrence (Kansas), 79

Wakarusa War: mention, 109; events of, 138-43; free-state men seek to avoid violence, 141; effects of, 143

Wakefield, John A.: judge, Actual Settlers Association, 73; candidate for territorial delegate, 98

Walker, Samuel: persuades Lane to leave Nebraska City, 195; attacks Ft. Titus, 200-01

Walter, George: superintendent, American Settlement Company, 67-68; handbook, History of Kansas, 68

Ward, William, part proprietor of Osawatomie, 82, 260

Waters, R. P.: member, Executive Committee, 31, 32, 251; vice president, 1862, 272; president, 1864, 274

Webb, Thomas H.: sketch, 13-14; stock subscription agent, 17; appointed secretary, 18; secretary under trusteeship, 26; secretary, New England Emigrant Aid Company, 30; negotiations for reduced fares, 35; interest in Manhattan (Kansas), 83, 123; temporary office, Massachusetts Historical Society, 111; visits Kansas, 116, 123; reports on Kansas, 116; reports on emigrant parties, 117-18; trouble with forwarding agents, 118-19; efforts to safeguard emigrants, 119-21; promises grist mill to Manhattan, 123; describes Dietzler's rifle mission, 124-25; orders Sharps rifles, 124-25; relief funds for Kansas, 161; work for defense fund, 164; illness, 166; comment on Cutter party, 192; elected director, 258; in drought relief, 1860, 266; work on hotel claim, 273; death, 276-77

Weston (Missouri), Bentonite meeting, 96

Westport (Missouri), anti-Benton meeting, 93-94

White, William A., stock subscription agent, 63-64

Whitfield, John W.: candidate for territorial delegate, 98; elected territorial delegate, 108

Whitman, E. B., stock subscription agent, 113, 161

Whittier, John G., "Song of the Kansas Emigrant," 62-63

Wilcox, the Rev. H. A., stock subscription agent, 115, 161

Williams, J. M. S.: sketch, 12-13; trustee, 26; vice president, New England Emigrant Aid Company, 30; loan to Herald of Freedom, 90; cash advances, 113; reports on Kansas, 116; guarantees salary of assistant treasurer, 117

Williston, J. P. (director), solicits funds in Northampton, 116

Wilson, Henry, defends Emigrant Aid Company in Senate, 150

Winchell, J. M., and Council City (Kansas), 85

Wisconsin State Kansas Emigration Aid Society, 212

Wood, Bartholomew, stock subscription agent, 115, 161

Wood, J. N. O. P., Lawrence claim dispute, 79, 80

Wood, Samuel N.: and Emigrant Aid Association of Northern Ohio, 69; Actual Settlers Association, 73; on early settlers, 73, 73n, 74; in Branson rescue, 138; escapes arrest, 156; returns to Kansas, 156; indicted for treason, 157; leads emigrant party to Kansas, 213

Woodson, Daniel: secretary, Kansas Territory, 139; calls out militia, 202-03; calls on Col. Cooke for troops, 205

Woodward, B. W., projector of Burlington (Kansas), 244

Worcester Academy, Eli Thayer, principal, 8

Wyandotte (Kansas), 85

Wyandotte floats: title to Lawrence townsite, 80; meaning of term, 80n; title to Manhattan townsite, 83; purchased by Emigrant Aid Company, 112

Yankees, New England settlers called, 76

Zeandale (Kansas): founding of, 85; founded by A. B. Marshall, 240